Grade 6

Addison-Wesley Mathematics

Robert E. Eicholz   **Phares G. O'Daffer**   **Randall I. Charles**
Sharon L. Young   **Carne S. Barnett**   **Charles R. Fleenor**

Stanley R. Clemens   **Carol A. Thornton**
Andy Reeves   **Joan E. Westley**

▲▼ Addison-Wesley Publishing Company

Menlo Park, California ■ *Reading, Massachusetts* ■ *New York*
Don Mills, Ontario ■ *Wokingham, England* ■ *Amsterdam* ■ *Bonn*
Sydney ■ *Singapore* ■ *Tokyo* ■ *Madrid* ■ *San Juan*

PROGRAM ADVISORS

John A. Dossey
Professor of Mathematics
Illinois State University
Normal, Illinois

Freddie Renfro
K-12 Mathematics
  Coordinator
La Porte Independent
  School District
La Porte, Texas

Bonnie Armbruster
Associate Professor
Center for the Study of
  Reading
University of Illinois
Champaign, Illinois

David C. Brummett
Educational Consultant
Palo Alto, California

William J. Driscoll
Chairman
Department of
  Mathematical Sciences
Central Connecticut State
  University
Burlington, Connecticut

Betty C. Lee
Assistant Principal
Ferry Elementary School
Detroit, Michigan

Irene Medina
Mathematics Coordinator
Tom Browne Middle School
Corpus Christi, Texas

Rosalie C. Whitlock
Educational Consultant
Stanford, California

CONTRIBUTING WRITERS

Betsy Franco
Marilyn Jacobson
Marny Sorgen
Judith K. Wells

Mary Heinrich
Ann Muench
Connie Thorpe

Penny Holland
Gini Shimabukuro
Sandra Ward

EXECUTIVE EDITOR

Diane H. Fernández

Cover Photo credit: Orion Press/West Light

TI-12 Math Explorer™ is a trademark of Texas Instruments.

ISBN: 0-201-27600-3

8 9 10 - DO - 95 94

Contents

DIVISION: WHOLE NUMBERS AND DECIMALS

7

ADDITION AND SUBTRACTION: FRACTIONS AND MIXED NUMBERS

8

MULTIPLICATION AND DIVISION: FRACTIONS AND MIXED NUMBERS

11

USING PERCENT

14

PERIMETER, AREA, AND VOLUME

15

PROBABILITY

16   INTRODUCTION TO ALGEBRA

RESOURCE BANK AND APPENDIX

Dear Student:

This year will be an exciting adventure in mathematics for you. The skills you learn will give you power, because they prepare you to solve important problems now and for the rest of your life!

For example, exploring percentages will let you calculate sale prices and discounts at the store. You can save money! You will also be introduced to probability and statistics, so you can better understand what graphs and charts mean and make better decisions.

Throughout the year, you will work in pairs and groups to solve problems, discover new concepts, and build on what you already know. You will practice these concepts by looking at your world in a new way. You will have fun with graph paper, geometry, integers, and more.

Be sure to check out the back of the book, where we have provided a Data Bank, a Calculator Bank, a Computer Bank, a Glossary, and a lot more to make this book useful and interesting for you.

Good luck. We are sure you will enjoy this year in mathematics.

From your friends at Addison-Wesley.

1

WHOLE NUMBERS, PROPERTIES, AND PLACE VALUE

MATH AND
SOCIAL STUDIES

DATA BANK

Use the Social Studies Data Bank on page 468 to answer these questions.

1 The earliest writing that we know of was done by the Sumerians. These ancient people lived in what is now southern Iraq. About how many years ago did the Sumerians write their numeral system?

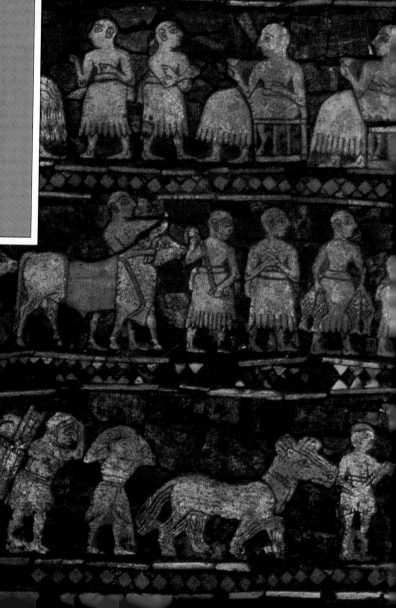

2 The ancient Egyptians were the first civilization to develop a numeral system based on 10. About how many years after the Sumerians wrote their number system did the Egyptians record theirs?

3 The ancient Hindus were the first people to use a code numeral system with zero as a placeholder. About how many years after the first written numeral system did people understand the usefulness of the placeholder zero?

4 **Using Critical Thinking** Look at the ways the Egyptians and Hindus wrote numerals. Write the number 2,079 in Egyptian and in Hindu. What are the advantages and disadvantages of each system? Which of the two would you use? Explain.

Place Value Through Thousands

EXPLORE Read the Information

About 5,000 years ago, the ancient Egyptian kingdom covered about 8,000 square miles. Today, the nation of Egypt covers 386,702 square miles. During the Age of Pyramids, more than 100,000 peasants labored for 20 years to complete the Great Pyramid. It covers an area of about 566,280 square feet.

TALK ABOUT IT

1. How many numbers in the information about Egypt are less than ten thousand?
2. Which numbers are greater than one hundred thousand?
3. Why might there be more people in Egypt today than in ancient times?

When we write large numbers, we use a comma to separate each group of three digits. A group of digits is called a **period.**

	Thousands Period			Ones Period			← Periods
We write, in standard form:	5	6	6	, 2	8	0	
	hundred thousands	ten thousands	thousands	hundreds	tens	ones	← Place Values

We read: "five hundred sixty-six thousand, two hundred eighty"

We write, in **expanded form:** 500,000 + 60,000 + 6,000 + 200 + 80

Read each number. Then use place value to tell what each red digit means.

1. 6,384
2. 502,749
3. 45,204
4. 72,521

5. 86,074
6. 197,600
7. 647,938
8. 425

Give the digit from the following number for each place value named below.

386,702 square miles   (the area of Egypt today)

1. ten thousands place   **2.** hundreds place   **3.** one thousands place

4. ones place   **5.** hundred thousands place   **6.** tens place

Write the number in standard form.

7. 40,000 + 600 + 70 + 8   **8.** 485 thousand 63   **9.** 369 thousand

10. five hundred thirty-two thousand, seven hundred sixty-five

Write in expanded form. Then write each number in words.

11. 267   **12.** 48,541   **13.** 924,687   **14.** 8,309

APPLY

MATH REASONING

Ten 10s make 100. How many 10s make   Ten 100s make 1,000. How many 100s make

15. 200   **16.** 500   **17.** 1,000   **18.** 2,000   **19.** 5,000   **20.** 10,000

PROBLEM SOLVING

21. Which numbers in the story on page 4 are between 5,000 and 380,000?

22. Social Studies Data Bank You will use the information on pages 468–483 for Data Bank problems throughout this book. Turn to the Social Studies Data Bank to find Egyptian numerals. Early Egyptian astronomers created a calendar with 365 days. Using hieroglyphics, write 365 in two ways to show that the Egyptian numeral system did not use place value.

▶ **USING CRITICAL THINKING   Give a Rule**

Roman numeral digits can be	6	VI	4	IV
combined in different ways	11	XI	9	IX
to make other numerals.	20	XX	40	XL
Here are some examples.	60	LX	90	XC
	110	CX	900	CM

Values of Some Roman Numeral Digits			
1	I	100	C
5	V	500	D
10	X	1,000	M
50	L		

23. Give rules that tell how the Roman numerals above are formed.

More Practice, page 500, set A

5

Larger Numbers Through Trillions

LEARN ABOUT IT

EXPLORE Examine the Data

Historians estimate that there were
10 million people on Earth 12,000 years
ago. The chart shows other estimates of
world population from the past.

TALK ABOUT IT

1. Is the world population increasing faster
   now than 200 years ago? How can you
   tell?
2. How many periods does the population
   of 200 years ago have?
3. How many periods does the population
   of 150 years ago have?

The diagram below shows the estimated future
world population for the year 2000. Periods
and place values are shown.

Estimated World Population

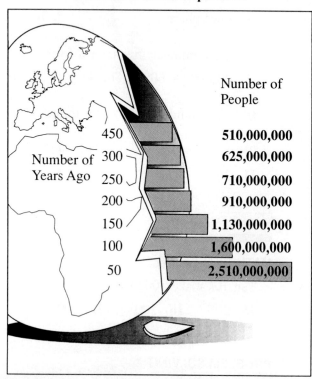

Number of Years Ago	Number of People
450	510,000,000
300	625,000,000
250	710,000,000
200	910,000,000
150	1,130,000,000
100	1,600,000,000
50	2,510,000,000

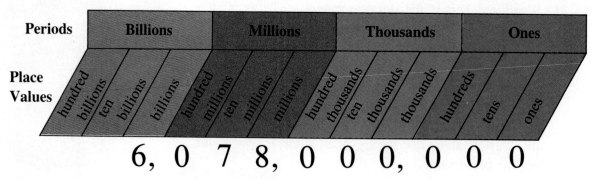

Periods	Billions				Millions				Thousands				Ones		
Place Values	hundred billions	ten billions	billions		hundred millions	ten millions	millions		hundred thousands	ten thousands	thousands		hundreds	tens	ones
	6,	0	7	8,	0	0	0,	0	0	0					

We think about the periods and read: "six billion, seventy-eight million."
The period after billions is trillions. 75 trillion is written 75,000,000,000,000.

TRY IT OUT

Give the digits in each period named, then read each number.

1. 238,938,000
   (Millions)

2. 22,391,000,000,000
   (Trillions)

3. 730,294,932,000,000
   (Billions)

For this number, give the digits that are in each period named below.

483,458,728,493

1. thousands period   **2.** millions period   **3.** ones period   **4.** billions period

Give the number in standard form.

5. 5,000,000 + 300,000 + 80,000 + 4,000 + 600 + 2

6. 3,000,000,000 + 400,000,000 + 70,000,000 + 6,000,000

7. Three billion, seven hundred six million, five hundred forty thousand

Write these in words.

8. 8,000,000   **9.** 80,000,000,000   **10.** 384,000,000

APPLY

MATH REASONING

Use mental math and place value.
Tell how much greater **A** is than **B**.

11. A = 39,824,000,000
B = 39,724,000,000

12. A = 538,490,000,000
B = 537,490,000,000

PROBLEM SOLVING

13. More Than One Answer Write two 12-digit numbers so that one is exactly one million more than the other.

14. Social Studies Data Bank Which numeral systems were developed during the Bronze Age, from 5,000 to 3,000 years ago? During the Middle Ages, from 1,500 to 500 years ago?

▶ **CALCULATOR**

Use your calculator and your understanding of place value to find these sums.

15. 41,257,000,000 + 37,122,000,000   **16.** 216,039,000,000 + 442,160,000,000

17. Did you try to enter the numbers on your calculator? What happened? How did you use your calculator to find the sums?

More Practice, page 500, set B

Comparing and Ordering

Fish Caught in California, 1980

Type	Numbers
Barracuda	27,909
Kelp and sand bass	585,432
Ling cod	89,349
Pacific mackerel	1,315,971
Pacific bonito	560,508
Salmon	64,500
White croaker	27,461
Yellowtail	44,246

EXPLORE **Compare the Data**

This list of fish caught is in alphabetical order.

TALK ABOUT IT

1. How can you quickly decide which type of fish was caught in the largest numbers?
2. Name five types of fish that were caught less often than Pacific bonito.

Here is a way to compare the number of bass with Pacific bonito. Line up the digits, starting with the ones place. Find the first place, left to right, in which the digits are different.

585,432
560,508 *the ten thousands place is different*

Compare the digits. The greater digit tells the greater number.

is greater than   *is greater than*   *is less than*   *is less than*

$8 > 6$ so $585,432 > 560,508$ or $6 < 8$ so $560,508 < 585,432$

To order a set of numbers, compare them two at a time.

Greatest → 157,823 ← Number with the most digits is greatest

$$\left.\begin{array}{l} 57,548 \\ 56,924 \\ \end{array}\right\} \begin{array}{l} 7 > 6 \\ 2 > 0 \end{array}$$

Least → 56,907

TRY IT OUT

Write >, <, or = for each ⬚.

1. 7,280 ⬚ 7,301
2. 789 ⬚ 802
3. 23,829 ⬚ 23,289
4. 5,623 ⬚ 6,123
5. 597 ⬚ six hundred one
6. 824,000 ⬚ 824 thousand

Write >, <, or = for each ▯.

1. 385,267 ▯ 385,249   **2.** 1,267,285 ▯ 1,273,285   **3.** 48,267 ▯ 48,304

4. 426,785 ▯ 397,876   **5.** 5,287,643 ▯ 5,290,588   **6.** 672,011 ▯ 672,008

7. Order the numbers in List A from greatest to least.

8. Order the numbers in List B from least to greatest.

9. Which numbers in List A are between 10,000 and 1,000,000?

10. Which number in List B is closest to 400,000?

11. Which is the greatest number in List C?

12. Which number in List C is closest to 1,300,000?

List A	List B	List C
45,258	424,468	1,298,121
4,467,395	423,849	1,287,287
425,426	421,490	1,310,246

MATH REASONING

Decide whether it makes sense to round each piece of data.

13. School phone number

14. Number of books in the library on any given day

15. Age of an ancient piece of pottery

16. Cost of a new bicycle

PROBLEM SOLVING

17. Write the largest and smallest number you can, using each of these digits once. 6, 2, 0, 3, 5

18. The number 28,356 is greater than the number 27,356. How much greater is it?

Add, subtract, multiply, or divide.

19. 9 + 6   **20.** 4 × 8   **21.** 90 − 30   **22.** 160 ÷ 4

23. 5,000 × 20   **24.** 10 + 3 + 7   **25.** 49 ÷ 7   **26.** 20,000 − 10,000

27. 400 + 800 + 10   **28.** 640 ÷ 8   **29.** 20 × 50   **30.** 180 ÷ 6

31. 26 + 9 + 11   **32.** 65 − 43   **33.** 86 + 7   **34.** 5 + 6 + 45

More Practice, page 500, set C

Problem Solving
Understanding the Operation

UNDERSTAND
ANALYZE DATA
PLAN
ESTIMATE
SOLVE
EXAMINE

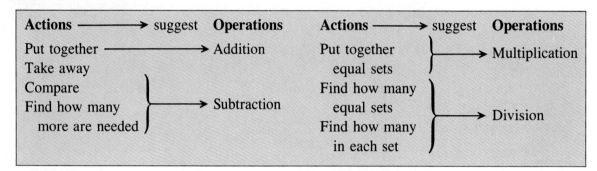

Actions	suggest	Operations		Actions	suggest	Operations
Put together	→	Addition		Put together equal sets	}	→ Multiplication
Take away				Find how many equal sets	}	
Compare	}	→ Subtraction				→ Division
Find how many more are needed				Find how many in each set		

The action in a problem suggests the operation needed to solve the problem. The box reviews the actions you learned about in earlier grades. Sometimes the actions in problems are not easy to recognize. Study the examples below.

Betsy and some friends played soccer. By late afternoon, 7 friends had gone home. That left only 15 to continue the game. How many players were there at the start of the game?

Since I need to find how many there were before some went away, I need to undo the subtraction. I'll add.

$15 + 7 = 22$

Betsy and 13 classmates worked on an art project. Some of them had to leave before lunch. That left only 8 to carry on the project. How many left early?

I want to know how many left early. I know the total, so I can subtract the number that are still left.

$14 - 8 = 6$

Name the operation you need to use. Then solve.

1. Nora's class formed 4 nature study groups. There were 8 students in each group. How many participated?

2. There were 15 parts in the class play and 24 students in the class. The ones not in the play were stagehands. How many were stagehands?

3. Jody's class of 24 went on a field trip. If they rode 4 to a car, how many cars were needed?

4. Three classes went on the field trip. One class had 27 students, another had 26, and the third had 24. How many students went on the trip?

Name the operation you need to use. Then solve.

1. At Sadako's school, there were 27 students in the chorus and 35 in the band. How many were in the two groups?

2. Luz's class earned $240 for charity. The class decided to give the same amount to each of 4 charities. How much did each charity get?

3. Wayne and 12 friends decided to play basketball. They wanted 18 players for two teams. How many more players do they need?

4. In the basketball game, Wayne made 5 two-point baskets. How many points did he score?

5. Keiko's new class has 26 students. There were only 17 present during a bad storm. How many were absent?

6. Steven needed to buy 40 hamburger buns for a class party. The buns come in packages of 8 for $1.29. How many packages should Steven buy?

7. At 6:00 p.m., 4 carloads of students showed up for the party. Steven counted 4 in the first, 5 in the second, 4 in the third, and 6 in the fourth. How many students got there at 6:00 p.m.?

8. One of the games at the class party had prizes that cost 8 cents each. There were 25 students who played the game and only 6 won a prize. How much did the prizes that were given away cost?

9. There are 180 school days in the school year. When Susan has finished 120 school days, how many are left?

10. **Write Your Own Problem** Write a question that you could answer by using the data below. Then answer your own question.
Bev's class: 13 girls, 11 boys
Everett's class: 12 girls, 15 boys
Maria's class: 14 girls, 13 boys

Mental Math
Compatible Numbers and Break Apart

EXPLORE Analyze the Process

Work in groups. Number properties can help you do certain calculations using mental math. How many of these sums and products can you find mentally?

A $2 \times 8 \times 5$ **B** $75 + 87 + 25$

C 4×35 **D** 3×125

TALK ABOUT IT

1. Did you discover an easy way to find the product in **A?** How did you do it?
2. Was there an easy way to find the sum in **B?**
3. How did you find the products in **C** and **D?**

Below are two methods you can use to do calculations mentally.

Compatible numbers are pairs of numbers that "go together" so that computing with them mentally is easy.

$2 \times 6 \times 15 = 6 \times 30 = 180$

Breaking apart numbers and using the distributive property can make certain mental calculations easier.

$$\overset{\overset{600}{\frown}}{} \quad \overset{\overset{100}{\frown}}{}$$

$2 \times 350 = (2 \times 300) + (2 \times 50) = 700$

Number Properties

Zero Property of Addition
The sum of a number and zero is that number.
$35 + 0 = 35$

Zero Property of Multiplication
The product of a number and zero is zero.
$21 \times 0 = 0$

One Property of Multiplication
The product of a number and one is that number.
$46 \times 1 = 46$

Commutative (Order) Property
Changing the order of addends or factors does not change the sum or product.
$20 + 4 = 24$ $4 + 20 = 24$
$10 \times 5 = 50$ $5 \times 10 = 50$

Associative (Grouping) Property
Changing the grouping of addends or factors does not change the sum or product.
$(4 + 8) + 2 = 14$ $4 + (8 + 2) = 14$
$(5 \times 6) \times 2 = 60$ $5 \times (6 \times 2) = 60$

Distributive Property
Multiplying a sum by a number is the same as multiplying each addend by the number and then adding the products.
$3 \times (20 + 5) = 75$
$(3 \times 20) + (3 \times 5) = 75$

Calculate using mental math.

1. $17 + 38 + 13$ 2. $9 \times 2 \times 50$ 3. $5 \times 27 \times 2$ 4. $80 + 43 + 20$

5. 6×35 6. 3×28 7. 3×104 8. 6×16

Use compatible numbers to find each sum or product mentally.

1. 22 + **14** + **6**

2. **30** + 48 + **70**

3. **25** + 45 + **25**

4. 130 + 150 + 150

5. 80 + 40 + 20

6. 375 + 138 + 125

7. 8 × 5 × 20

8. 25 × 6 × 4

9. 35 × 50 × 2

10. 500 × 35 × 2

11. 9 × 25 × 4

12. 5 × 15 × 20

Break apart the numbers to find each product mentally.

13. 5 × 15

14. 4 × 17

15. 325 × 2

16. 52 × 6

17. 5 × 43

18. 72 × 3

19. 125 × 3

20. 5 × 208

APPLY

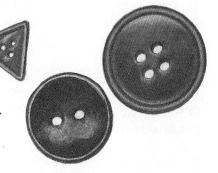

MATH REASONING

21. Does the commutative property apply to subtraction? To division? Give examples to support your answers.

PROBLEM SOLVING

22. Ricardo collects buttons. He has 52 sets of 4 buttons. How many buttons does Ricardo have in his collection?

23. Write Your Own Problem Use break apart or compatible numbers to write a problem that has an answer of 6,480.

▶ **ALGEBRA**

Suppose the letter A = $1, B = $2, C = $3, ..., Z = $26. What is the "value" of a name?

Example: S +   U +   S +   A +   N
           $19 + $21 + $19 + $1 + $14
            "Susan" has a value of $74.

24. Find the value of your name. Can you find some names worth $100 or more?

More Practice, page 500, set D

Order of Operations

LEARN ABOUT IT

EXPLORE Analyze the Examples

Sometimes solving a problem involves using more than one operation. The answer you get may depend on the order in which you do the operations. Here are some examples:

A $4 + 5 \times 3$ **B** $12 \div 4 - 1$ **C** $8 + 4 \div 2$

TALK ABOUT IT

1. What is the answer for **A** if you add first? If you multiply first?
2. Can you get two different answers for **B**? Explain.
3. **C** can be either 6 or 10. How?

Mathematicians have developed rules about the order in which we do operations. If we follow those rules, we get exactly one answer.

> **Order of Operations**
>
> ■ Compute inside parentheses first.
>
> ■ Multiply and divide next, from left to right.
>
> ■ Add and subtract last, from left to right.

Examples

A $(14 - 4) \times 2$ (Compute inside parentheses.)
    ↓
    10×2 (Multiply next.)
    ↓
    20

B $14 - 4 \times 2$ (Multiply first.)
    ↓
    $14 - 8$ (Subtract next.)
    ↓
    6

PRACTICE

Solve.

1. $12 \div (3 + 1)$
2. $12 \div 3 + 1$
3. $5 \times (3 + 4)$

4. $5 \times 3 + 4$
5. $6 + 10 \div 2$
6. $(6 + 10) \div 2$

7. $(5 + 4) \times 2$
8. $5 + 4 \times 2$
9. $9 \div 3 + 6$

10. $9 \div (3 + 6)$
11. $(8 - 2) \times 3$
12. $8 - 2 \times 3$

13. $6 \times (4 - 3)$
14. $6 \times 4 - 3$
15. $5 + 8 \div 2$

More Practice, page 500, set E

MIDCHAPTER REVIEW/QUIZ

For each number, name the place and give the value for the digit 5.

1. 4,253

2. 1,500,724

3. 75,268,401

Write the number in standard form and in expanded form.

4. twelve thousand forty-two

5. 257 trillion, 5 million, 2

Write >, <, or = for each ⅷ.

6. 2,537 ⅷ 537

7. 1,000,012 ⅷ 1,000,120

8. 13,452 ⅷ 13,542

Use the numbers from the chart.

9. Find the numbers between 725,000 and 1,000,000. List them from greatest to least.

980,274	724,109	7,243,154
742,835	1,000,012	570,246

Compute mentally.

Use compatible numbers: **10.** 275 + 125 + 248   **11.** 4 × 9 × 25   **12.** 15 × 5 × 20

Use break apart: **13.** 3 × 72

14. 52 × 4

15. 450 × 2

PROBLEM SOLVING

Tell which operation is suggested by each question.

16. How many more people live in Egypt today than lived in ancient Egypt 5,000 years ago?

17. If the Egyptians could build a pyramid in 20 years, how long would it take to build 4 pyramids?

18. What is the total population of all the countries in the Middle East?

19. If each Egyptian farmer plowed 4 acres, how many farmers would be needed to plow 112 acres?

Use the chart showing the estimated population for 5-year intervals.

20. How much greater was the population estimate in 1985 than in 1980?

21. Write a number that is exactly 1 billion more than the estimate for 1980. During which interval might you expect the estimated population to reach the number you wrote?

Estimated World Population	
1980	4,473,000,000
1985	4,873,000,000
1990	5,259,000,000
1995	5,643,000,000
2000	6,078,000,000

Estimating Sums and Differences
Using Rounding

You can use estimation when you need only to find an answer that is close. You can also use estimation to check on the reasonableness of an exact answer.

EXPLORE Solve to Understand

The electricity that we use is measured in kilowatt-hours. The graph shows the number of kilowatt-hours of electricity some appliances use in a year. About how many kilowatt-hours do an air conditioner and a clothes dryer together use in a year?

TALK ABOUT IT

1. Does the problem ask for an exact answer or an estimate? How did you decide?
2. What numbers do you need from the graph?

Average Kilowatt Hours per Year

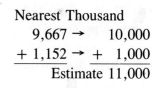

You can estimate a sum or difference by rounding. Look at the digit to the right of the place to which you want to round. If it is 5 or more, round up. If it is less than 5, write zeros there and in all other places to the right and round down.

Nearest Ten	Nearest Hundred	Nearest Thousand
48 → 50	$318 → $300	9,667 → 10,000
+ 72 → + 70	+ 589 → + 600	+ 1,152 → + 1,000
Estimate 120	Estimate $900	Estimate 11,000

TRY IT OUT

Estimate the sums and differences.

Round to the nearest ten: **1.** 55 + 87   **2.** 147 − 23

Round to the nearest thousand: **3.** 8,638 + 9,299   **4.** 15,386 − 6,899

Round to the nearest dollar: **5.** $9.89 + $5.27   **6.** $13.39 − $8.53

Estimate by rounding to the nearest ten.

1.	69	**2.**	48	**3.**	132
	+ 44		+ 75		− 57

Estimate by rounding to the nearest hundred.

4.	546	**5.**	775	**6.**	1,458
	+ 808		− 199		+ 376

Estimate by rounding to the nearest thousand.

7.	16,552	**8.**	8,446	**9.**	12,916
	+ 8,263		+ 8,595		− 5,878

Estimate by rounding to the nearest dollar.

10.	$7.74	**11.**	$16.89	**12.**	$13.67
	+ 6.23		− 8.39		− 6.99

MATH REASONING

Which estimate is an overestimate and which is an underestimate?

13.	$7.95	→	$8.00
	+ 6.79	→	+ 7.00
		Estimate	$15.00

14.	$10.00	→	$10.00
	− 6.79	→	− 7.00
		Estimate	$3.00

PROBLEM SOLVING

15. About how many kilowatt-hours do the water heater and space heater together use per year?

16. About how much more electricity does the water heater use per year than the refrigerator?

Write >, <, or = for each ⫼.

17. 6,378 ⫼ 6,380   **18.** 67,012 ⫼ 67,102   **19.** 6,000,000,001 ⫼ 5,829,125

Multiply or divide. Use mental math when possible.

20. 9 × 80   **21.** 100 × 8   **22.** 84 ÷ 4   **23.** 2,000 ÷ 5

24. 345 ÷ 15   **25.** 687 × 73   **26.** 8,009 × 6   **27.** 979 ÷ 11

28. 8 × 506   **29.** 9 × 25 × 4   **30.** 4 × 82   **31.** 5 × 76 × 20

Reviewing Addition and Subtraction
Whole Numbers

LEARN ABOUT IT

In this lesson, you will review the paper and pencil procedures for adding and subtracting numbers. The examples will help you review these skills.

A Add 7,562 + 4,386.

Line up the numbers.
Start with the ones place.
Trade if necessary.

$$\begin{array}{r} 1 \\ 7,562 \\ + 4,386 \\ \hline 1\,1,948 \end{array}$$

14 tens = 1 hundred plus 4 tens

B 1,243 + 825 + 432 + 2,289

$$\begin{array}{r} 1\ 1\ 1 \\ 1,243 \\ 825 \\ 432 \\ + 2,289 \\ \hline 4,789 \end{array}$$

C Subtract 358 from 400.

$$\begin{array}{r} 3\ 9\ 10 \\ \cancel{400} \\ - 358 \\ \hline 42 \end{array}$$

40 tens = 39 tens and 10 ones

D 7,253 − 2,796

$$\begin{array}{r} 6\ 11\ 14\ 13 \\ \cancel{7253} \\ - 2,796 \\ \hline 4,457 \end{array}$$

TRY IT OUT

Add or subtract.

1. $\begin{array}{r} 3,524 \\ + 5,832 \end{array}$	**2.** $\begin{array}{r} 4,380 \\ + 1,464 \end{array}$	**3.** $\begin{array}{r} 700 \\ - 561 \end{array}$	**4.** $\begin{array}{r} 5,352 \\ + 2,355 \end{array}$	**5.** $\begin{array}{r} 23 \\ 6,345 \\ 9,567 \\ + 825 \end{array}$
6. $\begin{array}{r} 37 \\ + 678 \end{array}$	**7.** $\begin{array}{r} 8,006 \\ - 491 \end{array}$	**8.** $\begin{array}{r} 33,903 \\ - 4,827 \end{array}$	**9.** $\begin{array}{r} 796 \\ + 8,245 \end{array}$	

10. 473 + 2,452 + 379   **11.** 3,513 + 1,385 + 311   **12.** 802 − 557   **13.** 5,482 − 495

14. 6,045 + 29,987   **15.** 37,600 − 841   **16.** 106 − 28   **17.** 720 − 152

Find the sums and differences.

HILLVIEW
HOSPITAL RAFFLE

1.   895
      − 237

2.   18
      + 75

3.   9,700
      − 8,148

4.   456
      + 212

5.   1,429
      − 674

6.   13,089
      − 3,865

7.   11,000
      − 5,989

8.   5,044
      − 3,897

9.   975
       123
      + 59

10.   875
        785
      + 367

11.   527
        717
      + 285

12.   3,757
        4,632
      + 5,508

13. 42,193 − 5,898   **14.** 1,020 − 429   **15.** 58,467 − 34,276   **16.** 1,672 + 854

17. Add: 3,425 + 726 + 1,258 + 1,193   **18.** Subtract 438 from 1,205.

19. Find the sum of 6,284, 1,358, 4,390, and 998.   **20.** Find the difference of 4,004 and 3,479.

APPLY

MATH REASONING

21. Do not add or subtract. Give the letters of the problems in order from smallest answer to largest answer.

A   6,729
      − 1,836

B   6,729
      + 1,836

C   6,729
      + 836

D   6,729
      − 836

PROBLEM SOLVING

22. A local charity had a goal of raising $7,500 during its fund-raising drive. So far, the charity has collected $5,687. How much more money is needed to reach the goal?

23. When the drive was over, the charity had exceeded the goal by $1,862. In honor of the success, a store gave another $150. How much money was raised?

▶ **USING CRITICAL THINKING   Use Careful Reasoning**

Copy each problem and supply the missing digits.

24.   ▨,6▨▨▨
      + 5,▨12
        9,5 0 6

25.   ▨,61▨
      − 2,8▨9
        2,▨78

26.   ▨,▨7▨
      −   3▨6
        7,6 7 8

27.   ▨,3▨9
      + 6,54▨
        ▨0,▨02

Problem Solving
Introduction

UNDERSTAND
ANALYZE DATA
PLAN
ESTIMATE
SOLVE
EXAMINE

LEARN ABOUT IT

Some problems can be solved by choosing one of the operations:
addition, subtraction, multiplication, or division. These are
called one-step problems. One-step problems can be solved using
the strategy **Choose the Operation.**

Some TV viewers named their favorite TV shows. How many named either *Clue* or *Western Days*?	**Favorite Prime-Time Shows**
	Western Days 51 *Clue* 58
	Newsmakers 49

Understand the Situation
> I want to find the total number of people who named *Clue* or *Western Days*.

Analyze the Data
> Number of people who named *Clue:* 58
> Number of people who named *Western Days:* 51

Plan the Solution
> I can add the two numbers to get the total.

Estimate the Answer
> 58 + 51 is about 60 + 50, or 110.

Solve the Problem
> 58 + 51 = 109
> The number of people who named *Clue* or *Western Days* was 109.

Examine the Answer
> 109 is close to the estimate of 110, so 109 is a reasonable answer.

TRY IT OUT

Choose the letter that shows how you could solve the problem. Do not solve.

1. How many viewers were asked to name their favorite show?

   A $58 + (51 + 49)$ **B** $58 - (51 - 49)$ **C** $58 \times (51 \times 49)$ **D** $58 \div (51 \div 49)$

2. How many more viewers named *Clue* than *Newsmakers?*

   A $58 + 49$ **B** $58 - 49$ **C** 58×49 **D** $58 \div 49$

Choose the operation you could use to solve the problem. Do not solve.

1. Tara watched TV for 6 nights in one week. Each night she watched TV for 2 hours. How many hours did Tara watch TV that week?

   A 6 + 2   B 6 − 2
   C 6 × 2   D 6 ÷ 2

2. Jon spent $18 to rent 6 videotapes. How much did each rental cost?

   A $18 + 6   B $18 − 6
   C $18 × 6   D $18 ÷ 6

3. Julie watched 6 comedy shows, 2 movies, and 3 quiz shows on TV one week. How many TV programs did Julie watch that week?

   A (6 + 2) + 3   B (6 − 2) − 3
   C (6 × 2) × 3   D (6 ÷ 2) ÷ 3

4. A TV program had 21 minutes of show time and 7 minutes of commercials. How much longer was the show time than the commercials?

   A 21 + 7   B 21 − 7
   C 21 × 7   D 21 ÷ 7

Solve these problems.

5. Television City is having a special sale. Use the price list to find how much a 27-in. color TV and a VCR together would cost.

6. Vic bought 3 6-packs of videotapes. How much did he spend?

7. How much would 1 package of videotape cost if you could buy just one?

8. Use the price list to find how much you can save if you buy a 21-in. color TV instead of a 27-in. color TV.

9. Kayla bought a portable TV. The tax came to $9. What was her total bill?

SPECIALS

27-inch color TV $525

21-inch color TV $319

Portable TV $150

VCR $289

Videotapes, 6-pack $24

10. **Understanding the Operations** Choose the operation you would use to solve this problem.

    Mario watched TV for 12 hours last week. He watched football for 4 hours and spent the rest of the time watching movies. How many hours did he spend watching movies?

    A 12 + 4   B 12 − 4   C 12 × 4   D 12 ÷ 4

More Practice, page 522, set B

Exploring Algebra
Variables and Algebraic Expressions

Throughout this book you will be studying topics from **algebra.**
One of the most important topics from algebra is the idea of a
variable. A **variable** is a letter, such as n, that keeps a place for
a number. An expression such as $n + 12$ that contains at
least one variable is called an **algebraic expression.**

To **evaluate** the algebraic expression $n + 12$ when $n = 26$,
you can follow the steps below.

Write the expression: $n + 12$
Replace the variable: $26 + 12$
Then compute: 38

TALK ABOUT IT

1. Can you evaluate $n + 12$ for $n = 3$? For $n = 79,312$?
   For any value?
2. In the expression $m + 3 + n$, do you think that m and n
   could have different values? The same value?
3. In the expression $m + 4 + m$, do you think the first m
   could equal 2 while the second m could equal 3? Explain.

Other Examples

A Evaluate $(3 \times c) + 5$ for $c = 9$
$$(3 \times c) + 5$$
$$(3 \times 9) + 5 \quad \text{Replace } c \text{ with 9.}$$
$$27 + 5$$
$$32 \quad \text{Compute inside parentheses first.}$$

B Evaluate $(m \times n) - 4$ for $m = 5$ and $n = 3$
$$(m \times n) - 4$$
$$(5 \times 3) - 4 \quad \text{Replace } m \text{ with 5 and } n \text{ with 3.}$$
$$15 - 4$$
$$11$$

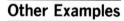

Evaluate each algebraic expression.

1. $35 - x$ for $x = 27$

2. $y \div 6$ for $y = 42$

3. $(a + b) - 6$ for $a = 22$ and $b = 25$

4. $p + 36$ for $p = 17$

5. $(6 \times z) + 8$ for $z = 5$

6. $(y - 3) \times z$ for $y = 33$ and $z = 2$

Evaluate each algebraic expression.

1. $r + 36$ for $r = 75$ **2.** $n - 16$ for $n = 61$ **3.** $z \div 6$ for $z = 36$

4. $b \times 4$ for $b = 3$ **5.** $29 - r$ for $r = 29$ **6.** $3 + x + 12$ for $x = 4$

7. $(2 \times y) + 3$ for $y = 8$ **8.** $10 - (c \div 5)$ for $c = 10$ **9.** $8 \times (7 - p)$ for $p = 3$

10. $17 + a$ for $a = 0$, and for $a = 20$ **11.** $2 \times g$ for $g = 0$, and for $g = 40$

Evaluate each algebraic expression for $a = 3$, $b = 7$, and $c = 4$.

12. $(a \times b) + 11$ **13.** $6 \times (b - c)$ **14.** $b + (a \times c)$

Copy and complete the table. Evaluate the algebraic expression for the given numbers.

	x	y	$(x \times y) - x$
	3	4	$(3 \times 4) - 3 = 9$
15.	10	5	
16.	20	30	
17.	0	6	

MATH REASONING

18. Each letter stands for one number. Different letters stand for different numbers. Use reasoning to tell what number each letter represents.

$E + C = 15$ $A \times B = A$ $D \times D = 16$ $D \times C = 24$ $A + B = 8$

PROBLEM SOLVING

19. Social Studies Data Bank Evaluate the following algebraic expressions in these ancient numeral systems.

$a - \text{𝟞} =$ for $a = 7\equiv$ (in Hindu)

$a + \text{𝟡∩∩}$ for $a = \text{∩∩∩|}$ (in Egyptian)

▶ **USING CRITICAL THINKING** **Discover a Relationship**

20. For what values of n will $2 \times n$ be an even number?

21. For what values of n will $n + 2$ be an even number?

22. For what values of n will $n + 1$ be an odd number?

Group Decision Making

Group Skills

Listen to Others
Encourage and Respect Others
Explain and Summarize
Check for Understanding
Disagree in an Agreeable Way

Working as part of a team means more than just doing your share of the work. It also means being responsible for helping and encouraging other members of the group. Some ways to help your team work together are shown in the chart.

Suppose someone in your group got discouraged while trying to solve a problem and said, "I'm quitting. This is too hard." Think of three or four things you could do to help this person in an encouraging and respectful way. Keep these ideas in mind while your group works on the activity.

Cooperative Activity

The challenge for your group is to find ways to make as many numbers from 1 to 20 as you can, using only fours. You can use as many fours as you want and any combination of addition, subtraction, multiplication, and division. For example, you could make the number 2 this way: $(4 + 4) \div 4 = 2$. Make a chart to show your methods. If you find more than one way for the same number put those ways in the chart also.

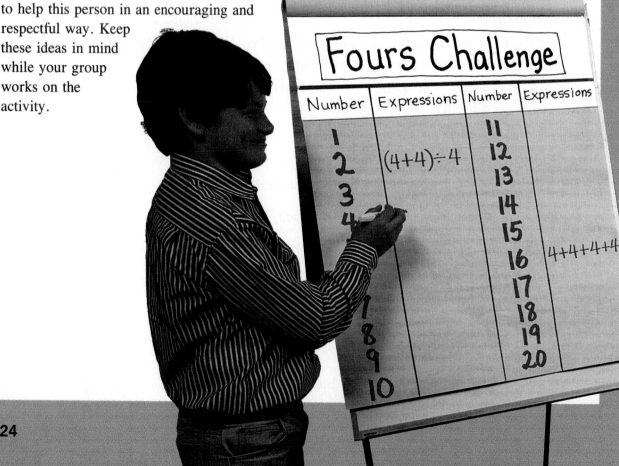

Fours Challenge

Number	Expressions	Number	Expressions
1		11	
2	$(4+4)\div4$	12	
3		13	
4		14	
		15	
		16	$4+4+4+4$
		17	
7		18	
8		19	
9		20	
10			

Fours Challenge

Number	Expressions	Number	Expressions
1		11	
2	(4+4)÷4	12	
3		13	
4		14	
5		15	
6		16	4+4+4+4
7		17	
8		18	
9		19	
10		20	

1. How many numbers were you able to make?
2. Which numbers did you find the most challenging to make?
3. Did you figure out any "tricks" for making the numbers? Explain.

Check Your Group Skills

4. Did any members of your group become discouraged? What did you do to help?

WRAP UP

Number Match

Match the number on the left with the expression on the right.

1. 6,500,030
2. 3,000,000,001,000
3. 85,025,362
4. 3,001,000
5. 85,250,003,620

a. three million, one thousand

b. eighty-five billion, two hundred fifty million, three thousand, six hundred twenty

c. six million, five hundred thousand, thirty

d. eighty-five million, twenty-five thousand, three hundred sixty-two

e. three trillion, one thousand

Sometimes, Always, Never

Decide which word should go in the blank: *sometimes, always,* or *never.* Explain your choices.

6. If the product of two factors is zero, both factors are ___ zero.

7. The rules for order of operations state that you ___ multiply before adding or subtracting.

8. If you work outside the parentheses first, your answer ___ will be the same as if you worked inside first.

9. It is ___ better to underestimate than to overestimate.

10. When you add two whole numbers, the answer is ___ less than either addend.

11. When you evaluate an algebraic expression, you ___ replace the variable with a number.

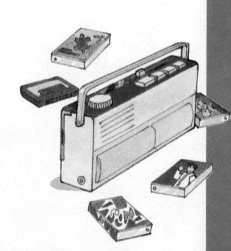

Project

Use the table to make up problems for classmates to solve. Include some that can be solved by using compatible numbers, and by applying the commutative, associative, and distributive properties.

Yvette's Cassettes

High-grade Videotapes	$5.75
Audiotapes	$3.29
Head Cleaners	$8.50
Good-grade Videotapes	$4.25
Club Membership	$35.00

CHAPTER REVIEW/TEST

Part 1   Understanding

Tell how much less the first number is than the second.

1. 56,549
   57,549

2. 347,926,000,000
   387,926,000,000

Estimate by rounding to the nearest dollar. Tell if the estimate is an overestimate or an underestimate of the exact answer.

3. $8.95
    + 4.69

4. $12.27
    −   5.29

Part 2   Skills

5. Write the number *ten billion, four hundred sixty million, seventy-three thousand, twelve*

Write >, <, or = for each ⫿⫿⫿ .

6. 64,423 ⫿⫿⫿ 64,433

7. 9,862,340 ⫿⫿⫿ 9,852,340

Solve mentally. Break apart the numbers or use compatible numbers.

8. $85 + 27 + 15$

9. 5×46

10. $20 \times 7 \times 5$

Solve.

11. $15 \div (7 - 4)$

12. $9 + 12 \div 4$

13. $389 + 28 + 9 + 715$

14. $503 - 267$

Evaluate.

15. $x \div 8$ for $x = 64$

16. $(a - 3) \times b$ for $a = 5$ and $b = 7$

Part 3   Applications

17. Name the operation you need to use. Then solve. There were 28 students in the bus and 34 students in the class. The students not in the bus were in the van. How many were in the van?

18. **Challenge**   Use the price list to solve. Juan has $300 to spend. Which two items can he buy and still have about $25 left over?

Stan's Sporting Goods	
Tennis racquet	$75.79
Squash racquet	$35.95
Golf clubs	$179.95
Golf bag	$59.95
Football	$29.95
Golf shoes	$94.99

27

ENRICHMENT
Base Five

In our number system, we group by tens, using the digits 0–9, but, Aurora's favorite number is five. She has five favorite TV stars, five pen pals, five pictures of the Beatles, and five gerbils. Aurora learned that number systems can be developed using grouping by numbers other than ten. She decided to try grouping by five. Aurora showed the base five number 14 (read as "one, four") by using a set of dots.

14_{five}

The set shows 1 five and 4 ones.
In base ten, this number is written as 9.

Aurora's set at the right shows the number 23_{five}. It shows 2 fives and 3 ones.

1. Show a set of dots to represent the base five number 31.

2. Does the base five number system use the same digits as the base ten system? Explain.

3. The number 10_{five} means 1 five and 0 ones, or 5 in base ten. If 20_{five} means 2 fives and 0 ones in base five, what does it mean in base 10? What does 30_{five} mean in base ten? 40_{five}?

The place-value chart for a base five number system is given. Use the chart to answer the questions.

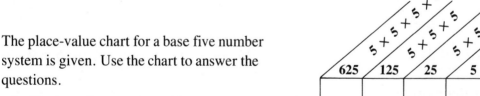

4. The base five number 100 means $1 \times (5 \times 5)$, or 25, in base ten. What do $1,000_{\text{five}}$ and $10,000_{\text{five}}$ mean in base ten?

Write each base five number in base ten.

5. 200_{five}

6. $3,000_{\text{five}}$

7. $40,000_{\text{five}}$

8. 32_{five}

9. 231_{five}

10. $1,223_{\text{five}}$

11. $3,111_{\text{five}}$

12. $21,342_{\text{five}}$

13. Write the current year in base five.

CUMULATIVE REVIEW

Add, subtract, multiply, or divide.

1. $808 + 433 + 272$

    A. 1,413   **B.** 1,513

    C. 1,613   **D.** 1,713

2. $6,517 - 79$

    A. 7,307   **B.** 5,808

    C. 6,438   **D.** 7,226

3. $5,062 - 483$

    A. 4,579   **B.** 5,579

    C. 5,545   **D.** 4,689

4. 363×9

    A. 2,661   **B.** 32,427

    C. 3,357   **D.** 3,267

5. $3 \overline{)1,527}$

    A. 509   **B.** 59

    C. 5,009   **D.** 508

6. A polygon having two pairs of sides the same length and four right angles is a

    A. right triangle   **B.** trapezoid

    C. pentagon   **D.** rectangle

7. A polygon with six sides is a

    A. pentagon   **B.** hexagon

    C. rhombus   **D.** sixagon

8. What type of angle is a 50° angle?

    A. right   **B.** obtuse

    C. scalene   **D.** acute

9. Give the digits in the billions period: 435,274,905,619,005.

    A. 905   **B.** 435

    C. 274   **D.** 619

10. Which number is closest to 600,000?

    A. 627,948   **B.** 672,881

    C. 629,156   **D.** 625,999

11. Use compatible factors to find the product mentally: $50 \times 18 \times 2$

    A. 136   **B.** 180

    C. 1,800   **D.** 1,000

12. Evaluate: $(a \times b) - 3$ for $a = 3$ and $b = 4$.

    A. 9   **B.** 3

    C. 4   **D.** 0

13. Eric paid $7.95 and $8.19 for tapes. About how much did he spend in all?

    A. about $17   **B.** about $16

    C. about $18   **D.** about $19

14. Dolores did homework for 3 hours each night for 18 nights. For how many hours did she do homework?

    A. 21   **B.** 6

    C. 15   **D.** 54

2

DECIMALS AND METRIC UNITS

MATH AND
HEALTH AND FITNESS

DATA BANK

Use the Health and Fitness
Data Bank on page 473 to
answer the questions.

1 If you listed the team sports
in order from least to
greatest number of possible
players on the field, which sport
would you list first? Where would
you place water polo?

2 Which is heavier: a bag containing a basketball and a volleyball or the same bag containing a field hockey ball and a water polo ball?

3 The game of volleyball, invented in 1895, was originally played using a basketball. How much heavier is a basketball than a volleyball?

4 **Using Critical Thinking** Suppose 43 football players broke up into five teams of the other sports listed. Each team was from a different sport and each player was on only one team. Which sports would be left out? Explain how you solved the problem.

Decimal Place Value
Tenths and Hundredths

You can use what you know about place value for whole numbers to help you understand decimals.

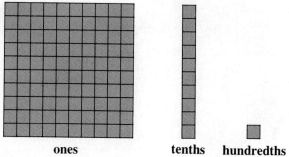

ones   tenths   hundredths

EXPLORE **Use Place Value Models**

Work in groups. Color graph paper to help you explain each of the following.
a. 3 tenths is the same as 30 hundredths.
b. 26 tenths is the same as 2 ones and 6 tenths.

TALK ABOUT IT

1. How many hundredths does it take to make 1 tenth?
2. How many tenths does it take to make 1 whole?
3. How many hundredths did you color to show 26 tenths?

Here is how to read and write decimals.

The graph paper is colored to show 2 ones and 67 hundredths.

ones	tenths	hundredths
2	6	7

We think:

We write:

Using a mixed number
$$2\frac{67}{100}$$

Using a decimal
2.67

We read: "two and sixty-seven hundredths"

TRY IT OUT

1. Color graph paper squares to show 2.36.
2. Color graph paper squares to show 3.04.

3. Write the decimal

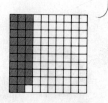

Write the decimal for the amount shown.

1.   **2.**   **3.**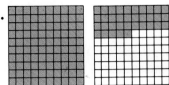

Write the decimal.

4. one and fifty hundredths

5. thirty-two hundredths

6. sixteen and sixty-three hundredths

7. seven hundredths

Write the word name for each decimal.

8. 0.4   **9.** 0.63   **10.** 1.25   **11.** 2.58

Between which two letters on the number line does each decimal fall?

12. 3.28   **13.** 3.82   **14.** 5.07   **15.** 5.70   **16.** 5.92   **17.** 6.29

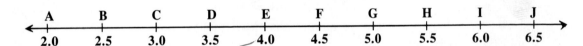

APPLY

MATH REASONING

18. Felipe said, "I know that 0.25 is the same as $\frac{1}{4}$." Color graph paper to prove that he is correct.

PROBLEM SOLVING

19. Michael colored small squares on a 10 by 10 square to show the decimal 0.37. Then he colored 25 more squares. What decimal part of the square was colored then?

▶ **ESTIMATION**

Write a decimal to estimate how full each jar is.

20.    **21.**    **22.**

More Practice, page 501, set C

33

Decimal Place Value
Thousandths

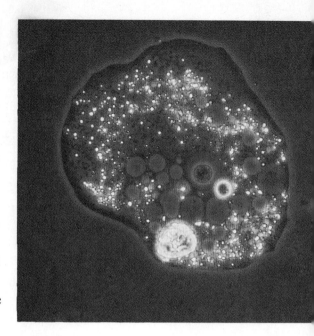

EXPLORE **Read the Information**

Amoebas are tiny, one-celled animals that range in size from 0.1 inch to 0.01 inch. A microscope is needed to see most amoebas. Kathleen used a microscope to look at an amoeba that she thought was between 0.02 inch and 0.03 inch wide. A more accurate measurement of the amoeba can be made using **thousandths.**

TALK ABOUT IT

1. Give the missing numbers:
   1 hundredth = 10 thousandths
   2 hundredths = ▓▓▓▓ thousandths
   3 hundredths = ▓▓▓▓ thousandths

2. Could the amoeba that Kathleen saw in the microscope have been 25 thousandths of an inch wide? Why?

The graph paper is colored to help you think about the size of thousandths.

We see: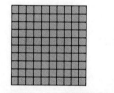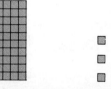

	ones	tenths	hundredths	thousandths
We think:	1	4	3	5

We write: 1.435

We read: "one and four hundred thirty-five thousandths"

We write in expanded form: 1 + 0.4 + 0.03 + 0.005

Read each decimal. Use place value to tell what each red digit means.

1. 5.263   **2.** 7.076   **3.** 0.324   **4.** 2.008   **5.** 0.029   **6.** 2.101

34

Read each decimal. Write it in expanded form. Then write the word name.

1. 4.286   **2.** 0.753   **3.** 0.042   **4.** 1.54   **5.** 7.008

6. 25.34   **7.** 4.622   **8.** 18.531   **9.** 0.427   **10.** 0.050

Write the decimal.

11. three hundred sixty-five thousandths

12. one and one hundred two thousandths

13. fifty-four thousandths

Write all the numbers from the box where:

14. the 4 has a value of 0.04

15. the 3 has a value of 0.003

16. the 8 has a value of 0.8

27.348	29.083
47.825	0.837
7.493	0.047

MATH REASONING

17. Put a decimal point in the number in red so that all these numbers are in order, smallest to largest. Example: 0.1 0.581 1

   A 1 215 10   **B** 10 5765 100   **C** 0.01 00384 .1

PROBLEM SOLVING

18. Study the decimal pattern. Skip count to write the next 5 decimals. 0.343, 0.346, 0.349, 0.352

19. Gina showed 0.74 by coloring a 10 by 10 square. Flora showed 0.49 on another 10 by 10 square. How many more small squares did Gina have to color than Flora?

▶ **CALCULATOR**

20. Try this game for two people. One player enters 123.456 on a calculator. The other player enters 654.321 on another calculator. The players take turns rolling a number cube. The player uses only the digit on the number cube and one or two zeros to make a number to subtract from the calculator number. The first player to reach zero is the winner.

More Practice, page 501, set D

Metric Units and Decimals

EXPLORE Examine the Figures

You can use decimals to compare metric units. A long step is about 1 meter. The figures below show three other units compared to the meter.

centimeters

0 1 2 3 4 5 6 7 8 9 10 11

1 decimeter (dm) = 0.1 meter (m)

1 centimeter (cm) = 0.01 m

1 millimeter (mm) = 0.001 m

TALK ABOUT IT

1. How many centimeters are in 1 decimeter? What decimal compares the centimeter to the decimeter?
2. How does the millimeter compare to the decimeter?
3. There are 1,000 meters in a **kilometer (km).** What decimal compares the meter to the kilometer?

1 meter (m)

Examples

These examples show some ways to use decimals with metric units.

A 10 mm = 1 cm
  9 mm = 0.9 cm
  39 mm = 3.9 cm

B 100 cm = 1 m
  75 cm = 0.75 m
  375 cm = 3.75 m
  375 cm = 3 m 75 cm

C 0.5 m = 5 dm
  0.5 m = 50 cm
  2.5 m = 2 m 5 dm

Give the missing numbers.

1. 1 cm = ▦ m

2. 1 m = ▦ km

3. 1 dm = ▦ m

4. 250 cm = ▦ m

5. 2,500 m = ▦ km

6. 25 dm = ▦ m

7. 3.4 m = ▦ cm

8. 3.4 km = ▦ m

9. 3.4 m = ▦ dm

Give each measurement in meters.

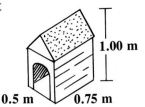

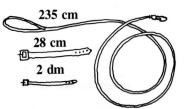

1. aquarium length
2. aquarium width
3. aquarium depth

4. dog leash
5. dog collar
6. cat collar

Give each measurement in centimeters.

7. doghouse length
8. doghouse width
9. doghouse height

10. rabbit pen length
11. rabbit pen width
12. fence height

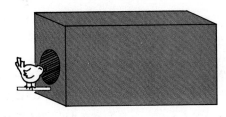

APPLY

MATH REASONING

The figure shows a side view of a birdhouse.

13. What is the height in centimeters?
14. Use the height as a benchmark. Estimate the length of the birdhouse in centimeters.

124 mm

PROBLEM SOLVING

15. The height of Erin's dog is 36 cm. Her cat is just 19 cm tall. How much taller is Erin's dog? Give your answer in meters.

MIXED REVIEW

Write in expanded form.

16. 245
17. 28,001
18. 1,080,000
19. 271,000

Give the digits that are in each period for the number 821,403,123,456.

20. thousands period
21. millions period
22. ones period

Evaluate each algebraic expression for $a = 15$ and $b = 26$.

23. $a + b$
24. $(2 \times a) + b$
25. $b - 17$
26. $(b + a) - 38$

Problem Solving
Draw a Picture

LEARN ABOUT IT

One strategy you can use to help you understand and solve problems is **Draw a Picture.**

Kelly walks past a park, a grocery store, a swimming pool, and a yogurt shop on her way to school. The park is next to the school. The pool is between the yogurt shop and the park. When she leaves home, she comes to the grocery store first. In what order does she pass each on her way to school?

First, I'll draw a line to show the route from her home to school.

Home   School

Then, I'll show the park next to the school.

Home   Park   School

Now, I'll show the swimming pool between the park and the yogurt shop.

Home   Yogurt Shop   Swimming Pool   Park   School

I'll show the grocery store first after Kelly's home.

Home   Grocery Store   Yogurt Shop   Swimming Pool   Park   School

Kelly passes the grocery store, then the yogurt shop, the swimming pool, and the park on her way to school.

TRY IT OUT

Read the problem and finish the solution.

Eric and his three friends had to wait in line to get into the swimming pool building. Eric was behind Juan. Bill was last. Dylan was ahead of Juan. Who got into the building first?

- Could Eric be first?
- Who was last?
- Who was ahead of Juan?

- Copy and finish drawing this picture to solve the problem.

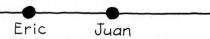

Eric   Juan

Draw a picture to solve each problem.

1. Five girls raced to the water slide in the park. Erica got there after Maria and Molly. Molly was first. Erica was between Dennie and Maria. Beth was last. In what order did the girls get to the water slide?

2. The frozen yogurt shop has 4 machines. French vanilla is in one of the middle machines. Chocolate is in the machine on the left. Both raspberry and mocha mint are to the right of the vanilla. Mocha mint is next to the vanilla. Garth chose the flavor in the machine on the farthest right. What did he get?

Solve. Choose a strategy from the list or use another strategy that you know.

Some Strategies

Act Out	Choose an Operation
Use Objects	Draw a Picture

3. On Saturday, 203 children came to the swimming pool. On Sunday, 128 children came. How many more children came to the pool on Saturday than on Sunday?

4. A ticket for the water slide costs 50¢. Kenji went down the slide 7 times in one day. How much did he spend for tickets?

5. The fence between the park and the school is 140 ft long. The students want to decorate the top of each post with a balloon for the school carnival. The posts are 10 ft apart and there is a post at each end. How many balloons do they need?

6. The carnival had four races. Each student participated in only one race. How many students participated?

Race	Students
3-legged	40
Wheelbarrow	28
Gunnysack	60
Backward	12

7. There were 24 students signed up for the roller skating relay. Each relay team had 3 members. How many teams were there?

8. Four teams competed in the over-the-wall contest. The Sun Devils came in second. The Marauders beat the Dragons. The Speed Demons won first prize. In what order did the four teams finish?

More Practice, page 522, set C

Decimals Through Hundred-Thousandths

LEARN ABOUT IT

EXPLORE Study the Information

Gold and silver can be hammered into sheets.
The sheets can be so thin that it would take
many of them piled on top of one another to
be as thick as a sheet of paper. It would take
70 sheets of silver 0.0001 cm (one ten-thousandth
centimeter) thick or 700 sheets of gold 0.00001 cm
(one hundred-thousandth centimeter) thick to be
as thick as this page.

TALK ABOUT IT

1. How many gold sheets would you need to pile on top of one
   another to be as thick as one silver sheet?
2. How thick are 10 silver sheets piled on top of one another?
3. What happens to the decimal point when you multiply a
   decimal by 10? Why? Example: 0.0001 × 10 = 0.001

The chart below will help you understand very small numbers such as 0.00025.

ones	tenths	hundredths	thousandths	ten-thousandths	hundred-thousandths
0 .	0	0	0	2	5

We read: "twenty-five hundred-thousandths"

Other Example

We write: 3.0286

We read: "three and two hundred eighty-six ten-thousandths"

> **Math Point**
> The word name of a decimal
> is determined by the place value
> of the digit in the last place.

TRY IT OUT

Read each decimal. Use place value to tell what each red digit means.

1. 0.0792
2. 0.00792
3. 0.792
4. 7.92

5. 3.00864
6. 3.0864
7. 3.864
8. 38.64

Read each decimal. Then write the word name.

1. 0.0006　　**2.** 0.00006　　**3.** 0.00645　　**4.** 14.02　　**5.** 6.007

6. 1.2005　　**7.** 12.0054　　**8.** 12.00540　　**9.** 0.9262　　**10.** 0.42873

Write the decimal.

11. nine hundred forty-five thousandths

12. six and fifteen ten-thousandths

13. two hundred six hundred-thousandths

Write all the numbers from the box where

14. the 7 has a value of 0.0007

15. the 2 has a value of 0.002

16. the 4 has a value of 0.00004

32.4625	0.34678
1.24354	567.283
5.0067	4.3628
4.00724	32.0865

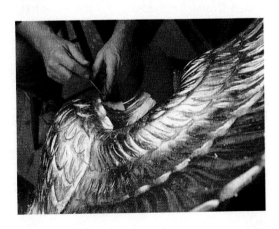

MATH REASONING

17. Write the next three decimals in the pattern.

5.2069
5.2168
5.2267
5.2366

PROBLEM SOLVING

18. A sheet of silver was 0.0025 cm thick. A sheet of gold was only one-tenth that thick. How thick was the gold sheet?

19. More Than One Answer Write a decimal that has 3 in the thousandths place and 7 in the hundred-thousandths place.

▶ **COMMUNICATION** **Understanding Math Words**

A length of 1 ten-thousandth centimeter is called a *micron*.

1 micron = 0.0001 cm

20. Gold and silver can be blended together and hammered into very thin sheets called gold leaves. Gold leaves can be used in artistic lettering and gilding. A gold leaf is 13 microns thick. How many centimeters thick is a leaf?

More Practice, page 502, set B

Comparing and Ordering Decimals

LEARN ABOUT IT

EXPLORE Compare the Data

A baseball batting average is the three-place decimal that you get when the number of hits the batter had is divided by the number of times at bat.

TALK ABOUT IT

1. If you put the averages in order from lowest to highest, what year would have the second highest average? The third highest average?

2. In which years were the batting averages between 0.330 and 0.340?

To compare two decimals, first line up the decimal points. Then follow the rules used for whole numbers.

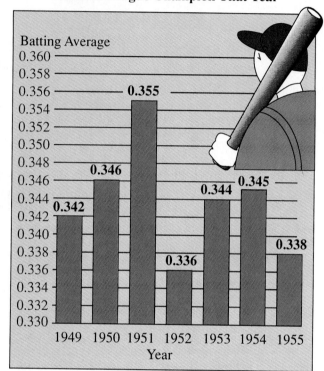

Old-Timer Batting Average For the National League Champion That Year

Examples

| 0.356 | $5 < 6$ |
| 0.362 | |

so 0.356 < 0.362
or 0.362 > 0.356

| 0.923 | $2 < 3$ |
| 0.93 | |

so 0.923 < 0.93
or 0.93 > 0.923

| 6.007 | $7 > 0$ |
| 6.0007 | |

so 6.007 > 6.0007
or 6.0007 < 6.007

TRY IT OUT

Write >, <, or = for each .

1. 9.05 ⦀ 9.01
2. 0.039 ⦀ 0.390
3. 0.90 ⦀ 0.89
4. 0.052 ⦀ 0.0520

5. 0.008 ⦀ 0.01
6. 4.96 ⦀ 5.02
7. 1.6840 ⦀ 1.685
8. 1.336 ⦀ 1.431

9. Order these decimals from least to greatest.
   3.549   3.954   3.459   3.594   4.359

42

Write >, <, or = for each .

1. 0.67 0.68   **2.** 0.742 0.80   **3.** 9.32 9.3   **4.** 0.006 0.0060

5. 0.7502 0.752   **6.** 3.0740 3.047   **7.** 4.7 4.6999   **8.** 2.0234 2.0243

Order each set of decimals from least to greatest.

9. 0.0375	**10.** 34.268	**11.** 0.3046
0.0369	34.259	0.3027
0.0381	34.264	0.3102
0.0372		0.3090
		0.3051

Match the decimals with the letters.

12. 0.437   **13.** 0.367   **14.** 0.473

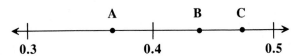

MATH REASONING

15. Sort these decimals into two sets, the ones greater than 0.5 and the ones less than 0.5.

0.496   0.5001   0.384   0.00069   1.0003   0.600

PROBLEM SOLVING

16. At the end of the community baseball season, the top three hitters were Jenny, Sam, and Bud. Jenny was batting 0.228, Sam was batting 0.232, and Bud was batting 0.227. Who won the batting title?

17. Health and Fitness Data Bank Stan Musial was National League batting champion seven times. What was his highest average? Over the years 1943 through 1948, did his batting improve or did it get worse?

18. Jamie and Georgia were batting under 0.300. Jamie's average was 0.298 and Georgia's was higher than Jamie's. What was Georgia batting?

▶ **ALGEBRA**

Write a decimal for *n*. There are many correct answers.

19. $2 < n < 3$ **20.** $0.3 < n < 0.8$ **21.** $1.4 < n < 1.5$ **22.** $0.36 < n < 0.37$

More Practice, page 502, set C   **43**

Rounding Decimals

LEARN ABOUT IT

EXPLORE Study the Information

It takes the moon an average of 27.32167 days
to revolve around the earth. To understand this
length of time, you may not need a decimal with
this many places. It may be sufficient to report
the decimal rounded to the nearest thousandth or
even the nearest tenth.

TALK ABOUT IT

1. Is this length of time closer to 27 or 28 days?
   Why?
2. Is the time closer to $27\frac{3}{10}$ days or to
   $27\frac{1}{2}$ days?

You round decimals using the same rules you used in rounding whole numbers.

Examples

Nearest Thousandth

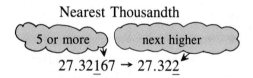

5 or more   next higher

27.32<u>1</u>67 → 27.32<u>2</u>

Nearest Tenth

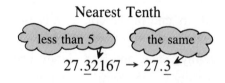

less than 5   the same

27.<u>3</u>2167 → 27.<u>3</u>

PRACTICE

Round to the nearest tenth.   **1.** 0.47   **2.** 5.662   **3.** 12.443   **4.** 0.6372

Round to the nearest hundredth.   **5.** 0.897   **6.** 5.006   **7.** 0.523   **8.** 22.2312

Round to the nearest whole number.   **9.** 4.73   **10.** 11.07   **11.** 0.58   **12.** 19.6

Round each number to the place of the underlined digit.

13. 2.<u>6</u>7   **14.** <u>8</u>.47   **15.** 5.4<u>7</u>8   **16.** 0.00<u>2</u>6   **17.** 42.<u>8</u>1

18. 2.8<u>2</u>4   **19.** 7.<u>3</u>19   **20.** 0.32<u>7</u>5   **21.** <u>0</u>.093   **22.** 0.8<u>8</u>4

MIDCHAPTER REVIEW/QUIZ

Use the decimals in the box.

0.00005
5.002
0.0520
5.2
0.500
0.052
2.5

1. In which decimals does the digit 5 have a value of 0.05?

2. Which decimals have a 2 in the thousandths place?

3. Which decimals are equal?

4. Which decimal is greatest?

5. Which decimal is least?

6. Which decimals are greater than 0.05?

7. Which decimals are less than 0.5? List them from greatest to least.

Carefully read each word name. Match each word name with its decimal from the list above.

8. fifty-two thousandths

9. five and two thousandths

10. five hundred twenty ten-thousandths

11. five hundred-thousandths

12. two and five tenths

13. five and two tenths

Write each measure as a number of meters.

14. 476 cm   15. 9 mm   16. 5 dm   17. 0.12 km

Write each measure as a number of centimeters.

18. 5 m   19. 2 mm   20. 3.8 dm   21. 1.25 dm   22. 2.175 mm

Write <, >, or = for each ⦀.

23. 6.08 ⦀ 6.008   24. 3.0250 ⦀ 3.052   25. 1.059 ⦀ 1.06

26. 5.1823 ⦀ 5.18023   27. 1.740 ⦀ 1.74   28. 6.12154 ⦀ 6.12145

PROBLEM SOLVING

29. Ben cycled 5 km north and 3 km west to reach the park from his house. Glenn left his house and cycled 3 km south and 5 km west to meet Ben. Describe a way to go from Ben's house to Glenn's house.

Problem Solving
Multiple-Step Problems

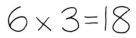

UNDERSTAND
ANALYZE DATA
PLAN
ESTIMATE
SOLVE
EXAMINE

LEARN ABOUT IT

Some problems can be solved using two or more of the operations: addition, subtraction, multiplication, and division. Because you need to use more than one step to solve them, these problems are called multiple-step problems.

The McKinleyville Soccer League has 6 teams. The teams play against teams from other leagues on Tuesdays and Saturdays. Each McKinleyville team plays 3 Tuesday games and 2 Saturday games every month. How many games a month does the league have scheduled for Tuesdays and Saturdays?

> First, I'll find the number of Tuesday games.

> Next, I'll find the number of Saturday games.

> Now, I'll add to find the number of games scheduled.

$$6 \times 3 = 18$$
$$6 \times 2 = 12$$
$$18 + 12 = 30$$

The McKinleyville Soccer League has 30 games scheduled a month.

TRY IT OUT

Solve. You may want to use a calculator.
Remember to follow the rules of order of operations.

1. The Red Boy Pizza team has 7 new members. The team can buy jerseys for $9 each and hats for $3 each. How much would jerseys and hats for all the new members cost?

2. The League had a soccer fundraiser one Saturday. They asked for a donation of $1 for each child and $3 for each adult. Laura's father gave a donation for 6 adults and 4 children. How much did he donate?

3. Elena's team has kicking drills twice a week. The first week they had drills for 35 min and 20 min. The next week the drills were 15 min and 25 min. How much longer were the kicking drills in the first week?

4. After each Saturday game, the 15 players on the Miracle Cleaners team go out for pizza and milk. A large pizza costs $12 and serves 3 players. How much does the team spend for pizzas?

46

Solve. Use any problem solving strategy. You may want to use a calculator.

1. The community center sponsors recreational activities. Use the table to find out how many more people participated in volleyball than in table tennis.

Activity	Number of People		
	Teens	Adults	Older Adults
Volleyball	55	31	46
Badminton	36	31	27
Tennis	21	24	15
Swimming	10	42	13
Table Tennis	37	35	30
Yoga	7	22	11

2. In the city-wide competition, Matt swam the 50-meter freestyle in a little more than 42 seconds. He finished the 100-meter freestyle in a little less than 69 seconds. About how much longer did it take Matt to swim the 100-meter freestyle?

3. A skydiver can free-fall at 185 miles an hour. A walker can walk at a pace of 5 miles an hour. How many times faster can the skydiver travel?

4. The first roller skate was invented in 1760. Then, 103 years later, a new roller skate like the ones we use today was invented. In what year was the new roller skate invented?

5. Four teams played for the soccer championship. The Stars came in third. The Comets placed after the Wizards, but ahead of the Stars. The Stars beat the Bears. Which team won the championship?

6. Pele scored a record 1,285 goals during his soccer career. Franz Binder scored 1,006 goals. About how many more goals did Pele score than Binder?

7. A volleyball has a circumference (distance around) of 67 centimeters. How many meters is that? How many millimeters?

8. **Suppose . . .** The parents' club bought snacks for after the game. They bought 20 raisin granola bars for $1 each and 4 large bottles of apple juice for $3 each. How much did they spend for snacks?

Suppose the facts were changed. Which of these facts would change the solution to the problem?
a. They bought 16 granola bars.
b. Each parent contributed $2.
c. Juice was on special at 2 bottles for $5.

More Practice, page 522, set D

47

Estimating Decimal Sums and Differences

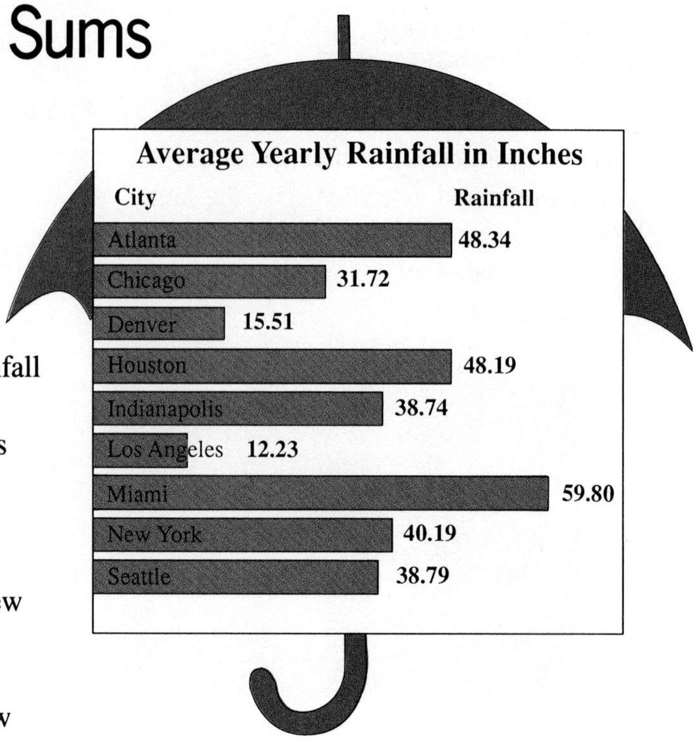

EXPLORE Examine the Data

The graph shows the average yearly rainfall for some American cities. Estimate how much more rain New York gets than Los Angeles.

TALK ABOUT IT

1. What is the amount of rainfall for New York to the nearest whole number?
2. What is it for Los Angeles?
3. About how much more rain does New York get than Los Angeles?

Average Yearly Rainfall in Inches	
City	Rainfall
Atlanta	48.34
Chicago	31.72
Denver	15.51
Houston	48.19
Indianapolis	38.74
Los Angeles	12.23
Miami	59.80
New York	40.19
Seattle	38.79

You have estimated the difference in the two decimals 12.23 and 40.19 by rounding to the nearest whole number. You can also estimate decimal sums and differences using front-end digits and compatible numbers.

Examples

Rounding

$$
\begin{array}{r}
72.89 \rightarrow 70 \\
+ 40.24 \rightarrow + 40 \\
\hline
110
\end{array}
$$

Front-end digits

$$
\begin{array}{r}
62.38 \\
+ 78.76 \\
\hline
130
\end{array}
$$

2 + 8

140
Improved

Compatible numbers

$$
\begin{array}{r}
24.92 \\
67.21 \\
+ 76.38 \\
\hline
167
\end{array}
$$

About 100

Estimate each sum and difference. Use any method you choose.

1.
$$
\begin{array}{r}
8.92 \\
+ 7.23
\end{array}
$$

2.
$$
\begin{array}{r}
48.32 \\
37.68 \\
+ 53.17
\end{array}
$$

3.
$$
\begin{array}{r}
\$92.87 \\
- 38.98
\end{array}
$$

4.
$$
\begin{array}{r}
7.832 \\
- 1.964
\end{array}
$$

5.
$$
\begin{array}{r}
\$74.89 \\
27.36 \\
+ 56.03
\end{array}
$$

Estimate each sum and difference.
Use any method you choose.

1. 4.63
    + 7.71

2. 12.4
    − 10.66

3. 19.89
    + 4.52

4. 19.055
    − 4.41

5. 32.79
    − 13.19

6. 4.53
    + 0.72

7. 20.263
     4.46
    + 19.55

8. 124.95
     59.50
    + 100.40

9. 60.88
    41.45
    + 9.95

10. 57.34
    + 26.59

11. 80.03
    + 46.57

12. 12.89
    − 5.24

APPLY

MATH REASONING

Which sum is more than 60?

13. 23.87
    + 35.92

14. 24.87
    +35.92

Which difference is less than 30?

15. 70.38
    − 39.99

16. 39.06
    − 9.95

PROBLEM SOLVING

17. What city has an average rainfall
    between that of New York and that of
    Atlanta?

18. During a dry year, Seattle had only
    24.96 inches of rain. The next year it
    had 39.87 inches. About how much
    rain did it have for the two years?

MIXED REVIEW

Estimate by rounding.

19. 28
    + 57

20. 189
    + 129

21. 80
    − 18

22. 851
    + 458

23. 256
    − 217

Evaluate the expression $(8 \times a) + (8 \times b)$ for the values given.

24. $a = 18$ and $b = 32$

25. $a = 25$ and $b = 15$

26. $a = 200$ and $b = 600$

More Practice, page 502, set E

Reviewing Addition and Subtraction
Decimals

Adding and subtracting decimals is very much like adding and subtracting whole numbers. These examples will help you review these skills.

A Add 17.6 and 38.93.

Line up the decimal points.
Trade if necessary.

```
  1 1↓
  1 7.6
+ 3 8.9 3
  5 6.5 3
```

15 tenths = 1 and 5 tenths

B 3.88 + 0.6 + 9.872

```
  2 1
  3.8 8
  0.6
+ 9.8 7 2
 1 4.3 5 2
```

C Subtract 2.617 from 7.342.

```
  6 13 3 12
  7̶.3̶ 4̶ 2̶
- 2.6 1 7
  4.7 2 5
```

1 hundredth and 2 thousandths = 12 thousandths

D 680.3 − 136.9

```
  7 9 13
  6 8̶ 0.3
- 1 3 6.9
  5 4 3.4
```

80 = 79 + 10 tenths

Add or subtract.

1. $\begin{array}{r} 0.68 \\ + 0.4 \\ \hline \end{array}$	**2.** $\begin{array}{r} 14.75 \\ + 72.88 \\ \hline \end{array}$	**3.** $\begin{array}{r} 265.3 \\ - 121.44 \\ \hline \end{array}$	**4.** $\begin{array}{r} 703.02 \\ - 98.86 \\ \hline \end{array}$	**5.** $\begin{array}{r} 12.5265 \\ 24.69 \\ 0.347 \\ + 6.8 \\ \hline \end{array}$
6. $\begin{array}{r} 61.3 \\ - 16.95 \\ \hline \end{array}$	**7.** $\begin{array}{r} 8.004 \\ - 2.5721 \\ \hline \end{array}$	**8.** $\begin{array}{r} \$42.69 \\ + 9.89 \\ \hline \end{array}$	**9.** $\begin{array}{r} \$0.73 \\ + 0.25 \\ \hline \end{array}$	

10. 4.7 + 8.8 + 0.45   **11.** 0.472 − 0.0892   **12.** 0.61 − 0.17   **13.** 5.9 + 6.057

14. 213.060 − 4.8   **15.** 1.04 − 0.9999   **16.** 439.6 + 7.049 + 12.32 + 0.0009

PRACTICE

Add or subtract.

1.	62.74 − 17.26	2.	0.362 − 0.19	3.	3.825 + 4.769	4.	375.2 − 183.9	5.	83.45 17.69 0.094 + 13.98

6.	32.6 + 78.9	7.	67.85 + 34.9	8.	0.862 − 0.195	9.	3.826 + 1.79

10.	803.7 − 136.9	11.	$19.95 − 8.89	12.	$10.00 − 5.98	13.	$5.00 − 3.95	14.	$20.00 − 13.88

15. 2.36 + 3.78 + 2.67

16. 0.381 + 0.2 + 0.377

17. 42.83 + 36.356 + 75.6

18. 36.2 − 27.75

19. 30.86 − 24.9

20. 92.03 − 29.28

21. Add 28.75 and 36.29.

22. Subtract 26.34 from 95.

23. Find the sum of 0.836 and 0.92.

24. Find the difference of 2.836 and 7.9.

APPLY

MATH REASONING

Use mental math and the first example to write answers only.

368 + 975 1,343	25.	0.368 + 0.975	26.	3.68 + 9.75	27.	13.43 − 9.75	28.	1.343 − 0.368

PROBLEM SOLVING

29. A pipe was 3.8629 cm in diameter. It needs to pass through a hole that is 3.8634 cm. Will it fit? By how much?

30. **Health and Fitness Data Bank** Which has a larger circumference, a soccer ball or a basketball? How much larger?

DATA BANK

▶ **USING CRITICAL THINKING   Support Your Conclusion**

31. Choose the correct answer. Give examples to support your conclusion.
   - The sum of two decimals less than 1 is always less than 1.

   - The sum of two decimals less than 1 is sometimes less than 1.

   - The sum of two decimals less than 1 is never less than 1.

More Practice, page 503, set A

Problem Solving
Choosing a Calculation Method

UNDERSTAND
ANALYZE DATA
PLAN
ESTIMATE
SOLVE
EXAMINE

LEARN ABOUT IT

When you solve a problem, you often need to decide on a calculation method. You might use different methods to solve different kinds of problems.

Calculation Methods
- Paper and Pencil
- Mental Math
- Calculator

SALE	ALL-STAR Sporting Equipment					SALE
	Reg. Price	**Sale Price**			**Reg. Price**	**Sale Price**
Fishing Rod & Reel	$80.00	$69.95	Golf Clubs—set of 12		$198.00	$144.50
Tennis Rackets	$75.00	$59.50	Running Shoes		$67.50	$47.50
Basketballs	$29.00	$20.00	Sleeping Bags		$127.40	$98.79

How much would you save by buying a basketball on sale?

$29.00 − $20.00. This is easy to do in my head. I can use mental math.

How much would you save by buying a sleeping bag on sale?

$127.40 − $98.79. I could use paper and pencil, but a calculator may be better.

Here are two general rules to follow when you are deciding on a calculation method.

- **First try mental math.** Look for numbers that can be computed easily in your head.
- **If you can't use mental math, choose between pencil and paper and a calculator.** Problems that require many trades or steps are often easier to solve by using a calculator.

TRY IT OUT

Tell which calculation method you would choose and why. Then solve.

1. $236.25 − $197.78

2. $100 − $75

3. 24.30 + 28.70

4. 8 × $37.95

5. 25 + 87 + 75

6. 426 + 38 + 111

7. 89 + 97 + 68 + 79

8. 2,003 − 1,876

9. $56.20 + $29.00

Choose an appropriate calculation method and tell why. Then solve.

1. 283 + 174

2. 50 + 93 + 50

3. $30.00 − $17.95

4. 134.15 − 17.89

5. 9 × 9,000

6. $69.95 + $95.00

7. 125 − 50

8. $38.59 × 6

9. 25 + 68 + 75

10. 39.83 ÷ 7

11. 784 − 58

12. $1.00 − $0.15

13. $20.00 − $7.95

14. 624 + 111

15. 4,007 − 1,888

16. 28 + 35 + 16

Solve. Choose an appropriate calculation method.

17. The tax on a basketball was $1.20. How much money will you need to buy the sale-price basketball?

18. The school coach bought 12 pairs of running shoes for the cross-country team on sale. How much were the shoes before tax?

19. How much money did the coach save by buying the 12 pairs of running shoes on sale?

20. The tax on a set of the golf clubs on sale was $8.67. What was the total cost for the golf clubs including tax?

21. **Data Hunt** Choose one of the items from the ad that you would like to have. Find out how much sales tax you would have to pay in your community. Then compute the total cost of the item at its regular price.

22. What is your total savings if you buy a fishing rod and reel and a tennis racket on sale?

23. Sleeping bags weren't selling well even at the sale price. The manager took another $10 off the sale price. How much did the sleeping bags cost then?

24. **Write Your Own Problem** Write and solve your own problem using data from the ad.

More Practice, page 523, set A

Data Collection and Analysis
Group Decision Making

UNDERSTAND
ANALYZE DATA
PLAN
ESTIMATE
SOLVE
EXAMINE

Doing a Survey
Group Skill
Listen to Others

Some television and radio advertisements use jingles (short verses or songs) to make the names of products and services easy to remember. You probably know jingles that advertise things like foods, perfumes, and soaps. What advertising jingles do you think are most effective in helping people remember names of products? Conduct a survey to find out.

Collecting Data

1. Work with your group to think of at least five advertising jingles. Number them and write them on a piece of paper. If the name of the product is mentioned in the jingle, replace the name with a blank.

2. Show your list of jingles to at least 20 people. Ask each person to name the product that each jingle advertises. Use tallies to record whether or not the people you survey recognize products when they see the jingles. Here is one way to tally your survey results.

	Can Recognize Product	Cannot Recognize Product
Jingle 1		
Jingle 2		
Jingle 3		
Jingle 4		
Jingle 5		

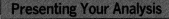
Presenting Your Analysis

3. Make a bar graph to show the data collected in your survey. Choose labels and a title. For each jingle that you used in the survey, draw a bar to show how many people recognized the product. Choose a scale for your graph that will give you enough space to show the largest number in your tally. Use the bar graph shown as an idea for starting your graph.

LABEL   TITLE

Jingle 1						
Jingle 2						
Jingle 3						
Jingle 4						
Jingle 5						

0 1 2 3 ? ? ?

4. Present your graph and give a brief oral report about your survey. In planning what to present in your report, think about the following:

- For which jingles did more than half of the people in the survey recognize the product?
- Which jingle do you think was most effective?
- Which was least effective?
- Were you surprised by the results of the survey? What would you predict about the results if you tried the survey again with a different group of people?

Wrap Up

Measure Match

Match each expression on the left with a measurement on the right.

1. another name for 0.023 meters

2. four and two thousandths meters

3. two and three hundredths centimeters

4. another name for 4.12 meters

5. two and three thousandths centimeters

6. four and two hundredths decimeters

7. the sum of 1.5 meters and 25 meters

8. the difference between 25 meters and 1.5 meters

a. 2.03 cm

b. 2.003 cm

c. 4.002 m

d. 4.02 dm

e. 26.5 m

f. 41.2 dm

g. 23.5 m

h. 2.3 cm

Sometimes, Always, Never

Decide which word should go in the blank: *sometimes*, *always*, or *never*.
Explain your choices.

9. The number 4.76 can _____ be rounded to 4.7.

10. The word name of a decimal is _____ determined by the place value of the digit in the last place.

11. The sum of two decimals, each less than 2, is _____ greater than 1.

12. The difference between two decimals, each less than 1, is _____ less than 1.

Project

Design a decimal game in which players make up problems to fit the clues they are given. An example of a clue is "two decimals whose sum is 8.43." A problem that fits the clue is "5.06 + 3.37." Include a name for the game, the rules, a playing board (if needed), how to time and score the game, and a way to record the scores.

CHAPTER REVIEW/TEST

Part 1   Understanding

Write a decimal to estimate how full each glass is.

1.

2.

3. Order these numbers from least to greatest.

    3.6508   3.665   0.3709   3.658   0.36589

Estimate each sum or difference. Is the answer more than 20?

4.	27.24	5.	13.6	6.	12.7	7.	42.29
	− 0.57		+ 4.5		+ 9.9		− 26.07

Part 2   Skills

Write the decimal.

8. two hundred thirty-six thousandths

9. four and twenty-nine hundred thousandths

Give the missing numbers.

10. 23 cm = ▓ mm

11. 45 dm = ▓ m

Compare. Write >, <, or = for each ▓.

12. 9.002 ▓ 9.02

13. 1.0330 ▓ 1.033

Round each number to the place of the underlined digit.

14. 24.4<u>7</u>6

15. 0.<u>3</u>682

16. 7<u>8</u>.453

Add or subtract.

17. 4.79 + 59.0398 + 0.847

18. 88.04 − 27.35

19. 71 − 39.09

Part 3   Applications

20. Tell which method you choose. Then solve the problem. Fran bought a poster for $3.50 and a greeting card for $1.50. How much did she spend?

21. Four divers competed in the belly flop contest. John made a bigger splash than Bo. Ann came in third. Meg came in first with the biggest splash. In what order did the divers finish?

22. **Challenge**   Kim worked five days for the math professor. Each day she was paid twice what she was paid the previous day. If she earned $10 on the third day, how much did she earn in all?

ENRICHMENT
Addition and Subtraction Patterns

In these problems there are hidden digits covered by black boxes.
Copy each problem without the boxes and replace the boxes with the
correct digits. Look for cases where there must be trades.

1.
```
   8.▓ 9
 + 6.▓ ▓
 1 5.9 6
```

2.
```
   ▓ ▓.6 ▓ 1
 +   7.▓ 1 ▓
 1 0 0.0 0 0
```

3.
```
   1 ▓.▓ ▓
 +   0.▓ 8
   2 ▓.9 0
```

4.
```
   4 ▓.0 ▓
 - ▓ 9.▓ 7
     6.6 8
```

5.
```
 7 0.0 ▓ 0
 - ▓.2 3 4
 6 8.7 6 ▓
```

6.
```
 1 3.▓ 0 ▓
 - ▓.4 ▓ 2
   4.1 2 2
```

7.
```
   ▓ ▓ ▓
   3 7 5
 + 6 1 9
 1,6 0 4
```

8.
```
   7,8 1 3
 - ▓ ▓ ▓ ▓
   2,9 0 5
```

Finish these magic squares. Each row, column, and diagonal adds to
the same magic sum.

9.
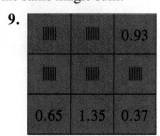

Magic Sum = ▓

10.
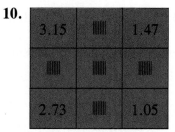

Magic Sum = 6.3

Use the numbers 151 through 159 to complete the magic square.

11.

▓	157	▓
159	▓	151
▓	153	▓

Magic Sum = ▓

CUMULATIVE REVIEW

Subtract or multiply.

1.
$$\begin{array}{r} 15 \\ -7 \\ \hline \end{array}$$

A. 22   B. 8

C. 9   D. 6

2. 9×7

A. 56   B. 16

C. 63   D. 2

3. A triangle that has no sides of the same length is called

A. equilateral   B. scalene

C. isosceles   D. rhombus

4. A quadrilateral with exactly one pair of parallel sides is a

A. square   B. rhombus

C. trapezoid   D. rectangle

5. How many 100s make 8,000?

A. 8   B. 80

C. 80,000   D. 800

6. In 436,907,364,321, find the digit in the millions place.

A. 6   B. 7

C. 0   D. 4

7. How much greater is 42,593 than 41,593?

A. 1   B. 100

C. 10   D. 1,000

8. Which numerical expression has an answer of 30?

A. $6 - 2 \times 3$ B. $6 \times 2 + 3$

C. $6 \times (2 + 3)$ D. $(6 + 2) \times 3$

Add or subtract.

9. $56{,}507 - 38{,}009$

A. 18,508   B. 28,498

C. 18,498   D. 94,516

10. $5{,}688 + 429 + 7{,}007$

A. 13,104   B. 13,224

C. 13,124   D. 13,114

11. Estimate by rounding to the nearest thousand: $18{,}213 + 6{,}775$

A. 24,000   B. 25,000

C. 27,000   D. 26,000

12. Find the decimal for thirty-four hundredths.

A. 0.034   B. 3,400

C. 0.34   D. 34.01

13. Carl's frog hopped 5.59 m. How many centimeters did it hop?

A. 55.9 cm   B. 500.59 cm

C. 0.559 cm   D. 559 cm

14. Find the decimal that has 4 in the thousandths place and 2 in the tenths place.

A. 4,127   B. 5.274

C. 0.2554   D. 4,006.2

3

MULTIPLICATION: WHOLE NUMBERS AND DECIMALS

MATH AND SCIENCE

DATA BANK

Use the Science Data Bank on page 475 to answer the questions.

1 Which of the planets is about the same size (has about the same surface area) as Earth? Which planet is about 90 times larger than Earth?

2 How much farther from the sun in astronomical units is Saturn than Jupiter? How much farther is Saturn than Mercury?

3 Which planet moves at a speed three times slower than Earth? Which planet moves six times slower than Earth?

4 **Using Critical Thinking** Suppose a new planet was discovered that was 50.18 AU from the sun. At about what speed do you predict it would move as it revolves around the sun? Use the data to justify your prediction.

Mental Math and Estimation of Products

EXPLORE Analyze the Process

On the sun, the gravitational pull is much stronger than on the earth. An astronaut who weighs 187 pounds on the earth would weigh about 28 times as much on the sun. About how much would the astronaut weigh on the sun?

You multiply because you need to find how many times as much. You can estimate the product by using rounding and mental math.

You can estimate this product,	28×187	if you can round these numbers	$28 \rightarrow 30$ $187 \rightarrow 200$	and find the product.	30×200

TALK ABOUT IT

1. How can you use the product 3×2 to find 30×200?
2. How many 0s does 30×200 have?
3. What is an estimate for 28×187?
4. Use a complete sentence to give a reasonable answer to the story problem.

Other Examples

A 7×814
↓
$7 \times 800 = 5,600$

B 25×319
↓   ↓
$30 \times 300 = 9,000$

C 462×536
↓   ↓
$500 \times 500 = 250,000$

TRY IT OUT

First round the numbers. Then find the special product to estimate.

1. 28×43 2. 7×394 3. $4 \times 2,876$ 4. 34×278 5. 298×216

Find the products.

1. 30 × 40 **2.** 3 × 600 **3.** 70 × 200 **4.** 60 × 80 **5.** 8 × 700

6. 600 × 300 **7.** 50 × 80 **8.** 400 × 900 **9.** 30 × 800 **10.** 5 × 400

Use rounding and mental math to estimate each product.

11. 38 × 45 **12.** 41 × 56 **13.** 74 × 38 **14.** 56 × 45 **15.** 38 × 56

16. 8 × 337 **17.** 7 × 375 **18.** 4 × 624 **19.** 6 × 924 **20.** 5 × 729

21. 41 × 624 **22.** 87 × 337 **23.** 45 × 589 **24.** 56 × 624 **25.** 74 × 337

26. 44 × 295 **27.** 382 × 516 **28.** 494 × 812 **29.** 276 × 48 **30.** 399 × 408

MATH REASONING

Use estimation to tell if the answer is reasonable or unreasonable.

31. 37 × 286 = 10,582 **32.** 8 × 798 = 4,384 **33.** 78 × 83 = 64,740

34. 286 × 844 = 24,138 **35.** 327 × 48 = 15,696 **36.** 584 × 672 = 592,440

PROBLEM SOLVING

Estimate answers to these problems.

37. The earth travels 30 km in a second. About how far does the earth travel in 13 minutes?

38. Science Data Bank About how far does Jupiter travel in 191 seconds?

▶ USING CRITICAL THINKING Supporting a Conclusion

Give a counterexample to show that the following statement is false.

39. When you round one number up and the other down, the estimate will always be less than the actual product.

Reviewing Multiplication
Whole Numbers

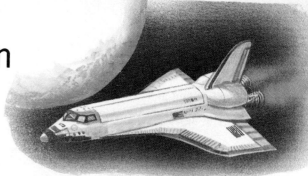

The examples below will help you review multiplication of whole numbers.

A $$\begin{array}{r} 6\ 6\ 3 \\ \$5,9\ 9\ 5 \\ \times\ \ \ \ \ \ \ 7 \\ \hline \$41,9\ 6\ 5 \end{array}$$ *7 × 5 = 3 tens and 5 ones*	**B** $$\begin{array}{r} 1\ 3\ 2 \\ 6,3\ 8\ 7 \\ \times\ \ \ \ \ \ \ 4 \\ \hline 2\ 5,5\ 4\ 8 \end{array}$$ *4 × 8 tens plus 2 tens = 34 tens*
C $$\begin{array}{r} 3\ 2 \\ 7,0\ 6\ 4 \\ \times\ \ \ \ \ 6\ 0 \\ \hline 4\ 2\ 3,8\ 4\ 0 \end{array}$$ *6 tens × 4 = 24 tens*	**D** $$\begin{array}{r} 9,2\ 8\ 6 \\ \times\ \ \ \ \ 5\ 3 \\ \hline 2\ 7\ 8\ 5\ 8 \\ 4\ 6\ 4\ 3\ 0\ 0 \\ \hline 4\ 9\ 2,1\ 5\ 8 \end{array}$$ *3 × 6 = 1 ten and 8 ones Write 8. Remember 1.*

Find the products.

1. $$\begin{array}{r} 3,684 \\ \times\ \ \ \ \ 6 \\ \hline \end{array}$$

2. $$\begin{array}{r} 365 \\ \times\ \ 27 \\ \hline \end{array}$$

3. $$\begin{array}{r} 6,843 \\ \times\ \ \ \ 74 \\ \hline \end{array}$$

4. $$\begin{array}{r} 4,006 \\ \times\ \ \ \ 37 \\ \hline \end{array}$$

5. $$\begin{array}{r} 7,284 \\ \times\ \ \ \ 30 \\ \hline \end{array}$$

6. $$\begin{array}{r} 1,093 \\ \times\ \ \ \ \ 5 \\ \hline \end{array}$$

7. $$\begin{array}{r} 12,720 \\ \times\ \ \ \ \ \ 73 \\ \hline \end{array}$$

8. $$\begin{array}{r} 21,139 \\ \times\ \ \ \ \ \ 51 \\ \hline \end{array}$$

9. 293 × 3

10. 468 × 37

11. 4,538 × 40

12. 8,217 × 52

13. 47 × 492

14. 6,250 × 76

15. 889 × 47

16. 354 × 76

17. 24 × 32

Find the products.

1.	86 × 8	2.	75 × 7	3.	86 × 4	4.	678 × 7	5.	394 × 5

6. 6,038 × 9
7. 7,954 × 3
8. 5,009 × 4
9. 32,947 × 8
10. 27,306 × 7

11. 965 × 6
12. 3,198 × 3
13. 94 × 30
14. 638 × 60
15. 4,387 × 40

16. 52 × 23
17. 96 × 74
18. 374 × 65
19. 1,537 × 28
20. 3,605 × 18

21. 74 × 25
22. 86 × 32
23. 27 × 205
24. 590 × 62

25. 54 × 618
26. 1,370 × 69
27. 83 × 2,431
28. 5,046 × 29

29. What is the product when 426 is multiplied by 37?

30. Find the product of 786 and 9.

MATH REASONING

31. If you know that $40 × 387 = 15,480$, how can you find $39 × 387$ without multiplying?

PROBLEM SOLVING

32. **Science Data Bank** How many Earth days does it take Venus to revolve around the Sun 12 times?

DATA BANK

▶ **CALCULATOR**

The product of a book's page numbers is 5,852 ($76 × 77$). To what pages would you need to open a book so that the product of the facing page numbers would be the numbers below? Use guess and check and your calculator.

33. 7,832
34. 2,162

35. 39,402

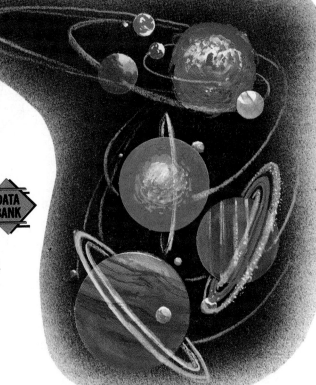

Problem Solving
Guess and Check

UNDERSTAND
ANALYZE DATA
PLAN
ESTIMATE
SOLVE
EXAMINE

LEARN ABOUT IT

To solve some problems, you have to do more than choose an operation. The strategy **Guess and Check** can often help you.

The Bell Canyon Bird Sanctuary has 35 booted and snake eagles. They have 7 more booted eagles than snake eagles. How many of each do they have?

I'll start by guessing the number of snake eagles.

Then I'll check my guess. It's too small.

Guess	Snake Eagles	Booted Eagles
	10	17
Check	10 + 17 = 27	

I'll guess again and pick a larger number.

Then I'll check my guess. It's too big.

Guess	Snake Eagles	Booted Eagles
	15	22
Check	15 + 22 = 37	

I'll guess again and pick a number between my other guesses. Then I'll check it.

This checks. The Bell Canyon Bird Sanctuary has 14 snake eagles and 21 booted eagles.

Guess	Snake Eagles	Booted Eagles
	14	21
Check	14 + 21 = 35	

TRY IT OUT

Complete the solution to the problem.

The Crestview Zoo has 2 bald eagles, a female and a male. Together they weigh 27 pounds. The female eagle weighs twice as much as the male eagle. How much does each eagle weigh?

- How much do the 2 eagles weigh together?

- Which eagle weighs more? How much more?

- Use guess and check and the table to solve this problem.

	Male		Female
Guess	5		10
Check		5 + 10 = 15	Too low
Guess	?		?
Check		?	

66

Solve by guessing and checking.

1. A golden eagle takes about 56 hours to hatch. It may take the chick 3 times as long to break out of the shell as to peck the first hole. How long does it take the chick to peck the first hole?

2. The bird sanctuary is open to the public on weekends. General admission tickets cost $3 each and student tickets cost $2 each. One Saturday, 36 tickets were sold and $93 was collected. How many of each kind of ticket were sold?

MIXED PRACTICE

Solve. Choose a strategy from the list or use another strategy that you know.

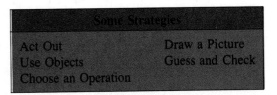

Some Strategies	
Act Out	Draw a Picture
Use Objects	Guess and Check
Choose an Operation	

3. A golden eagle weighs about 3 ounces at birth. In less than 2 months it weighs 40 times as much. How much does it weigh then?

4. The feathers on a bald eagle weigh a little less than 21 ounces. If there are 349 feathers in 1 ounce, about how many feathers does the eagle have?

5. Use the table to find the total number of eagles.

Groups of Eagles	
Name	Number
Fish and sea eagle	11
Harpy eagle	6
Snake eagle	12
Booted eagle	30

6. The Philippine monkey-eating eagle is the second largest eagle. The Australian little eagle is smaller than a snake eagle. The harpy eagle is bigger than the snake eagle. Which of the four eagles is the largest? The smallest?

7. A large eagle eats 12 pounds of food a day. How many pounds of food are needed to feed 8 large eagles for a year?

8. The animal rescue center received 152 injured birds in 4 weeks. It received 8 more birds the second week than the first week, 8 more birds in the third week than the second week, and 8 more birds the fourth week than the third week. How many birds did the center receive in the first week?

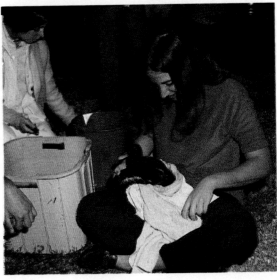

Estimating Decimal Products

You can use whole number facts to help you estimate decimal products.

EXPLORE **Analyze the Process**

Carmen rode her bicycle in a long-distance bicycling race. During the race, she averaged 18.9 miles per hour for 3.75 hours. How many miles did she ride during that time? Three students calculated the answer to the problem.

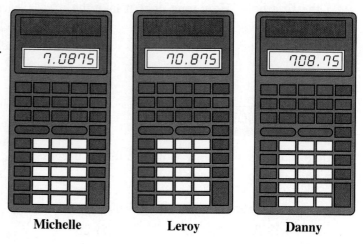

| Michelle | Leroy | Danny |

Michelle: 7.0875   Leroy: 70.875   Danny: 708.75

TALK ABOUT IT

1. Why is Michelle's answer unreasonable?
2. Do you think you could drive a car more than 700 miles in 4 hours? What does this tell you about Danny's answer?
3. If you round 18.9 to 20 and 3.75 to 4, what estimate do you get for 18.9 × 3.75? Is Leroy's answer reasonable?
4. Explain how Michelle, Leroy, and Danny found three such different answers.

Other Examples

A Round to estimate.
42.86 × 2.93
↓   ↓
40   ×   3   = 120

B Find compatible numbers to estimate.
27.48 × 3.96
↓   ↓
25   ×   4   = 100

TRY IT OUT

Estimate by rounding.

1. 3.92 × 8.19   **2.** 32.9 × 8.6   **3.** 17.9 × 43.82   **4.** 56.3 × 8.97

Estimate by finding compatible numbers.

5. 27.87 × 3.56   **6.** 56.3 × 1.87   **7.** 18.97 × 4.95   **8.** 24.6 × 4.28

Estimate each product. Choose any method you know.

1. 3.7 × 8.3 **2.** 6.47 × 7.19 **3.** 8.96 × 4 **4.** $48.36 × 5

5. 71.974 × 8.6 **6.** 67.46 × 39.28 **7.** 319.3 × 86.76 **8.** $909.36 × 6.2

9. 7.4 × 3.826 **10.** 9.324 × 6.7 **11.** 57.8 × 9.15 **12.** 6.45 × 8.59

APPLY

MATH REASONING

Look at this product:
4,837 × 729 = 3,526,173.
Use estimation to choose **a, b,** or
c as the correct answer.

13. 48.37 × 7.29
   a. 3526.173 **b.** 352.6173 **c.** 35.26173

14. 4.837 × 0.729
   a. 3.526173 **b.** 35.26173 **c.** 0.3526173

15. 48.37 × 72.9
   a. 352.6173 **b.** 35.26173 **c.** 3526.173

PROBLEM SOLVING

16. Chris rode 2.5 hours into the wind at an average speed of 12.96 miles per hour. Then he rode with the wind at 19.67 miles per hour for 1.75 hours. About how far did he ride?

17. The bike trails at the state park were 12.9, 17.6, 14.9, and 15.6 miles. Flora rode two of them for 30.5 miles. Which two trails did she ride?

MIXED REVIEW

Round 241.71284 to the given place.

18. tenth **19.** thousandth **20.** hundred **21.** hundredth **22.** whole number

Estimate.

23. 4.812 + 2.142 **24.** 28.02 − 26.7 **25.** 2.06 + 17.83

26. 9.187 + 2.87 + 10 **27.** 800 − 30.007 **28.** 23.1998 + 14.6 + 36.512

Using Critical Thinking

FUNCTION MACHINE

? ? ? ? ?

Function Rule

input 4

output 8

LEARN ABOUT IT

Erin and Doug are playing a game that they call Guess My Rule. Erin explained, "The best way to understand our game is to think of a function machine. A number is put in, something happens to it, and the result comes out."

Erin said, "Input 4."

Doug said, "Output 8."

Erin replied, "The function is × 2."

Doug said, "That's not the function. Try another input number."

TALK ABOUT IT

1. What was the input number? The output number?
2. Could Erin's guess of the rule be correct? Can you be sure of the rule from this one example? Why or why not?
3. Erin said "7" and Doug answered "11." Then Erin said "15" and Doug answered "19." Now do you think you know the rule? What is it?

In	Out
10	22
5	12
4	10
2	6
0	2
3	8

In	Out
50	150
4	12
2	6
0	0
22	6
15	

TRY IT OUT

Think of the cards as a recording of the game. Give the rule being used and any missing numbers.

1.

In	Out
10	22
5	12
4	10
2	6
0	2
3	8

2.

In	Out
50	150
4	12
2	6
0	0
22	66
15	45

3.

In	Out
8	15
6	11
9	17
3	▓▓
2	▓▓
1	▓▓

4.

In	Out
6	20
5	17
3	11
9	▓▓
▓▓	2
4	▓▓

5. Play Guess My Rule with a classmate.

MIDCHAPTER REVIEW/QUIZ

Find the products.

1. 30 × 8 **2.** 60 × 70 **3.** 80 × 900 **4.** 5 × 600 **5.** 200 × 500

Use rounding and mental math to estimate the products.

6. 6 × 786 **7.** 27 × 43 **8.** 49 × 51 **9.** 207 × 81 **10.** 427 × 68

11. 12 × 258 **12.** 3 × 419 **13.** 898 × 906 **14.** 327 × 682 **15.** 507 × 198

Find the products.

16. 423   **17.** 94   **18.** 607   **19.** 2,198   **20.** 35,386
    × 6   × 51   × 83   × 30   × 7

21. 23   **22.** 672   **23.** 80   **24.** 3,406   **25.** 12,856
    × 2   × 94   × 87   × 65   × 3

26. 18 × 32 **27.** 25 × 476 **28.** 89 × 567 **29.** 1,231 × 54 **30.** 3,805 × 36

Round or use compatible numbers to estimate the products.

31. 2.7 × 4.5   **32.** 15.98 × 2.3   **33.** 4 × $26.54

34. 432.6 × 7   **35.** 28.54 × 43.95   **36.** 825.9 × 124.8

37. 12.125 × 93.984   **38.** 503.27 × 390.841   **39.** 8.23 × 6.459

PROBLEM SOLVING

Solve by guessing and checking.

40. Latisha is twice as old as her sister Lavonne. The sum of their ages is 24. How old are the sisters?

41. For a school fundraiser, Andrew sold greeting cards at $5 per box. He sold stationery at $4 per box. Andrew sold 12 boxes and raised $52. How many boxes of each type did he sell?

42. Larry has $1 in change in his pocket. He has 9 coins and his largest coin is a quarter. What coins does he have?

43. Susan is training for a marathon. Each week she will run 5 km more than her distance the previous week. In the next four weeks, she plans to run 130 km. How much will she run during each of the weeks?

Multiplying Decimals
Making the Connection

LEARN ABOUT IT

EXPLORE Use Decimal Models

- Work with a partner. Outline a 10 by 10 square on graph paper. You and your partner decide who will use a red crayon and who will use a blue one.
- The person using the blue crayon colors some but not all rows of the square. Record the decimal part of the square that was colored.
- The person using red then colors some but not all columns red. Record the decimal part that was colored.
- Decide together the decimal part that is purple. (Blue and red make purple.) Record that decimal.

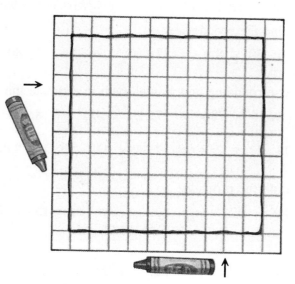

Color some rows (→) blue.
Color some columns (↑) red.

TALK ABOUT IT

1. Each row is what decimal part of the square?
2. What are the possible decimal parts you could color by coloring some but not all rows?
3. How does the decimal for the purple part compare to the decimal for the rows? For the columns?

You have colored decimal parts of a square and figured out the decimal part colored by both colors. Now you will see how to record what you have done. This will help you understand how to find a decimal part of a decimal, or products such as 0.5 × 2.6.

What You Do   **What You Record**

■ Color rows of the squares blue to show 2.6.

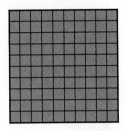 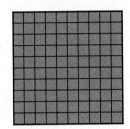 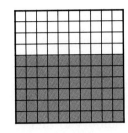

2.6

■ Color 0.5 of the columns with the red crayon.

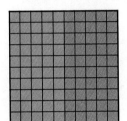 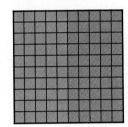 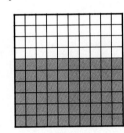

0.5 of 2.6
is 1.30

■ Explain how the purple part of the figure shows 1.30.

Math Point
Finding the decimal part of a decimal is like multiplying decimals.
0.5 of 2.6 is 1.30 → 0.5 × 2.6 = 1.30

TRY IT OUT

Use graph paper and crayons to show each of these. Then solve.

1. 0.5 of 2.8 → 0.5 × 2.8 = n **3.** 0.6 of 0.9 → 0.6 × 0.9 = n
2. 0.4 of 1.5 → 0.4 × 1.5 = n **4.** 0.2 of 0.4 → 0.2 × 0.4 = n

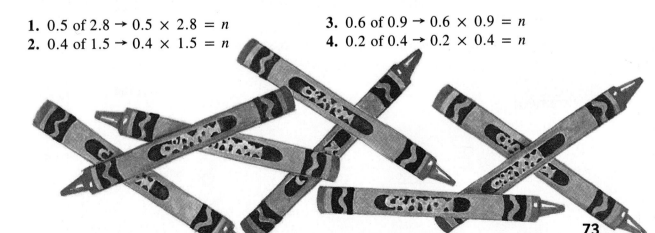

Multiplying Decimals

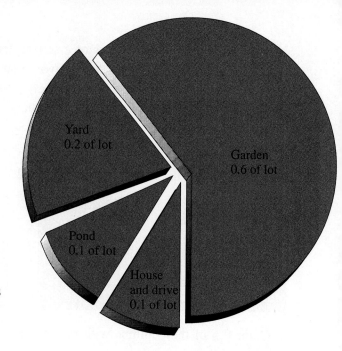

Yard
0.2 of lot

Garden
0.6 of lot

Pond
0.1 of lot

House
and drive
0.1 of lot

EXPLORE Analyze the Process

The circle graph shows how Jason uses a
2.3-acre lot. How large is his garden?

You know what part of Jason's lot is
garden. You know the total number of acres
in Jason's lot. You need to multiply to find
the number of acres the garden occupies.

Multiply as with whole numbers.	$\begin{array}{r} 2.3 \\ \times\ 0.6 \\ \hline 138 \end{array}$	Write the product so it has as many decimal places as the sum of the decimal places in the factors.	$\begin{array}{r} 2.3 \leftarrow \text{1 decimal place} \\ \times\ 0.6 \leftarrow \text{1 decimal place} \\ \hline 1.38 \leftarrow \text{2 decimal places} \end{array}$

TALK ABOUT IT

1. Do the decimal parts of Jason's lot add to 1? Should they?
2. Explain how you know that 13.8 and 138 would be unreasonable answers to the problem.
3. Use a complete sentence to give a reasonable answer to the story problem.

Other Examples

A $\begin{array}{r} 9.43 \leftarrow \text{2 decimal places} \\ \times\ 0.6 \leftarrow \text{1 decimal place} \\ \hline 5.658 \leftarrow \text{3 decimal places} \end{array}$

B $\begin{array}{r} 0.276 \\ \times\quad 3 \\ \hline 0.828 \end{array}$

C $\begin{array}{r} 1.32 \\ \times\ 0.87 \\ \hline 924 \\ 10560 \\ \hline 1.1484 \end{array}$

Multiply.

1. $\begin{array}{r} 4.27 \\ \times\ 0.7 \\ \hline \end{array}$

2. $\begin{array}{r} 1.374 \\ \times\quad 6 \\ \hline \end{array}$

3. $\begin{array}{r} 2.41 \\ \times\ 0.68 \\ \hline \end{array}$

4. $\begin{array}{r} 3.45 \\ \times\ 2.4 \\ \hline \end{array}$

5. $\begin{array}{r} \$9.56 \\ \times\ 0.15 \\ \hline \end{array}$

Multiply.

1.	4.3	**2.**	2.7	**3.**	0.53	**4.**	3.28	**5.**	25.6
	× 0.6		× 5.9		× 6		× 9		× 0.46

6.	2.675	**7.**	3.64	**8.**	0.56	**9.**	$7.25	**10.**	$7.23
	× 8		× 2.9		× 8.41		× 1.89		× 5.4

11. 6.8 × 3.2   **12.** 9.7 × 0.56   **13.** 4.75 × 0.9   **14.** 5.62 × 3.84

15. Estimate, then find 8.6 × 2.4.   **16.** Estimate, then find 28.67 × 72.46.

MATH REASONING

Without multiplying, tell which product is greater, **a** or **b**.

17. a.	3.7	**b.**	0.37		**18. a.**	28.6	**b.**	28.6
	× 5.8		× 5.8			× 0.395		× 0.4

PROBLEM SOLVING

19. How many acres do Jason's garden and pond occupy?

20. **Write Your Own Problem** Write and solve a problem about Jason's lot. Use numbers from the circle graph.

Give the missing numbers.

21. 1 cm = ▓▓▓ m   **22.** 5 m = ▓▓▓ cm

23. 1 m = ▓▓▓ km   **24.** 18 m = ▓▓▓ km

Add or subtract.

25. 2.13 + 1.48 + 8.01   **26.** 18.02 + 6.8 + 14   **27.** 30.48 − 24.82

28. 10 + 4.56 + 0.002   **29.** 200 − 1.28   **30.** 81.1 − 0.482

More Practice, page 503, set C

More Multiplying Decimals

LEARN ABOUT IT

Your work with placing the decimal point in multiplying decimals will help you understand the special cases in this lesson.

EXPLORE Analyze the Process

The pages in a large encyclopedia were 0.007 cm thick. In a large dictionary, the pages were only half, or 0.5, that thick. How thick were the dictionary pages?

TALK ABOUT IT

1. What is there about this problem that suggests that you should multiply?
2. Will the pages of the dictionary be more than or less than 0.007 cm thick? How do you know?

$$
\begin{array}{r}
0.007 \leftarrow \text{3 decimal places} \\
\times \quad 0.5 \leftarrow \text{1 decimal place} \\
\hline
0.0035 \leftarrow \text{4 decimal places}
\end{array}
$$

Write as many extra zeros on the left as are needed to show the correct number of decimal places in the product.

The thickness of each page in the large dictionary is 0.0035 cm.

Other Examples

A
$$
\begin{array}{r}
0.08 \\
\times \ 0.4 \\
\hline
0.032
\end{array}
$$

B
$$
\begin{array}{r}
0.03 \\
\times 0.02 \\
\hline
0.0006
\end{array}
$$

C
$$
\begin{array}{r}
435 \\
\times 0.0002 \\
\hline
0.0870
\end{array}
$$

D
$$
\begin{array}{r}
\$0.73 \\
\times \ 0.05 \\
\hline
\$0.0365
\end{array}
$$
or $0.04 (rounded to the nearest cent)

TRY IT OUT

Multiply.

1.
$$
\begin{array}{r}
2.3 \\
\times 0.004
\end{array}
$$

2.
$$
\begin{array}{r}
\$0.59 \\
\times \ 0.06
\end{array}
$$

3.
$$
\begin{array}{r}
0.006 \\
\times \ 0.05
\end{array}
$$

4.
$$
\begin{array}{r}
0.012 \\
\times \quad 1.1
\end{array}
$$

5. 0.036×0.4

6. 0.016×2.1

7. 0.007×0.002

8. $\$12.25 \times 0.004$

Multiply.

1.	3.4 × 5.7	**2.**	0.05 × 0.08	**3.**	3.2 × 0.004	**4.**	5.765 × 7.2	**5.**	6.2 × 0.0005
6.	1.2 × 0.04	**7.**	6.375 × 0.03	**8.**	0.007 × 4.3	**9.**	5.67 × 1.98	**10.**	$4.77 × 0.05
11.	0.0012 × 6.4	**12.**	238 × 0.01	**13.**	50 × 0.8	**14.**	$9.65 × 0.20	**15.**	$46.06 × 0.06

16. 0.08×0.015 **17.** 8.46×9.573 **18.** 0.0054×0.025

19. 0.075×5.75 **20.** 1.34×5.062 **21.** $0.205 \times \$9.67$

22. What is the product when 0.016 is multiplied by 0.025?

23. Estimate, then find the product of the factors 3.87 and 19.605.

MATH REASONING

24. Multiply 0.0075 by 10. Multiply by 10 again. Multiply by 10 again. What is happening to the decimal point?

PROBLEM SOLVING

25. Suppose the sales tax is 0.06. How much tax will you pay on a $97.95 bicycle? Round to the nearest cent.

26. **Missing Data** You spend $87.49 on a TV. What will it cost you including tax? Make up the missing data and complete the problem.

▶ ESTIMATION

When you eat in a nice restaurant, you are expected to tip the server about 0.15 of the total bill. You can use estimation and mental math to find out how much to tip.

Example: 0.15 × $38.95

   Think: 0.10 × $40 plus half that

          $4 + $2, which is $6

Estimate the tips.

27. $19.95   **28.** $59.89   **29.** $24.12

Problem Solving
Extra Data

UNDERSTAND
ANALYZE DATA
PLAN
ESTIMATE
SOLVE
EXAMINE

LEARN ABOUT IT

Sometimes a problem has extra data. This data is not needed to solve the problem.

Meteor Crater in Arizona is 1,219 meters across and 174 meters deep. Scientists think the meteorite that blasted this hole probably weighed about 100,000 tons. How much wider is the crater than it is deep?

> First, I'll find the data I need to solve this problem.

> The other data is extra.

> Now, I'll solve the problem using only the needed data.

The crater is 1,219 meters across and 174 meters deep.

The weight of the meteorite is not needed.

$1,219 - 174 = 1,045.$

Meteor Crater is 1,045 meters wider than it is deep.

TRY IT OUT

Solve. Which data is extra?

1. A meteoroid travels through space at 19 kilometers per second. It becomes visible from the earth when it is 96 kilometers above the ground. How far does a meteoroid travel in 60 seconds?

2. The temperature on the moon can reach 243°F when the sun is overhead, but drops to 58°F by sunset. During the night it can drop to as low as 260° below zero. How much can the temperature change between the time the sun is overhead and sunset?

3. The Skygazer's Club has 12 members. They counted 17 meteors one night and 9 meteors the second night. How many meteors did they see?

Solve. Use any problem solving strategy.

1. Use the table to find the combined weight of the three largest known meteorites.

Largest Known Meteorites	
Location	*Weight*
SW Africa	69 tons
New York	34 tons
Oregon	15 tons

2. Earth is 148.8 million kilometers from the Sun. Jupiter is 5.2 times farther from the Sun. Find the distance between Jupiter and the Sun.

3. The number of known asteroids is about 1,600. Astronomers believe that about 20 times that many exist. How many asteroids do astronomers think exist?

4. Earth takes a little more than 365 days to travel around the Sun. Mars takes 687 Earth days. How much longer does it take Mars to go around the Sun than it takes Earth?

5. The world's largest telescope has a 984.3-centimeter reflector. The next largest telescope has a 590.5-centimeter reflector and weighs 78 tons. How much larger is the reflector on the larger telescope?

6. Admission to Hall's planetarium costs $4.50 for adults and $2.75 for students. Mr. Emery took his class of 27 students to a show. How much did Mr. Emery and his class spend for tickets?

7. Use the sign to find how many shows Hall's Planetarium has each week.

Hall's Planetarium
Hours   Shows
Thursday-Sunday   2 p.m.
1 p.m. to 10 p.m.   4 p.m.
             8 p.m.

8. Talk About Your Solution The science classes at Mimi's school took a field trip to the planetarium. Sixty-five students went. There were 13 more sixth graders than seventh graders. How many sixth graders went on the field trip? Explain to a classmate how you reached your solution. Did you and your classmate get the same answer?

Exponents

LEARN ABOUT IT

EXPLORE   Discover a Pattern

Sometimes a number is used as a factor several times. See if you can discover the multiplication pattern for these sequences. Give the next number to show that you have found the pattern.

2,4,8,16, |||||

3,9,27,81, |||||

5,25,125,625, |||||

TALK ABOUT IT

1. How many times is 2 used as a factor to get 16?
2. What is the result if 3 is used as a factor 5 times?
3. What do you get when 5 is used as a factor 3 times?

An **exponent** tells how many times a number, called the **base,** is used as a factor.

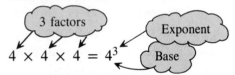

$4 \times 4 \times 4 = 4^3$

Read: "4 to the third power" or "4 cubed"

$3 \times 3 = 3^2$

Read: "3 to the second power" or "3 squared"

Other Examples

$6 \times 6 \times 6 = 6^3$

$7 \times 7 \times 7 \times 7 \times 7 = 7^5$

$100 \times 100 = 100^2$

$4^2 = 4 \times 4 = 16$ ← Standard form

$8^4 = 8 \times 8 \times 8 \times 8 = 4{,}096$

$10^5 = 10 \times 10 \times 10 \times 10 \times 10 = 100{,}000$

TRY IT OUT

Write the exponent and the standard form.

1. $2 \times 2 \times 2 \times 2 \times 2 = 2^{|||||}$

2. $10 \times 10 \times 10 \times 10 = 10^{|||||}$

Write each number in standard form.

3. 2^6
4. 0.2^2
5. 30^2
6. 4^4
7. 7^5

Write the base, the exponent, and the standard form.

1. $5 \times 5 \times 5 \times 5 \times 5 \times 5$　　　　**2.** $7 \times 7 \times 7 \times 7$

3. $2 \times 2 \times 2 \times 2 \times 2 \times 2 \times 2$　　　　**4.** $8 \times 8 \times 8$

Write the numbers in standard form.

5. 3^3　　　**6.** 4^2　　　**7.** 5^4　　　**8.** 10^6　　　**9.** 0.3^2　　　**10.** 0.2^3

11. 1^7　　　**12.** 2^3　　　**13.** 6^3　　　**14.** 0^8　　　**15.** 9^2　　　**16.** 7^3

Write in words.

17. 25^2　　　**18.** 204^3

APPLY

MATH REASONING

Are these numbers getting larger or smaller?

19. $2^2, 2^3, 2^4, 2^5, \ldots$　　　　**20.** $0.3^2, 0.3^3, 0.3^4, 0.3^5, \ldots$

PROBLEM SOLVING

21. The figure shows how to find the volume of a cube. What is the volume if $a = 2.8$ cm?

22. What is each side if the volume is 8 cubic cm?

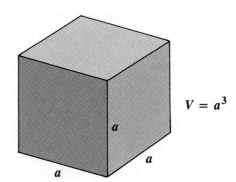

$V = a^3$

▶ **CALCULATOR**

Use the multiplication constant on your calculator to find the standard form of each of these numbers.

Example:　$6^4 \longrightarrow$ | ON/AC | 6 | × | 6 | = | = | = | $\rightarrow$ **1,296**

　　　　　　　　　　　　　　　　　　6^2　6^3　6^4

23. 8^5　　　**24.** 0.8^5　　　**25.** 12^5　　　**26.** 1.2^5　　　**27.** 10^7　　　**28.** 0.1^7

Estimate the standard form. Check with your calculator.

Example:　$9.6^3 \rightarrow$ Think: About 10^3, or 1,000

29. 2.9^2　　　**30.** 1.9^3　　　**31.** 5.1^2　　　**32.** 9.75^4　　　**33.** 98.6^2　　　**34.** 49.3^2

More Practice, page 503, set E

Prime Numbers and Prime Factorization

EXPLORE **Analyze the Data**

Candice is sorting the whole numbers greater than 1 into two sets. Can you figure out what is special about the two sets?

Set P: 2, 3, 5, 7, 11, 13,...
Set C: 4, 6, 8, 9, 10, 12, 14, 15,...

TALK ABOUT IT

1. Without using 1, can you find numbers that multiply together to give a number in P? What is the next number in P?
2. Without using 1, can you find numbers that multiply together to give a number in C? What are some examples? What is the next number in C?

The **factors** of a number are those numbers that multiply together to give that number.
Example: $1 \times 6 = 6$ $2 \times 3 = 6$
      Factors of 6 → 1, 2, 3, 6

Prime numbers have exactly two factors, themselves and 1.
Examples: $1 \times 3 = 3$ $1 \times 5 = 5$ $1 \times 13 = 13$

Composite numbers have more than two factors.
Example: $1 \times 6 = 6$ and $2 \times 3 = 6$ → 6 is composite.

Each composite number can be expressed as a product of prime factors. This is the **prime factorization** of the composite number 40. A factor tree may help you find the prime factors of a number. The lowest row of the tree contains only prime numbers.

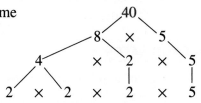

You can write prime factorizations using exponents. $40 = 2 \times 2 \times 2 \times 5$
$40 = 2^3 \times 5$

Make a factor tree to show that each of these prime factorizations is correct.

1. $28 = 2^2 \times 7$ 2. $30 = 2 \times 3 \times 5$ 3. $45 = 3^2 \times 5$
4. Give the prime factorization of 24. Use exponents when possible.

Write all the factors of each number. Then write *prime* or *composite* for each number.

1. 8

2. 10

3. 19

4. 20

5. 23

6. 25

Copy and complete each factor tree. Then write the prime factorization. Use exponents when possible.

7.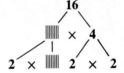

8.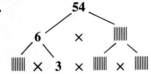

9.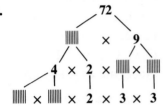

Make a factor tree for each number. Then write the prime factorization. Use exponents when possible.

10. 44

11. 81

12. 66

13. 80

APPLY

MATH REASONING

Find *n*.

14. a prime number *n* if $n > 52$ and $n < 55$

15. $n = 5^2 \times 3$

PROBLEM SOLVING

16. Science Data Bank The speed of Planet X can be written as 3×2^4 kilometers per second. Which planet is Planet X?

▶ **USING CRITICAL THINKING** Support Your Conclusion

17. Some pairs of prime numbers have a difference of 2. For example, $19 - 17 = 2$. These pairs are called **twin primes.** Why might they be called *twin* primes? How many twin primes are there between 2 and 35? Which numbers are they?

More Practice, page 504, set A

Exploring Algebra
Algebraic Expressions

LEARN ABOUT IT

Phrases that suggest an operation can be written as expressions. A **numerical expression** is a name for a number. You can use what you already know about numerical expressions like $23 + 16$ and $(340 + 12) - 15$ to work with **algebraic expressions.**

Numerical Expression		*Algebraic Expression*	
5 increased by 3	$\rightarrow 5 + 3$	a number increased by 3	$\rightarrow n + 3$
4 less than 12	$\rightarrow 12 - 4$	4 less than a number	$\rightarrow n - 4$
2 times 8	$\rightarrow 2 \times 8$	2 times a number	$\rightarrow 2 \times n$
10 divided by 2	$\rightarrow 10 \div 2$	a number divided by 2	$\rightarrow n \div 2$

TALK ABOUT IT

1. Give another phrase that can be written as $5 + 3$. Give another phrase that can be written as $n + 3$.
2. Can 4 less than 12 be written as the same expression as 12 less than 4? Can 4 less than a number be written as the same expression as a number less than 4?
3. Four students wrote 7 times a number, each in a different way. Can all four of them be correct? Explain.

> **Math Point**
> Algebraic expressions involving multiplication can be written in four different ways. Each of the following shows "2 times a number":
> $2 \times n \qquad 2 \cdot n \qquad 2(n) \qquad 2n$

Other Examples

A six more than twelve $\rightarrow 12 + 6$

B the product of eight and a number $\rightarrow 8n$

TRY IT OUT

Write as an algebraic expression.

1. a number plus 4

2. a number decreased by 9

3. 11 more than a number

4. the product of a number and 7

5. 6 times a number

6. 34 less than a number

Write as a numerical expression.

1. the sum of 15 and 6

2. 16 divided by 8

3. 8 times 21

4. the product of 11 and 5

5. the difference of 14 and 6

6. subtract 9 from 10

Write as an algebraic expression.

7. twice as much as a number

8. 5 less than a number

9. a number decreased by 6

10. a number times 15

11. the sum of four and a number

12. double a number

13. a number minus 8

14. 9 more than a number

APPLY

MATH REASONING

Match each phrase with the algebraic expression.

15. 3 increased by twice a number

16. 3 more than twice a number

17. 2 less than 3 times a number

18. 3 less than double a number

$3 + 2n$
$2n - 3$
$2n + 3$
$3n - 2$

PROBLEM SOLVING

19. Roger hiked for a number of miles. Then he hiked for 6 more miles. Write an algebraic expression to tell how far he hiked?

▶ **USING CRITICAL THINKING   Discover a Rule**

20. Analyze the product $x \cdot y$. Suppose that x and y are replaced by odd or even numbers. Copy and complete the table to tell whether the product is *odd* or *even*.

21. For which values of m will $m + 1$ be even?

22. For which values of n will $2n$ be even? Be odd?

x	y	$x \cdot y$
even	even	
odd	odd	
even	odd	
odd	even	

Applied Problem Solving
Group Decision Making

UNDERSTAND
ANALYZE DATA
PLAN
ESTIMATE
SOLVE
EXAMINE

Group Skill
Check for Understanding

In order to raise $500 to pay for field trips, your school is having a reading marathon. This means students will read books and ask people to sponsor them. Each sponsor will pledge to pay a certain amount of money for each book read. After all the books are read, the students will collect the money from their sponsors. You need to figure out how many books and how many sponsors each student should try to get in order to meet the goal of $500.

Facts to Consider

- Sponsors usually pledge about $0.10 to $0.30 per book read.
- Students have 6 weeks to read.
- There are about 75 students participating in the fundraiser.
- A sample sponsor sheet is shown below.

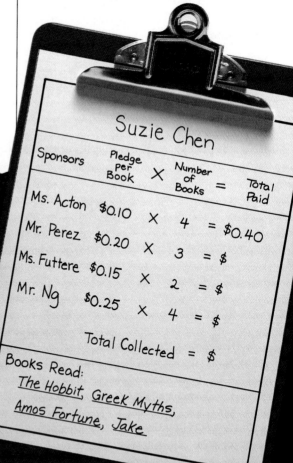

Suzie Chen

Sponsors	Pledge per Book	X	Number of Books	=	Total Paid
Ms. Acton	$0.10	X	4	=	$0.40
Mr. Perez	$0.20	X	3	=	$
Ms. Futtere	$0.15	X	2	=	$
Mr. Ng	$0.25	X	4	=	$

Total Collected = $

Books Read:
The Hobbit, _Greek Myths_, _Amos Fortune_, _Jake_

1. What is a reasonable number of books for one student to read?
2. About how much money does each student need to earn?
3. How much money do you think an average sponsor will pledge per book?
4. If you get 2 sponsors and each pledges $0.15 per book, how much would you earn in all?
5. How could the strategy Guess and Check help you solve this problem?

What is your recommendation for the number of sponsors and books each student should try to get? Show how the school will be able to meet its goal by using your recommendation.

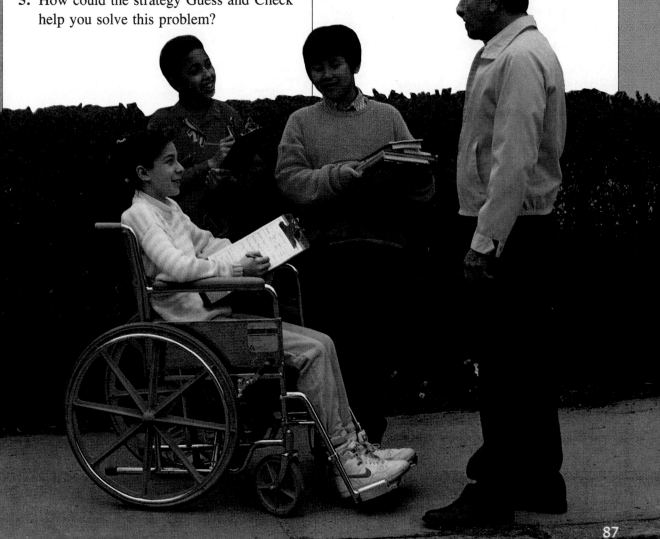

WRAP UP

Language Match

Match the statement with the number or algebraic expression.

1. an estimated product of 9.8 and 21.37

2. the sum of a number and 6

3. 98.98 rounded to the nearest tenth

4. twice a number decreased by 6

5. a number minus 9

6. an estimated product of 28 and 11

7. 9 more than a number

8. an estimated product of 22.9 and 5.1

a. $n + 6$

b. $n - 9$

c. $n + 9$

d. 200

e. 300

f. $2n - 6$

g. 100

h. 99

Sometimes, Always, Never

Decide which word should go in the blank: *sometimes*, *always*, or *never*. Explain your choices.

9. The product of two decimals is _____ greater than either of the factors.

10. To find a decimal part of a decimal you can _____ multiply.

11. You can _____ determine the number of decimal places in the product by adding the number of decimal places in the factors.

12. An algebraic expression _____ suggests an operation.

Project

Use a calculator to help you investigate patterns that happen when numbers are raised to different powers.

1. Find each standard number for 4^1, 4^2, 4^3, and so on up to 4^9. Look at the digit in the ones place for each. Find a pattern. Predict the ones digit for 4^{43}.

2. Find each standard number for 7^1, 7^2, 7^3, and so on up to 7^9. Look at the ones digits and the tens digits. Find patterns. Predict the ones digit for 7^{34} and the tens digit for 7^{66}.

3. Try other powers. What patterns do you find?

CHAPTER REVIEW/TEST

Part 1 Understanding

Use estimation to tell if the product is reasonable or unreasonable.
Use rounding or compatible numbers.

1. $47 \times 61 = 2{,}867$

2. $21.22 \times 4.87 = 103.3414$

3. $1.9 \times 24.7 = 25.63$

Write in words. Use two different ways.

4. 32^2

5. 817^3

Write as an algebraic expression.

6. a number decreased by 6

7. 2 more than 3 times a number

Part 2 Skills

Use rounding and mental math to estimate each product.

8. 86×47

9. 534×7

10. 466×921

Estimate by rounding or by finding compatible numbers.

11. 39.8×9.2

12. 26.28×4.34

13. 48.1×1.64

14. 6.6×5.5

Multiply.

15. 39×9

16. 48×56

17. 728×45

18. $1{,}085 \times 90$

19. 0.47×21.4

20. 6.4×5.2

21. 0.003×4.1

22. 0.06×0.007

Write the base, the exponent, and the standard form.

23. $2 \times 2 \times 2 \times 2$ **24.** $5 \times 5 \times 5$

Part 3 Applications

25. Give the prime factorization for 63. Use exponents when possible.

26. Ken's mother is 4 times as old as he is. The sum of their ages is 45. How old are they?

27. Challenge For the picnic, Sue spent $8.50 on sandwiches, $1.75 each for 4 desserts, $5.95 for insect repellent, and $2.60 on salad. How much did she spend on food for the picnic?

ENRICHMENT
Russian Peasant Multiplication

Russian Peasant Multiplication was one of the first methods used to find the product of two numbers. Here it is used to find the product of 27 × 63.

	A	B
	27	63
Step 1	13	126
Step 2	6	252
Step 3	3	504
Step 4	1	1,008

In Step 1, the number in column A is halved. The remainder is ignored. The number in column B is doubled.

$27 \div 2 = 13$; R1 is ignored
$63 \times 2 = 126$

In Steps 2–4, the process is repeated.

1. What happens in Step 2?

2. What happens in Step 3?

3. What happens in Step 4?

Once all of the numbers have been halved or doubled, each row with an even number in column A is marked out.

4. Which row or rows should be marked out?

5. Add all of the numbers in column B that are not marked out. What is the total?

6. Multiply in the usual way to check the final product.

7. Summarize the Russian Peasant Multiplication method in your own words.

Use Russian Peasant Multiplication. Show your steps.

8. 12 × 42

9. 23 × 35

10. 18 × 49

11. 78 × 96

12. 54 × 73

13. 101 × 101

14. 365 × 42

15. 546 × 695

CUMULATIVE REVIEW

Add, multiply, or divide.

1. $200 + 43 + 1,650$

    A. 2,280   **B.** 1,893

    C. 1,993   **D.** 1,807

2. 37×395

    A. 14,585   **B.** 3,950

    C. 13,615   **D.** 14,615

3. $1,001 \div 11$

    A. 910   **B.** 90

    C. 91   **D.** 100

4. $250 \times 13 \times 4$

    A. 13,000   **B.** 4,250

    C. 1,300   **D.** 1,052

5. $\begin{array}{r} 0.83 \\ \times\ \ 0.7 \\ \hline \end{array}$

    A. 5.81   **B.** 0.581

    C. 0.0581   **D.** 0.00581

6. 0.0004×0.08

    A. 0.000032   **B.** 0.00032

    C. 0.0032   **D.** 0.0000032

7. How much greater than 41.555 is 41.557?

    A. 0.02   **B.** 0.002

    C. 2   **D.** 0.2

8. Which is the estimated product of 43×587?

    A. 30,000   **B.** 20,000

    C. 2,400   **D.** 24,000

9. What is the product when 4,097 is multiplied by 86?

    A. 342,342   **B.** 352,342

    C. 351,242   **D.** 342,352

10. Use estimation to choose the correct product for 23.7×3.95.

    A. 69.35   **B.** 93.615

    C. 103.65   **D.** 936.635

11. Which expression has an answer of 43?

    A. $8 \times 7 + 5$ **B.** $(8 + 5) \times 7$

    C. $8 \times 5 + 7$ **D.** $8 + 5 \times 7$

12. In which number does the 6 have a value of 0.06?

    A. 0.056   **B.** 34.675

    C. 6.587   **D.** 0.963

Solve.

13. Admission to the aquarium costs $2.25 for students and $4.75 for adults. The teacher and one parent took a class of 23 students. How much did the group spend on the tickets?

    A. $61.25   **B.** $51.75

    C. $56.25   **D.** $42.25

14. Louise has a ribbon 180 cm long. She wants to cut the ribbon into pieces 20 cm long. How many cuts will she have to make?

    A. 10 cuts   **B.** 8 cuts

    C. 9 cuts   **D.** 90 cuts

4

DIVISION:
WHOLE
NUMBERS
AND
DECIMALS

MATH AND
SOCIAL STUDIES

DATA BANK

Use the Social Studies Data
Bank on page 470 to answer
the questions.

Use the Social Studies Data
Bank on page 470 to answer
the questions.

1 Earth's surface can be
divided into several large
land masses and several
large ocean areas. Which land mass
has the largest surface area? Which
ocean has the largest surface area?

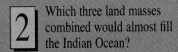 **2** Which three land masses combined would almost fill the Indian Ocean?

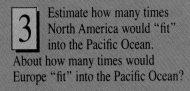 **3** Estimate how many times North America would "fit" into the Pacific Ocean. About how many times would Europe "fit" into the Pacific Ocean?

4 **Using Critical Thinking** Some people call Earth the water planet. Do you agree or disagree with them? Use numbers to explain why.

Mental Math
Special Quotients

Newspapers Collected

Russ
Kris
Liz
Phil
Tanya
Cory

Each 📚 means 30 lb

EXPLORE Examine the Data

Six students collected newspapers for recycling. The table shows the approximate number of pounds each person collected. Liz decided to make a pictograph to show the results of the project. How many bundles of paper should she draw for Kris?

TALK ABOUT IT

1. Did Liz draw the right number of bundles for Russ? How do you know?
2. How can Liz decide on the number of bundles for Kris?
3. How can you use basic division facts to help you find quotients like 240 ÷ 30?

If you know this division fact: 24 ÷ 3
you can find this quotient: 240 ÷ 30
   24 ÷ 3 = 8, so 240 ÷ 30 = 8

Newspapers Collected	
Student	Pounds (lb)
Russ	150 lb
Kris	240 lb
Liz	180 lb
Phil	120 lb
Tanya	210 lb
Cory	180 lb

Other Examples

A   48 ÷ 6 = 8
   so 4,800 ÷ 6 = 800

B   40 ÷ 5 = 8
   so 40,000 ÷ 50 = 800

C $9\overline{)63}$ gives 7 so $90\overline{)6,300}$ gives 70

TRY IT OUT

Divide.

1. 32 ÷ 4
   320 ÷ 4
   3,200 ÷ 4
   32,000 ÷ 4

2. 35 ÷ 7
   350 ÷ 70
   3,500 ÷ 70
   35,000 ÷ 70

3. 210 ÷ 7

4. 420 ÷ 70

5. 540 ÷ 60

6. 3,600 ÷ 40

7. $6\overline{)420}$

8. $6\overline{)4,200}$

9. $60\overline{)4,200}$

10. $30\overline{)2,400}$

Find the quotients mentally. Use pencils for answers only.

1. $240 \div 6$ **2.** $420 \div 60$ **3.** $5,400 \div 9$ **4.** $1,800 \div 9$

5. $400 \div 5$ **6.** $180 \div 20$ **7.** $240 \div 30$ **8.** $4,000 \div 80$

9. $180 \div 3$ **10.** $2,400 \div 80$ **11.** $4,200 \div 70$ **12.** $2,400 \div 60$

13. $4,800 \div 8$ **14.** $3,500 \div 5$ **15.** $2,800 \div 40$ **16.** $18,000 \div 60$

17. $24,000 \div 60$ **18.** $5,400 \div 60$ **19.** $1,800 \div 30$ **20.** $4,200 \div 6$

21. $3\overline{)210}$ **22.** $6\overline{)4,800}$ **23.** $4\overline{)3,600}$ **24.** $7\overline{)350}$

25. $50\overline{)3,000}$ **26.** $80\overline{)32,000}$ **27.** $30\overline{)1,200}$ **28.** $60\overline{)3,600}$

APPLY

MATH REASONING

For each pair, tell if they are equal or tell which is greater.

29. $280 \div 7$ **30.** $350 \div 50$ **31.** $4,200 \div 7$ **32.** $7,200 \div 80$
     $2,800 \div 70$ $3,500 \div 50$ $4,200 \div 70$ $720 \div 8$

PROBLEM SOLVING

33. More Than One Answer Tiffany collected 180 pounds of paper. She wanted to bundle the paper so she could have fewer than 10 bundles. She wanted each bundle to be equal in weight but to weigh no more than 40 pounds. How could she do this?

34. Brad's class collected 3,600 pounds of paper. The students wrapped the papers in 40-pound bundles. How many bundles did they have?

▶ **USING CRITICAL THINKING**   **Drawing Conclusions**

35. Our product is 1,200. Our sum is 70. Who are we?

36. I'm both the quotient and the divisor. The number being divided is 4,900. Who am I?

Estimating Quotients
Using Compatible Numbers

LEARN ABOUT IT

EXPLORE Compare the Data

Some cities spread out over a large land area.
Others build upward over a small land area.
The table shows Texas cities with large land
areas and large populations. Miami, Florida
has a small land area (89 km²) and a large
population. Estimate how many times the
area of Miami would "fit" into the area
of San Antonio.

TALK ABOUT IT

1. What data do you need from the table to
   solve the problem?
2. What is there in the problem that suggests
   that you should divide to find an answer?
3. What is the answer to the problem?

Texas City	Land Area, in Square Kilometers (km²)
Austin	300
Dallas	979
El Paso	621
Fort Worth	622
Houston	1,501
San Antonio	697

You can estimate a quotient by rounding or by using compatible
numbers. Sometimes you can find the compatible numbers to use
by rounding first.

	Round	Choose a Compatible Number
Estimate 697 ÷ 89	700 ÷ 90 ⟶	720 ÷ 90 = 8

Other Examples

A $537 \div 6$
  $540 \div 6 = 90$
  ↑ Estimate

B $3,640 \div 9$
  $3,600 \div 9 = 400$
  ↑ Estimate

C $23,465 \div 82$
  $24,000 \div 80 = 300$
  ↑ Estimate

TRY IT OUT

Choose compatible numbers to estimate the quotients.

1. $249 \div 6$
2. $174 \div 3$
3. $274 \div 40$
4. $4,906 \div 8$

5. $90\overline{)727}$
6. $63\overline{)480}$
7. $33\overline{)1,710}$
8. $76\overline{)36,104}$

Give the best replacement for each bold number so that a basic
fact can be used to estimate the quotient. Then, give the estimate.

1. 259 ÷ 50   **2. 3,437** ÷ 7   **3. 6,234** ÷ 9   **4. 5,565** ÷ 60

5. 270 ÷ **32**   **6. 8,215** ÷ 9   **7.** 6,400 ÷ **79**   **8. 4,325** ÷ 11

Choose compatible numbers to estimate the quotients.

9. 125 ÷ 3   **10.** 427 ÷ 6   **11.** 163 ÷ 2   **12.** 306 ÷ 50   **13.** 342 ÷ 70

14. 8)3,372   **15.** 9)4,567   **16.** 4)3,517   **17.** 90)6,400   **18.** 60)4,325

19. 6)54,631   **20.** 8)62,479   **21.** 5)46,235   **22.** 60)29,247   **23.** 70)54,896

MATH REASONING

One answer is correct. Use estimation to find it.

24. 1,722 ÷ 6   **a.** 187   **b.** 287   **c.** 387
25. 4,952 ÷ 8   **a.** 619   **b.** 519   **c.** 719
26. 19,560 ÷ 40   **a.** 389   **b.** 589   **c.** 489

PROBLEM SOLVING

27. Every 24 hours, more than 3,600 acres
of the earth's green space (trees,
forests, marshes, and so forth) are
replaced by buildings. About how many
acres is this every hour? Every year?

28. Social Studies Data Bank
In the United States, the
shortest river that has a
name is the D River in
Oregon. It is 0.133 km
long. How much shorter
is the D River than the Red River?

DATA BANK

▶ ESTIMATION

The length of the small rod is 2 units. The long rod is 12 units.
Estimate the length of the other rods.

 2 units   12 units

29.

30.

Reviewing Division
One-Digit Divisors

The examples below will help you review whole number division.

A
```
    163 R3
4)655
    4
    25
    24
    15
    12
     3
```
$25 \div 4 = 6$ R1

B
```
    46
6)276
   24
   36
   36
    0
```
$2 \div 6$. Not enough hundreds. Start with the tens.

C
```
    608 R2
7)4,258
  4 2
    05
     0
    58
    56
     2
```
$05 \div 7 = 0$ R5

D Short Division
```
     3 7 5 R2
6)2,2⁴5³2
```
$22 \div 6 = 3$ R4

Write the remainder beside the next digit. Then divide in that place. $(45 \div 6)$

Copy and complete the division problem.

1.
```
    2
3)87
  6
  27
```

2.
```
    7
8)576
  56

   0
```

3.
```
    84
5)4,215
  4 0
    21
    20
     1
```

4.
```
    4 6 9
6)28⁴15⁷
```

Divide.

5. 7)99

6. 4)317

7. 8)4,608

8. 6)25,091

98

Divide. Use long or short division.

1. $6\overline{)84}$ **2.** $3\overline{)86}$ **3.** $9\overline{)198}$ **4.** $4\overline{)332}$ **5.** $6\overline{)380}$

6. $3\overline{)547}$ **7.** $2\overline{)972}$ **8.** $6\overline{)278}$ **9.** $5\overline{)2,076}$ **10.** $2\overline{)19,712}$

Find the quotients.

11. $875 \div 5$ **12.** $3,604 \div 4$ **13.** $2,880 \div 6$ **14.** $30,065 \div 5$

15. Divide 4,242 by 7. **16.** Divide 2,760 by 4.

17. Estimate, then find: $8,865 \div 3$ **18.** Estimate, then find: $23,574 \div 6$

APPLY

MATH REASONING

Answer *sometimes, always* or *never*.

19. The remainder is _____ greater than the divisor.

20. When the remainder is 0, the divisor time the quotient is _____ equal to the dividend.

21. The remainder is _____ less than the quotient.

PROBLEM SOLVING

22. On a trip from Los Angeles to New York, a plane averaged 547 miles per hour for 2 hours and 498 miles per hour for 3 hours. How far did it fly on its trip?

23. On a trip from Honolulu to Chicago, a plane traveled 4,304 miles in 8 hours. What was the average distance covered each hour?

▶ USING CRITICAL THINKING Analyze the Situation

Each example has something wrong. Choose which of the statements is true. Do not divide.

A There are too many digits in the quotient. **C** The remainder is too large.
B There are not enough digits in the quotient.

24. $7\overline{)8,326}$ 189 R3 **25.** $4\overline{)1,705}$ 425 R5 **26.** $8\overline{)14,804}$ 185 R4 **27.** $5\overline{)62,304}$ 1,246 R4 **28.** $5\overline{)2,648}$ 5,293

More Practice, page 504, set D

Problem Solving
Choosing A Calculation Method

UNDERSTAND
ANALYZE DATA
PLAN
ESTIMATE
SOLVE
EXAMINE

When you are solving a problem, you will often need to decide on a calculation method.

Calculation Methods
- Mental Math
- Pencil and Paper
- Calculator

Model T Ford Facts	
Originally built in 1908	Most popular car for nearly 20 years
Price in 1908: $850	Production speed: 5 cars per
Price in 1916: $400	8-hour shift
(due to mass production)	

How much did the price come down by 1916?

$850 − $400. That's easy to do in my head. I'll use mental math.
$850 − $400 = $450

How many minutes did it take to make one car?

8 × 60 min. Then divide by 5. I could use pencil and paper, but a calculator might be better.
8 × 60 min = 480 min
480 min ÷ 5 = 96 min

When you have to choose a calculation method

- First try mental math. See if you can do the calculation in your head.
- If you can't use mental math, choose between pencil and paper and a calculator. Problems that require many steps and trades are often better solved with a calculator.

Tell what calculation method you choose and why. Then solve.

1. 7×38.96

2. $4,000 \div 50$

3. $7.638 - 1.296$

4. $20,286 \div 9$, then add 10

5. $468 \div 2$

6. $\$3,600 - \$1,600$

7. $\$4,003 - \$768.40$

8. $\$12.21 - \$3.50$, then double

9. $0.58 + 0.42 + 3.5$

Choose a calculation method and tell why. Then solve.

1. $3,200 \div 80$ **2.** $384 - 169$ **3.** 60×700 **4.** $7,040 - 3,876$

5. $57.69 + 287.92$ **6.** $6,000 + 7,000$ **7.** 248×3 **8.** $395 + 287$

9. $693 \div 3$ **10.** $7,074 \div 9$ **11.** $912 \div 2$ **12.** $540 \div 60$

13. 283.89×27 **14.** $120 - 50$ **15.** $627 + 89 + 495$ **16.** 372×4

17. $28,000 \div 7$ **18.** $482 - 258$ **19.** $6,636 \div 7$ **20.** $23 + 56$

Choose an appropriate calculation method. Do not solve.

21. A Model T cost $850 in 1908. By 1990, a low-cost compact auto cost 9 times that much. How much less did a Model T cost than the auto in 1990?

22. An auto company in 1903 made 600 autos in 6 months. What is the average number of autos made in one month?

23. In 1900, about 350 autos were built each month. Fifty years later, 1,909 times as many were built. How many autos were built in 1950?

24. The first gasoline-driven automobile was patented in 1886. The first American automobile was built 6 years later. What year was that?

25. Felipe started driving at the park and drove 9 blocks west, 12 blocks north, 15 blocks east, and 20 blocks south. How many blocks did he drive?

26. In 1908, workmen could build a Model T in about $12\frac{1}{2}$ hours. By 1914, assembly line techniques had cut the time to about $1\frac{1}{2}$ hours. How much time was saved?

Choose an appropriate calculation method. Then solve.

27. Extra Data In 1914, a worker in an auto factory could earn $5.04 for an 8-hour shift. By 1984, just 70 years later, a worker might earn as much as $112 for 8 hours. How much more did the 1984 worker earn in an 8-hour shift than the worker in 1914?

Finding Averages

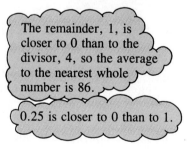

EXPLORE Analyze the Process

Tina threw four balls and received scores
of 25, 15, 10, and 10. What is her average
score? Use your calculator if you want.

To find the average score, you need to find the score you would
get if you got the same score each time.

Find the sum of the numbers.	Divide by the number of addends.	The quotient is the average of the numbers.
25 + 15 + 10 + 10 = 60	$\dfrac{15}{4\overline{)60}}$	15

TALK ABOUT IT

1. What was Tina's total score for the game?
2. Could Tina's average score be less than 10? More than 25? Explain.
3. Find another way that Tina could have thrown the ball four times and have an average score of 15.

ON/AC	25	+	15	+

10	+	10	=	÷	4	=

Other Example

Find the average of these test scores to the nearest whole number.

Test	1	2	3	4
Score	87	79	92	87

$87 + 79 + 92 + 87 = 345$

$$\begin{array}{r} 8\ 6\ \text{R1} \\ 4\overline{)34^25} \end{array}$$

The remainder, 1, is closer to 0 than to the divisor, 4, so the average to the nearest whole number is 86.

86.25

0.25 is closer to 0 than to 1.

Find the average of these test scores to the nearest whole number.
Use your calculator if you want.

1. 74, 86, 90, 86   **2.** 64, 76, 85, 92, 96   **3.** 72, 74, 84, 96, 84, 72

Find the average of these sets of numbers to the nearest whole number.

1. 76, 84, 96, 80

2. 97, 91, 86, 89

3. 70, 72, 62

4. 67, 84, 86, 92, 95

5. 70, 75, 86, 94, 82, 75

6. 87, 98, 79, 80, 67

7. 92, 88, 96, 97, 89, 100

8. 74, 86, 92, 82, 79

9. 64, 73, 71, 61

APPLY

MATH REASONING

10. One of the numbers below is the average of the set of numbers on the left. Without finding the average, how can you be sure which one it is?

Set	Average
54, 63, 47, 58, 49, 65	46 56 66

PROBLEM SOLVING

11. What is Hector's average bowling score for the 3 games?

12. How much higher is Hector's highest bowling score than his average?

13. What is the average height of the students? The average mass?

14. What is the difference between the average height of the girls and the average height of the boys?

Hector's Bowling Scores

Game	Score
1	174
2	190
3	158

Name	Height (cm)	Mass (kg)
Doug	149	40
Juanita	148	38
Raul	143	35
Ann	152	42
Vance	145	37
Joan	155	39

MIXED REVIEW

Estimate.

15. 432×48 **16.** $389 - 213$ **17.** $1,688 + 210$ **18.** 8.91×4.15 **19.** 42.3×18.8

Find the answers.

20. $\begin{array}{r} 2.19 \\ + 8.01 \\ \hline \end{array}$

21. $\begin{array}{r} 8.12 \\ \times \quad 9 \\ \hline \end{array}$

22. $\begin{array}{r} 2.17 \\ \times 1.01 \\ \hline \end{array}$

23. $\begin{array}{r} 851.8 \\ - 458.21 \\ \hline \end{array}$

24. $\begin{array}{r} 256 \\ \times \quad 17 \\ \hline \end{array}$

More Practice, page 504, set E

Problem Solving
Make a Table

UNDERSTAND
ANALYZE DATA
PLAN
ESTIMATE
SOLVE
EXAMINE

To solve some problems, it helps to put the data in a table. This problem solving strategy is called **Make a Table.**

Sean works at Bradley Video. One Saturday night he noticed that for every 2 old videos rented, they rented 5 new releases. If they rented 12 old videos, how many new releases did they rent?

> I'll make a table using the data in the problem.

> Then, I'll look for a pattern in the table to help me find the answer.

> Now, I'll finish filling in the table and find the answer.

Bradley Video rented 30 new video releases.

Data given in the problem

Old	2	4	6	8	10	12
New	5					

Old	2	4	6	8	10	12
New	5	10	15	20		

Answer to the problem

Old	2	4	6	8	10	12
New	5	10	15	20	25	30

TRY IT OUT

Read the problem and find the solution.
Videos that were released more than a year ago can be rented at a special weekend rate of 3 videos for $7. Last weekend, Bradley Video rented 21 videos at the special rate. How much rent did they collect?

- What is the special weekend rate?
- At this rate, how much rent would they get for 6 videos?
- How many videos did they rent at the special rate?
- Copy and complete this table to solve the problem.

VIDEOS

Number of videos	3	6		
Cost		$7		

Solve by making a table.

1. Video Mania gives its members a card to punch each time they rent a video. For every 8 punches, the members get 1 free video. Last week, members turned in cards with a total of 72 punches. How many free videos were given out?

2. For every 3 comedy videos rented, the store rents 5 drama videos. If the store rents 35 drama videos, how many comedy videos does it rent?

MIXED PRACTICE

Solve. Choose a strategy from the list or use another strategy that you know.

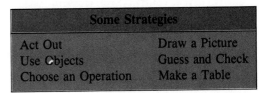

Some Strategies	
Act Out	Draw a Picture
Use Objects	Guess and Check
Choose an Operation	Make a Table

STARBURST VIDEO

New Releases	Other	Specials
$26.50	$21.95	$19
Rentals	Rentals	Exercise
$4 each	$3 each	Happy Forever
2 for $7	2 for $5	Cartoon Classics

3. Use the sign to find how much more you have to pay to buy a new release video than to buy other videos.

4. Starburst Video sold 11 exercise videos. About how much money did they collect?

5. Each time Jen rented a video she got 2 new releases. During October she spent $35. How many new release videos did she rent?

6. During a 4-week period, Starburst Video collected $525 for single rentals of other videos. How many rentals of other videos did they have?

7. Use the table below to find the average number of children's videos rented per day.

	Children's Videos		
Day	Number Rented	Day	Number Rented
Sun.	10	Thurs.	9
Mon.	5	Fri.	12
Tues.	8	Sat.	15
Wed.	4		

8. The store sold 43 videos. They sold 7 more dramas than comedies. How many of each did they sell?

Reviewing Division
Two-Digit Divisors

Your estimation skills are especially useful
when you divide by a two-digit number.
These examples will help you review these skills.

A
```
        3 2 4
6 0)1 9,4 4 0
    1 8 0
      1 4 4
      1 2 0
        2 4 0
        2 4 0
            0
```
> 194 ÷ 60
> Think: 19 ÷ 6

B 70
```
          6 R 7
7 2)4 3 9
    4 3 2
        7
```
> 439 ÷ 72
> Think: 43 ÷ 7

C
```
      1 4 3
4 6)6,5 7 8
    4 6
      1 9 7 ←
      1 8 4
        1 3 8
        1 3 8
            0
```
> 197 ÷ 46 =
> 4 R13

D
```
              3 0 7 R8
4 3)1 3,2 0 9
    1 2 9
        3 0 9
        3 0 1
            8
```
> Zero tens.
> Write 0 in quotient.

Copy and complete each problem.

1.
```
      14
68)9,658
   6 8
   2 85
   2 72
     138
```

2.
```
        61
42)25,762
   25 2
      56
```

3.
```
        30
43)13,201
   12 9
     301
```

4.
```
        40
57)22,971
   22 8
     171
```

Find the quotients.

5. 26)2,744

6. 53)425

7. 34)50,112

8. 15)16,001

106

Find the quotients.

1. $60\overline{)252}$ 2. $30\overline{)2,520}$ 3. $20\overline{)14,160}$ 4. $67\overline{)217}$

5. $62\overline{)558}$ 6. $19\overline{)6,097}$ 7. $76\overline{)460}$ 8. $64\overline{)350}$

9. $43\overline{)2,322}$ 10. $68\overline{)1,564}$ 11. $20\overline{)1,030}$ 12. $27\overline{)1,975}$

13. $78\overline{)3,120}$ 14. $85\overline{)88,740}$ 15. $46\overline{)9,752}$ 16. $92\overline{)37,998}$

17. $57\overline{)19,762}$ 18. $34\overline{)21,270}$ 19. $62\overline{)58,967}$ 20. $25\overline{)24,951}$

21. $9,374 \div 86$ 22. $782 \div 34$ 23. $9,658 \div 58$ 24. $94,725 \div 75$

25. $1,836 \div 27$ 26. $2,668 \div 58$ 27. $7,875 \div 35$ 28. $48,269 \div 79$

29. Divide 31,605 by 49.   30. Divide 57,932 by 28.

MATH REASONING

Do not divide. Just tell which quotient is greater.

31. $4,367 \div 68$ 32. $25,384 \div 62$
    $4,367 \div 62$ $24,384 \div 62$

PROBLEM SOLVING

33. In 1986, Voyager flew non-stop around the world. It carried 1,200 gallons of fuel in 17 tanks. How many gallons were in each tank?

▶ CALCULATOR

Here's how to use a calculator to find the quotient and remainder for $8,712 \div 64$.

Divide. The whole number part is the quotient.

8712 ÷ 64 = $\boxed{136.125}$

Multiply the quotient by the divisor.

136 × 64 = $\boxed{8704}$

Subtract the product from the dividend to find the remainder. 8712 − 8704 = $\boxed{8}$

Use a calculator to find these quotients and remainders.

34. $76\overline{)12,787}$ 35. $38\overline{)27,694}$ 36. $96\overline{)38,948}$

More Practice, page 504, set F

Estimating Decimal Quotients

LEARN ABOUT IT

Two of the estimation methods you know, rounding and using compatible numbers, can be used to estimate decimal quotients.

EXPLORE Examine the Data

The greatest recorded rainfall in a 24-hour period was 73.62 inches at a recording station near the Indian Ocean. This happened in March 1952. Estimate the average amount of rain that fell per hour.

TALK ABOUT IT

1. What is the data you need to solve the problem?
2. What is there about the problem that suggests that you should divide to find the answer?

To estimate 73.62 ÷ 24, you can use compatible numbers.

$$73.62 \div 24$$
$$\downarrow \qquad \downarrow$$
$$75 \div 25 = 3$$

About 3 inches of rain fell per hour.

Other Examples

Rounding	Compatible Numbers
A 412.88 ÷ 5.2	**B** 362.76 ÷ 6.9
$\downarrow \qquad \downarrow$	$\downarrow \qquad \downarrow$
400 ÷ 5 = 80	350 ÷ 7 = 50

PRACTICE

Estimate each quotient. Use rounding or compatible numbers.

1. 283.64 ÷ 4
2. 478.34 ÷ 6
3. 724.62 ÷ 8
4. 265.98 ÷ 3

5. 14.862 ÷ 3.2
6. 322.47 ÷ 7.6
7. 355.93 ÷ 5.8
8. 536.71 ÷ 9.1

9. 55.982 ÷ 7.8
10. 483.7 ÷ 63
11. 34.967 ÷ 4.7
12. 55.63 ÷ 9.25

More Practice, page 505, set A

MIDCHAPTER REVIEW/QUIZ

Divide.

1. 270 ÷ 9 **2.** 540 ÷ 60 **3.** 5,600 ÷ 800 **4.** 4,800 ÷ 60 **5.** 18,000 ÷ 90

6. 2,400 ÷ 80 **7.** 40,000 ÷ 50 **8.** 36,000 ÷ 90 **9.** 63,000 ÷ 7 **10.** 10,000 ÷ 50

11. 30)$\overline{2,100}$ **12.** 4)$\overline{3,200}$ **13.** 700)$\overline{4,900}$ **14.** 80)$\overline{640}$ **15.** 70)$\overline{35,000}$

Divide and check.

16. 6)$\overline{96}$ **17.** 7)$\overline{249}$ **18.** 4)$\overline{725}$ **19.** 8)$\overline{8,320}$ **20.** 9)$\overline{24,354}$

21. 3,402 ÷ 6 **22.** 13,015 ÷ 5 **23.** 22,244 ÷ 3 **24.** 4,993 ÷ 7 **25.** 24,028 ÷ 2

Find the average of these sets of numbers, to the nearest whole number.

26. 12, 17, 22, 18, 21 **27.** 41, 54, 60, 44

28. 7, 6, 8, 9, 3, 6, 5 **29.** 89, 97, 85, 80, 91, 93

Divide.

30. 80)$\overline{4,097}$ **31.** 54)$\overline{330}$ **32.** 23)$\overline{7,251}$ **33.** 38)$\overline{27,000}$

34. 78)$\overline{16,070}$ **35.** 62)$\overline{31,620}$ **36.** 26)$\overline{21,034}$ **37.** 47)$\overline{18,824}$

PROBLEM SOLVING

Choose a calculation method, then solve. Try the strategy **Make a Table.**

38. During Donna's first year on the softball team, she got on base 3 times for every 7 times she was at bat. How many times was Donna at bat if she was on base 21 times?

39. During baseball season, Gordon hit 2 fly balls for every 3 grounders. If he had a total of 30 fly balls, how many total hits did he have?

40. If Sue walks 4 miles in 1 hour, about how far does she walk in 2 hours? About how far in 25 minutes?

41. When Jeannie swims laps, she does twice as many laps swimming the side stroke as she does swimming the crawl. If she swam 18 side stroke laps, how many laps would she swim the crawl?

42. During basketball season, Arne made 4 free throws for every 5 times he was at the free-throw line. If he ended the season making 40 free throws, how many times was he at the line? How many times did he miss?

43. Geraldo got 566 points in 3 bowling games. What was his average score?

Dividing Decimals
Making the Connection

EXPLORE Use a Decimal Model

Work in groups. Use play dollars, dimes, and pennies.

- Show 4 one-dollar bills and 2 dimes.
- How many ways can your group find to share the money equally? For example, could the money be shared equally 2 ways? Three ways?
- Make trades to show each of the ways you find. Record how many shared the money and how much each one got.

Trades

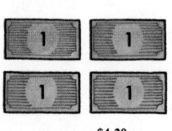

$4.20

1 dollar = 10 dimes

1 dime = 10 pennies

TALK ABOUT IT

1. Use play money and describe some of the trades you needed to make as you shared the money in different ways.
2. Did you find a way to share the money so you didn't have to make any trades at all?
3. Suppose some money can be shared equally 3 ways and also 5 ways. Who would get more, those in the group of 3 or those in the group of 5? Why?

You have found ways of sharing money equally among different size groups. Here is a convenient way to record what you have done. This work with money will help you understand decimal divisions such as $8.25 ÷ 3 or 8.25 ÷ 3.

$$3\overline{)\$8.25}$$

What You Do

1. Share the dollars.

How many dollars are left to be traded for dimes?

Trade

What You Write

$$\begin{array}{r} \$2 \\ 3\overline{)\$8.25} \\ \underline{6} \\ 22 \end{array}$$

2. Share the dimes.

How many dimes are left to be traded?

Trade

$$\begin{array}{r} \$2.7 \\ 3\overline{)\$8.25} \\ \underline{6} \\ 22 \\ \underline{21} \\ 15 \end{array}$$

3. Share the pennies.

How many pennies are left over?

$$\begin{array}{r} \$2.75 \\ 3\overline{)\$8.25} \\ \underline{6} \\ 22 \\ \underline{21} \\ 15 \\ \underline{15} \\ 0 \end{array}$$

4. How much money is in each set? What is $8.25 divided by 3?

TRY IT OUT

Use dollars, dimes, and pennies to divide these amounts. Record what you did as in the examples above.

1. Divide $7.38 by 2.

2. Divide $7.38 by 3.

3. Make up and solve your own division problem.

Dividing a Decimal by a Whole Number

Olympic Speed Skating: 500-Meter Winners

Year	Winner	Time, seconds
1988	Bonnie Blair	39.10
1984	Christa Rothenburger	41.02
1980	Karin Enke	41.78
1976	Sheila Young	42.76

EXPLORE Analyze the Process

In the 1988 Olympics, Bonnie Blair set a new record for women's 500-meter speed skating. What was her average time for each 100 meters?

Why would you divide to find the answer to the problem?

Divide the whole number part.	Place the decimal point. Divide the tenths.	Divide the hundredths.
$\begin{array}{r} 7 \\ 5\overline{)39.10} \end{array}$	$\begin{array}{r} 7.8 \\ 5\overline{)39.10} \\ \underline{35} \\ 4\ 1 \\ 4\ 0 \end{array}$	$\begin{array}{r} 7.82 \\ 5\overline{)39.10} \\ \underline{35} \\ 4\ 1 \\ 4\ 0 \\ 10 \\ \underline{10} \\ 0 \end{array}$

TALK ABOUT IT

1. How do you know that 782, 78.2, and 0.782 are unreasonable answers?
2. How could you estimate the division mentally to see if the answer is reasonable?
3. How could you use multiplication to check your answer?
4. Use a complete sentence to give a reasonable answer to the story problem.

Divide. Check your answers.

1. $4\overline{)25.92}$

2. $9\overline{)5.166}$

3. $32\overline{)\$45.76}$

4. $3\overline{)0.87}$

5. $5\overline{)24.55}$

6. $2\overline{)72.238}$

7. $57\overline{)59.85}$

8. $26\overline{)13.104}$

Divide. Check your answers.

1. $2\overline{)6.42}$ **2.** $4\overline{)32.67}$ **3.** $3\overline{)18.25}$ **4.** $4\overline{)20.16}$ **5.** $7\overline{)123.85}$

6. $6\overline{)2.898}$ **7.** $8\overline{)8.344}$ **8.** $9\overline{)0.5733}$ **9.** $4\overline{)93.04}$ **10.** $3\overline{)168.6}$

11. $19\overline{)28.5}$ **12.** $24\overline{)59.28}$ **13.** $43\overline{)165.55}$ **14.** $26\overline{)244.4}$ **15.** $35\overline{)819.7}$

16. $2\overline{)19.6}$ **17.** $7\overline{)17.738}$ **18.** $5\overline{)1.835}$ **19.** $8\overline{)288.24}$ **20.** $6\overline{)340.2}$

21. $37\overline{)9.361}$ **22.** $85\overline{)158.95}$ **23.** $73\overline{)\$33.58}$ **24.** $3\overline{)\$50.25}$ **25.** $24\overline{)\$245.28}$

26. $61.38 \div 9$ **27.** $9.506 \div 7$ **28.** $68.8 \div 8$ **29.** $4.737 \div 3$ **30.** $4.842 \div 6$

31. Estimate, then find: $8.85 \div 3$ **32.** Estimate, then find: $381.6 \div 9$

MATH REASONING

Find the missing number without dividing.

33. $3\overline{)}$ 71 R1   **34.** $53\overline{)2{,}496}$ 47 R   **35.** $7\overline{)}$ 2.84

PROBLEM SOLVING

36. How much less was Bonnie Blair's time than Christa Rothenburger's time in the 1984 Olympics?

37. What is the average time for this race in the Olympics from 1976 through 1988?

▶ **MENTAL MATH**

Find each quotient. Use a calculator if you want. Look for a pattern.

38. $7{,}386.4 \div 10$
$7{,}386.4 \div 100$
$7{,}386.4 \div 1{,}000$

39. $296.54 \div 10$
$296.54 \div 100$
$296.54 \div 1{,}000$

40. $28{,}374 \div 10$
$28{,}374 \div 100$
$28{,}374 \div 1{,}000$

Use the pattern you discovered to give these answers mentally.
Write answers only.

41. $9.6 \div 10$ **42.** $27.54 \div 10$ **43.** $75 \div 10$ **44.** $34.2 \div 100$

45. $536.5 \div 100$ **46.** $278 \div 100$ **47.** $496.4 \div 1{,}000$ **48.** $387.25 \div 1{,}000$

Problem Solving
Deciding When to Estimate

UNDERSTAND
ANALYZE DATA
PLAN
ESTIMATE
SOLVE
EXAMINE

LEARN ABOUT IT

When you solve problems, you should decide if
you need an **estimate** or an **exact answer.**

Suppose you are in charge of ordering soft
drinks to sell at your school's holiday party.
You figure that at least 190 students will
attend and that you will sell an average of
$1\frac{1}{2}$ drinks per person. How many drinks
should you order?

> Since I'm not positive of the number
> attending and the amount they will drink,
> I can estimate how many to buy.

You will be charged 18¢ a can for the
drinks you actually sell. How much will it
cost you if you sell 286 drinks?

> I need to know the exact amount so I
> will know how much I'll have to pay.

You need to understand the situation in the problem before you
can decide if you need an exact answer or if an estimate will be
enough to answer the question.

TRY IT OUT

Use the situation above to decide whether an estimate or an exact
answer is needed. Tell why.

1. You report to your class the profit made
   by selling drinks at the party.

2. You tell your class whether the average
   number of drinks per person was more
   or less than 2.

Decide if you need an estimate or an exact answer. Tell why.

1. You tell someone the amount of money you intend to make selling drinks at the school Valentine's Day party.

2. You tell someone the amount of money you made on each soft drink you sold.

3. You tell your class how much money you will receive if each person attending the Valentine's Day party spends 95¢ on drinks.

4. You tell your class how much it will cost to buy 350 drinks from the supplier.

5. You want to find out if the average sixth grader spent more or less than $2.00 at the last party.

6. You want to know how much it would cost a student to buy a sandwich and 2 soft drinks.

7. You tell your class about how much it costs to buy the ingredients to make 25 sandwiches.

8. At a fifth grade party, 69 students spent $152 on food and soft drinks. The sixth graders had 56 students at their party and they spent $149. Who spent more per student, the fifth graders or the sixth graders?

9. Jason had to pay 19¢ each for his soft drinks. He sold 358 drinks for 35¢ each. What was his profit if he had to pay $15 for ice and cups?

10. **Missing Data** Make up the missing data and solve the problem. Amanda made 18¢ on each turkey sandwich and 21¢ on each tuna sandwich. How much did she make on these sandwiches?

Rounding Decimal Quotients

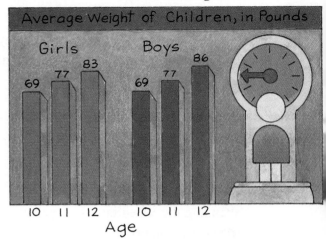

National Average

Average Weight of Children, in Pounds

LEARN ABOUT IT

EXPLORE Solve to Understand

Six 11-year-old students weighed 69, 82, 78, 68, 75, and 83 pounds, for a total of 455 pounds. What was their average weight to the nearest tenth of a pound?

Since we want an average, we divide the total by the number of addends.

Divide.	Divide to one place beyond the place to which you are rounding.	Round the quotient. If the last digit is less than 5, drop it. If it is 5 or more, drop it and round up.

Divide.

```
    75.8
6)455.0
    42
    35
    30
    50
    48
     2
```

Write zeros as needed to complete the dividing.

Divide to one place beyond the place to which you are rounding.

```
     75.83
6)455.00
    42
    35
    30
    50
    48
     20
     18
      2
```

Round the quotient. If the last digit is less than 5, drop it. If it is 5 or more, drop it and round up.

75.83 → 75.8

Round to the nearest tenth.

TALK ABOUT IT

1. Why can you write zeros after the decimal point without changing the problem?
2. How could you convince someone that 75.8 is a reasonable average for the given weights? Hint: Look at the table above.
3. Use a complete sentence to give a reasonable answer to the story problem.

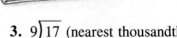

TRY IT OUT

Divide. Round as indicated.

1. $9\overline{)24}$ (nearest tenth) **2.** $25.43 \div 7$ (nearest cent) **3.** $9\overline{)17}$ (nearest thousandth)

Divide. Round to the nearest tenth.

1. $3\overline{)11}$ **2.** $7\overline{)5}$ **3.** $9\overline{)4}$ **4.** $6\overline{)13}$ **5.** $8\overline{)3}$

6. $14\overline{)7.34}$ **7.** $18\overline{)6.45}$ **8.** $25\overline{)3}$ **9.** $27\overline{)96}$ **10.** $43\overline{)287}$

Find the quotients. Round to the nearest hundredth or cent.

11. $6\overline{)5}$ **12.** $6\overline{)31}$ **13.** $7\overline{)5}$ **14.** $19\overline{)6}$ **15.** $20\overline{)87.2}$

16. $8\overline{)\$10.06}$ **17.** $3\overline{)\$19.06}$ **18.** $7\overline{)\$3.94}$ **19.** $25\overline{)\$64.75}$ **20.** $36\overline{)\$38.93}$

MATH REASONING

Use the whole number quotient to give each decimal quotient. Write answers only.

$$\begin{array}{r} 1{,}428 \text{ R4} \\ 7\overline{)10{,}000} \end{array}$$

21. $10 \div 7$ (nearest tenth)   **22.** $10 \div 7$ (nearest hundredth)

23. $100 \div 7$ (nearest tenth)   **24.** $1 \div 7$ (nearest thousandth)

PROBLEM SOLVING

Use data from the opposite page to solve these problems.

25. By how much did the average weight of the six students miss the national average for 11-year-olds?

26. More Than One Answer Three students weigh different amounts. Find possible weights for them so their average weight is 75 pounds.

27. Seven students weigh a total of 481 pounds. Find their average weight to the nearest tenth. What age do you think they might be?

28. Data Hunt Get a group of 3, 4, or 5 classmates. Find the average weight of your group to the nearest tenth.

▶ **CALCULATOR**

You can write a decimal for a fraction by dividing.   **Example:** $\frac{3}{8} = 3 \div 8 = 0.375$

Use your calculator to write a decimal for each fraction. Round to the nearest thousandth when necessary.

29. $\frac{1}{8}$ **30.** $\frac{5}{8}$ **31.** $\frac{7}{8}$ **32.** $\frac{1}{6}$ **33.** $\frac{5}{6}$

34. $\frac{1}{3}$ **35.** $\frac{2}{3}$ **36.** $\frac{1}{12}$ **37.** $\frac{5}{12}$ **38.** $\frac{1}{16}$

Problem Solving
Understanding the Question

UNDERSTAND
ANALYZE DATA
PLAN
ESTIMATE
SOLVE
EXAMINE

LEARN ABOUT IT

One of the first steps in solving a problem is understanding the question. Sometimes it helps to ask the question in a different way.

Yellowstone National Park has 120 named geysers and about 60 unnamed geysers. How many geysers are there in the Park?

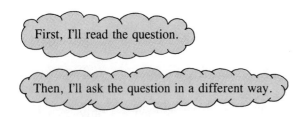

First, I'll read the question.

Then, I'll ask the question in a different way.

How many geysers are there in the park?

What is the total number of geysers in the park?

TRY IT OUT

Read each problem. Then decide which question asks the same thing.

1. Norris Geyser Basin has at least 24 active geysers. Lower Geyser Basin has at least 18. How many geysers are there in the two basins?
   a. How many geysers do the two basins have altogether?
   b. How many more geysers does Norris Basin have?

2. Valentine Geyser erupts up to 75 feet. Minute Geyser erupts up to 20 feet. How much higher does Valentine erupt?
   a. How many feet do the 2 geysers erupt together?
   b. How much lower is Minute's eruption?

Now write a question to complete each problem.

3. A group of sixth graders came to see the geysers. There are 12 girls and 9 boys in the group.

4. The students watched one geyser erupt for about 4 minutes and another erupt for about 7 minutes.

Solve. Use any problem solving strategy.

1. Lower Yellowstone Falls is 310 feet high. Ribbon Falls in Yosemite is 1,612 feet high and is the highest waterfall in the United States. How much higher is Ribbon Falls?

2. Use the data in the chart to find how many gallons of water Old Faithful discharges in one day.

3. The park gift shop sells picture postcards for 3 for 50¢. Stacy bought 21 postcards. How much did she spend?

4. Little Cub Geyser erupts about every 1.8 hours. About how many times does it erupt in 24 hours?

Old Faithful (each eruption)
Erupts 116 to 175 feet
Erupts for about 4 minutes every hour
Discharges about 12,000 gallons of water

5. Mei bought souvenirs for some friends. He spent $23.85 for 3 T-shirts and $7.50 on posters. How much did each T-shirt cost?

6. Darryl's family drove to Yellowstone National Park last summer. The trip took 3 days. They drove 425 miles the first day, 378 miles the second day, and 214 miles the third day. Find the average number of miles driven each day.

7. The family stayed in a campground for 12 days. The camping fee was $4.50 a day. How much did it cost them to camp?

8. **Social Studies Data Bank** The Yellowstone River is 318.4 km shorter than the Brazos River. What is its length?

9. **Understanding the Operations**
Name the operation you would use to solve this problem.

A group of people were watching Old Faithful erupt. Five of them left. Then there were 8 people watching Old Faithful. How many people were in the original group?

Dividing by a Decimal

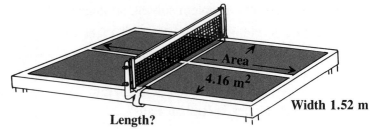

Area
4.16 m²

Width 1.52 m

Length?

LEARN ABOUT IT

EXPLORE Solve to Understand

The area of this table tennis table is
4.16 square meters, and the width of
the table is 1.52 meters. What is the
length of the table to the nearest hundredth?

Since we know the area and one side, we divide to find the other side.

Multiply the divisor by a power of 10 to make it a whole number.	Multiply the dividend by the same power of 10.	Divide.

× 100

$1.5\,2\,\overline{)4.1\,6}$

× 100

$1.5\,2_\wedge\overline{)4.1\,6_\wedge}$

Multiplying the divisor and the
dividend by the same number
does not change the quotient.
See these whole number
examples.

$$\begin{array}{ccc} 7 & 7 & 7 \\ 6\overline{)42} & 60\overline{)420} & 600\overline{)4,200} \end{array}$$

```
              2.7 3 6
1.5 2∧)4.1 6∧0 0 0
        3 0 4
        1 1 2 0
        1 0 6 4
          5 6 0
          4 5 6
          1 0 4 0
            9 1 2
            1 2 8
```

TALK ABOUT IT

1. Why is dividing by a decimal like dividing by a whole number
   except for placement of the decimal point?
2. Use a complete sentence to give a reasonable answer to the story problem.

TRY IT OUT

Divide. Round to the nearest hundredth when necessary.

1. $4.3\overline{)201.24}$ **2.** $0.7\overline{)6.65}$ **3.** $0.54\overline{)4.433}$ **4.** $0.038\overline{)3.0666}$

Divide. Round to the nearest hundredth when necessary.

1. $3.4\overline{)12.92}$ **2.** $0.8\overline{)26.08}$ **3.** $0.67\overline{)3.643}$ **4.** $0.03\overline{)0.294}$

5. $9.5\overline{)0.8265}$ **6.** $0.6\overline{)0.576}$ **7.** $0.09\overline{)34.283}$ **8.** $0.08\overline{)7.221}$

9. $0.7\overline{)224}$ **10.** $0.003\overline{)5.1}$ **11.** $0.007\overline{)0.0868}$ **12.** $0.046\overline{)3.0084}$

Find the quotients. Round to the nearest hundredth when necessary.

13. $1.44 \div 0.45$ **14.** $0.3904 \div 0.061$ **15.** $0.5318 \div 0.49$

16. $42 \div 0.06$ **17.** $12 \div 0.005$ **18.** $32.2 \div 0.46$

19. Estimate, then find the quotient: $63.96 \div 7.8$

20. Estimate, then find the quotient: $242 \div 0.55$

MATH REASONING

Use your knowledge of whole number division to find these quotients. Write answers only.

$\begin{array}{r} 6 \\ 5\overline{)30} \end{array}$

21. $0.5\overline{)30}$ **22.** $0.05\overline{)30}$ **23.** $0.005\overline{)30}$

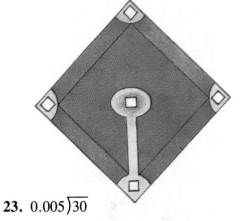

PROBLEM SOLVING

24. A tennis court is 10.97 m wide. It has an area of 260.75 m². What is the length of the court to the nearest hundredth?

25. A baseball diamond is a square that is 27.45 m on each side. What is the area of the diamond?

Evaluate the expressions for $a = 20$ and $b = 30$.

26. $(a \times b) + a$ **27.** $1.2 \times a$ **28.** $3 \times (a + b)$ **29.** $(3 \times a) + (3 \times b)$

Write as an algebraic expression.

30. a number increased by 4   **31.** double a number   **32.** 5 less than a number

Problem Solving
Using a Calculator

UNDERSTAND
ANALYZE DATA
PLAN
ESTIMATE
SOLVE
EXAMINE

LEARN ABOUT IT

To do accurate comparison shopping, you need to understand and be able to calculate unit prices. Such calculations are most easily done with a calculator.

The price for 1 unit (one ounce, one pound, and so forth) of an item is called the **unit price.**

The simple problem below will help you understand how to find unit prices when you know the total price and the number of units.

A 20-pound bag of potatoes costs $1.98. Find the unit price per pound. Round to the nearest cent.

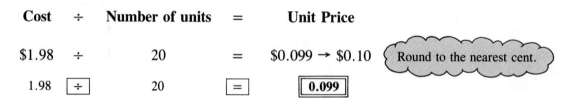

Cost	÷	Number of units	=	Unit Price	
$1.98	÷	20	=	$0.099 → $0.10	Round to the nearest cent.
1.98	÷	20	=	**0.099**	

TRY IT OUT

Use your calculator to find the unit price. Round to the nearest cent.

1.

CRACKERS
9.5 oz $1.19

2.

TOMATOES
15 oz $0.89

3.

TUNA
5.5 oz $0.99

4.

FLOUR
5 lbs $1.29

Solve. Use any problem solving strategy.

1. Alejandro bought a package of 80 paper napkins for $1.69. How much was each napkin? Round to the nearest cent.

2. Liz paid $11.06 for 12.3 gallons of gasoline. How much did she pay per gallon? Round to the nearest tenth of a cent.

3. Muriel bought an 18-pound watermelon for $3.00. To the nearest cent, what was the unit price per pound?

4. Ms. Washington drove from her house to the grocery store, a distance of 2.2 miles. She then drove to the medical center for a dental appointment. The medical center is 4.2 miles from the grocery store. After that she drove 5.3 miles to visit her mother. How many miles did Ms. Washington travel?

5. Tim had twice as many baseball cards as Tom. Sally had 9 cards, four fewer than Tom. How many cards did Tim have?

6. Baseball cards were on sale at the grocery store. Packages containing 5 cards sold for 25¢ while packages containing 4 cards sold for 20¢. Ginger spent $1.20 on baseball cards. How many baseball cards did she buy?

7. A five-pound bag of cat food sells for $1.25. Sam's cats eat 2 bags of food every month. What is the unit price of the cat food?

8. A 38-oz box of pancake mix costs $2.49. A 24-oz box costs $1.79. Compare unit costs to determine the better buy.

9. Apples cost $0.39 per pound. Maurice bought 5 pounds. How much did he pay for the apples?

10. Cindy bought 2 pounds of bananas at 29¢ per pound and 6 pounds of pears at 69¢ per pound. She gave the cashier $5. What change did she receive?

11. **Determining Reasonable Answers** Ginny, George, and Rina each figured the unit price for this grape juice. Tell why Ginny and George have unreasonable answers. Is Rina correct?

Ginny

George

Rina

Data Collection and Analysis
Group Decision Making

UNDERSTAND
ANALYZE DATA
PLAN
ESTIMATE
SOLVE
EXAMINE

Doing a Simulation

Group Skill

Encourage and Respect Others

In a group of six people, is it likely that two of them were born in the same month? Predict whether you think there will be a month match less than half the time, more than half the time, or about half the time. You and your group will conduct a **simulation** in which you will act out the situation to see what is likely to happen in the real world.

Collecting Data

1. Work with your group to cut out 12 small cards and write the name of each month on a card.
2. Draw a month card at random to represent the month of birth for one person. Record the month. Replace the card and draw another to simulate the second person in the group. Continue until six months have been drawn and recorded. This completes your first series of draws, or one **trial.** Did any of the six months match? Make a table like the one below to keep a record for 30 trials.

Number of Draws						Match?
1st	2nd	3rd	4th	5th	6th	
Trial 1	Mar.	Jan.	Nov.	Aug.	July	Feb.	no
Trial 2	July	June	May	April	May	Dec.	y*
Trial 3	Sept.	Oct.	June	Jan.	Feb.	Oct.	y*
Trial 4							
Trial 5							

3. Count the total number of matches and the total number of nonmatches. Make a bar graph to compare the two totals.

```
-----------Title----------
Outcomes
  Matches
No Matches
         0 2 4 6 8 - - - - -
         -------Label------
```

4. Compare the results to your predictions. Write a summary about what your group found out.

5. Did other groups get similar results? Do you think you would get similar results if you tried the simulation with a larger number of trials? Why or why not?

WRAP UP

Estimation and Mental Math Terms

Which estimation or mental math technique is used in each example?
Choose: *compatible numbers, clustering, break-apart, rounding.*

1. $247 \div 7 \rightarrow 240 \div 8$

2. $87 + 78 + 83 + 90 \rightarrow 4 \times 80$

3. $587 + 562 + 615 \rightarrow 590 + 560 + 620$

4. $\$24.84 \div 4 \rightarrow (\$24.00 \div 4) + (8 \text{ dimes} \div 4) + (4 \text{ pennies} \div 4)$

5. $554.6 \div 66 \rightarrow 560 \div 70$

6. $2{,}427 \div 3 \rightarrow (2{,}400 \div 3) + (27 \div 3)$

7. $5{,}982 + 6{,}305 + 6{,}019 \rightarrow 3 \times 6{,}000$

Sometimes, Always, Never

Decide which word should go in the blank: *sometimes, always,* or
never. Explain your choices.

8. An estimated quotient is ____ sufficient to give the correct
answer.

9. The remainder in division is ____ less than the divisor.

10. If the divisor is greater than 1, the number being divided is
____ greater than the quotient.

11. The average of a set of numbers is ____ less than the smallest
number.

Project

You want to open a grocery store. To begin, you look at ads for
some local stores. You compare unit prices on items sold by 2s, 3s,
4s, and so on. For example, grapefruit might sell at 4 for $1.25. You
want to sell your items for about $.02 less than the lowest price you
find at the other stores. You will only sell in packages of 5. Decide
on a store name and a slogan. Make a table that lists the unit price
and the package price for 10 items you will sell.

Grapes

seedless•red & green

Corn-on-the-Cob

just picked

Apples

5 varieties

Broccoli

crisp, fresh

CHAPTER REVIEW/TEST

Part 1   Understanding

Tell which quotient is greater without dividing.

1. $2,482 \div 41$ or $2,482 \div 51$

2. $16,667 \div 47$ or $12,667 \div 47$

3. Without dividing, choose the number that is the average of this set of numbers: 44, 53, 37, 48, 39, 55   **a.** 36   **b.** 46   **c.** 56

Decide if you need an estimate or an exact answer.

4. You tell someone the amount of money your lemonade stand will probably earn next weekend.

5. You want to know what it will cost to buy 100 cups for your lemonade stand.

Part 2   Skills

Find the quotients mentally.

6. $320 \div 8$

7. $24,000 \div 60$

Estimate each quotient. Use rounding or compatible numbers.

8. $423.96 \div 6$ **9.** $552.5 \div 8.13$ **10.** $217 \div 7$ **11.** $3,466 \div 50$

Choose a calculation method. Then solve.

12. 371×5

13. $2,800 \div 70$

Divide.

14. $26,452 \div 8$ **15.** $58,966 \div 55$ **16.** $36.729 \div 21$ **17.** $0.0444 \div 0.006$

18. Divide \$5.35 by 3. Round to the nearest cent.

19. Divide 70.2 by 0.96. Round to the nearest hundredth.

Part 3   Applications

20. Horace bowled games of 132, 152, 108, and 140. What is his average score for the 4 games?

21. For every 5 western videos rented, the store rents 8 sports videos. If the store rents 48 sports videos, how many western videos are rented?

22. Challenge   A 6-pound bag of dog food sells for \$2.70. Kay has 3 dogs. She bought 3 bags. What is the price per pound for the dog food?

ENRICHMENT
Scientific Notation

The sun is 93,000,000 miles from Earth. This is such a long distance that it takes light from the sun over 8 minutes to reach us. Distances throughout the universe are so huge that scientists use a special measurement, the **light year,** to describe them. A light year is the distance light travels in 1 year, about 6,000,000,000,000 miles.

Can you display the distance from Earth to the sun in standard form on your calculator? The distance light travels in 1 year? Explain.

$$93,000,000 = 9.3 \times 1,000,000 = 9.3 \times 10^7$$
$$6,000,000,000,000 = 6 \times 1,000,000,000,000 = 6 \times 10^{12}$$

A number written in scientific notation is the product of two factors. One factor is a number between 1 and 10. The other is a power of ten and is written with exponents.

1. Does writing a number in scientific notation change its value? Explain.

Write in scientific notation.

2. 4,700

3. 210,000

4. 6,800,000

5. 345,000,000,000

Solve.

6. Pluto has a diameter of 1,500 miles. Write that number in scientific notation.

7. The largest crater on the moon is called Bailly. It covers an area of about 26,000 square miles. Express its area using scientific notation.

8. Light travels at a speed of 186,000 miles per second. Write this speed in scientific notation.

9. Astronomers agree that the universe started about 15,000,000,000 years ago. Write this number in scientific notation.

10. The Orion Nebula, which can be seen with the naked eye, is 1.6×10^3 light years away from us. Write the distance in light years in standard form.

11. The moon revolves around the earth from an average distance of 2.39×10^5 miles. Write this number in standard form.

CUMULATIVE REVIEW

Find the number.

1. eighty thousand

   A. 8,000   **B.** 80,000

   C. 8,000,000   **D.** 800,000

2. eight billion

   A. 8,000,000,000   **B.** 8,000,000

   C. 800,000   **D.** 80,000,000,000

3. Choose the number that correctly completes $1,684,328 <$ ▓.

   A. 1,684,328   **B.** 1,684,229

   C. 1,684,332   **D.** 1,684,325

4. Write the decimal: one and thirty-two hundredths.

   A. 0.132   **B.** 1.032

   C. 13.2   **D.** 1.32

5. Write the next number in the sequence: 0.214, 0.234, 0.254, 0.274

   A. 0.314   **B.** 0.294

   C. 0.254   **D.** 0.239

6. $4.3 \text{ m} =$ ▓ cm

   A. 43   **B.** 0.43

   C. 430   **D.** 4,300

7. Find $25 + 37 + 75$ mentally.

   A. 87   **B.** 63

   C. 137   **D.** 40

8. Meg sang for a number of minutes. Then she sang for 5 more minutes. Which expression tells how long she sang?

   A. $n + 5$ **B.** $n - 5$

   C. $5 - n$ **D.** $n \times 5$

9. What is the value of the 6 in the decimal 2.0346?

   A. 0.0006   **B.** 0.006

   C. 0.6   **D.** 0.06

10. Round 2.381 to the nearest hundredth.

   A. 2.39   **B.** 2.38

   C. 2.40   **D.** 2.9

11. Estimate the sum: $14.04 + 7.89$.

   A. 14.7   **B.** 21

   C. 6   **D.** 22

12. Which is the prime factorization for 78?

   A. 2×39 **B.** 7×2^3

   C. $7 \times 10 \times 2^3$ **D.** $2 \times 3 \times 13$

13. Adult tickets cost $3 each. Student tickets cost $1.50 each. Ten tickets were sold and $24 was collected. How many of each kind of ticket were sold?

   A. 4 adult, 6 student

   B. 5 adult, 5 student

   C. 6 adult, 4 student

   D. 4 adult, 4 student

14. Which factors would give the product shown in the drawing?

   A. 0.9×0.8

   B. 9×0.8

   C. 0.09×0.08

   D. 0.09×0.8

5

DATA,
GRAPHS,
AND
STATISTICS

MATH AND
HEALTH AND FITNESS

DATA BANK

Use the Health and Fitness
Data Bank on page 474 to
answer the questions.

1 Which team sport uses the
most calories per hour?
Which team sport uses the
fewest calories per hour?

2 A single scoop of ice cream can easily contain 100 calories. Which activities could you do by yourself to use those calories in 15 minutes or less?

3 Make a simple bar graph. Show how many activities use 200, 300, 400, and 500 calories in an hour.

4 **Using Critical Thinking** Do you think you use more than or less than 2,500 calories in a 24-hour day during the school week? How could you use the chart to help you decide? Explain your thinking.

Reading Graphs

EXPLORE Study the Data

Every week, Jose tries to improve his swimming times. This **double bar graph** shows his best times for two different weeks and three different events. The numbers along the bottom of the graph are called the **scale** of the graph.

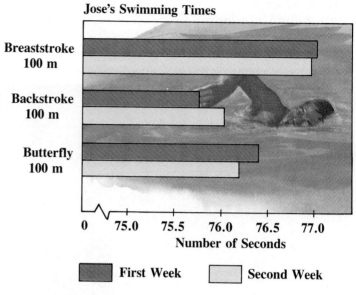

Jose's Swimming Times

Breaststroke 100 m

Backstroke 100 m

Butterfly 100 m

0 75.0 75.5 76.0 76.5 77.0

Number of Seconds

First Week   Second Week

TALK ABOUT IT

1. Why do you think the graph above is called a double bar graph?
2. What numbers are missing along the scale? Why do you think they were left out?
3. What do the two bars for each event compare?

- A squiggle at the beginning of a scale means that part of the scale has been omitted.
- On most graphs you must estimate to find the approximate number represented by the bar or point on a graph.

The bar represents about 76.2 on the scale.

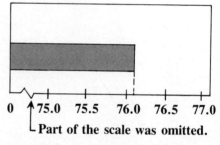

0 75.0 75.5 76.0 76.5 77.0

Part of the scale was omitted.

TRY IT OUT

1. In how many seconds did Jose swim the breastroke the first week? The second week?

2. For which events did he improve his time the second week? Which showed the greatest improvement?

3. Approximately what was his best time for the backstroke?

132

Use the graph on the opposite page for exercises 1–3.

1. For which event did Jose have a time of about 76.2 seconds? Was it the first or the second week?

2. For which event were his times about the same both weeks?

3. Do you think Jose swam faster the first or the second week? Use data to support your conclusion.

Jose trained for six weeks to get ready for a big swimming meet. This pictograph shows how many hours per week he trained.

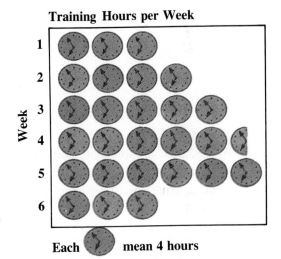

Training Hours per Week

4. How many hours did Jose train the third week?

5. What do you think the half-clock means for the fourth week? How many hours did Jose train that week?

6. What week did he train 16 hours?

7. Why do you think Jose only trained 12 hours the sixth week?

Each ⏱ mean 4 hours

MATH REASONING

8. If means 10 hours, estimate the amount of time for ⏱ .

PROBLEM SOLVING

9. **Health and Fitness Data Bank** If Jose swims 10 hours every week, about how many more calories does he use swimming competitively than if he were to swim for relaxation?

DATA BANK

▶ **USING CRITICAL THINKING** Evaluate the Situation

10. Tell why this graph misleads you about how close the race actually was.

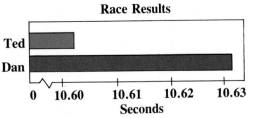

Race Results

133

Range and Scales

Number of Calories (per cup)

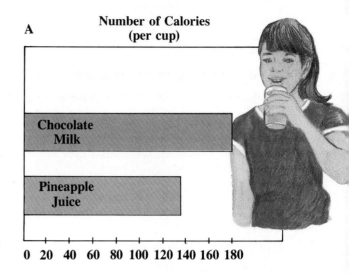

EXPLORE Study the Data

A glass of chocolate milk (180 calories) contains about 45 more calories than a glass of pineapple juice (135 calories). The two graphs show how different the data can appear depending on the scale.

0 20 40 60 80 100 120 140 160 180

TALK ABOUT IT

1. What numbers are represented on each of the scales?
2. Which scale exaggerates the difference in calories?
3. Which scale would you need to use if you wanted to include skim milk (90 calories) and tomato juice (45 calories)?

B

Number of Calories (per cup)

0   130 140   150   160   170   180

The **range** of a set of numbers is the difference between the highest and lowest numbers in the set. The range for the set of numbers 180, 135, 90, 45 is (180 − 45), or 135.

The **interval** of a graph is the number of units between spaces on the scale. The interval for Graph A is 20 and Graph B is 5.

This is how to create a scale.

- First decide if you will show the entire scale or will omit some numbers at the beginning.
- Decide how many intervals you will use.
- Determine the size of each interval depending on the range of numbers to be graphed.

Numbers: 19.5, 17.8, 18.0, 16.4, 17.1   Use 8 intervals, 0.5 each.
Range: About 20 − 16, or 4

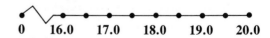

0   16.0   17.0   18.0   19.0   20.0

1. Create a scale for the set of numbers 17, 12, 32, 26.
2. Create a scale for the range from 40 to 110. Make the interval 10.

1. What is the approximate range of numbers represented in this graph?

2. How many intervals are there?

3. What is the number of units in each interval?

4. Create a scale for the data in this graph if the scale is to omit the numbers less than 40.

0   40

Calories per Cup

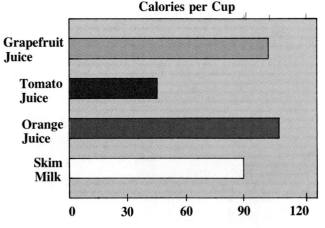

0	30	60	90	120	

5. Draw a scale for a range from 0.2 to 2.0. Make 10 intervals.

MATH REASONING

6. What operation would you use to get the approximate interval size if you have a range of 200 and you plan to use 7 intervals?

PROBLEM SOLVING

7. What interval would you use if you were going to graph the calorie content of the chocolate milk on the opposite page and the skim milk above?

8. **Health and Fitness Data Bank** Create a scale, mark the intervals, and make a bar graph for the number of calories used in walking, jogging, and running. Include all types.

DATA BANK

Estimate.

9. 289×68 **10.** 8.79×22.13 **11.** $326 \div 5$ **12.** $812 \div 18$ **13.** $82.551 \div 3.576$

Find the answers.

14. 305×400 **15.** 4.73×8.4 **16.** $72\overline{)597.6}$ **17.** $89\overline{)0.2047}$

More Practice, page 505, set E

Reading and Making Line Graphs

LEARN ABOUT IT

EXPLORE Study the Data

This table shows how your heart rate might change
as you go from resting, to exercising, and back to resting.
A **line graph** has been started to show the data in the table.

Time	Pulse Rate
0 min	70
5 min	127
10 min	142
15 min	158
20 min	130
25 min	87

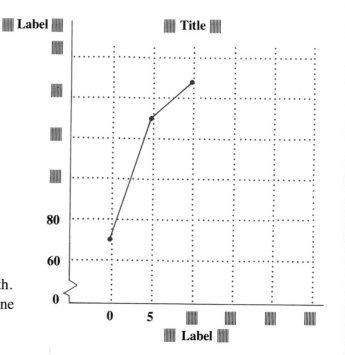

TALK ABOUT IT

1. What do the numbers on the bottom
   scale show?
2. What is shown on the side scale?
3. Which numbers in the table are shown
   by the three points on the graph?
   What point would you show next?

This is how to make a line graph.

- Choose a label for each scale.
- Create each scale so that the data will fit
  and the scales will be about the same length.
- Plot the points for the data and draw the line
  connecting the points.
- Title the graph.

TRY IT OUT

1. Copy and complete the graph above.
2. Look at your graph. What does the descending part of the
   line graph show?

1. This table shows how certain cats with heart disease improved the pumping ability of their hearts with medication given over a 10-week period. Use this data to make a line graph. The figure below will help you start the graph.

Number of Weeks	Units of Blood Pumping Ability
0	0.23
1–2	0.26
3–4	0.34
5–6	0.35
7–8	0.37
9–10	0.40

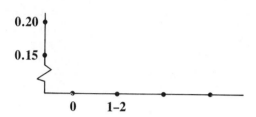

2. Which of these line graphs shows no change moving from left to right?

3. Which shows a decrease?

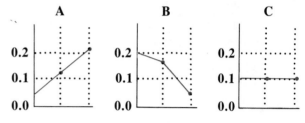

APPLY

MATH REASONING

4. Suppose this is the pay scale for a job. It shows how many hours you need to work to earn $100. Would you like your line graph to increase or decrease over the years? Why?

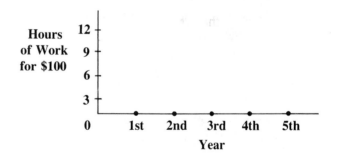

PROBLEM SOLVING

5. How much did the pumping ability of the cats improve over the 10-week period?

6. Use the graph and table from the opposite page to estimate when the pulse rate will return to 70.

▶ ALGEBRA

7. If you graph the data in the table below, will your line graph increase or decrease as n becomes larger?

n	2	3	4	5	...
$2 \times n - 3$					

$2 \times n - 3$

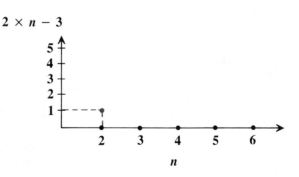

Reading and Making Circle Graphs

LEARN ABOUT IT

What you know about estimating fraction and decimal parts can help you understand information in **circle graphs.**

EXPLORE Study the Graphs

Many nutrition experts believe that a diet low in fats is healthier than one high in fats. The two circle graphs show the diets of two different people.

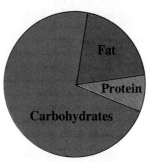

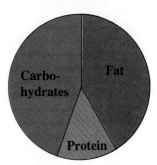

Person A's Diet   **Person B's Diet**

TALK ABOUT IT

1. According to the experts, which person do you think has the healthier diet? How can you tell?
2. What makes up for the fat in Person A's diet, protein or carbohydrates? How can you tell?
3. Which diet is more than half carbohydrates? How can you tell?

In a circle graph, the circle represents the whole, or 1. You can show how the whole is broken into parts by shading or coloring parts of the circle. You can make circle graphs by estimating the parts to show the data. Folding and marking a circle into eighths will help you estimate the parts. The example shows how the data in the chart is shown on the circle.

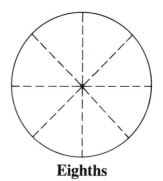

Eighths   **Sources of Grain**

Sources of Grain

Breads	0.48	→	about $\frac{1}{2}$
Cereals	0.37	→	about $\frac{3}{8}$
Other	0.15	→	about $\frac{1}{8}$

TRY IT OUT

1. Make a circle graph showing the data in this chart.

Nutrients in Trout

Protein	0.3	→	a little more than $\frac{1}{4}$
Carbohydrates	0.0	→	0
Fat	0.7	→	a little less than $\frac{3}{4}$

138

PRACTICE

Use the four circle graphs to answer the questions.

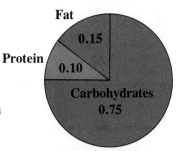

1. Which of the four foods is highest in carbohydrates?

2. Can you tell which food is lowest in fat just by looking at the graphs? Which do you think is lowest?

3. Which food is highest in protein?

4. Which foods are more than $\frac{3}{4}$ carbohydrates?

5. Make two circle graphs to show this data about hamburger meat. Assume that hamburger meat contains no carbohydrates.

Soda Crackers

Fat 0.15
Protein 0.10
Carbohydrates 0.75

White Bread

Protein 0.15
Fat
Carbohydrates 0.80

Spaghetti

Carbohydrates 0.85
Protein 0.13
Fat

Peas

Fat
Protein 0.30
Carbohydrates 0.68

Regular Hamburger

Protein	0.70
Fat	0.30

Extra Lean Hamburger

Protein	0.85
Fat	0.15

APPLY

MATH REASONING

6. How can you find out how much fat is in white bread? How much is there? What is the sum of the parts of a circle graph?

PROBLEM SOLVING

7. Halibut is 0.95 protein while whitefish is 0.86 protein. Assume neither has any carbohydrates. How much more of whitefish is fat than halibut?

8. Health and Fitness Data Bank
Roast chicken has 216 calories per serving, baked potato has 145, and green beans have 30. How many hours of sleeping would it take to use all the calories in one serving of each?

▶ CALCULATOR

9. Blue = 0.46875. Orange = 0.2512. Red = Yellow. What is the value of Red?

Exploring Algebra
Understanding Variables

LEARN ABOUT IT

You have learned that a variable can stand for one number.
A variable can also stand for a range of numbers.

EXPLORE Solve to Understand

"I want to spend my whole $12 on
bowling," said Fran. "Me too!" said
Danielle. Copy and complete the table
at the right to find how many games
they can each bowl.

Number of games	Cost for games ($2 each)	Cost for shoes ($1)	Total cost
1	2	1	3
2	4	1	5
3	6	1	7
4	▨	1	▨
5	▨	1	▨
6	▨	▨	▨

TALK ABOUT IT

1. How much does it cost to rent shoes?
2. As the number of games increases does
   the cost of shoes increase?
3. As the number of games increases, what
   happens to the total cost?

In the situation above, the number of games and the total cost both
vary. Let g stand for the number of games. Let c stand for the total
cost. The letters g and c are variables. In this situation they vary.
You can give a rule that tells how to find the cost, c, if you know
the number of games, g: Multiply g by 2 and add 1 to find c.

TRY IT OUT

1. In the situation above, find c if g is 8.
   Find c, if g is 10.

2. How do you find the entry fee if you
   know the number of students?

3. Use variables to give a rule for finding
   the total cost if you know the number of
   students.

4. What is the total cost for 5 students?

Number of students (n)	Entry fee ($5 each)	Team photo ($2)	Total cost (c)
1	5	2	7
2	10	2	12
3	15	2	17
4	20	2	22
5	▨	▨	▨

140

The line graph shows how much the Chin family spent on groceries the first 6 months of last year. The table shows the values for the remainder of the year. Copy and complete the graph to show the year's grocery expenses.

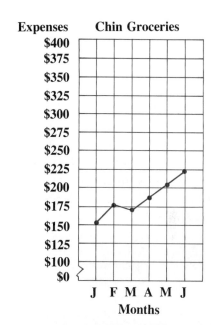

Expenses   Chin Groceries

Months

1. What does the squiggle at the beginning of the scale mean?

2. What is the range of the data? What interval is used?

3. About how much did the Chins spend each of the first 3 months?

4. Between which two months did the amount spent increase the most?

5. Which months might the Chin twin boys have been home from college?

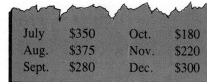

July	$350	Oct.	$180
Aug.	$375	Nov.	$220
Sept.	$280	Dec.	$300

Use the circle graph to answer this question.

6. During which 4-month period did the Chins spend about $\frac{1}{4}$ of their year's grocery money? About $\frac{1}{3}$? About $\frac{2}{5}$?

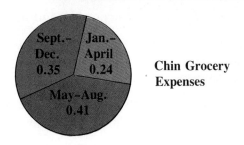

Chin Grocery Expenses

PROBLEM SOLVING

The pictograph shows 4 weeks of grocery bills.

7. Decide how much was spent each week and tell the range of the data.

8. Make a bar graph to display the data. Be sure to label the parts of the graph. What interval did you use?

9. Draw a circle graph showing that about 0.58 of the money was spent in the first two weeks. What part was spent in the second two weeks?

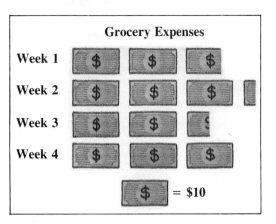

Grocery Expenses

Week 1
Week 2
Week 3
Week 4

$= \$10$

141

Problem Solving
Solve a Simpler Problem

There are 18 basketball teams playing in a tournament. Each team plays until it loses. How many games must be played to determine the champions?

LEARN ABOUT IT

When a problem has large numbers, sometimes it helps to solve the same problem but with smaller numbers. This strategy is called **Solve A Simpler Problem.**

I'll start with 3 teams (A, B, and C) and see how many games must be played.

A plays B.
Winner plays C.

3 teams.
2 games.

Next, I'll try 4 teams (A, B, C, and D) and find how many games must be played.

A plays B and
C plays D.

4 teams.

Aha! The number of games is 1 less than the number of teams.

Winner of A-B plays winner of C-D.

3 games.

There must be 17 games played to determine the champions.

TRY IT OUT

There were 10 girls and 10 boys at a party. Each girl shook hands with each boy one time. How many handshakes were there?

1. How many girls were at the party? How many boys?

2. How many handshakes did each girl have with each boy?

3. How many handshakes did each boy have with each girl?

4. Suppose there were only 2 girls and 2 boys. How many handshakes would 1 girl have? How many would 2 girls have?

5. What relationship do you see between the number of boys and the number of handshakes a girl can have? Use the relationship to solve the problem.

Solve. Try finding a simpler problem.

1. Mr. Aaron bought enough rope to make 18 jump ropes. How many cuts will he have to make?

2. Bea's gym class has 9 boys and 9 girls playing badminton. Each boy plays each girl once. How many games are played?

MIXED PRACTICE

Solve. Choose a strategy from the list or use another strategy that you know.

3. Karna swam the same number of laps every morning for 5 days. She swam 325 laps altogether. How many laps did she swim each day?

4. Membership in the Seals Swim Club costs $250. Each member also pays monthly dues of $35. How much are the dues altogether for one year?

5. An exercise survey asked 500 people how many days each week they exercise. Use the graph to find how many people exercise more than 4 days each week.

Some Strategies	
Act Out	Guess and Check
Use Objects	Make a Table
Choose an Operation	Solve a Simpler Problem
Draw a Picture	

6. There are 15 teams in a volleyball tournament. Each team plays until it loses. How many games are needed to decide the champions?

7. The fitness center offers exercise classes that meet once a week. There are 3 classes on Tuesday and 4 on Saturday. Each class has 20 people. How many people take part in an exercise class at the center each week?

8. In the rope climbing exercise, Rick climbed 2 feet higher than Kim. Ethan was only 4 feet from the top. Kim was 3 feet below Ethan. How much higher did Ethan climb than Rick?

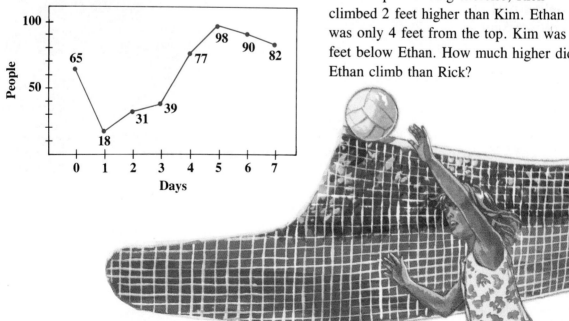

Data Collection
Writing Questions

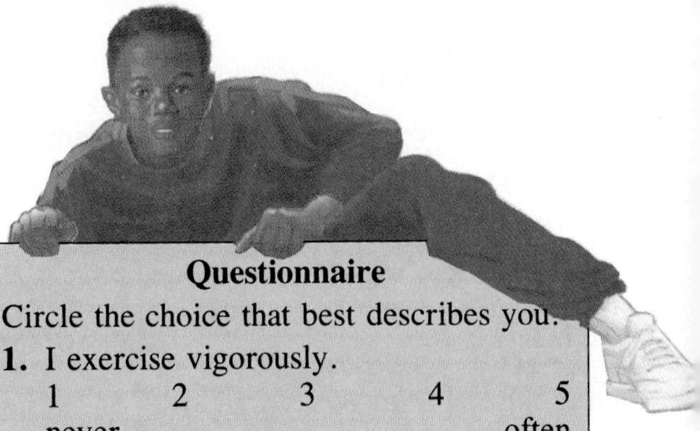

LEARN ABOUT IT

EXPLORE **Think About the Situation**

Here is a **questionnaire** to find out about students' concern for their own physical health.

Questionnaire

Circle the choice that best describes you.

1. I exercise vigorously.

1	2	3	4	5
never				often

2. I try to eat healthy foods.

1	2	3	4	5
seldom				often

3. My average amount of sleep is

6	7	8	9	10
		hours		

4. My favorite sport is
(a) football (b) baseball (c) track
(d) basketball (e) soccer (f) other

TALK ABOUT IT

1. Do you think these four questions will help you find out what you want to know?
2. Which question do you think tells you the least about a person's health habits?
3. Which do you think tells the most?

The two types of questions used on the questionnaire are shown below.

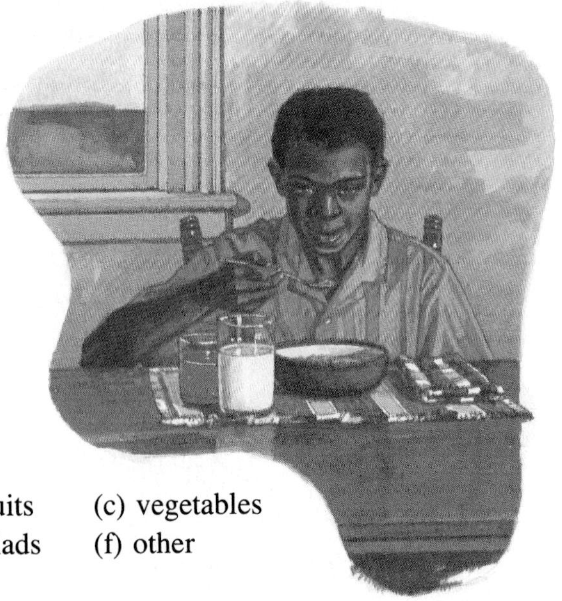

Rating Response

I eat breakfast 1 2 3 4 5
never ... always

Multiple Choice

My favorite types of food are (a) fish (b) fruits (c) vegetables
(d) meats (e) salads (f) other

TRY IT OUT

1. Write a rating response question about health.
2. Write a multiple-choice question about health.

Finish the rating scale for each rating response.

1. I think eating vegetables is   1   2   3   . . .

not so
important

2. I exercise   0   1   2   3   . . .

times per . . .

3. List four choices for this question: My favorite fruit snack is. . . .

4. Write a rating response question about diet.

5. Write a multiple-choice question about sleep habits.

6. Write a health question in your choice of form.

APPLY

MATH REASONING

7. Jan exercises at least 1 hour a day and at most 2 hours a day. One month Jan exercised less than 30 hours. What month was it?

PROBLEM SOLVING

8. Todd's normal pulse rate is 72 beats per minute. When he swims, his rate increases by 59 beats per minute. How many times does his heart beat during a 5-minute swim?

9. Each week, Ed jogs 4 miles more than Shelly. Shelly jogs 7 miles less than Chip. In 3 weeks, how many more miles than Ed does Chip jog?

MIXED REVIEW

Use mental math to find the answers.

10. $360 \div 6$ **11.** 5×307 **12.** $999 + 999$ **13.** $450 \div 50$ **14.** 300×80

Find the quotients. Round to the nearest hundredth.

15. $18\overline{)32.074}$ **16.** $31\overline{)1.1679}$ **17.** $0.7\overline{)8.012}$ **18.** $4.8\overline{)18.1}$

Interpreting Data
Mean, Median, and Mode

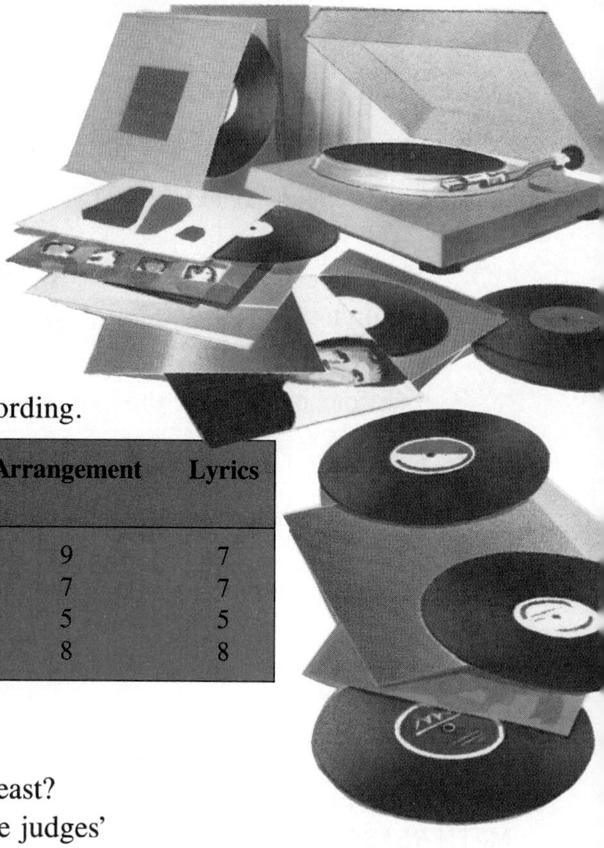

EXPLORE Study the Chart

This chart shows how four judges rated a new recording.

	Audience Appeal	Vocal Quality	Instrumental Quality	Arrangement	Lyrics
Judge 1	9	6	7	9	7
Judge 2	8	7	8	7	7
Judge 3	5	4	5	5	5
Judge 4	8	7	8	8	8

TALK ABOUT IT

1. Which judge appears to like the recording the least?
2. What one number would you use to describe the judges' opinion of audience appeal? Of lyrics?

Here are three ways to use one number to describe a set of numbers.
Set of numbers: 7, 8, 8, 9, 8, 6

Mean or Average

Add the values and divide by the number of values.

$7 + 8 + 8 + 9 + 8 + 6 = 46$
$46 \div 6 = 7.66$, or about 7.7
So 7.7 is the average, or mean.

Median

Put the numbers in order. Find the middle number. If no one middle number exists, add the two middle numbers and divide by 2.

6, 7, 8, 8, 8, 9
The two middle numbers are 8.
$(8 + 8) \div 2 = 8$.
So 8 is the median.

Mode

Find the value that occurs most often.

8 is the value that occurs most often.
So 8 is the mode.

Use the data in the chart above to answer these questions.

1. What is the median score for instrumental quality for all four judges?

2. What is the mode for the scores given on lyrics?

Use the data table below to answer the questions.

Motocross Bike Ratings					
	Durability	Appearance	Weight	Warranty	Price
Pro Rider	30 points	42 points	31 lbs	2 years	$178
Dirt Wheels	48 points	25 points	32 lbs	10 years	$210
Lightning V	32 points	36 points	28 lbs	1 year	$146
2XK Climber	43 points	40 points	29 lbs	5 years	$188
Free Wheeler	45 points	45 points	32 lbs	2 years	$250

1. Find the median number of points for durability ratings on the bikes.

2. Find the mode for the weights of the bikes.

3. What is the mean appearance score?
   Which bike is closest to the mean score?

4. What is the median appearance score?

Copy and complete this table.

	Median	Mean
5. Prices for all five bikes	_____	_____
6. Prices for all but the highest priced bike	_____	_____

MATH REASONING

7. In exercises 5 and 6, did the median and mean go up or down when the highest priced bike was removed from the list?

PROBLEM SOLVING

8. **Missing Data** This problem has some missing data. Tell what is needed to solve the problem.

Jimmy added all of his test scores together and got a sum of 415. What is his average test score?

▶ **CALCULATOR**

Use guess and check and a calculator to find each missing number.

9. The mean of five numbers is 18. Four of the numbers are 12, 25, 18, and 17.

10. The mean of four numbers is 203. Three of the numbers are: 235, 188, and 172.

More Practice, page 506, set C

Using Critical Thinking

Erica and Devin each bought an 8-inch tall box of popcorn before the movie started. They started eating as soon as they sat down.

After a while, Erica said, "I'm getting full. Let me give you some of mine." Devin held his box as Erica poured in some of her popcorn.

Then Erica said, "I'll bet you still finish before I do." Devin exclaimed, "No way! I have a lot of extra popcorn to eat."

The two graphs show the amount of popcorn in the two boxes during the first 24 minutes.

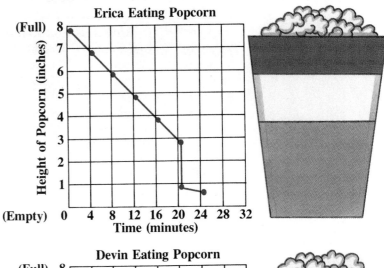

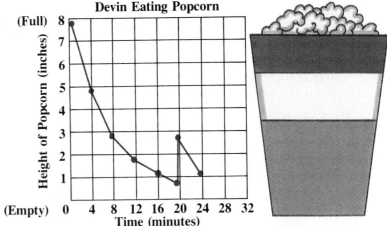

TALK ABOUT IT

1. Who eats faster, Erica or Devin? How can you tell?
2. How long had they been eating before Erica gave Devin some of her popcorn? How can you tell?
3. After examining the graphs, who do you think will finish first? Can you be sure? Explain.

These two graphs show Raul and Dana eating popcorn. Predict
when each of them will finish.

1.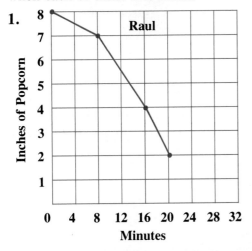

2.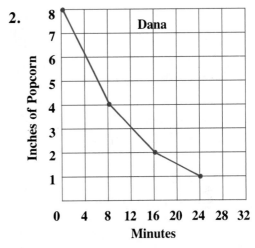

These two graphs show Amy and Cory eating popcorn. Examine
the graph and tell what you think might have happened.

3.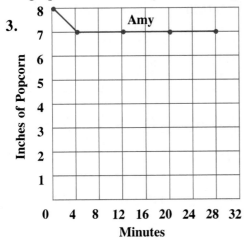

4.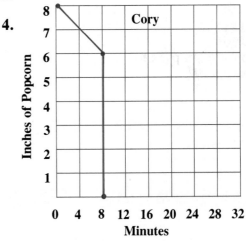

These two graphs show Brett and Trudy eating popcorn.

5. Which person had a friend drop by and help
eat the popcorn? How can you tell?

6. Which person was not very hungry? How can
you tell?

7. Predict when, if at all, each person will finish.

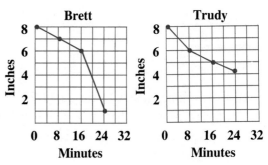

Problem Solving
Data From a Table

UNDERSTAND
ANALYZE DATA
PLAN
ESTIMATE
SOLVE
EXAMINE

LEARN ABOUT IT

To solve some problems you need data from a table, a graph, or some other source outside the problem.

Charlie weighs 95 pounds. His body needs about 45 grams of protein every day. How many cups of skim milk would Charlie have to drink to get all 45 grams?

Food	Serving Size	Grams of Protein	Food	Serving Size	Grams of Protein
Beef, lean cooked	2 ounces	16	Oatmeal	1 cup	5
Bread, whole wheat	2 slices	5	Pancakes	3 pancakes	6
Cheese, cheddar	1 ounce	7	Peanut butter	2 tablespoons	8
Cheese, cottage	½ cup	15	Pizza	¼ med. pizza	16
Chicken, drumstick	1 small	12	Potato	7 ounces	4
Corn	½ cup	3	Rice, brown	1 cup cooked	5
Eggs	2 medium	11	Spaghetti	1 cup	7
Lentils	½ cup	8	Tuna, canned	3 ounces	24
Macaroni	1 cup cooked	7	Walnuts	6 large	4
Milk, skim	1 cup	9	Yogurt, low-fat	1 cup	8

First, I'll look for the data I need in the problem.

Then I'll look for the data I need in the table.

Now I'll use the data to solve the problem.

Charlie needs 45 grams of protein.

A cup of milk has 9 grams.

$45 \div 9 = 5$

Charlie would have to drink 5 cups of skim milk.

TRY IT OUT

Solve.

1. Erin's father needs to eat about 70 grams of protein every day. For dinner he ate 4 chicken drumsticks. How many more grams does he need?

2. For lunch, Zack ate 1 cup of cottage cheese and 3 walnuts. How many grams of protein did he eat?

Solve. Use data from the table on the opposite page when needed.

1. Jeff wants to eat at least 15 grams of protein for lunch. He has a cup of milk and a peanut butter sandwich made with 2 tablespoons of peanut butter. Does his lunch have enough protein?

2. Ken made macaroni and cheese using 2 cups of macaroni and 4 ounces of cheddar cheese. How many grams of protein does his macaroni and cheese have?

3. Peter kept a record of the number of grams of protein he ate during one week. Use his data to find the mean number of grams he ate per day.

Grams of Protein	
Monday	37
Tuesday	41
Wednesday	36
Thursday	45
Friday	49
Saturday	42
Sunday	44

4. A restaurant has 35 small square tables to use for banquets. Each table can seat only one person on each side. If they put the small tables together to make one long table, how many people can they seat?

5. A pound of turkey has 144 grams of protein and will serve 4 people. How many grams of protein will each person get?

6. An adult who weighs 150 pounds needs about 0.36 grams of protein per pound each day. How many grams of protein does the adult need?

7. A 12-year-old needs about 1,200 mg of calcium every day. A glass of milk has about 350 mg. Sherry drank 3 glasses of milk. How many milligrams of calcium did she get?

8. **Write Your Own Problem** Write a problem that can be solved using data from this table.

Recommended Calories		
Age	Weight (lb)	Calories
4–6	44	1,700
7–10	62	2,400
11–14	100	2,220 (girls)
		2,700 (boys)

Applied Problem Solving
Group Decision Making

UNDERSTAND
ANALYZE DATA
PLAN
ESTIMATE
SOLVE
EXAMINE

Group Skill

Listen to Others

You are doing an investigation to find the best buy in pizza. You have been asked to write an article about your findings for the December edition of the school newspaper.

Facts to Consider

1. Here are some prices at Papa's Pizza.

Papa's Pizza Menu

Pizza	Small	Medium	Large
One topping	$5.00	$7.85	$9.85
Each additional topping	$0.65	$1.00	$1.20
Combination pizza	$6.95	$10.85	$13.65

Drinks			
Small	Medium	Large	Pitcher
$0.55	$0.70	$0.90	$2.75

COUPON – Papa's Pizza
$1.50 off Large Pizza
Valid until 12–31

COUPON – Papa's Pizza
$1.00 off Medium Pizza
Valid until 12–31

2. Here is some information about Pizza Alley.

- They are offering a special this month of $10.60 for a large pizza with one topping and a pitcher of lemonade.
- They usually charge $9.99 for a large pizza and $2.70 for a pitcher of lemonade.
- They charge $1.40 for each additional topping and $3.60 extra for a combination pizza.

3. Your classmates rated the pizza parlors on a scale of 1 to 5, where 1 is the best rating and 5 is the worst. The average rating for Papa's was 1. The average rating for Pizza Alley was 2.
4. There are video games at Pizza Alley.

Some Questions to Answer

1. How much does it usually cost for a large pizza with one topping at Papa's? At Pizza Alley?

2. How much does a pitcher of lemonade and a large pizza cost this month at Papa's? At Pizza Alley?

3. Complete a table like the one below to help you compare the two pizza parlors.

	Papa's	Pizza Alley
Pitcher of lemonade		
Large pizza with one topping		
Additional topping		
Large pizza with two toppings		
Large pizza with pitcher w/coupon		
Combination pizza		
Combination pizza w/coupon		
Ratings		
Extras		

What Is Your Decision?

Write a newspaper article comparing both pizza parlors and include your recommendation.

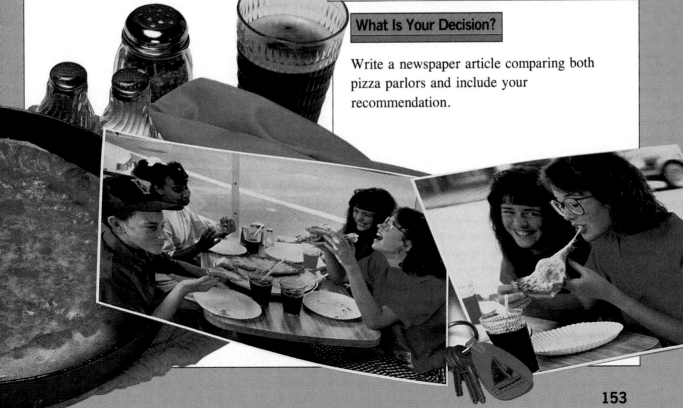

WRAP UP

Language Exercise

Over a 7-day period, Felicia did 18, 24, 26, 33, 37, 37, and 42 sit-ups. Complete each statement. Use the data and these words: *intervals, line, mode, range, scale, median, mean.*

1. The ____ of this set of numbers is from 18 to 42, or 24.

2. A ____ graph is used to display information that changes over time.

3. A reasonable ____ for the vertical axis might be 0–50.

4. ____ of 5 could be used for this scale.

5. The ____ for this set of numbers is 37.

6. The ____ for this set of numbers is 31.

7. The ____ for this set of numbers is 33.

Sometimes, Always, Never

Decide which word should go in the blank: *sometimes, always,* or *never.* Explain your choices.

8. A line graph should ____ have a vertical scale and a horizontal scale.

9. The sum of all parts of a circle graph should ____ be 1.

10. The interval of a scale is ____ greater than the range of the scale.

11. The mode and the median for a set of numbers are ____ the same.

12. The mode for a set of numbers is ____ greater than the mean.

Project

Make a prediction, then survey ten classmates to find out how many hours each spends in a week watching television. Display the results in a bar graph. Give the mean, median, and mode for the data. Explain how the actual results compare with your prediction.

POWER PRACTICE/TEST

Part 1   Understanding

1. The numbers along the side or bottom of a graph are called the ____ .

2. Describe 4 steps for making a line graph.

3. What kind of graph represents a whole broken into its parts?

4. Dan bowled r games at a cost of $2 a game, and rented shoes for $1. Represent what he spent using a variable.

Part 2   Skills

Five judges gave Barking Dog the following ratings for vocal quality on their hit single: 9, 7, 9, 8, and 5.

5. What is the range of the ratings?

6. What is the mean rating?

7. What is the median?

8. What is the mode?

Part 3   Applications

9. A tennis tournament has 12 boys and 12 girls. Each girl plays each boy once. How many games are played?

10. The lowest score is 3. The highest is 72. You plan to use 5 intervals in a scale for a graph. What is the best size for each interval?

11. Write a rating response question to find out how often students watch TV after school. Write a multiple choice question to find out what kinds of after-school programs students watch.

12. **Challenge**   Jan had a serving of oatmeal with half a cup of skim milk and 2 eggs for breakfast. For lunch she had a tuna sandwich and two servings of milk. How many grams of protein did she get?

Food	Serving	Protein
Bread	2 slices	5 g
Eggs	2 medium	11 g
Milk, skim	1 cup	9 g
Oatmeal	1 cup	5 g
Tuna, canned	3 ounces	24 g

ENRICHMENT
Using Scattergrams

A scattergram is a graph of a set of points. By looking at all of the points, you may be able to see if two sets of data are related.

Is the amount of time students listen to the radio related to their ages? A group of students was surveyed. They were asked their ages and how many minutes they spend listening to the radio each day. The resulting number pairs (age, radio time) are presented in a scattergram.

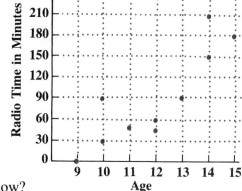

Radio Listening Time by Students

1. How many minutes each day does the 13 year-old listen? The two 10 year-olds?

2. How many students were surveyed? How do you know?

3. Do you think listening time is related to age? Explain how the graph shows this.

If the points on a scattergram cluster or group together, in a particular pattern, the two sets of data are probably related.

Look at the two scattergrams at the right.

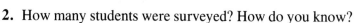

A   B

4. Which one shows a pattern? Describe the pattern.

5. How would you describe the points on the other graph?

6. Choose any two of the things listed in the table that you think are related. Write a questionnaire.

■ Age	■ Test scores
■ Number of books read	■ Homework time
■ Bedtime	■ Hours watching TV

7. Survey at least 12 students to see if your choices were related. Organize your data. Then display the results in a scattergram.

CUMULATIVE REVIEW

1. In line for the movies, Tom was ahead of Sonya. Henry was last. Kate was behind Sonya. Who got into the theater first?

   A. Henry   B. Sonya

   C. Tom   D. Kate

2. The 12 members of the travel club went out for chow mein. One container cost $4 and served 3 people. How much did the club spend for chow mein?

   A. $20   B. $16

   C. $48   D. $12

3. Use rounding and mental math to estimate the product: 492×81.

   A. 4,000   B. 60,000

   C. 32,000   D. 40,000

4. Use rounding to estimate the difference: $82.06 - 29.4$.

   A. 80   B. 50

   C. 60   D. 110

5. Write 4^3 in standard form.

   A. 64   B. 12

   C. 7   D. 81

6. Find the sum of 0.784 and 0.76.

   A. 8.384   B. 0.86

   C. 1.544   D. 0.1544

7. Find the quotient mentally: $42,000 \div 60$.

   A. 7   B. 7,000

   C. 70   D. 700

8. Use compatible numbers to estimate the quotient: $472 \div 8$.

   A. 5   B. 60

   C. 50   D. 6

9. Find the average of the set to the nearest whole number: 54, 38, 49, 44.

   A. 44   B. 45

   C. 47   D. 46

10. Find the quotient: $13,708 \div 24$.

    A. 5.714   B. 570 R4

    C. 571 R4   D. 572

11. Divide 130.52 by 26.

    A. 5.2   B. 5.02

    C. 0.502   D. 5.002

12. Divide 86 by 31. Round to the nearest tenth.

    A. 2.8   B. 2.7

    C. 3.0   D. 2.78

6

MATH AND SCIENCE

DATA BANK

Use the Science Data Bank on page 476 to answer the questions.

UNDERSTANDING FRACTIONS AND CUSTOMARY UNITS

1 Weather forecasters can predict what the weather will likely be by analyzing what it has been in the past. In an average year in Miami, how many days are usually clear?

2 Weather conditions can vary from season to season. There are 91 days in autumn. How many autumn days in Miami are unlikely to be clear?

3 In an average spring in Miami, are more than or fewer than half the days partly cloudy?

4 **Using Critical Thinking** Complete the statement. Use the word *increases* or *decreases*. In Miami, as the number of clear days increases, the average temperature _____ and the average amount of precipitation _____.

159

Understanding Fractions

EXPLORE Analyze the Process

Tampa, Florida averages 48.60 inches of precipitation each year. In 1956, one of the driest years on record, Tampa received only 28.89 inches. The calendar colors show which months had below-average (red) and which had above-average (yellow) precipitation.

A **Region:** Part of the calendar is red.

JAN	FEB	MAR	APRIL	MAY	JUNE
JULY	AUG	SEPT	OCT	NOV	DEC

A **Set:** Part of the squares are red.

TALK ABOUT IT

1. How many of the 12 squares are red?
2. Does the number of red squares change when they are removed from the calendar?
3. Would you say that the part of the region that is red is the same as the part of the set that is red?

We think: 10 of the 12 equal squares

We write: $\dfrac{10}{12}$ ← numerator
← denominator

We read: "Ten twelfths of the calendar is red."

- When we talk about the fractional part of an object or region, we think of the object as divided **equally** into the same number of parts as the denominator.

We think: 10 of the 12 squares

We write: $\dfrac{10}{12}$ ← numerator
← denominator

We read: "Ten twelfths of the squares are red."

- When we talk about the fractional part of a set, the objects in the set may or may not be equal in size.

TRY IT OUT

Write the fraction for each picture.

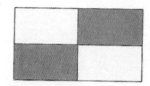

1. ▓ of the balls are baseballs.

2. ▓ of the flag is blue.

3. ▓ of the apples are green.

160

Write the fraction for each picture.

1. ▦ of the strip is green.

2. ▦ of the balls are footballs.

3. ▦ of the schedule board is filled.

4. ▦ of the stars are blue.

5. ▦ of the circle is yellow.

6. ▦ of the shapes are triangles.

Write the fraction.

7. three fifths

8. four sixths

9. one fourth

10. seven tenths

MATH REASONING

11. A unit fraction has a numerator of 1. Suppose you choose a unit fraction other than $\frac{1}{2}$. If you shade that fractional part of a square, will you shade more than half, less than half, or exactly half of that square? Try it with other unit fractions. Is your answer always the same? Explain why or why not?

PROBLEM SOLVING

12. In 1959, Tampa set a record with 76.57 inches of rainfall. Nine months had above average rainfall. What fraction of the year had average or below-average rainfall?

13. Science Data Bank During which season does Miami have the highest average temperature? How much higher is that temperature than the average yearly temperature?

DATA BANK

▶ USING CRITICAL THINKING Take a Look

14. Fold a sheet of paper 3 times. Before you unfold, color one side of the folded paper. Guess what fraction of the paper you colored. Then, take a look.

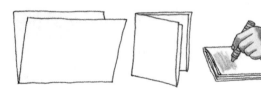

161

Equivalent Fractions

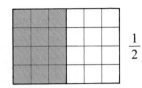 $\frac{1}{2}$

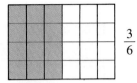 $\frac{3}{6}$

LEARN ABOUT IT

EXPLORE Use a Fraction Model

Work in groups. The figures on the right show how some 4 by 6 graph paper can be used to show different names for the same amount.

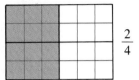 $\frac{2}{4}$

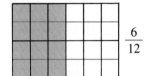 $\frac{6}{12}$

The figure below shows $\frac{2}{3}$ on a 4 by 6 graph paper model. Use graph paper to show other fractions that name the same amount. Try to find as many as possible.

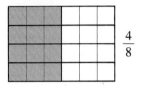 $\frac{4}{8}$

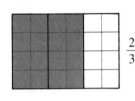 $\frac{2}{3}$

TALK ABOUT IT

1. Look at the figure that shows $\frac{6}{12}$. Tell how $\frac{6}{12}$ is like $\frac{1}{2}$. Name some other fractions that show the same amount.
2. Look at the figure that shows $\frac{2}{3}$. Tell how many fractions you found that name the same amount as $\frac{2}{3}$.
3. Could you show the fraction $\frac{18}{24}$ on a 4 by 6 model? Explain.

■ Different fractions that name the same amount are **equivalent fractions.**

You can find equivalent fractions by multiplying the numerator and denominator by the same number (not zero).

$$\frac{1}{2} = \frac{3}{6}$$

Think: $\frac{1}{2}$ — $\boxed{\times 3}$ → $\frac{3}{6}$

TRY IT OUT

Find equivalent fractions.

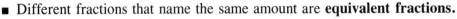

1. $\frac{3}{4}$ — $\boxed{\times 2}$ → ‖‖‖

2. $\frac{3}{5}$ — $\boxed{\times 4}$ → ‖‖‖

3. $\frac{5}{4}$ — $\boxed{\times 3}$ → ‖‖‖

Write two equivalent fractions for the red part.

1.

2.

3.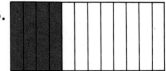

Write an equivalent fraction by multiplying the numerator and denominator by 2.

4. $\frac{1}{2} = \frac{}{}$ 5. $\frac{7}{10} = \frac{}{}$ 6. $\frac{5}{8} = \frac{}{}$ 7. $\frac{1}{6} = \frac{}{}$ 8. $\frac{2}{3} = \frac{}{}$

Find the missing numerator or denominator.

9. $\frac{2}{5} = \frac{}{20}$ 10. $\frac{3}{10} = \frac{}{100}$ 11. $\frac{2}{2} = \frac{}{8}$ 12. $\frac{2}{3} = \frac{40}{}$ 13. $\frac{7}{8} = \frac{28}{}$

Write one fraction equivalent to the given fraction.

14. $\frac{4}{5}$ 15. $\frac{7}{8}$ 16. $\frac{3}{8}$ 17. $\frac{5}{6}$ 18. $\frac{3}{4}$ 19. $\frac{1}{10}$ 20. $\frac{5}{12}$

MATH REASONING

Use mental math to write the next 3 fractions. Look for patterns.

21. $\frac{1}{5}, \frac{2}{10}, \frac{3}{15}, \frac{}{}, \frac{}{}, \frac{}{}$

22. $\frac{3}{8}, \frac{6}{16}, \frac{9}{24}, \frac{}{}, \frac{}{}, \frac{}{}$

PROBLEM SOLVING

23. One week it rained $\frac{1}{2}$ inch on Monday, $\frac{1}{3}$ inch Tuesday, $\frac{5}{10}$ inch Wednesday, and only $\frac{1}{8}$ inch on Thursday. Which two days had the same amount of rainfall?

24. On the average, in Orlando, Florida, 2 days out of every 5 days are partly cloudy. Use equivalent fractions to find out how many days a year are partly cloudy.
Hint: $\frac{2}{5} = \frac{}{365}$

▶ **USING CRITICAL THINKING   Discover a Counterexample**

Jessica said, "Since I can find equivalent fractions by multiplying both the numerator and denominator of a fraction by the same number, I can also find equivalent fractions by adding."

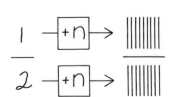

25. Use graph paper to see if Jessica is correct or incorrect. Explain.

More Practice, page 506, set D

Greatest Common Factor

LEARN ABOUT IT

Knowing how to find the greatest common factor of two numbers will help you find lowest-terms fractions in the next lesson.

EXPLORE Study the Information

When two whole numbers (not zero) are multiplied, each of the numbers is a factor of the product. For example, 5 and 7 are both factors of 35 because $5 \times 7 = 35$.

Factor	Factor	Product
5	× 7	= 35

How many numbers other than 2 can you find that are factors of both 60 and 72? You may want to use your calculator.

2 is a factor of both these numbers.
$2 \times 30 = 60$
$2 \times 36 = 72$

TALK ABOUT IT

1. How can you use division to show that 4 is a factor of both 60 and 72?
2. Can you prove that 1 is a factor of every number?
3. What is the largest number you found that is a factor of both 60 and 72?

- The **greatest common factor (GCF)** of two numbers is the largest number that is a factor of both numbers.

Here are two methods for finding the greatest common factor of two numbers such as 24 and 36.

List the Factors	Prime Factorization
$24 \rightarrow$ 1, 2, 3, 4, 6, 8, 12, 24 $36 \rightarrow$ 1, 2, 3, 4, 6, 9, 12, 18, 36	$24 = 2 \cdot 2 \cdot 2 \cdot 3$ $36 = 2 \cdot 2 \cdot 3 \cdot 3$
Common factors $\rightarrow$ 1, 2, 3, 4, 6, 12 Choose the largest. GCF = 12	The product $2 \cdot 2 \cdot 3$ is common to both. GCF = $2 \cdot 2 \cdot 3 = 12$

TRY IT OUT

Find the GCF for each pair. Try both methods.

1. 8 and 24   **2.** 15 and 25   **3.** 7 and 20   **4.** 12 and 54

Find the GCF for each pair. The factors of each number are given.

1. 12 and 30
   $12 \rightarrow$ 1, 2, 3, 4, 6, 12
   $30 \rightarrow$ 1, 2, 3, 5, 6, 10, 15, 30

2. 30 and 50
   $30 = 2 \cdot 3 \cdot 5$
   $50 = 2 \cdot 5 \cdot 5$

Find the GCF for each pair of numbers.

3. 4 and 8   **4.** 3 and 12   **5.** 18 and 30   **6.** 20 and 50

7. 6 and 7   **8.** 18 and 38   **9.** 12 and 36   **10.** 9 and 32

11. 42 and 36   **12.** 10 and 50   **13.** 15 and 45   **14.** 14 and 63

15. 21 and 60   **16.** 45 and 72   **17.** 20 and 36   **18.** 18 and 24

19. 20 and 27   **20.** 12 and 60

21. 28 and 42   **22.** 42 and 56

APPLY

MATH REASONING

Use your calculator to find the GCF of these numbers.

23. 238, 102, 170   **24.** 147, 343, 392   **25.** 231, 105, 189

PROBLEM SOLVING

26. Donna made a row of tiles that was 96 inches long. Lori's row was 84 inches long. What is the largest size tile they might have been using if all the tiles were the same size?

27. The sum of two numbers is 156. Their product is 900. What are the numbers?

▶ **ALGEBRA**

Suppose that ★ between two numbers means:
Multiply the first number by itself and add the second to this product.
So, $2 \star 1 = 5$, $3 \star 2 = 11$, and $4 \star 2 = 18$.

Solve the equations.

28. $2 \star 4 = n$ **29.** $5 \star 1 = n$ **30.** $6 \star 6 = n$ **31.** $1 \star 1 = n$

32. $9 \star 2 = n$ **33.** $3 \star 9 = n$ **34.** $4 \star 8 = n$ **35.** $7 \star 8 = n$

More Practice, page 507, set A

Lowest Terms

LEARN ABOUT IT

EXPLORE Use Fraction Models

Analyze the equivalent fraction strip that starts with $\frac{3}{4}$.

$\frac{3}{4}$	$\frac{6}{8}$	$\frac{9}{12}$	$\frac{12}{16}$	$\frac{15}{20}$	$\frac{18}{24}$	$\frac{21}{28}$	$\frac{24}{32}$	$\frac{27}{36}$	$\frac{30}{40}$

Below are three other fraction strips. Try to find the fraction that is first on each of these strips.

a.  $\frac{5}{10}$ b. 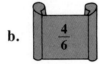 $\frac{4}{6}$ c. $\frac{3}{12}$

TALK ABOUT IT

1. What can you say about each fraction on the same strip?
2. Did you discover a method for finding the first fraction on the strip? Explain?

- A fraction is in **lowest terms** when the greatest common factor of the numerator and denominator is 1.

Here are two methods for finding the lowest-terms fractions.

- To reduce a fraction to lowest terms: Divide the numerator and the denominator by any common factor and continue to divide until you find the lowest-terms fraction.	- Divide the numerator and the denominator by the greatest common factor (GCF) to find the lowest-terms fraction.
$\frac{6 \div 2}{24 \div 2} = \frac{3}{12} \rightarrow \frac{3 \div 3}{12 \div 3} = \frac{1}{4}$	6 is the GCF. $\frac{6 \div 6}{24 \div 6} = \frac{1}{4}$ 1 is the only common factor of 1 and 4

TRY IT OUT

Reduce to lowest terms.

1. $\frac{25}{50}$ 2. $\frac{27}{30}$ 3. $\frac{6}{9}$ 4. $\frac{7}{35}$ 5. $\frac{6}{30}$ 6. $\frac{18}{24}$

Tell whether the fraction is in lowest terms. Write *yes* or *no*.

1. $\frac{5}{8}$ **2.** $\frac{5}{10}$ **3.** $\frac{5}{12}$ **4.** $\frac{5}{15}$ **5.** $\frac{4}{5}$ **6.** $\frac{4}{6}$ **7.** $\frac{4}{8}$ **8.** $\frac{4}{10}$

9. $\frac{6}{9}$ **10.** $\frac{6}{10}$ **11.** $\frac{6}{11}$ **12.** $\frac{6}{15}$ **13.** $\frac{3}{5}$ **14.** $\frac{3}{6}$ **15.** $\frac{3}{8}$ **16.** $\frac{3}{9}$

Reduce to lowest terms if the fraction is not already in lowest terms.

17. $\frac{12}{16}$ **18.** $\frac{2}{15}$ **19.** $\frac{20}{30}$ **20.** $\frac{8}{15}$ **21.** $\frac{14}{21}$ **22.** $\frac{16}{20}$ **23.** $\frac{4}{9}$

24. $\frac{18}{20}$ **25.** $\frac{6}{15}$ **26.** $\frac{9}{24}$ **27.** $\frac{12}{18}$ **28.** $\frac{7}{8}$

MATH REASONING

29. See how many numbers you can find for n in $\frac{n}{12}$. Each number must be less than 12, and the fraction must be in lowest terms.

PROBLEM SOLVING

30. During a thunderstorm, it would not be unusual for $\frac{5}{10}$ inch of rain to fall in less than an hour. Describe in lowest terms how much rain would fall.

31. If $\frac{1}{2}$ inch of rain falls as dry, fluffy snow, it would amount to as much as 15 inches of snow. If an inch of rain falls as snow, about how many inches of snow would there be?

Solve.

32. $\begin{array}{r} 37,489 \\ + 86,938 \\ \hline \end{array}$ **33.** $\begin{array}{r} 54,305 \\ - 8,578 \\ \hline \end{array}$ **34.** $\begin{array}{r} 65.256 \\ + 89.68 \\ \hline \end{array}$ **35.** $\begin{array}{r} 906.46 \\ - 567.8 \\ \hline \end{array}$ **36.** $\begin{array}{r} 807 \\ \times 275 \\ \hline \end{array}$

37. $\begin{array}{r} 9.38 \\ \times 6.4 \\ \hline \end{array}$ **38.** $8\overline{)360.16}$ **39.** $\begin{array}{r} 4.567 \\ \times 0.035 \\ \hline \end{array}$ **40.** $7.6\overline{)9.3936}$ **41.** $86\overline{)26,144}$

Write as an expression.

42. 8 more than a number **43.** the quotient of 4 and 20 **44.** the product of 2 and a number

More Practice, page 507, set B

Least Common Multiple (Denominator)

EXPLORE Think About the Process

The cricket and the grasshopper start together and jump along the same path. The cricket always jumps 9 cm and the grasshopper always jumps 12 cm. Will they ever land on the same spot again? Where?

TALK ABOUT IT

1. Where will the cricket and grasshopper be after 2 jumps? 3 jumps?
2. What was the first spot they both landed on?

- The **multiples** of a number are the whole-number products when that number is a factor. Multiples of 3: 0, 3, 6, 9, 12, . . .
- The **least common multiple** (LCM) of two numbers is the smallest number that is a multiple of both numbers.

Here are two methods for finding the least common multiple of two numbers such as 9 and 12.

List Some Multiples	Prime Factorization
$9 \rightarrow$ 9, 18, 27, 36, 45, . . . $12 \rightarrow$ 12, 24, 36, 48, 60, . . .	$9 = 3 \cdot 3$ $12 = 2 \cdot 2 \cdot 3$
Choose the smallest multiple common to both. LCM = 36	Write the smallest factorization containing both prime factorizations. $2 \cdot 2 \cdot 3 \cdot 3 = 36$ LCM = 36

- The **least common denominator** (LCD) of two fractions is the least common multiple of their denominators.

  Example: the LCD for $\frac{5}{9}$ and $\frac{7}{12}$ is 36.

Find the LCM of the whole numbers and the LCD of the fractions. Try both methods.

1. 2, 4 $\left(\frac{1}{2}, \frac{1}{4}\right)$ **2.** 6, 8 $\left(\frac{1}{6}, \frac{3}{8}\right)$ **3.** 3, 6 $\left(\frac{2}{3}, \frac{1}{6}\right)$ **4.** 9, 6 $\left(\frac{2}{9}, \frac{1}{6}\right)$

Find the least common multiple (LCM) for each pair of numbers.

1. 2, 8   **2.** 6, 4   **3.** 6, 3   **4.** 4, 10   **5.** 6, 9

6. 5, 10   **7.** 3, 5   **8.** 8, 4   **9.** 10, 12   **10.** 8, 10

Find the least common denominator (LCD) for each pair of fractions.

11. $\frac{1}{2}, \frac{3}{5}$ **12.** $\frac{5}{6}, \frac{1}{4}$ **13.** $\frac{1}{6}, \frac{2}{3}$ **14.** $\frac{3}{4}, \frac{3}{10}$ **15.** $\frac{5}{6}, \frac{8}{9}$

16. $\frac{2}{5}, \frac{7}{10}$ **17.** $\frac{2}{3}, \frac{3}{5}$ **18.** $\frac{1}{8}, \frac{1}{4}$ **19.** $\frac{3}{10}, \frac{7}{12}$ **20.** $\frac{5}{8}, \frac{1}{10}$

Find the LCD for each set of fractions.

21. $\frac{1}{2}, \frac{2}{3}, \frac{1}{6}$ **22.** $\frac{1}{2}, \frac{1}{4}, \frac{3}{8}$ **23.** $\frac{1}{3}, \frac{3}{4}, \frac{5}{6}$ **24.** $\frac{2}{3}, \frac{5}{6}, \frac{7}{9}$ **25.** $\frac{1}{4}, \frac{3}{8}, \frac{7}{16}$

The least common denominator for each pair of fractions is given.
Find the numerators.

26. $\frac{1}{2} = \frac{\text{▓}}{6}$ **27.** $\frac{2}{3} = \frac{\text{▓}}{12}$ **28.** $\frac{4}{5} = \frac{\text{▓}}{10}$ **29.** $\frac{5}{6} = \frac{\text{▓}}{18}$

     $\frac{1}{3} = \frac{\text{▓}}{6}$ $\frac{1}{4} = \frac{\text{▓}}{12}$ $\frac{3}{10} = \frac{\text{▓}}{10}$ $\frac{4}{9} = \frac{\text{▓}}{18}$

MATH REASONING

Find the pattern. Give the missing fraction.

30. $\frac{2}{3}, \frac{3}{4}, \frac{4}{5}, \frac{5}{6}, \frac{\text{▓}}{\text{▓}}, \frac{\text{▓}}{\text{▓}}, \cdots \frac{\text{▓}}{100}$

31. $\frac{1}{8}, \frac{2}{10}, \frac{3}{8}, \frac{4}{10}, \frac{5}{8}, \frac{\text{▓}}{\text{▓}}, \frac{\text{▓}}{\text{▓}}, \frac{\text{▓}}{\text{▓}}, \cdots$

PROBLEM SOLVING

32. Suppose the cricket and grasshopper jump 12 cm and 16 cm instead of 9 cm and 12 cm. Starting at 0, what will be the first spot they both land on?

33. Suppose the cricket jumps 6 cm each time and the grasshopper jumps 8 cm. They will eventually both land on 192 cm. Which will take more jumps? How many more jumps?

▶ **CALCULATOR**

34. How old is someone who is a million minutes old? About

    a. 2 months   **b.** 2 years   **c.** 20 years   **d.** 200 years

    Estimate first. Then check using your calculator.

More Practice, page 507, set C

Comparing and Ordering Fractions

EXPLORE Use Fraction Models

Mona used fraction pieces to compare fractions. She showed these two **inequality statements.**

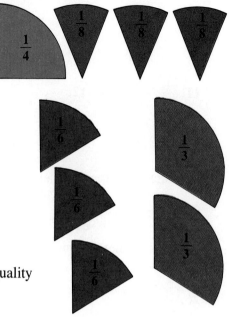

She read: "$\frac{1}{2}$ is greater than $\frac{2}{8}$, or $\frac{2}{8}$ is less than $\frac{1}{2}$"

She wrote: $\frac{1}{2} > \frac{2}{8}$, or $\frac{2}{8} < \frac{1}{2}$

Use the fraction pieces to show and write 6 different inequality statements. Put together only pieces of the same color.

TALK ABOUT IT

1. How could you show that $\frac{1}{3}$ is greater than $\frac{2}{8}$ and less than $\frac{3}{8}$?
2. If the numerators of two fractions are both 1, what can you say about the fraction with the greater denominator?

Here are two methods for comparing fractions without using fraction pieces.

■ If the fractions have different denominators, write equivalent fractions with common denominators. The fraction with the greater numerator is greater.

$$\left.\begin{array}{l} \frac{1}{3} = \frac{8}{24} \\[2mm] \frac{3}{8} = \frac{9}{24} \end{array}\right\} \quad \boxed{8 < 9} \quad \frac{1}{3} < \frac{3}{8}$$

■ Compare **cross products.** If the first product (down) is greater, the first fraction is greater. If they are equal, the fractions are equivalent. Otherwise, the second fraction is greater.

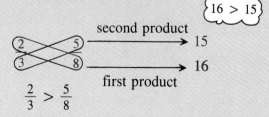

$$\frac{2}{3} > \frac{5}{8}$$

$16 > 15$

second product → 15

first product → 16

TRY IT OUT

Compare. Write $>$, $<$, or $=$ for each ⦀ . Try both methods for each comparison.

1. $\frac{1}{4}$ ⦀ $\frac{2}{10}$ 2. $\frac{5}{8}$ ⦀ $\frac{3}{4}$ 3. $\frac{2}{3}$ ⦀ $\frac{3}{4}$ 4. $\frac{2}{3}$ ⦀ $\frac{5}{8}$ 5. $\frac{6}{10}$ ⦀ $\frac{3}{5}$

Write $>$, $<$, or $=$ for each . Use equivalent fractions for problems 1–10. Use cross products for problems 11–20.

1. $\frac{1}{2}$ ▥ $\frac{1}{3}$ 2. $\frac{1}{2}$ ▥ $\frac{2}{3}$ 3. $\frac{1}{4}$ ▥ $\frac{1}{3}$ 4. $\frac{1}{4}$ ▥ $\frac{1}{6}$ 5. $\frac{1}{3}$ ▥ $\frac{1}{5}$

6. $\frac{2}{5}$ ▥ $\frac{1}{3}$ 7. $\frac{2}{5}$ ▥ $\frac{2}{3}$ 8. $\frac{8}{12}$ ▥ $\frac{2}{3}$ 9. $\frac{2}{3}$ ▥ $\frac{4}{5}$ 10. $\frac{5}{8}$ ▥ $\frac{1}{2}$

11. $\frac{1}{2}$ ▥ $\frac{3}{8}$ 12. $\frac{4}{10}$ ▥ $\frac{6}{15}$ 13. $\frac{7}{10}$ ▥ $\frac{3}{4}$ 14. $\frac{7}{10}$ ▥ $\frac{2}{3}$ 15. $\frac{5}{6}$ ▥ $\frac{7}{12}$

16. $\frac{3}{10}$ ▥ $\frac{7}{10}$ 17. $\frac{1}{4}$ ▥ $\frac{3}{10}$ 18. $\frac{1}{6}$ ▥ $\frac{1}{10}$ 19. $\frac{1}{6}$ ▥ $\frac{2}{10}$ 20. $\frac{6}{8}$ ▥ $\frac{18}{24}$

Compare two at a time. Then list them in order from least to greatest.

21. $\frac{1}{2}$, $\frac{1}{3}$, $\frac{1}{4}$ 22. $\frac{2}{3}$, $\frac{13}{18}$, $\frac{7}{9}$, $\frac{5}{6}$

23. $\frac{3}{4}$, $\frac{3}{8}$, $\frac{3}{7}$

24. $\frac{3}{5}$, $\frac{1}{2}$, $\frac{1}{4}$, $\frac{2}{5}$

MATH REASONING

The numerators are the same for each pair of fractions. Write $>$, $<$, or $=$ for each ▥ .

25. $\frac{1}{2}$ ▥ $\frac{1}{5}$ 26. $\frac{2}{5}$ ▥ $\frac{2}{3}$ 27. $\frac{7}{16}$ ▥ $\frac{7}{12}$ 28. $\frac{5}{8}$ ▥ $\frac{5}{12}$ 29. $\frac{9}{20}$ ▥ $\frac{9}{17}$

PROBLEM SOLVING

30. Jane rides her bicycle $\frac{1}{2}$ mile to the park. Marilyn rides her bike $\frac{3}{10}$ mile to the park. Which girl travels farther?

▶ **CALCULATOR**

When the fractions to be compared have large numerators and denominators, your calculator and the cross product method will be useful.

Compare these fractions. Write $>$, $<$, or $=$ for each ▥ .

31. $\frac{5}{16}$ ▥ $\frac{185}{592}$ 32. $\frac{42}{50}$ ▥ $\frac{336}{350}$ 33. $\frac{75}{92}$ ▥ $\frac{300}{552}$ 34. $\frac{243}{512}$ ▥ $\frac{27}{64}$ 35. $\frac{37}{100}$ ▥ $\frac{259}{700}$

More Practice, page 507, set D

Improper Fractions and Mixed Numbers

EXPLORE Study the Data

Anthony is a chef in a large restaurant. He uses butter that is packaged in 1-pound boxes with quarter-pound sticks in each box. A dessert recipe calls for $2\frac{3}{4}$ pounds of butter.

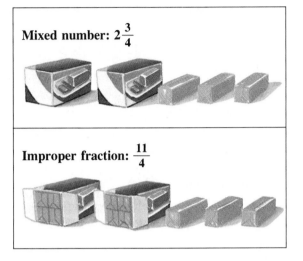

Mixed number: $2\frac{3}{4}$

Improper fraction: $\frac{11}{4}$

TALK ABOUT IT

1. How many full-pound boxes and how many extra sticks did Anthony need for the recipe?

2. How many quarter-pound sticks are needed for the recipe?

■ To change an improper fraction to a mixed number, divide the numerator by the denominator.

$$\frac{21}{4} \rightarrow 4\overline{)21} \xrightarrow{} 5\frac{1}{4}$$

5 ← wholes

−20

1 ← extra fourths

■ To change a mixed number to an improper fraction, first multiply the whole number and the denominator. Then add the numerator.

$$6\frac{3}{4} \rightarrow 6 \times 4 + 3 \rightarrow \frac{27}{4}$$

PRACTICE

Write each improper fraction as a mixed number or whole number.

1. $\frac{18}{5}$ **2.** $\frac{14}{2}$ **3.** $\frac{13}{4}$ **4.** $\frac{16}{3}$ **5.** $\frac{14}{4}$ **6.** $\frac{20}{6}$ **7.** $\frac{20}{5}$

Write each mixed number as an improper fraction.

8. $3\frac{1}{5}$ **9.** $2\frac{1}{8}$ **10.** $7\frac{1}{2}$ **11.** $6\frac{1}{4}$ **12.** $3\frac{1}{8}$ **13.** $5\frac{1}{10}$ **14.** $6\frac{7}{8}$

More Practice, page 507, set E

MIDCHAPTER REVIEW/QUIZ

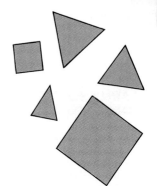

1. Write fractions to complete this statement:
▥ of the shapes are triangles and ▥ of the shapes are squares.

2. Write two equivalent fractions for the red part.
What part is not red?

Find the greatest common factor for each pair of numbers.

3. 6, 8   **4.** 15, 25   **5.** 7, 21   **6.** 18, 36   **7.** 9, 16

Find the least common denominator (LCD) for each set of fractions.

8. $\frac{3}{10}, \frac{3}{4}$ **9.** $\frac{1}{4}, \frac{1}{6}$ **10.** $\frac{5}{6}, \frac{2}{9}$ **11.** $\frac{3}{7}, \frac{4}{21}$ **12.** $\frac{3}{10}, \frac{3}{8}$

Reduce to lowest terms if the fraction is not already in lowest terms.

13. $\frac{6}{36}$ **14.** $\frac{12}{40}$ **15.** $\frac{13}{17}$ **16.** $\frac{5}{100}$ **17.** $\frac{2}{16}$ **18.** $\frac{2}{8}$

Use the fractions from the box.

19. Which fractions are greater than $\frac{1}{2}$?

20. Choose three fractions. Order them from smallest to largest.

| $\frac{2}{3}$ | $\frac{7}{12}$ | $\frac{1}{4}$ | $\frac{3}{9}$ | $\frac{6}{8}$ |
| $\frac{5}{6}$ | $\frac{2}{10}$ | $\frac{3}{6}$ | $\frac{1}{10}$ | $\frac{7}{10}$ |

Write >, < or = for each ▥.

21. $\frac{3}{8}$ ▥ $\frac{3}{4}$ **22.** $\frac{1}{6}$ ▥ $\frac{1}{5}$ **23.** $\frac{2}{3}$ ▥ $\frac{3}{4}$ **24.** $\frac{9}{15}$ ▥ $\frac{6}{10}$ **25.** $\frac{5}{8}$ ▥ $\frac{9}{12}$

PROBLEM SOLVING

26. There are 15 boys in a class of 27 students. Using lowest terms, what fraction of the students are boys? What fraction are girls?

27. A deep-dish pizza was cut into 24 pieces. Eight boys shared the pizza equally. Write two equivalent fractions to show each boy's share.

Problem Solving
Make an Organized List

UNDERSTAND
ANALYZE DATA
PLAN
ESTIMATE
SOLVE
EXAMINE

LEARN ABOUT IT

To solve some problems, it helps to write down all the possibilities in a special order. This strategy is called **Make an Organized List.**

> First, I'll write down all the combinations that have black stretch pants.

> Then, I'll write down the combinations with white pants and with red pants.

Brenda wants to buy a new parka and stretch pants for her ski trip. She found stretch pants in black, white, and red. She found parkas in yellow, white, red, green, and fuchsia. How many different combinations of parka and pants are possible?

Black – Yellow	Black – Green
Black – White	Black – Fuchsia
Black – Red	

BY	WY	RY
BW	WW	RW
BR	WR	RR
BG	WG	RG
BF	WF	RF

There are 15 different combinations of parka and pants possible.

TRY IT OUT

Read this problem and finish the solution.

The 12 members of the cross-country ski team want to put 2-digit numbers on the backs of their parkas. They decided to use only the digits, 1, 3, 5, and 7. Can each team member have a different number?

- How many members are on the team?
- How many digits do they want to put on each parka?
- What 2-digit numbers are possible beginning with 1?
- Copy and complete this organized list to help you solve the problem.

11	31
13	33
15	35
17	?

174

Make an organized list to solve these problems.

1. Zu found ski sweaters in white, pink, beige, and navy. She found bib pants in black, forest green, and pink. She wants bib pants and a sweater. How many different combinations are possible?

2. At the ski resort, Vic bought lunch at a snack bar. He got a sandwich, fruit, and a drink. What were the possible lunches he could choose from this menu?

Sandwiches	Drinks
Cheese	Milk
Turkey	Juice
Ham	Hot Chocolate

Fruit
Apple
Banana

MIXED PRACTICE

Solve. Choose a strategy from the list or use another strategy that you know.

Some Strategies

Act Out	Guess and Check
Use Objects	Make a Table
Choose an Operation	Solve a Simpler Problem
Draw a Picture	Make an Organized List

3. Cross-country skis that usually sell for $120 are on sale. The discount on Mountain King skis is $\frac{1}{5}$. The discount on Snow Imp skis is $\frac{1}{4}$. Which brand has the larger discount?

4. Erin bought skis, bindings, and a pair of boots on special. Use the price list to find how much money she saved.

SPECIALS

Boots
Reg. $170
Sale $119.99

Skis
Reg. $325
Sale $199.95

Bindings
Reg. $145
Sale $99.95

5. Len's family is headed for the mountains. To get to the freeway, they can take Fifth Street, Magnolia Avenue, Arlington Avenue, or Victoria Street. From the freeway to the lodge they can take Forest Drive or Crest Road. How many different ways can they go to the lodge?

6. The ski shop has 28 pairs of gloves on sale. Rick found 7 pairs of leather gloves and 12 pairs of wool gloves. What fraction of the pairs are wool?

7. Mrs. Kuan has a special coupon for after-ski clothes. The coupon is good for $2 off every $10 spent. She spent $140. How much did she save?

More Practice, page 524, set D

Reading Fraction Scales

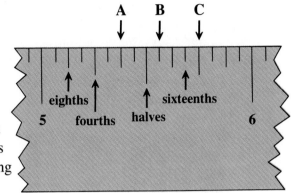

A   B   C

eighths   sixteenths

5   fourths halves   6

LEARN ABOUT IT

EXPLORE Study the Data

Examine the enlarged picture of the scale from an inch ruler. Notice the different length marks on the scale. They help you read measures using lowest-terms fractions.

TALK ABOUT IT

1. Explain why the mark at **A** is for a length of $5\frac{3}{8}$ inches.
2. The mark at **B** is for sixteenths. What length would you read for **B**?
3. Give the length for **C**.
4. You know there are 8 eighths in 1. Tell why there are only 4 eighths marks shown on the drawing of the 1-inch ruler.

The figure at the right shows how to read the ruler for a length of $3\frac{5}{8}$ inches.

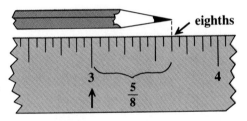

eighths

3    $\frac{5}{8}$ 4

Read: 3 and $\frac{5}{8}$ inches.

Other Examples

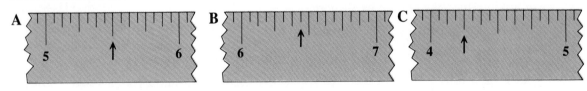

Read: $5\frac{1}{2}$ inches   Read: $6\frac{7}{16}$ inches   Read: $4\frac{1}{4}$ inches

TRY IT OUT

Give each length using lowest terms.

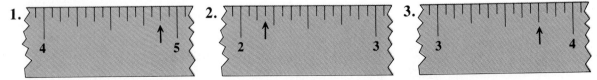

1.   4   5   2.   2   3   3.   3   4

Give each length using lowest terms.

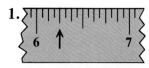

1. 6 7

2. 1 2

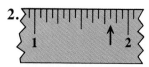

3. 7 8

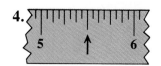

4. 5 6

5. 2 3

6. 4 5

Draw a line segment for each length.

7. $2\frac{1}{8}$ **8.** $3\frac{9}{16}$ **9.** $1\frac{5}{8}$ **10.** $2\frac{3}{4}$ **11.** $1\frac{11}{16}$ **12.** $4\frac{3}{8}$

MATH REASONING

Answer **A** if the length is between 1 and 2 inches, **B** if it is between 2 and 3 inches, and **C** if it is between 3 and 4 inches. Use mental math and estimation to decide.

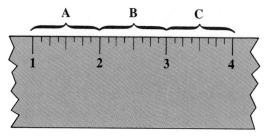

13. $\frac{20}{16}$ inches   **14.** $\frac{26}{8}$ inches   **15.** $\frac{35}{16}$ inches   **16.** $\frac{15}{4}$ inches   **17.** $\frac{40}{16}$ inches

PROBLEM SOLVING

18. Measure five objects in your classroom. Name and record the length of each object to the nearest sixteenth of an inch. Use only lowest-terms fractions.

19. Anthony mailed some recipes to a friend. The package weighed $\frac{13}{4}$ ounces. Mailing charges were 25 cents for each ounce plus 20 cents for any additional fraction of an ounce. How much was the postage?

 MIXED REVIEW

Estimate.

20. $8,379 + 5,786$ **21.** $576 \div 8$ **22.** $386 + 402 + 415 + 378 + 377$

23. Copy and complete the table. Write a rule for the pattern.

people	1	2	3	4	5	p
cost	4	8		16		

Writing a Decimal for a Fraction

EXPLORE Use a Fraction Model

Alan used graph paper to show how many hundredths are equal to $\frac{1}{4}$. Use graph paper to show how many hundredths are equal to $\frac{3}{10}$. To $\frac{4}{5}$. To $\frac{1}{2}$. Now try $\frac{1}{3}$.

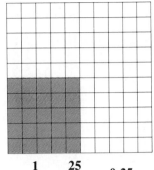

$$\frac{1}{4} = \frac{25}{100} = 0.25$$

TALK ABOUT IT

1. Tell why it is difficult to show how many hundredths are equal to $\frac{1}{3}$ using graph paper.
2. Think of $\frac{1}{3} = \frac{n}{100}$. What number for n makes $\frac{n}{100}$ close to $\frac{1}{3}$? Tell how you found it. Then write a decimal close to $\frac{1}{3}$.

■ You could find the decimal for $\frac{3}{8}$ by using equivalent fractions.

$$\frac{3}{8} = \frac{3 \times 125}{8 \times 125} = \frac{375}{1,000} = 0.375$$

■ Or you could use a calculator to divide.

ON/AC 3 ÷ 8 = 0.375

Both answers are the same. Therefore, $\frac{3}{8} = 0.375$.

■ To change a fraction to a decimal, divide the numerator by the denominator.

Other Examples

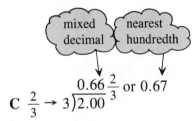

A $\frac{3}{4} \rightarrow 4\overline{)3.00}$ ⟶ 0.75

B $\frac{8}{5} \rightarrow 5\overline{)8.0}$ ⟶ 1.6

C $\frac{2}{3} \rightarrow 3\overline{)2.00}$ ⟶ $0.66\frac{2}{3}$ or 0.67

mixed decimal   nearest hundredth

Write a decimal for each fraction.

1. $\frac{2}{5}$ 2. $\frac{5}{8}$ 3. $\frac{5}{10}$ 4. $\frac{7}{5}$ 5. $\frac{1}{4}$ 6. $\frac{3}{16}$

Write a mixed decimal for each fraction.

7. $\frac{1}{7}$ 8. $\frac{5}{6}$ 9. $\frac{1}{3}$ 10. $\frac{5}{3}$ 11. $\frac{1}{6}$ 12. $\frac{5}{9}$

Write a decimal rounded to the nearest hundredth for each fraction.

13. $\frac{7}{8}$ 14. $\frac{7}{3}$ 15. $\frac{1}{6}$ 16. $\frac{5}{16}$ 17. $\frac{3}{8}$ 18. $\frac{5}{12}$

Write a decimal or a mixed decimal for each fraction.

1. $\frac{9}{10}$ **2.** $\frac{7}{20}$ **3.** $\frac{17}{100}$ **4.** $\frac{1}{2}$ **5.** $\frac{7}{16}$ **6.** $\frac{1}{8}$

7. $\frac{3}{7}$ **8.** $\frac{5}{8}$ **9.** $\frac{1}{3}$ **10.** $\frac{17}{6}$

Write a decimal rounded to the nearest hundredth for each fraction.

11. $\frac{1}{3}$ **12.** $\frac{6}{7}$ **13.** $\frac{5}{12}$ **14.** $\frac{2}{15}$ **15.** $\frac{10}{3}$ **16.** $\frac{5}{6}$

17. $\frac{7}{8}$ **18.** $\frac{11}{6}$ **19.** $\frac{7}{15}$ **20.** $\frac{3}{8}$ **21.** $\frac{4}{9}$ **22.** $\frac{7}{16}$

APPLY

MATH REASONING

Use estimation to match the fraction to the decimal.

23. $\frac{9}{16}$ **a.** $0.81\frac{1}{4}$ **b.** $0.56\frac{1}{4}$ **c.** $0.31\frac{1}{4}$

24. $\frac{31}{36}$ **a.** $0.69\frac{4}{9}$ **b.** $0.36\frac{1}{9}$ **c.** $0.86\frac{1}{9}$

PROBLEM SOLVING

25. In one of the worst blizzards of the century, Maine received 40 inches of snow in 24 hours. If one inch of snowfall represents about 0.1 inch of water, about how much water did the blizzard produce?

26. Science Data Bank Use the U.S. rainfall map. Write the range of the numbers for each colored section in feet. Use lowest-terms fractions. About what fraction of the map averages more than $3\frac{1}{3}$ feet of rain in one year?

▶ **USING CRITICAL THINKING   Create a Rule**

Study these examples. Then give a rule that tells how to change a decimal to a fraction.

$0.75 = \frac{75}{100} = \frac{3}{4}$ $0.4 = \frac{4}{10} = \frac{2}{5}$ $4.125 = 4\frac{125}{1000} = 4\frac{1}{8}$

Try out your rule by giving the lowest-terms fraction for each decimal.

27. 0.25   **28.** 0.6   **29.** 1.75   **30.** 4.375   **31.** 7.5

More Practice, page 508, set A   **179**

Problem Solving
Determining Reasonable Answers

| UNDERSTAND |
| ANALYZE DATA |
| PLAN |
| ESTIMATE |
| SOLVE |
| EXAMINE |

LEARN ABOUT IT

An important part of evaluating your thinking and work when you solve problems is to check your work. This chart shows some questions you can use to help you do this.

Wayne used this table of high and low temperatures published in the *Westview Times*. He calculated the difference between the high and low temperature in Acapulco to be 27°F. Decide if his answer is reasonable or not. Tell why.

Check Your Work

- Is the arithmetic correct?
- Did you use the strategies correctly?
- Is the answer reasonable?

DAILY TEMPERATURES		
City	High	Low
Acapulco	87°F	70°F
Calgary	31°F	14°F
London	64°F	35°F
Hong Kong	63°F	53°F
Melbourne	65°F	47°F
Montreal	14°F	−18°F
Nassau	82°F	64°F

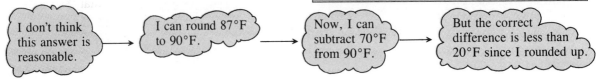

I don't think this answer is reasonable. → I can round 87°F to 90°F. → Now, I can subtract 70°F from 90°F. → But the correct difference is less than 20°F since I rounded up.

27°F is not a reasonable answer.

TRY IT OUT

Do not solve the problem. Decide if the answer given is reasonable. If it is not reasonable, explain why.

1. How much higher was the high temperature in Nassau than the high temperature in Montreal?

   Answer: The high temperature in Nassau was 78°F higher.

2. At noon the temperature in Hong Kong was 63°F. It dropped 7°F by evening. What was the temperature in the evening?

   Answer: The temperature in the evening was 56°F.

3. The temperature at Wayne's house dropped to 56°F. How much lower was the low temperature in Melbourne?

   Answer: The temperature in Melbourne was 19°F lower.

Solve. Use any problem solving strategy.

Average Monthly Temperature(°F)

City	Jan.	April	July	Oct.
Anchorage, AK	13.0	35.5	58.1	34.6
Boston, MA	29.6	48.7	73.5	54.8
Dallas, TX	44.0	65.9	86.3	67.9
Helena, MT	18.1	42.3	67.9	45.1
Jacksonville, FL	53.2	67.7	81.3	69.5
Madison, WI	15.6	45.8	70.6	49.5
Mobile, AL	50.8	68.0	82.2	68.5
New York, NY	31.8	51.9	76.4	57.5
Phoenix, AZ	52.3	68.1	92.3	73.4
San Francisco, CA	48.5	54.8	62.2	60.6
Toledo, OH	23.1	47.8	71.8	51.7

1. Use the temperature chart to find how much higher the average July temperature is in Dallas than in Helena.

2. Use the chart to find the average of the 4 monthly temperatures for Phoenix to the nearest tenth of a degree.

3. In Mobile how much lower is the average monthly temperature in January than in July?

4. For 32 years the average annual rainfall at Mt. Waialeale in Hawaii was 460 in. At Death Valley, California, the 42-year average was 1.63 in. How much greater was the average annual rainfall at Mt. Waialeale?

5. The students at the weather station measured $\frac{3}{5}$ in. of rain on Tuesday. On Wednesday they measured 0.72 in. Which day had the most rain?

6. Len's class measured 1.62 in. of rain on Monday and 0.87 in. of rain on Tuesday. He estimated that more than 3 in. of rain fell during this period of time. Is his estimate reasonable? Explain your answer.

7. Each of the 23 students helping with the school weather station has a 3-digit code number. The code numbers use only the digits 2, 5, and 9, but digits can be repeated. Can each student have a different code number?

8. **Missing Data** Tell what data is needed to solve this problem. Between July 1, 1988 and January 5, 1989, San Francisco got 8.98 in. of rain. How many more in. of rain must the city get to reach the season normal?

Data Collection and Analysis
Group Decision Making

Doing a Questionnaire

Group Skill:
Explain and Summarize

Have you or someone you know ever had an accident on a bicycle? Have you ever been injured? What information might have helped prevent the accident or injury? Make a **questionnaire** (a list of written questions) to gather information to make some recommendations for preventing accidents and injuries.

Collecting Data

1. Talk with your group to decide what specific information you might need to have about bicycle accidents. You may want to know about the accident conditions, the injury, or the bicycle. Make a list of the ideas and then decide which will be most useful.

2. Write at least four **multiple-choice questions** similar to the examples given below. A multiple-choice question usually lists 3 or 4 answer choices. Other types of questions may also be included.

Questionnaire on Bicycle Accidents

____ age

Check one choice for each question.

1. How serious was your injury?
    ____ not serious at all
    ____ somewhat serious
    ____ very serious
2. Where did the accident take place?
    ____ on a paved street
    ____ on a gravel or dirt roadway or path
    ____ on a sidewalk
    ____ other
3. Were you wearing a bicycle helmet at the time of the accident?
    ____ yes
    ____ no
    ____ I don't remember

3. Test your questionnaire on a few classmates. Revise questions that are unclear.
4. The group of people you give your questionnaire to is called your **sample.** For your sample, select at least 20 people who have had bicycle accidents. Discuss why you might want to include about the same number of males and females. Do you want the people in your sample to have the same age or different ages?
5. Make copies of your questionnaire and give it to the members of your sample.

6. Make a table to show the results of each question in your questionnaire. Mark a tally for the response on each questionnaire in your table. Count the total number of responses. An example is shown below.

1. How serious was your injury?

		Total
Not very serious	ⅢⅠ ⅢⅠ ⅢⅠ	15
Somewhat serious	ⅢⅠ ⅢⅠ	8
Very serious	ⅠⅠ	2

Presenting Your Analysis

7. Write a summary of your results. What recommendations would you make for preventing serious injuries on bicycles?
8. Write at least one question which you would like to explore further.

183

WRAP UP

Language Match

Find the term that matches the description.

1. a number that names a part of a region or set

2. the number below the line in a fraction

3. a fraction for which the greatest common factor of the numerator and denominator is 1

4. the largest number that is a factor of two numbers

5. a fraction with a numerator of 1

6. a fractional number greater than 1

a. unit fraction
b. greatest common factor
c. improper fraction
d. fraction
e. lowest-terms fraction
f. denominator

Sometimes, Always, Never

Decide which word should go in the blank: *sometimes, always,* or *never.* Explain your choices.

7. Equivalent fractions can _____ be found by multiplying both the numerator and the denominator by the same non-zero number.

8. Dividing the numerator and denominator of a fraction by a common factor will _____ reduce the fraction to lowest terms.

9. Improper fractions can _____ be written as mixed numbers or whole numbers.

10. When a fraction is reduced to lowest terms, its value _____ decreases.

Project

Design a card game to match fractions and money amounts. One set of cards should contain money questions such as "What part of a dollar is 3 quarters and a nickel?" The other set should have fraction answers to the questions in lowest terms. Make up a name, playing rules, and a scoring system for the game.

CHAPTER REVIEW/TEST

Part 1   Understanding

Write the next three equivalent fractions.   **1.** $\frac{3}{4}, \frac{6}{8}, \frac{9}{12}$, ▓, ▓, ▓

Is each fraction in the lowest terms? Write *yes* or *no*. **2.** $\frac{7}{12}$ **3.** $\frac{4}{28}$ **4.** $\frac{8}{32}$
If you write *no*, reduce the fraction to the lowest terms.

5. List these fractions in order $\frac{2}{3}, \frac{2}{7}, \frac{2}{5}, \frac{2}{9}$
from least to greatest.

6. Which picture shows $\frac{3}{5}$ of the set is shaded.   A 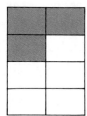 B

7. Which picture shows $\frac{3}{8}$ of the region is shaded?

Part 2   Skills

Find the greatest common factor (GCF) for each set of numbers.

8. 8 and 12   **9.** 15 and 20

10. Find the least common multiple (LCM) for 3 and 8.

11. Find the least common denominator (LCD) for $\frac{1}{3}$ and $\frac{2}{5}$.

12. Write $\frac{17}{4}$ as a mixed number.   **13.** Write $3\frac{3}{8}$ as an improper fraction.

14. Write $\frac{9}{20}$ as a decimal.   **15.** Write $\frac{13}{6}$ as a decimal rounded to the
nearest hundredth.

Part 3   Applications

16. Uniform tops are red, white, or pink. Pants are blue or black. How many different combinations of tops and pants are possible?

17. Fernando hiked 1.8 km on Monday, 1.7 km on Tuesday, and 2.4 km on Wednesday. He estimated that he hiked more than 8 km in all. Is his estimate reasonable? Explain.

18. Challenge   Sue has a batting average of 0.400. Batting average is found by dividing hits by number of times at bat. If Sue was at bat 15 times, how many hits did she get?

ENRICHMENT
The Tangram Puzzle

The seven shapes pictured here are the pieces of an old Chinese puzzle called the **tangram puzzle.** The pieces can be fit together to form many interesting shapes. Several of them can be grouped together to fit inside other pieces. In particular, all of the puzzle pieces will fit exactly into the unshaded square below.

Trace and cut out the tangram pieces. Show how they fit into the square.

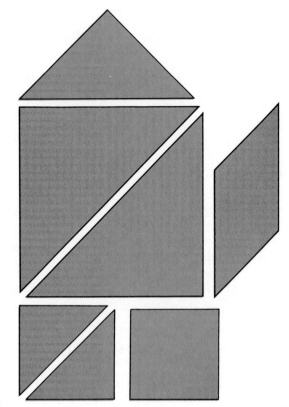

1. Which of the other shapes can you make by fitting the two small triangles together?

2. How many different ways can you make one of the largest triangles using three of the smaller pieces? Tell which pieces you used.

3. Which pieces fit into the parallelogram?

4. Suppose the area of the unshaded square is 1. Use the relationships from the questions above to write what fractional part each piece is of the square.

CUMULATIVE REVIEW

1. Choose the best estimate: 73×805.
   - A. 560
   - B. 5,600
   - C. 56,000
   - D. 560,000

2. Write an algebraic expression for: double a number.
   - A. $n + 2$
   - B. $\frac{n}{2}$
   - C. $2n$
   - D. $2 + n$

3. Use compatible numbers to estimate the quotient: $3,865 \div 80$.
   - A. 40
   - B. 50
   - C. 500
   - D. 400

4. A store rents 5 comedy videos for every 3 westerns. If it rents 21 westerns, how many comedies does it rent?
   - A. 26
   - B. 16
   - C. 15
   - D. 35

5. What is the range of this set of numbers: 14, 73, 29, 56?
   - A. 59
   - B. 73
   - C. 4
   - D. 87

6. Sara's normal pulse rate is 75 beats per minute. When she jogs, her rate increases by 50 beats per minute. How many times does her heart beat during a 20-minute run?
   - A. 2,500
   - B. 1,000
   - C. 3,750
   - D. 1,500

7. Find the product of 2.53 and 0.18.
   - A. 45.54
   - B. 0.4554
   - C. 0.0455
   - D. 4.554

8. Find the quotient mentally: $2,400 \div 6$.
   - A. 400
   - B. 40
   - C. 4,444
   - D. 4,000

9. Three ski jackets cost $144.36. What is the cost of one jacket?
   - A. $58.12
   - B. $47.12
   - C. $148.12
   - D. $48.12

10. There are 64 teams in a tournament. Each team plays one other team until it loses. How many games are needed to decide the champion?
    - A. 32
    - B. 64
    - C. 31
    - D. 63

11. What is the median of the following set of scores: 75, 68, 87, 83, 87?
    - A. 75
    - B. 83
    - C. 87
    - D. 80

12. A serving of lean beef has 16 grams of protein. Mary's mother needs 60 grams of protein every day. For lunch she ate 2 servings of beef. How many more grams of protein does she need?
    - A. 14
    - B. 28
    - C. 60
    - D. 32

7

MATH AND
LANGUAGE ARTS

DATA BANK

Use the Language Arts Data
Bank on page 478 to answer
the questions.

1 A layout is a plan that shows
how text and art will be
arranged on a page of a
magazine. The layout shown is for
a creative writing magazine. How
wide is the right margin? How
wide is the space for the photo
labeled *Art 1?*

ADDITION AND SUBTRACTION: FRACTIONS AND MIXED NUMBERS

2 Five lines of text will fit in each inch of the page length. If the poem "Searching" is used in the larger block marked for story or poem, about how much space will be left over?

3 Describe or sketch another layout using the same blocks of space for art, and for stories and poems. How did you find out if your new arrangement would work?

4 **Using Critical Thinking**
Use the layout to explain how you know that
$$\frac{5}{16} + 5\frac{1}{2} + 1\frac{3}{16} = 7.$$

Adding and Subtracting Fractions and Mixed Numbers
Common Denominators

EXPLORE Analyze the Process

This magazine page has art that is $5\frac{3}{8}$ inches wide and a column of text that is $2\frac{3}{8}$ inches wide. What is the total number of inches required for the width of both?

Here is how to find the sum of two mixed numbers when the denominators are the same.

Look at the denominators. $\begin{array}{r}5\frac{3}{8}\\+2\frac{3}{8}\\\hline\end{array}$ same	Add the fractions. Write the sum of the numerators over the common denominator. $\begin{array}{r}5\frac{3}{8}\\+2\frac{3}{8}\\\hline\frac{6}{8}\end{array}$	Add the whole numbers. Reduce if possible. $\begin{array}{r}5\frac{3}{8}\\+2\frac{3}{8}\\\hline 7\frac{6}{8}=7\frac{3}{4}\end{array}$

TALK ABOUT IT

1. How could you use fraction pieces to show that $\frac{3}{8} + \frac{3}{8} = \frac{6}{8}$ or $\frac{3}{4}$?
2. Use a complete sentence to give a reasonable answer to the story problem.

Find the sums and differences.

1. $\begin{array}{r}\frac{2}{11}\\+\frac{3}{11}\\\hline\end{array}$
2. $\begin{array}{r}\frac{6}{9}\\-\frac{4}{9}\\\hline\end{array}$
3. $\begin{array}{r}5\frac{3}{8}\\+2\frac{1}{8}\\\hline\end{array}$
4. $\begin{array}{r}6\\-2\frac{5}{10}\\\hline\end{array}$
5. $\begin{array}{r}3\frac{3}{7}\\+5\frac{6}{7}\\\hline\end{array}$
6. $\begin{array}{r}8\frac{13}{15}\\+2\frac{5}{15}\\\hline\end{array}$

Find the answers. Reduce if possible.

1. $\dfrac{7}{10}$
$-\dfrac{2}{10}$

2. $\dfrac{3}{4}$
$+\dfrac{3}{4}$

3. $\dfrac{9}{8}$
$-\dfrac{2}{8}$

4. $\dfrac{3}{16}$
$+\dfrac{5}{16}$

5. $\dfrac{1}{6}$
$+\dfrac{5}{6}$

6. $\dfrac{11}{12}$
$-\dfrac{5}{12}$

7. $\dfrac{2}{5}$
$+\dfrac{2}{5}$

8. $\dfrac{3}{8}$
$+\dfrac{7}{8}$

9. $\dfrac{7}{8}$
$-\dfrac{4}{8}$

10. $\dfrac{4}{6}$
$-\dfrac{1}{6}$

11. $10\dfrac{3}{10}$
$+\ 3$

12. $9\dfrac{4}{5}$
$-3\dfrac{1}{5}$

13. $\dfrac{19}{20} - \dfrac{13}{20}$

14. $\dfrac{14}{24} + \dfrac{10}{24}$

15. $3\dfrac{1}{8} + 8\dfrac{4}{8}$

16. $18\dfrac{1}{5} + 29\dfrac{3}{5}$

17. $8\dfrac{5}{6} - 5\dfrac{1}{6}$

18. $7\dfrac{5}{6} - 5\dfrac{2}{6}$

19. $21\dfrac{1}{4} + 14$

20. $19\dfrac{7}{8} - 12\dfrac{7}{8}$

21. $42\dfrac{5}{10} + 28\dfrac{3}{10}$

22. Find the sum of $7\dfrac{1}{6}$ and $3\dfrac{3}{6}$.

23. How much greater is $8\dfrac{7}{8}$ than $\dfrac{5}{8}$?

MATH REASONING Write $+$ or $-$ for each ▥.

24. $\dfrac{7}{8}$ ▥ $\dfrac{1}{8} = \dfrac{3}{4}$

25. $\dfrac{9}{10}$ ▥ $\dfrac{3}{10} = 1\dfrac{1}{5}$

26. $\dfrac{7}{12}$ ▥ $\dfrac{3}{12} = \dfrac{1}{3}$

27. $\dfrac{6}{9}$ ▥ $\dfrac{3}{9} = 1$

PROBLEM SOLVING

28. **Language Arts Data Bank** Suppose two poems will be printed in the larger space for story or poem. One poem uses $3\dfrac{5}{16}$ inches of the total length. The poems must be $\dfrac{3}{16}$ inches apart. How much room is left for the second poem?

▶ **MENTAL MATH**

Find a fraction for x.

29. $\dfrac{1}{2} + x = 1$

30. $\dfrac{3}{5} + x = 1$

31. $\dfrac{8}{8} - x = \dfrac{5}{8}$

32. $1 - x = \dfrac{3}{4}$

33. $\dfrac{3}{4} + x = 1$

34. $\dfrac{7}{8} - x = 0$

35. $\dfrac{5}{8} + x = \dfrac{5}{8}$

36. $3 + x = 3\dfrac{7}{8}$

Exploring Algebra
Solving Equations Using Mental Math

EXPLORE Examine the Equations

The hands are hiding numbers. Use mental math to figure out what numbers are under the hands. Each statement is correct.

A $8 + $  $= 15$

B $\dfrac{2}{4} + $ = $\dfrac{3}{4}$

C $6 \times $ = 18

D $12 - $ = 7

TALK ABOUT IT

1. How did you figure out what number is being hidden in **A**?
2. What is the denominator for **B**? What is the numerator?
3. Explain how you figured out **C** and **D**.

An **equation** is a mathematical sentence that says that two expressions stand for the same value. An equation uses the equality sign ($=$).

An equation: $2 + 18 + 20 = 40$ $\qquad$ Not an equation: $2 + 18 + 20$
$\qquad\qquad\quad\ 2 + 18 + x = 40$ $\qquad\qquad\qquad\qquad\quad\ 2 < 18$

When you have equations to solve, you can think of the letter, or variable, as "hiding" the number that makes the sentence true. To find the **solution** to an equation like $x + 6 = 10$ means to find a value for x that makes the left side stand for the same number as the right side. Some equations can be solved using mental math.
Example: Solve $x + 6 = 10$
$\qquad\qquad 4 + 6 = 10$, so $x = 4$

Other Examples

A $\dfrac{7}{8} - n = \dfrac{3}{8}$ $\qquad\qquad\qquad$ **B** $12 \div s = 3$

$\dfrac{7}{8} - \dfrac{4}{8} = \dfrac{3}{8}$ so, $n = \dfrac{4}{8}$ $\qquad\qquad 12 \div 4 = 3$, so $s = 4$

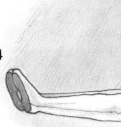

Solve. Use mental math.

1. $m - 12 = 10$ $\qquad$ 2. $b + \dfrac{1}{4} = \dfrac{3}{4}$ $\qquad$ 3. $6 \times c = 48$ $\qquad$ 4. $d - \dfrac{3}{8} = \dfrac{1}{8}$

5. $35 + k = 55$ $\qquad$ 6. $64 - p = 30$ $\qquad$ 7. $35 = 7 \times h$ $\qquad$ 8. $y \div 20 = 4$

1. $n + 20 = 50$

2. $70 - x = 6$

3. $40 + t = 100$

4. $a - 17 = 0$

5. $6 \times b = 30$

6. $3 \cdot c = 30$

7. $5d = 20$

8. $u - \frac{1}{5} = \frac{3}{5}$

9. $\frac{7}{12} + e = \frac{11}{12}$

10. $5 \div d = 1$

11. $4 = 28 \div w$

12. $m \div 1 = 13$

13. $6 \times m = 120$

14. $85 - r = 60$

15. $t + 50 = 90$

16. $u - 80 = 10$

17. $\frac{9}{10} - g = \frac{3}{10}$

18. $\frac{7}{8} + f = 1$

19. $14 \div z = 1$

20. $\frac{9}{10} = \frac{2}{10} + a$

21. Write an addition equation that has 10 as a solution.

22. Write a multiplication equation that has 4 as a solution.

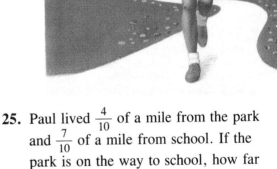

APPLY

MATH REASONING

23. Do not solve. Which is greater, a or b?
$324 \div a = 81$ $324 \div b = 108$

PROBLEM SOLVING

24. Rhonda walked $\frac{1}{4}$ of a mile. Then she started jogging. In all, she walked and jogged $\frac{3}{4}$ of a mile. Write and solve an equation to find out how far Rhonda jogged.

25. Paul lived $\frac{4}{10}$ of a mile from the park and $\frac{7}{10}$ of a mile from school. If the park is on the way to school, how far is the park from school?

▶ CALCULATOR

26. Find numbers for x and y from those in the ring. Your calculator will help.
$x + y = 762$

277 393
469 385
282 293

Estimating Sums and Differences
Fractions and Mixed Numbers

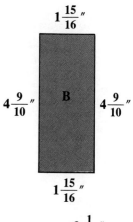

LEARN ABOUT IT

EXPLORE Study the Figures

Look at the figures. Estimate which figure
has the greatest perimeter and which has the
least. The **perimeter** is the distance around
the figure.

TALK ABOUT IT

1. Which of the fractions are close to 0?
   Close to $\frac{1}{2}$? Close to 1?
2. Did you have a method for finding
   your estimate? Explain.
3. Which figure has a perimeter very
   close to 14 inches?

Here are three methods you might use when
you estimate fraction sums and differences.

- Substitute compatible numbers.
  (Use numbers close to 0, $\frac{1}{2}$, and 1.)

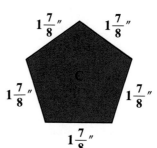

$$3\frac{7}{8} + 3\frac{1}{10} + 2\frac{3}{8} \text{ is about } 9\frac{1}{2}$$

- Use the whole numbers. Then adjust.

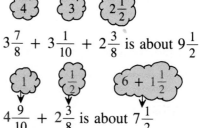

$$4\frac{9}{10} + 2\frac{3}{8} \text{ is about } 7\frac{1}{2}$$

- Use rounding.

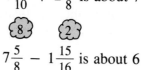

$$7\frac{5}{8} - 1\frac{15}{16} \text{ is about } 6$$

TRY IT OUT

Estimate each sum and difference.

1. $4\frac{9}{10} + 3\frac{1}{8}$

2. $7\frac{15}{16} - 2\frac{1}{10}$

3. $6\frac{4}{10} + 3\frac{1}{12}$

4. $8\frac{1}{16} - 4\frac{7}{8}$

5. $6\frac{7}{16} + 2\frac{1}{10} + 3\frac{1}{12}$

6. $\frac{1}{20} + 2\frac{7}{15} + \frac{3}{7}$

7. $6\frac{9}{20} - \frac{6}{13}$

8. $4\frac{1}{20} + 5\frac{1}{11} + 9\frac{5}{12}$

9. $6\frac{1}{2} - \frac{1}{3}$

Estimate each sum or difference.

1. $5\frac{1}{10} + 7\frac{3}{4}$

2. $6\frac{7}{8} - 2\frac{1}{10}$

3. $4\frac{9}{10} + 6\frac{1}{4}$

4. $3\frac{1}{2} + 7\frac{11}{12}$

5. $5\frac{1}{8} - \frac{15}{16}$

6. $3\frac{3}{4} - 1\frac{9}{10}$

7. $6\frac{11}{12} + 3\frac{1}{8}$

8. $7\frac{2}{15} + 1\frac{8}{9}$

9. $8\frac{1}{4} - 3\frac{9}{10}$

10. $6\frac{9}{10} - 3\frac{7}{8}$

11. $5\frac{1}{6} + 8\frac{5}{8}$

12. $9 - 2\frac{9}{10}$

13. $6\frac{11}{12} + 3\frac{1}{4}$

14. $8\frac{7}{8} - 1\frac{1}{10}$

15. $6\frac{3}{4} + 3\frac{1}{5} + 2\frac{9}{10}$

16. $8\frac{15}{16} - 3\frac{1}{8}$

17. $7\frac{7}{16} + 3\frac{1}{10}$

18. $5\frac{1}{8} - 1\frac{11}{12}$

19. $2\frac{9}{10} + 3\frac{8}{9}$

20. $6\frac{1}{5} + 3\frac{5}{6} + 4\frac{1}{10}$

APPLY

MATH REASONING

Estimate to decide which answer is correct.

21. $\frac{15}{16} + \frac{7}{8} + \frac{3}{4}$ **a.** $3\frac{9}{16}$ **b.** $2\frac{9}{16}$ **c.** $1\frac{9}{16}$

PROBLEM SOLVING

22. A square garden is $24\frac{11}{12}$ feet on each side. About how long would a fence have to be to go around the garden?

23. A rectangular garden is twice as long as it is wide. The fence around the outside of the garden is 90 feet. How long and how wide is the garden?

▨ MIXED REVIEW

Reduce each fraction to lowest terms.

24. $\frac{10}{15}$ 25. $\frac{7}{21}$ 26. $\frac{9}{72}$ 27. $\frac{3}{18}$ 28. $\frac{10}{40}$ 29. $\frac{2}{10}$

Write each improper fraction as a mixed or whole number.

30. $\frac{32}{5}$ 31. $\frac{40}{8}$ 32. $\frac{82}{4}$ 33. $\frac{24}{7}$ 34. $\frac{32}{8}$ 35. $\frac{24}{3}$

Adding and Subtracting Fractions
Making the Connection

LEARN ABOUT IT

EXPLORE Use Fraction Models

Work with a partner.

- Outline a rectangle on graph paper that has an area of 20 square units.
- You and your partner select different color crayons. Each of you color some of the small squares in the rectangle so that not all of it is colored. Each of you should color different squares.
- Each of you write a fraction in lowest terms for the part of the rectangle that you colored.
- Write a fraction in lowest terms for the total part of the rectangle that was colored.

TALK ABOUT IT

1. Give a pair of equivalent fractions that you could show on the rectangle.
2. What about the activity above suggests that you are adding fractions?
3. Can both you and your partner color more than half of the rectangle? Why or why not?

You have colored two fractional parts of a rectangle. You have figured out the total fractional part you colored. Now you will see how to record what you have done. This will help you understand adding and subtracting fractions.

What You Do

What You Write

- Outline a rectangle with an area equal to the least common denominator.

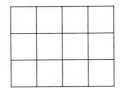

$$\dfrac{3}{4}$$ Think: LCD = 12

$$+\dfrac{1}{6}$$

1. Is there more than 1 kind of rectangle with an area of 12?

- Color $\dfrac{3}{4}$ one color and $\dfrac{1}{6}$ another.

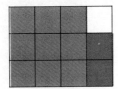

$$\dfrac{3}{4} = \dfrac{9}{12}$$

$$+\dfrac{1}{6} = \dfrac{2}{12}$$

2. How many squares make $\dfrac{3}{4}$ of 12? $\dfrac{1}{6}$ of 12?

- Count how many squares are colored.

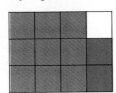 11

$$\dfrac{3}{4} = \dfrac{9}{12}$$

$$+\dfrac{1}{6} = \dfrac{2}{12}$$

$$= \dfrac{11}{12}$$

3. What fraction of the rectangle is colored?

4. What is the sum of $\dfrac{3}{4}$ and $\dfrac{1}{6}$?

5. How could you use graph paper to show $\dfrac{3}{4} - \dfrac{1}{6}$?

TRY IT OUT

Color graph paper to help you find each sum and difference. Record what you did. Use the above example for ideas.

1. $\dfrac{1}{2} + \dfrac{1}{3}$ **2.** $\dfrac{1}{2} - \dfrac{1}{3}$ **3.** $\dfrac{2}{3} + \dfrac{1}{4}$ **4.** $\dfrac{2}{3} - \dfrac{1}{4}$

Adding and Subtracting Fractions
Unlike Denominators

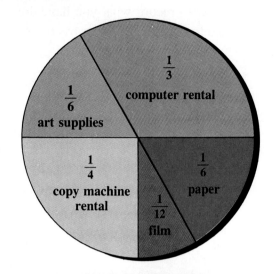

The circle graph:
- $\frac{1}{6}$ art supplies
- $\frac{1}{3}$ computer rental
- $\frac{1}{4}$ copy machine rental
- $\frac{1}{12}$ film
- $\frac{1}{6}$ paper

LEARN ABOUT IT

EXPLORE Analyze the Process

The circle graph shows the expenses for the Northside School creative writing magazine. What part of the total expenses was for renting a computer and a copy machine?

Since you want to find the total part of the expenses spent on computer and copy machine rental, you add.

Look at the denominators.	Find the least common denominator.	Write equivalent fractions with this denominator.	Add the fractions. Reduce if possible.
$\frac{1}{3}$ ← not the $+\frac{1}{4}$ ← same	The LCD of 3 and 4 is 12.	$\frac{1}{3}=\frac{4}{12}$ $+\frac{1}{4}=\frac{3}{12}$	$\frac{4}{12}$ $+\frac{3}{12}$ $\frac{7}{12}$

TALK ABOUT IT

1. Why is the sum $\frac{4}{12}+\frac{3}{12}$ the same as the sum $\frac{1}{3}+\frac{1}{4}$?

2. How could you use graph paper to find the sum $\frac{1}{3}+\frac{1}{4}$?

3. Use a complete sentence to give a reasonable answer to the story problem.

TRY IT OUT

Add or subtract.

1. $\frac{5}{6}$
$+\frac{1}{4}$

2. $\frac{7}{8}$
$-\frac{1}{4}$

3. $\frac{4}{5}$
$+\frac{3}{4}$

4. $\frac{1}{3}$
$-\frac{2}{7}$

5. $\frac{2}{5}$
$+\frac{2}{3}$

6. $\frac{1}{2}$
$-\frac{1}{10}$

Add or subtract. The LCD is given.

1. $\dfrac{3}{10}$ ⟨10⟩
$+\dfrac{2}{5}$

2. $\dfrac{5}{6}$ ⟨12⟩
$-\dfrac{1}{4}$

3. $\dfrac{7}{8}$ ⟨24⟩
$+\dfrac{1}{3}$

4. $\dfrac{5}{8}$ ⟨24⟩
$-\dfrac{1}{6}$

Add or subtract.

5. $\dfrac{4}{5}$
$+\dfrac{1}{2}$

6. $\dfrac{3}{2}$
$-\dfrac{1}{4}$

7. $\dfrac{3}{4}$
$-\dfrac{3}{8}$

8. $\dfrac{5}{3}$
$-\dfrac{1}{2}$

9. $\dfrac{4}{5}$
$-\dfrac{1}{6}$

10. $\dfrac{5}{6}$
$+\dfrac{1}{3}$

11. $\dfrac{1}{2} + \dfrac{1}{3} + \dfrac{1}{4}$

12. $\dfrac{3}{4} + \dfrac{1}{2} + \dfrac{1}{8}$

13. $\dfrac{1}{4} + \dfrac{3}{8} + \dfrac{3}{4}$

14. $\dfrac{3}{4} + \dfrac{1}{6} + \dfrac{1}{3}$

15. Add $\dfrac{7}{8}$ to $\dfrac{3}{4}$.

16. Find the difference between $\dfrac{1}{8}$ and $\dfrac{3}{12}$.

APPLY

MATH REASONING

Do not add. Tell if the answer is more than 1 or less than 1.

17. $\dfrac{1}{2} + \dfrac{3}{4}$ **18.** $\dfrac{3}{8} + \dfrac{2}{5}$ **19.** $\dfrac{5}{8} + \dfrac{1}{2}$

PROBLEM SOLVING

20. For every person in the U.S., almost 20 magazine copies are published each year. About how many copies would this be for a class of 30 students?

21. Language Arts Data Bank
Two poems have been written for the page. One is $1\dfrac{3}{4}$ inches long. The other is $1\dfrac{1}{8}$ inches long. Will both fit into the smaller space for the text?

DATA BANK

▶ **ALGEBRA**

Find a number for x. Many answers are possible.

22. $\dfrac{3}{4} + x < 1$ **23.** $\dfrac{3}{4} + x > 1$ **24.** $\dfrac{3}{4} - x < \dfrac{1}{2}$ **25.** $\dfrac{3}{4} - x > \dfrac{1}{2}$

More Practice, page 508, set D

Using Critical Thinking

LEARN ABOUT IT

Carmella and Anthony were reviewing their number facts. Anthony asked, "What is 72 divided by 8?" Carmella answered, "It is 8 *or* it is 9." Anthony replied, "You are both right *and* wrong. But now I am trying to decide if your answer is *true* or *false*."

- In mathematics, when **and** connects two statements, both statements must be true for the combined statment to be true.

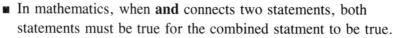

$$\text{T} \quad + \quad \text{T} \rightarrow \text{True} \qquad\qquad \text{T} \quad + \quad \text{F} \rightarrow \text{False}$$
Examples: **A** $2 + 3 = 5$ **and** $2 \times 3 = 6$ **B** $12 - 4 = 8$ **and** $12 \div 4 = 2$

- In mathematics, when **or** connects two statements, the combined statement is always true unless both parts are false.

$$\text{F} \quad + \quad \text{T} \rightarrow \text{True} \qquad\qquad \text{F} \quad + \quad \text{F} \rightarrow \text{False}$$
Examples: **C** $48 \div 8 = 5$ **or** $48 \div 8 \neq 5$ **D** $32 \div 8 = 5$ **or** $32 \div 8 = 6$
(Read, "is not equal to" for $\neq$)

TALK ABOUT IT

1. Examine Carmella's answer. How many statements does it contain? What joins her statements together?
2. Is the first part of Carmella's answer true? Is the second part of Carmella's answer true?
3. Should Anthony call Carmella's answer true?
4. Suppose Carmella had answered, "It is 8 *and* it is 9." Would her answer then be true or false? Explain.

TRY IT OUT

Use the rules of mathematical logic to decide if the student's statement is true or false.

1. Courtney declared that "Adding 0 to a number does not change the number **and** subtracting 0 from a number does not change the number."

2. Jen said, "My dad is going to take me to the park **or** to the zoo on Saturday." (Her dad took her to the park.)

3. Li said, "Multiplying a number by 1 does not change the number **and** multiplying by 0 does not change the number."

4. Joshua said, "I'm going swimming **and** to a movie this afternoon." (He went swimming only.)

MIDCHAPTER REVIEW/QUIZ

Solve these equations using mental math.

1. $x \cdot 15 = 150$ **2.** $\frac{3}{8} + n = 1$ **3.** $\frac{7}{9} - z = \frac{4}{9}$ **4.** $h \div 2 = 40$ **5.** $r - 2\frac{1}{4} = 3\frac{3}{4}$

Estimate each sum or difference.

6. $4\frac{5}{8} + 1\frac{3}{7}$ **7.** $6\frac{2}{5} - 3\frac{1}{2}$ **8.** $2\frac{1}{6} - \frac{7}{8}$ **9.** $3\frac{7}{9} + 8\frac{1}{8} + 4\frac{4}{7}$

Copy the rectangle. Finish by shading or crossing out.

10. $\frac{3}{4} + \frac{1}{6}$

Add or subtract. Reduce if possible.

11. $\begin{array}{r} \frac{3}{8} \\ -\frac{1}{8} \\ \hline \end{array}$ **12.** $\begin{array}{r} \frac{11}{12} \\ +\frac{5}{12} \\ \hline \end{array}$ **13.** $\begin{array}{r} \frac{7}{2} \\ -\frac{3}{2} \\ \hline \end{array}$ **14.** $\begin{array}{r} 5\frac{2}{3} \\ -1\frac{2}{3} \\ \hline \end{array}$ **15.** $\begin{array}{r} \frac{3}{4} \\ -\frac{3}{8} \\ \hline \end{array}$ **16.** $\begin{array}{r} \frac{2}{5} \\ +\frac{1}{4} \\ \hline \end{array}$

17. $\begin{array}{r} \frac{9}{10} \\ +\frac{5}{8} \\ \hline \end{array}$ **18.** $\begin{array}{r} 6\frac{2}{5} \\ +4\frac{3}{5} \\ \hline \end{array}$ **19.** $\begin{array}{r} \frac{2}{3} \\ -\frac{1}{2} \\ \hline \end{array}$ **20.** $\begin{array}{r} 3\frac{5}{6} \\ +2\frac{5}{6} \\ \hline \end{array}$ **21.** $\begin{array}{r} 8\frac{11}{12} \\ -4\frac{5}{12} \\ \hline \end{array}$ **22.** $\begin{array}{r} \frac{5}{6} \\ -\frac{5}{9} \\ \hline \end{array}$

23. $\frac{1}{6} + \frac{2}{9} + \frac{1}{2}$ **24.** $\frac{3}{4} + \frac{1}{2} + \frac{5}{8}$ **25.** $\frac{3}{2} + \frac{4}{5} + \frac{1}{3}$ **26.** $\frac{5}{6} + \frac{3}{8} + \frac{7}{12}$

PROBLEM SOLVING

27. *Meteor* magazine has 16 pages. $3\frac{1}{2}$ pages are poems and $7\frac{1}{2}$ pages are short stories. How many pages are not poems or stories?

28. The artist for *Meteor* bought a technical pen for $8.95, black ink for $4.67, and rubber cement for $5.39. How much did she spend for these supplies?

Adding Mixed Numbers
Unlike Denominators

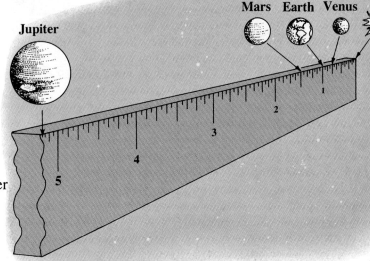

Jupiter

Mars   Earth   Venus

EXPLORE

If you think of Earth as being 1 inch from the Sun, the ruler shows how far away some other planets are. Jupiter is $5\frac{1}{5}$ inches away and Saturn (not shown) is $4\frac{3}{10}$ inches farther away than Jupiter. How far away is Saturn?

To solve the problem, you will need to add. You will need to put together amounts to find the total. Here is how to find the sum.

Look at the denominators.	Write equivalent fractions with a common denominator.	Add the fractions.	Add the whole numbers. Reduce fractions if possible.
$5\frac{1}{5}$ ← not the same $+\,4\frac{3}{10}$ ←	$5\frac{1}{5} = 5\frac{2}{10}$ $+\,4\frac{3}{10} = 4\frac{3}{10}$	$5\frac{2}{10}$ $+\,4\frac{3}{10}$ $\frac{5}{10}$	$5\frac{2}{10}$ $+\,4\frac{3}{10}$ $9\frac{5}{10} = 9\frac{1}{2}$

TALK ABOUT IT

1. How is adding mixed numbers different from adding fractions?
2. Estimate the sum using rounding.
3. Give a reasonable answer to the story problem using a complete sentence.

Find the sums.

1. $2\frac{1}{2}$
   $+\,4\frac{3}{4}$

2. $7\frac{9}{10}$
   $+\,4\frac{1}{2}$

3. $2\frac{2}{3}$
   $+\,12\frac{1}{2}$

4. $2\frac{1}{7} + 3\frac{1}{2} + 4\frac{3}{14}$

5. $5\frac{2}{3} + 1\frac{3}{4} + 2\frac{5}{8}$

Find the sums.

1. $2\frac{3}{8}$
   $+ 4\frac{3}{4}$

2. $3\frac{3}{4}$
   $+ 4\frac{1}{2}$

3. $7\frac{1}{4}$
   $+ 3\frac{1}{6}$

4. $10\frac{3}{5}$
   $+ 5\frac{4}{5}$

5. $4\frac{7}{8}$
   $+ 1\frac{1}{2}$

6. $6\frac{5}{8}$
   $+ 7\frac{3}{4}$

7. $6\frac{7}{10}$
   $+ 11\frac{3}{10}$

8. $3\frac{5}{6}$
   $+ 8\frac{1}{2}$

9. $61\frac{1}{2}$
   $+ 81\frac{1}{8}$

10. $28\frac{7}{10}$
    $+ 23\frac{1}{2}$

11. $3\frac{1}{2} + 8\frac{1}{4} + 6\frac{1}{8}$

12. $4\frac{1}{6} + 2\frac{1}{3} + 8\frac{2}{3}$

13. $16\frac{1}{4} + 7\frac{1}{5} + 9\frac{7}{10}$

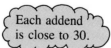

MATH REASONING

Find x.

14. $\frac{1}{2} + x = 1\frac{1}{2}$

15. $2\frac{3}{4} - x = 1\frac{1}{4}$

16. $x - \frac{3}{8} = \frac{5}{8}$

17. $\frac{3}{10} + x = \frac{1}{2}$

PROBLEM SOLVING

18. Mars is $1\frac{1}{2}$ inches from the Sun. Pluto is $37\frac{9}{10}$ inches farther away than Mars. How far away is Pluto?

19. Mercury (not shown) is $\frac{2}{5}$ of an inch away. Venus is $\frac{3}{4}$ of an inch away. Which of these planets is farther from the Sun?

▶ **ESTIMATION**

Estimate each sum by clustering.

Each addend is close to 30.

Example: $28\frac{3}{4} + 31\frac{1}{8} + 29\frac{5}{6} + 32\frac{1}{10} \rightarrow 4 \times 30 = 120$ Estimate

20. $57\frac{7}{10} + 61\frac{8}{9} + 63\frac{1}{4} + 59\frac{1}{2}$

21. $24\frac{7}{8} + 25\frac{1}{6} + 26\frac{1}{10} + 24\frac{11}{12}$

22. $9\frac{5}{8} + 11\frac{1}{4} + 10\frac{9}{10} + 9\frac{5}{6} + 10\frac{7}{16}$

23. $6\frac{2}{3} + 7\frac{1}{8} + 6\frac{9}{10} + 7\frac{1}{12} + 6\frac{7}{8} + 7\frac{1}{10}$

More Practice, page 509, set A

Subtracting Mixed Numbers
Unlike Denominators

LEARN ABOUT IT

EXPLORE **Analyze the Process**

Stephanie is baking oatmeal applesauce muffins. The recipe calls for $2\frac{3}{4}$ cups of applesauce. She has a can of applesauce that holds $7\frac{1}{3}$ cups. How many cups of applesauce will Stephanie have left after baking 1 batch?

You can answer the question by subtracting to find out how much is left.

Look at the denominators.	Write equivalent fractions with a common denominator.	Rename if necessary. Subtract the fractions.	Subtract the whole numbers. Reduce fractions if possible.
$7\frac{1}{3}$ $-2\frac{3}{4}$	$7\frac{1}{3} = 7\frac{4}{12}$ $-2\frac{3}{4} = 2\frac{9}{12}$	$6\frac{16}{12}$ $\left(7\frac{4}{12} = 6\frac{16}{12}\right)$ $-2\frac{9}{12}$ $\overline{\quad\frac{7}{12}}$	$6\frac{16}{12}$ $-2\frac{9}{12}$ $\overline{4\frac{7}{12}}$

TALK ABOUT IT

1. Why did $7\frac{4}{12}$ need to be renamed?

2. Tell why $7\frac{4}{12} = 6\frac{16}{12}$.

3. How could you estimate $7\frac{1}{3} - 2\frac{3}{4}$?

4. Use a complete sentence to give a reasonable answer to the story problem.

TRY IT OUT

Subtract.

1. $7\frac{1}{2}$
   $-5\frac{1}{4}$

2. $9\frac{3}{4}$
   $-1\frac{1}{6}$

3. $7\frac{1}{4}$
   $-1\frac{5}{6}$

4. 9
   $-3\frac{1}{4}$

5. $14\frac{3}{8}$
   $-5\frac{3}{4}$

Subtract.

1. $5\frac{7}{10}$
$-2\frac{3}{5}$

2. $6\frac{1}{2}$
$-5\frac{1}{3}$

3. $7\frac{1}{5}$
$-4\frac{1}{2}$

4. $9\frac{5}{9}$
$-7\frac{2}{9}$

5. $12\frac{1}{2}$
$-3\frac{3}{4}$

6. $8\frac{3}{4}$
$-\frac{1}{5}$

7. $7\frac{1}{4}$
$-6\frac{5}{6}$

8. $3\frac{7}{10}$
$-1\frac{1}{5}$

9. 8
$-5\frac{3}{4}$

10. $14\frac{3}{4}$
-5

11. $9\frac{2}{3} - 7\frac{1}{12}$

12. $8\frac{1}{8} - 1\frac{3}{4}$

13. $14 - 9\frac{7}{10}$

14. $7\frac{3}{5} - 2\frac{9}{10}$

MATH REASONING

Without subtracting, tell if the difference is > 5 or < 5.

15. $5\frac{1}{2} - \frac{1}{3}$

16. $5\frac{1}{2} - \frac{5}{8}$

17. $5\frac{3}{4} - \frac{7}{8}$

18. $5\frac{3}{4} - \frac{2}{3}$

19. $5\frac{3}{8} - \frac{1}{2}$

PROBLEM SOLVING

20. A number 300 can holds $13\frac{7}{8}$ ounces. A number $2\frac{1}{2}$ can holds 28 ounces. How many more ounces does a $2\frac{1}{2}$ can hold than a number 300 can?

21. Justin has 7 different sizes of cans. 4 of them are orange juice and 3 are pineapple juice. How many different pineapple-orange mixtures can he make using 1 can of each?

▶ **CALCULATOR**

The M+ key adds a number to the calculator's memory.
The M− key subtracts a number from the calculator's memory.

Example: $\frac{7}{8} - \frac{3}{10}$

| ON/AC | 7 | ÷ | 8 | = | M+ | 3 | ÷ | 10 | = | M− | MR |

Add or subtract.

22. $\frac{1}{4} + \frac{3}{5}$

23. $\frac{9}{10} - \frac{3}{4}$

24. $\frac{2}{5} + \frac{3}{8}$

More Practice, page 509, set B

Mental Math
Sums and Differences of Fractions and Mixed Numbers

EXPLORE Analyze the Situation

Examine the sums and differences in the box.
How many of them can you find mentally?

A $8\frac{1}{2} + 7$ **C** $12\frac{7}{8} - 2\frac{7}{8}$

B $6\frac{5}{8} + \frac{3}{8} + \frac{2}{5}$ **D** $7 - 3\frac{4}{5}$

TALK ABOUT IT

1. Which one did you think was easiest? How did you do it?
2. Did you discover any special methods for solving these mentally? Explain your methods.

Here are some methods you can use to mentally find sums and differences of fractions and mixed numbers.

Break Apart   **Compatible Numbers**   **Compensation**

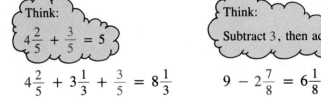

Think:
$7 - 3$ plus $\frac{5}{8} - \frac{2}{8}$

Think:
$4\frac{2}{5} + \frac{3}{5} = 5$

Think:
Subtract 3, then add $\frac{1}{8}$

$7\frac{5}{8} - 3\frac{2}{8} = 4\frac{3}{8}$ $4\frac{2}{5} + 3\frac{1}{3} + \frac{3}{5} = 8\frac{1}{3}$ $9 - 2\frac{7}{8} = 6\frac{1}{8}$

Find the sums and differences mentally. Write answers only.

1. $8\frac{3}{10} - 5$ 2. $7 - 1\frac{9}{10}$ 3. $4\frac{3}{8} + \frac{5}{8} + 6\frac{1}{5}$

4. $10 - 2\frac{1}{8}$ 5. $9\frac{5}{6} - 2\frac{1}{6}$ 6. $5\frac{7}{10} + 3\frac{5}{8} + 1\frac{3}{10}$

7. $6\frac{3}{5} + 2\frac{1}{5}$ 8. $2\frac{1}{5} + 3\frac{4}{5} + 9\frac{1}{6}$ 9. $12 - 5\frac{7}{8}$

Solve mentally. Try break apart.

1. $6\frac{5}{8} + 3$ **2.** $4 + 3\frac{1}{2}$ **3.** $7\frac{3}{4} - \frac{3}{4}$ **4.** $15\frac{3}{4} - 7\frac{1}{4}$

Solve mentally. Try compatible numbers.

5. $\frac{2}{5} + 3\frac{1}{2} + 1\frac{3}{5}$ **6.** $4\frac{3}{10} + 6\frac{7}{8} + \frac{7}{10}$ **7.** $6\frac{1}{8} + \frac{7}{8} + 2\frac{1}{3}$

Solve mentally. Try compensation.

8. $10 - 4\frac{7}{8}$ **9.** $7 - 3\frac{1}{4}$ **10.** $7 - 3\frac{5}{6}$ **11.** $12 - 7\frac{1}{8}$

Solve mentally. Use any method you want.

12. $\frac{5}{6} + 3\frac{1}{6} + 4\frac{1}{8}$ **13.** $14 - 5\frac{9}{10}$ **14.** $8\frac{5}{6} - 8$ **15.** $10 - 3\frac{1}{5}$

16. $6\frac{7}{10} - 2\frac{4}{10}$ **17.** $2\frac{4}{5} + 6\frac{5}{6} + \frac{1}{5}$ **18.** $5\frac{3}{4} + 3\frac{2}{3} + \frac{1}{4}$ **19.** $2\frac{3}{8} + 5\frac{4}{8}$

APPLY

MATH REASONING Without adding, tell if the sum is < 10 or > 10.

20. $9\frac{1}{4} + \frac{1}{2}$ **21.** $9\frac{5}{8} + \frac{1}{2}$ **22.** $9\frac{3}{10} + \frac{1}{2}$ **23.** $9\frac{7}{12} + \frac{1}{2}$

PROBLEM SOLVING

24. Bill read $\frac{1}{4}$ of a book the first day, $\frac{1}{2}$ the second day, and $\frac{1}{8}$ the third. He finished the book on the fourth day. What part of the book did Bill read on the fourth day?

MIXED REVIEW

Find the greatest common factor for each pair of numbers.

25. 8, 24 **26.** 12, 3 **27.** 15, 25 **28.** 7, 21 **29.** 12, 24 **30.** 18, 30

Write a decimal for each fraction.

31. $\frac{2}{5}$ **32.** $\frac{3}{8}$ **33.** $\frac{4}{10}$ **34.** $\frac{7}{20}$ **35.** $\frac{8}{16}$ **36.** $\frac{8}{25}$

Problem Solving
Work Backward

UNDERSTAND
ANALYZE DATA
PLAN
ESTIMATE
SOLVE
EXAMINE

LEARN ABOUT IT

Some problems can be solved by starting with a given number and reversing the actions in the problem. This strategy is called **Work Backward.**

The sixth graders at Edgeville School had a reading contest. Melissa won the contest. Nick read 9 fewer books than Melissa. Scott read 2 more books than Nick. Opal read twice as many books as Scott. Opal read 12 books. How many books did Melissa read?

It often helps to make a flowchart and then a reverse flowchart for the problem.

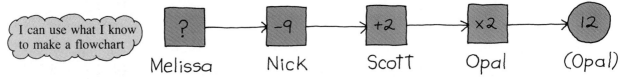

I can use what I know to make a flowchart

? — -9 — +2 — ×2 — 12

Melissa   Nick   Scott   Opal   (Opal)

Remember: ■ Adding and subtracting "undo" each other.
■ Multiplying and dividing "undo" each other.

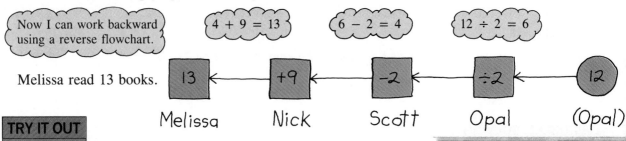

Now I can work backward using a reverse flowchart.

4 + 9 = 13   6 − 2 = 4   12 ÷ 2 = 6

Melissa read 13 books.   13 ← +9 ← -2 ← ÷2 ← 12

Melissa   Nick   Scott   Opal   (Opal)

TRY IT OUT

Read this problem and finish the solution.

Ricardo, Ann, Mike, and Tina each read a story. Ann's story was 5 pages longer than Ricardo's story. Mike's story was 3 times as long as Ann's. Tina's story was 8 pages shorter than Mike's. Tina's story was 13 pages long. How long was Ricardo's story?

■ What operation does "3 times as long" suggest?
■ What operation does "8 pages shorter" suggest?
■ How can you "undo" + 5?
■ Copy and complete the flowcharts to help you solve the problem.

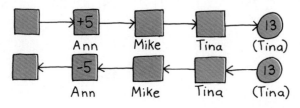

□ — +5 → □ → □ → 13
   Ann   Mike   Tina   (Tina)

□ ← -5 ← □ ← □ ← 13
   Ann   Mike   Tina   (Tina)

Solve by working backward.

1. The width of a bookcase is half its length. The bookcase is 8 inches wider than it is deep. It is 12 inches deep. How long is the bookcase?

2. Mikko bought some books and magazines. She spent $4.25 on magazines and 4 times that amount on books. She had $7.35 left. How much money did Mikko have before she bought the books and magazines?

MIXED PRACTICE

Solve. Choose a strategy from the list or use another strategy that you know.

3. Jesse made a book for creative writing from green cardboard. The cover is $14\frac{1}{2}$ inches long and $9\frac{3}{4}$ inches wide. How much longer is the cover than it is wide?

4. Each Friday, Ms. Newby asks her students to record on a wall chart the number of hours they spent reading during the week. Use the chart to find how many hours Keri and Alex together spent reading the third week.

Hours Spent Reading			
	Week 1	Week 2	Week 3
Alex	4¼	5	6 5/12
Consuela	2½	7¾	5½
Keri	5	2⅓	8¾
Rosa	4¾	2½	3
James	3½	5¼	7⅔

5. Use the chart to find how many more hours James spent reading during the first 2 weeks than Rosa.

Some Strategies	
Act Out	Make a Table
Use Objects	Solve a Simpler Problem
Draw a Picture	Make an Organized List
Guess and Check	Work Backward

6. The library displays its new books on a special shelf. They group them by type: fiction, adventure, or other. How many different ways can they arrange the 3 types?

7. Each student in Kim's reading group gave every other student in the group one book to read. There are 9 students in the group. How many books were exchanged?

8. Janice wants to buy some brocade ribbon $1\frac{1}{2}$ inches wide to make bookmarks. She wants to make one bookmark $7\frac{1}{8}$ inches long and the other $9\frac{13}{16}$ inches long. About how many inches of ribbon should Janice buy?

Applied Problem Solving
Group Decision Making

UNDERSTAND
ANALYZE DATA
PLAN
ESTIMATE
SOLVE
EXAMINE

Group Skill
Disagree in an Agreeable Way

Your aunt is a veterinarian and many of her customers are interested in having you watch their pets while they are on vacation. You need to decide what fees you will charge per day for each animal. You also need to figure out three different combinations of animals you could care for during the first week since you cannot fit all the customers into your schedule.

Facts to Consider

1. You received calls this week from 3 dog owners, 3 cat owners, 1 fish owner, and 2 bird owners.
2. You have $1\frac{1}{2}$ hours per day to devote to your job.
3. The customers live 10 minutes biking time from each other.
4. Animals need different kinds of care.

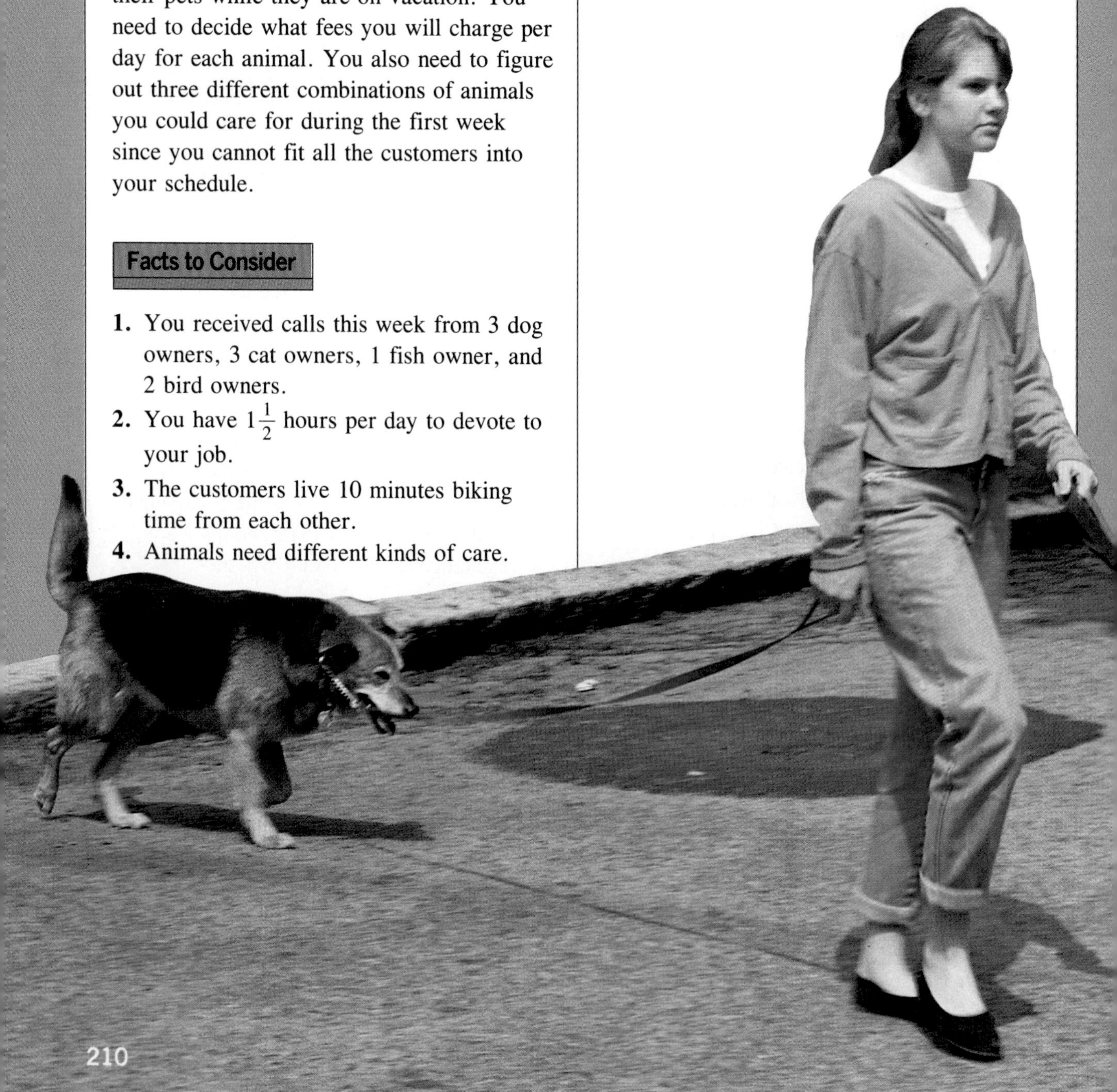

Dogs need: $\frac{1}{2}$ hour walking and playing time 2 times a day.

$\frac{1}{6}$ hour feeding time 2 times a day.

Cats need: $\frac{1}{4}$ hour feeding and playing time 2 times a day.

$\frac{1}{4}$ hour changing litter box every other day.

Fish need: $\frac{1}{6}$ hour feeding time 2 times a day.

Birds need: $\frac{1}{4}$ hour feeding and attention 2 times a day.

$\frac{1}{6}$ hour changing paper in cage every other day.

Some Questions to Answer

1. Which animal takes the most time? Which takes the least time?
2. How long would it take per day to care for two dogs?
3. If you take care of a cat, what is the most time it would take you in one day?
4. How long would it take per day to care for a cat and a dog?
5. If you charge $3 an hour, how much would you charge for a dog per day?
6. Do you like certain animals better than others? How will this affect your decision?

What Is Your Decision?

What will you charge for each animal? Use a table to show three possible combinations of animals you could care for the first week.

WRAP UP

Choose the Method

For each calculation below, first decide which can be solved using mental math. Then solve all of the problems using mental math or paper and pencil. Tell which method you used: *compatible numbers, break-apart, compensation,* or *finding the least common denominator.*

1. $8 - 3\frac{6}{7}$

2. $\frac{4}{5} + \frac{7}{9} + \frac{1}{5}$

3. $9\frac{5}{6} - 7\frac{1}{6}$

4. $2\frac{7}{10} + 5\frac{1}{4} + 4\frac{3}{10}$

5. $\frac{7}{8} - \frac{1}{6}$

6. $9 - 5\frac{1}{8}$

7. $4\frac{2}{3} + \frac{4}{5}$

8. $7\frac{4}{9} + 1\frac{4}{9}$

9. $8\frac{2}{3} - 2\frac{1}{4}$

Sometimes, Always, Never

Decide which word should go in the blank: *sometimes, always,* or *never.* Explain your choices.

10. The least common denominator of two fractions is _____ the product of the two denominators.

11. If each of two fractions is less than $\frac{1}{2}$ then their sum is _____ less than 1.

12. If one fraction is less than $\frac{1}{2}$ and the other is between $\frac{1}{2}$ and 1, the sum is _____ greater than 1.

13. The sum of two proper fractions is _____ found by adding the numerators and adding the denominators.

Project

Pretend you work for a wax museum. Make a map of the exhibits that shows visitors from one wax figure to another. Decide who your figures will be (classmates, pets, or famous people make interesting choices). Decide how far it is from one figure to the next. All distances must be given in fractions and mixed numbers. Then make up problems for others to solve based on the information in your map.

CHAPTER REVIEW/TEST

Part 1   Understanding

Solve. Use mental math.

1. $\frac{1}{4} + n = 1$

2. $\frac{5}{6} - n = 0$

3. $5b = 35$

4. $\frac{3}{8} + c = \frac{5}{8}$

Estimate to decide which answer is correct.

5. $\frac{5}{8} + \frac{7}{8} + \frac{3}{4}$ **a.** $1\frac{1}{4}$ **b.** $2\frac{1}{4}$ **c.** $3\frac{1}{4}$

6. $8\frac{4}{5} - 5\frac{1}{10}$ **a.** $1\frac{7}{10}$ **b.** $2\frac{7}{10}$ **c.** $3\frac{7}{10}$

Without adding or subtracting, tell if the answer is greater than 4 or less than 4.

7. $1\frac{5}{8} + 1\frac{3}{4}$

8. $8\frac{1}{6} - 3\frac{1}{3}$

9. $3\frac{1}{4} + 1\frac{1}{6}$

Part 2   Skills

Find the sums and differences mentally. Use break apart, compatible numbers, or compensation.

10. $9 - 2\frac{1}{6}$

11. $5\frac{7}{8} - 3\frac{4}{8}$

12. $\frac{3}{10} + 4\frac{5}{8} + 2\frac{7}{10}$

Find the sums and differences. Reduce if possible.

13. $2\frac{1}{8} + 7\frac{5}{8}$

14. $12 - 4\frac{7}{9}$

15. $\frac{2}{3} + \frac{1}{2} + \frac{1}{4}$

16. $\frac{7}{8} - \frac{1}{4}$

17. $2\frac{1}{4} + 4\frac{4}{5} + 8\frac{3}{10}$

18. $18\frac{1}{8} + 5\frac{5}{6}$

19. $7\frac{5}{6} - 3\frac{5}{12}$

20. $13\frac{1}{4} - 6\frac{5}{8}$

Part 3   Applications

21. Deirdre hiked $\frac{5}{8}$ miles on one trail. Then she hiked on another trail. In all, she hiked $\frac{7}{8}$ miles. Write and solve an algebraic equation to find out how far Deirdre hiked.

22. Challenge Comics take up half of Ben's bookshelf. Mysteries fill up $\frac{1}{3}$ as much space as comics. If the shelf is 6 feet long, how much space remains?

ENRICHMENT
Egyptian Fractions

With one exception, every fraction the ancient Egyptians used was a unit fraction. Its numerator was 1. The only fraction the Egyptians used that was not a unit fraction was $\frac{2}{3}$. To represent other fractions, the Egyptians combined unit fractions.

This is how the fraction $\frac{3}{8}$ was formed: $\frac{3}{8} = \frac{1}{4} + \frac{1}{8}$

The Egyptians always used the least possible number of fractions to find sums.

1. Which would the Egyptians use for $\frac{5}{8}$?

   a. $\frac{1}{8} + \frac{1}{8} + \frac{1}{8} + \frac{1}{4}$ b. $\frac{1}{8} + \frac{1}{2}$

2. Suggest a possible reason for the Egyptians using $\frac{2}{3}$ when all of the other fractions were unit fractions.

3. How would Egyptians form $\frac{5}{6}$?

Use the Egyptian fraction system to form each of the following fractions.

4. $\frac{1}{2}$

5. $\frac{3}{4}$

6. $\frac{5}{8}$

7. $\frac{5}{9}$

8. $\frac{4}{5}$

9. $\frac{3}{10}$

10. $\frac{7}{8}$

11. $\frac{7}{12}$

12. $\frac{11}{15}$

The Egyptians also used pictures to represent numbers. They wrote a staff | for 1 and a heel ∩ for 10. To write a numerator of a unit fraction, they used this picture: ⬭

To write the fractions $\frac{1}{5}$ and $\frac{1}{12}$, the Egyptians used: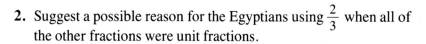

Write each of the following fractions in Egyptian symbols.

13. $\frac{1}{6}$ 14. $\frac{1}{10}$ 15. $\frac{1}{30}$ 16. $\frac{1}{25}$ 17. $\frac{1}{42}$ 18. $\frac{1}{55}$

CUMULATIVE REVIEW

1. Choose a calculation method and solve: $40 \times 5{,}000$.
   - A. 2,000,000
   - B. 20,000
   - C. 2,000
   - D. 200,000

2. Use compatible numbers to estimate the quotient: $36.902 \div 4.3$.
   - A. 80
   - B. 9
   - C. 10
   - D. 7

3. Write $\dfrac{13}{5}$ as a mixed number.
   - A. $2\dfrac{3}{5}$
   - B. $1\dfrac{3}{5}$
   - C. $2\dfrac{3}{13}$
   - D. $1\dfrac{5}{13}$

4. Which is one of the steps in the procedure for making a line graph?
   - A. plot points
   - B. draw the bars
   - C. choose symbols for the data
   - D. color parts to show the data

5. What is the mode for this set of numbers: 42, 65, 42, 18, 65, 42?
   - A. 47
   - B. 65
   - C. 18
   - D. 42

6. Write the word name for $\dfrac{5}{6}$.
   - A. six fifths
   - B. five sixths
   - C. one sixth
   - D. five elevenths

7. Find the quotient: $29{,}666 \div 7$.
   - A. 4,238
   - B. 4,138
   - C. 5,138
   - D. 5,238

8. Which is equivalent to $\dfrac{3}{8}$?
   - A. $\dfrac{8}{24}$
   - B. $\dfrac{6}{11}$
   - C. $\dfrac{8}{3}$
   - D. $\dfrac{9}{24}$

9. Which is the GCF for 12 and 27?
   - A. 9
   - B. 3
   - C. 27
   - D. 12

10. Which is in lowest terms?
    - A. $\dfrac{5}{40}$
    - B. $\dfrac{4}{18}$
    - C. $\dfrac{3}{21}$
    - D. $\dfrac{25}{36}$

11. Which is the LCD for the set: $\dfrac{1}{2}, \dfrac{3}{5}, \dfrac{3}{4}$?
    - A. 10
    - B. 5
    - C. 20
    - D. 40

12. Carlos wrote a set of 3 fractions in correct order from least to greatest. Which set is it?
    - A. $\dfrac{1}{4}, \dfrac{3}{8}, \dfrac{1}{8}$
    - B. $\dfrac{11}{12}, \dfrac{5}{58}, \dfrac{1}{4}$
    - C. $\dfrac{2}{3}, \dfrac{1}{6}, \dfrac{2}{9}$
    - D. $\dfrac{5}{11}, \dfrac{5}{9}, \dfrac{5}{6}$

13. Felix divided $4.23 evenly among 3 of his friends. How much did each receive?
    - A. $1.07
    - B. $12.69
    - C. $1.21
    - D. $1.41

14. The numbers along the bottom of a bar graph with horizontal bars are called the
    - A. bar numbers
    - B. scale
    - C. title
    - D. range

8

MULTIPLICATION AND DIVISION: FRACTIONS AND MIXED NUMBERS

MATH AND LANGUAGE ARTS

DATA BANK

Use the Language Arts Data Bank on pages 479 and 480 to answer the questions.

1 Use the research figures estimating the number of commercials seen by the average child in this country. How many commercials might a typical child see in one week? In one day?

2 The frames in a storyboard show each picture and dialogue for TV programs and advertisements (commercials). What part of the ad shown in the storyboard would be finished after the third frame? After the eighth frame?

3 How many frames would you need to add to the storyboard to expand the commercial to 45 seconds? To one minute?

4 **Using Critical Thinking**
Present a plan for dividing 5 minutes of commercial time into a number of advertisements of different lengths. Use the two most common lengths and any others you want. What did you consider in planning?

Mental Math
Fraction of a Number

EXPLORE Study the Graph

Wes is making a graph. He wants to divide
the bottom scale of his graph into fifths.
There are 20 spaces, so he needs to know
how many spaces there would be in each of
5 equal parts.

TALK ABOUT IT

1. How many spaces do you think Wes will
   choose for each fifth? Explain your answer.
2. Think about sharing 20 things equally among
   5 groups. Tell what operation you would use.
3. Use the graph to explain this statement: To
   find $\frac{1}{5}$ of 20, divide 20 by 5.

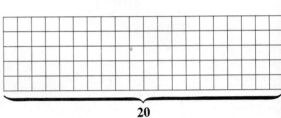

20

- To find a fractional part of a number, you can divide
  by the denominator and multiply by the numerator.

Other Examples

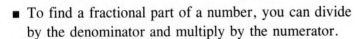

A

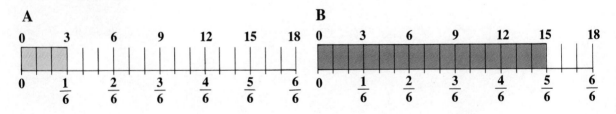

$\frac{1}{6}$ of 18 is 3, or $\frac{1}{6} \times 18 = 3$

B

$\frac{5}{6}$ of 18 is 15, or $\frac{5}{6} \times 18 = 15$

TRY IT OUT

Use mental math to find each answer.

1. $\frac{1}{2}$ of 12   2. $\frac{2}{3}$ of 12   3. $\frac{3}{5}$ of 15   4. $\frac{1}{8}$ of 16

5. $\frac{3}{8} \times 16$ 6. $\frac{1}{6} \times 24$ 7. $\frac{5}{6} \times 24$ 8. $\frac{7}{8} \times 24$

Use mental math to find each answer.

1. $\frac{1}{2} \times 20$ **2.** $\frac{3}{4} \cdot 36$ **3.** $\frac{1}{3}$ of 12   **4.** $\frac{2}{3} \times 9$

5. $\frac{1}{8} \times 32$ **6.** $\frac{3}{8}$ of 32   **7.** $\frac{1}{10} \times 40$ **8.** $\frac{2}{5} \times 25$

9. $\frac{5}{6} \times 30$ **10.** $\frac{4}{5} \times 40$ **11.** $\frac{1}{8} \cdot 24$ **12.** $\frac{5}{8} \cdot 40$

13. $\frac{2}{9}$ of 18   **14.** $\frac{9}{10}$ of 50   **15.** $\frac{1}{3} \times 27$ **16.** $\frac{7}{10} \cdot 100$

17.

1 hour = 60 minutes

$\frac{1}{2}$ of an hour = ▥ minutes

18.

1 dozen = 12

$\frac{3}{4}$ of a dozen = ▥

19.

1 foot = 12 inches

$\frac{2}{3}$ of a foot is ▥ inches.

APPLY

MATH REASONING

Which is greater? Tell how you know without finding the actual answer.

20. $\frac{1}{3}$ of 405 or $\frac{1}{5}$ of 405?   **21.** $\frac{1}{8}$ of 1,296 or $\frac{1}{6}$ of 1,296?   **22.** $\frac{1}{10}$ of 1,760 or $\frac{1}{2}$ of 1,760?

PROBLEM SOLVING

23. Shauna's graph has 24 spaces along the bottom. She divides it into eighths. How many spaces will there be in 3 of the 8 parts?

24. Clayton is making a large display graph that is 1 yard along the bottom. He wants to divide it into ninths. How many inches will there be in each of the equal parts?

▶ **ESTIMATION**

You can estimate the fractional part of certain numbers by choosing a compatible number. For example, $\frac{1}{3}$ of 25 is about $\frac{1}{3}$ of 24. So the answer is about 8. Estimate each answer.

25. $\frac{1}{5}$ of 16   **26.** $\frac{1}{4}$ of 13   **27.** $\frac{1}{3}$ of 20   **28.** $\frac{1}{6}$ of 19   **29.** $\frac{1}{4}$ of 27

More Practice, page 509, set D

Multiplying Fractions
Making the Connection

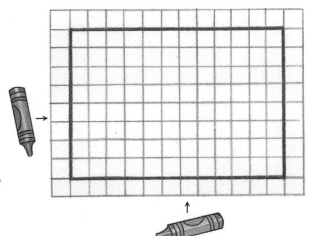

EXPLORE Use Fraction Models

Work in groups.

- Make an 8 by 12 rectangle on graph paper. Decide who will use a red crayon, who will use a blue one, and who will record the results.
- Color some but not all the rows of the rectangle red. Then write the fractional part of the rectangle that was colored red.
- Color some but not all of the columns blue. Write the fractional part of the rectangle that was colored blue.
- As a group, decide what fractional part is purple. (Blue and red make purple.) Write the fraction.
- Try this several times. Be sure to record your results.

Color some rows (→) red.
Color some columns (↑) blue.

TALK ABOUT IT

1. Each row is what fractional part of the rectangle?
2. Each column is what fractional part of the rectangle?
3. Is the fraction for the purple part ever greater than 1? Tell why you think your answer is true.

You have colored overlapping parts of a rectangle and then figured out what part was colored with both colors. Now you will see how to record what you have done. This procedure will help you understand how to find a fractional part of a fraction or a product such as $\frac{2}{5} \times \frac{3}{4}$.

What You Do   **What You Record**

1. Outline a rectangle with sides equal to the denominators of the fractions.

   THINK: 4 × 5

2. Think about how many small squares there are in the rectangle. Color $\frac{3}{4}$ of them blue.

   20 small squares.
   $\frac{3}{4}$ of 20 is 15.
   15 blue squares

3. Think about how many small squares are blue. Color $\frac{2}{5}$ of the $\frac{3}{4}$ with red.

   15 blue squares.
   $\frac{2}{5}$ of 15 is 6.

   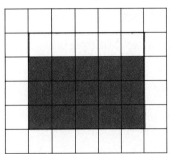

   $\dfrac{2}{5} \times \dfrac{3}{4}$

4. Think about how many small squares turned out purple. Decide what fraction of the total is purple.

   6 squares are purple. So 6 out of 20 squares are purple. You can write the fraction as $\frac{6}{20}$.

   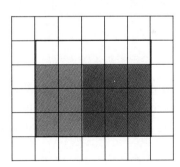

   $\dfrac{2}{5} \times \dfrac{3}{4} = \dfrac{6}{20}$

TRY IT OUT

Use graph paper and coloring to find each of these products.
Can you think of a rule that you could use to multiply fractions?

1. $\frac{1}{3} \times \frac{1}{4}$ 2. $\frac{2}{3} \times \frac{3}{4}$ 3. $\frac{2}{5} \times \frac{2}{3}$ 4. $\frac{3}{4} \times \frac{4}{5}$ 5. $\frac{1}{2} \times \frac{5}{8}$

Multiplying Fractions

EXPLORE **Analyze the Process**

The Comic Kids Show fills $\frac{5}{6}$ of a television hour. The rest of the hour is advertisements. A clown act uses $\frac{2}{3}$ of the Comic Kids Show. How much of the hour is devoted to the clown act

To answer the question, you multiply because you want to find a fractional part of a fraction. Below are two methods.

Reducing **after** Multiplying

Multiply the numerators. Multiply the denominators.	Reduce if possible.
$\frac{2}{3} \times \frac{5}{6} = \frac{10}{18}$	$\frac{2}{3} \times \frac{5}{6} = \frac{10}{18} = \frac{5}{9}$

Reducing **before** Multiplying

Reduce. Divide a numerator and a denominator by the same number.	Multiply the numerators. Multiply the denominators.
$\overset{1}{\cancel{2}} \times \frac{5}{\cancel{6}} \quad \overset{2 \div 2}{\underset{6 \div 2}{}}$	$\frac{\overset{1}{\cancel{2}}}{3} \times \frac{5}{\underset{3}{\cancel{6}}} = \frac{5}{9}$

TALK ABOUT IT

1. Which method do you like better? Why?
2. Would you have estimated more than or less than 1 for the product?
3. Use a complete sentence to give a reasonable answer to the story problem.

Other Examples

> Two numbers whose product is 1 are **reciprocals** of each other.

A $\frac{\overset{1}{\cancel{2}}}{3}$ of $\frac{7}{\underset{2}{\cancel{4}}} = \frac{7}{6} = 1\frac{1}{6}$ **B** $12 \cdot \frac{2}{3} = \frac{\overset{4}{\cancel{12}}}{1} \cdot \frac{2}{\underset{1}{\cancel{3}}} = \frac{8}{1} = 8$ **C** $\frac{3}{5} \times \frac{5}{3} = \frac{15}{15} = 1$

Multiply. Use either method.

1. $\frac{3}{4} \times \frac{6}{15}$ 2. $\frac{5}{8} \times \frac{8}{5}$ 3. $8 \times \frac{5}{12}$ 4. $\frac{7}{8} \cdot \frac{8}{7}$ 5. $\frac{3}{5}$ of $\frac{15}{18}$

Multiply. Reduce to lowest terms.

1. $\frac{2}{5} \times \frac{1}{6}$ **2.** $\frac{1}{2}$ of $\frac{1}{4}$ **3.** $\frac{3}{4} \times \frac{5}{8}$ **4.** $\frac{2}{3} \times 9$

5. $\frac{5}{8} \times \frac{2}{3}$ **6.** $\frac{2}{3} \times 36$ **7.** $\frac{2}{3} \times \frac{3}{5}$ **8.** $\frac{7}{4} \cdot \frac{3}{2}$

9. $\frac{4}{5} \times \frac{5}{4}$ **10.** $\frac{3}{4} \times \frac{1}{3}$ **11.** $4 \times \frac{3}{4}$ **12.** $\frac{3}{5} \times \frac{7}{8}$

13. $\frac{3}{4} \times 24$ **14.** $\frac{3}{8} \cdot \frac{4}{9}$ **15.** $\frac{1}{6} \times \frac{6}{7}$ **16.** $\frac{4}{3} \cdot \frac{5}{2}$

17. $\frac{5}{6} \times \frac{3}{4}$ **18.** $\frac{7}{8}$ of 4 **19.** $\frac{5}{8}$ of 16 **20.** $\frac{5}{6} \cdot \frac{3}{10}$

Give the reciprocal of each number.

21. $\frac{2}{3}$ **22.** $\frac{1}{2}$ **23.** 3 **24.** $\frac{7}{5}$

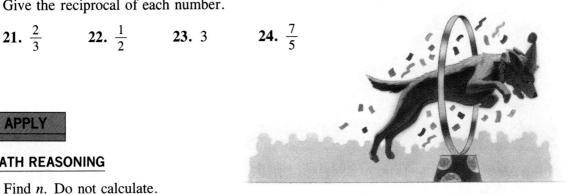

MATH REASONING

Find n. Do not calculate.

25. $\frac{2}{5} \times n = 1$ **26.** $\frac{7}{4} \times n = 1$ **27.** $3 \times n = 1$ **28.** $\frac{1}{8} \times n = 1$

PROBLEM SOLVING

29. The Scientific Mysteries program sells 12 minutes of program time to advertisers. The Mental Marvel game company bought $\frac{5}{6}$ of the ad time. How many minutes did the game company buy?

30. Language Arts Data Bank How many hours per year does the average household have its TV set on?

Find the mean to the nearest tenth, the median, and the mode.

31. 101, 114, 98, 100, 114 **32.** 10, 7, 7, 6, 8, 2, 7, 10, 1, 2

Solve. Use mental math.

33. $a + 7 = 17$ **34.** $b + \frac{1}{8} = \frac{5}{8}$ **35.** $r - 8 = 12$ **36.** $5a = 25$

More Practice, page 510, set A

223

Problem Solving
Look for a Pattern

UNDERSTAND
ANALYZE DATA
PLAN
ESTIMATE
SOLVE
EXAMINE

LEARN ABOUT IT

To solve this problem, it helps to make a table from the given information first. Then you can use the problem-solving strategy called **Look for a Pattern.**

On the show "Trivia Fortunes" correct answers win money. If you answer the first question, you win only $1. Your answer to the second question wins $2, the third wins $4, the fourth $8, and so on. Which question will have a payoff of over $10,000?

> I'll start by making a table from the given information.

Question number	1	2	3	4
Amount of money	$1	$2	$4	$8

> Then, I'll look for a pattern. Aha! The amount of money doubles each time the next question is answered.

Question number	1	2	3	4	5	6	7	8	9	10	11	12	13	14	15
Amount of money	$1	$2	$4	$8	$16	$32	$64	$128	$256	$512	$1,024	$2,048	$4,096	$8,192	$16,384

Question 15 will have a payoff of over $10,000.

TRY IT OUT

Another game show also pays for correct answers. If you answer the first question, you win $10. Your answer to the second question wins $13, the third wins $16, the fourth $19, and so on. How much would you get for answering the 8th question correctly?

1. How much do you get for answering the first question? The second question? The fifth question?
2. Copy and complete this table to solve the problem. Be sure to look for a pattern to help you.

Question number	1	2	3	4	5
Amount of money	$10	$13	$16	$19	?

Solve by first making a table. Then look for a pattern.

1. A public broadcasting radio station started a telephone campaign to get new subscribers. The first hour they got 2 new subscribers, the second hour they got 6, and the third hour they got 18. At this rate, how many new subscribers will they get in the eighth hour?

MIXED PRACTICE

Solve. Choose a strategy from the list or use another strategy that you know.

3. A survey was given to 120 students. The graph shows the fraction of sixth graders watching TV for different time periods during one week. How many of them watch TV for 10–19 hours a week?

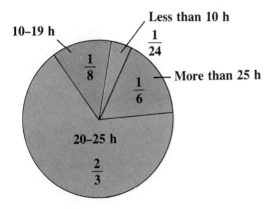

10–19 h

Less than 10 h
$\frac{1}{24}$

$\frac{1}{8}$

More than 25 h
$\frac{1}{6}$

20–25 h
$\frac{2}{3}$

4. Use the graph to predict how many sixth graders in a group of 150 watch for 20 hours or more each week.

5. The magazine *TV Today* costs $0.45 a week. Subscriptions cost $19.75 for 1 year and $35.50 for 2 years. Would you save more than or less than $8 each year if you buy a 1-year subscription instead of buying the magazine each week?

2. Berta participated in a TV-watching contest. She watched TV for 1 hour the first day and 2 more hours each day than the day before. How many hours did she watch on the twelfth day?

Some Strategies	
Act Out	Solve a Simpler
Use Objects	Problem
Choose an Operation	Make an Organized
Draw a Picture	List
Guess and Check	Work Backward
Make a Table	Look for a Pattern

6. Jason wants to learn as many Beatles songs as he can. He already knows 2 songs. After 1 week he knew 3 songs, at the end of 2 weeks he knew 5 songs, and after 3 weeks he knew 8. At this rate, how many songs will he know at the end of 12 weeks?

7. KTOP radio is giving 2 free concert tickets to the first caller to solve this problem: "We gave away 8 tickets the first day, twice as many the second day, and 4 more the third day than the second day. We have 6 tickets left. How many tickets did we have when we started?" What would your answer be when you call?

More Practice, page 525, set C

225

Estimating Mixed-Number Products by Rounding

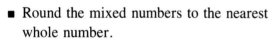

LEARN ABOUT IT

EXPLORE **Understand the Situation**

Cal wants to carpet a hallway that is $18\frac{11}{12}$ feet long and $4\frac{1}{6}$ feet wide. Estimate the area.

TALK ABOUT IT

1. Is $18\frac{11}{12}$ closer to 18 or to 19? Tell how you know.
2. Is $4\frac{1}{6}$ closer to 4 or 5? Why?
3. What operation do you use to find area? Explain.

Here is how you can estimate the product for $18\frac{11}{12} \times 4\frac{1}{6}$.

- Round the mixed numbers to the nearest whole number.

$$19 \times 4$$

- Round again if necessary.

$$20 \times 4 = 80$$

The area is about 80 square feet.

PRACTICE

Estimate each product by rounding.

1. $9\frac{5}{6} \times 3\frac{1}{8}$
2. $7\frac{3}{4} \times 2\frac{7}{8}$
3. $8\frac{1}{10} \times 3\frac{7}{8}$

4. $5\frac{1}{4} \times 9\frac{1}{2}$
5. $7\frac{9}{10} \cdot 3\frac{1}{4}$
6. $29\frac{1}{4} \times 3\frac{5}{6}$

7. $26\frac{8}{9} \cdot 3\frac{1}{3}$
8. $5\frac{6}{7} \times 31\frac{1}{4}$
9. $6\frac{11}{12} \times 31\frac{1}{12}$

10. $26\frac{8}{9} \times 6\frac{1}{6}$
11. $41\frac{5}{8} \times 3\frac{3}{4}$
12. $6\frac{7}{8} \cdot 36\frac{9}{10}$

13. $7\frac{1}{2} \cdot 81\frac{1}{4}$
14. $3\frac{9}{10} \times 49\frac{9}{10}$
15. $61\frac{1}{4} \times 8\frac{1}{10}$

Estimate each area by rounding.

16. $27\frac{3}{4}$ inches by $14\frac{3}{16}$ inches 17. $39\frac{1}{6}$ feet by $13\frac{7}{12}$ feet 18. $18\frac{1}{2}$ yards by $24\frac{1}{3}$ yards

226

More Practice, page 510, set B

MIDCHAPTER REVIEW/QUIZ

Use mental math to find the fraction of the number.

1. $\frac{1}{3}$ of 12   **2.** $\frac{7}{10} \times 60$ **3.** $\frac{5}{6} \times 18$ **4.** $\frac{3}{8} \times 24$ **5.** $\frac{2}{9} \times 36$

Copy the rectangle. Finish by shading
or crossing out. Then solve the equation.

6. $\frac{1}{5} \times \frac{2}{3} = n$

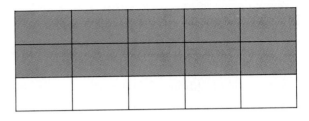

Multiply. Reduce to lowest terms.

7. $\frac{1}{3}$ of $\frac{1}{6}$ **8.** $20 \times \frac{5}{2}$ **9.** $\frac{2}{3} \times 6$ **10.** $\frac{5}{6} \times \frac{3}{4}$

11. $\frac{3}{5} \times \frac{5}{3}$ **12.** $\frac{3}{4} \cdot \frac{8}{15}$ **13.** $6 \times \frac{1}{6}$ **14.** $\frac{7}{8} \times 4$

15. $\frac{3}{10}$ of 15   **16.** $\frac{7}{8} \times \frac{8}{7}$ **17.** $\frac{3}{7} \cdot \frac{21}{28}$ **18.** $\frac{4}{9} \times \frac{4}{9}$

19. $\frac{13}{5} \times \frac{2}{5}$ **20.** $\frac{8}{3} \times \frac{15}{16}$ **21.** $\frac{5}{12} \times \frac{9}{10}$ **22.** $40 \cdot \frac{2}{5}$

Give the reciprocal of each number.

23. $\frac{3}{5}$ **24.** $\frac{1}{4}$ **25.** $\frac{2}{9}$ **26.** 3   **27.** $\frac{4}{3}$

PROBLEM SOLVING

28. Nami practiced violin for $\frac{3}{4}$ hour. How many minutes is that?

29. Devin measured his stride. In 3 steps he walks 2 meters.
About how far is it to Torren's house, 24 steps away?

30. Ariana uses the price list below for her babysitting charges.
How much will she charge for an 8-hour job? For an
$8\frac{1}{2}$-hour job?

up to 1 hour = $5.00
1 hour up to 2 hours = $7.50
2 hours up to 3 hours = $10.00

Multiplying Mixed Numbers

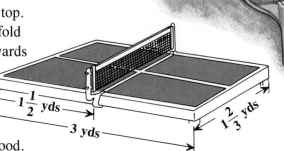

EXPLORE Analyze the Process

Crystal is buying plywood to make a table tennis top.
She is making the table in two pieces so she can fold
it in half for storage. What is the area in square yards
for each sheet of plywood Crystal needs?

To find the area of a sheet of plywood, you
need to multiply the length and the width.

Here's how to find the area for one sheet of plywood.

| Write the mixed numbers as improper fractions. | $1\frac{1}{2} \times 1\frac{2}{3} = \frac{3}{2} \times \frac{5}{3}$ | Multiply the fractions. | $\frac{1\cancel{3}}{2} \times \frac{5}{\cancel{3}_1} = \frac{5}{2} = 2\frac{1}{2}$ |

TALK ABOUT IT

1. Explain this statement: The first step changes the problem
   to one we already know how to do.
2. Tell how to get $2\frac{1}{2}$ from $\frac{5}{2}$.
3. How do you think you could have estimated the product?
4. Use a complete sentence to give a reasonable answer
   to the story problem.

Other Examples

A

$$6 \times 4\frac{3}{8} = \frac{\overset{3}{\cancel{6}}}{1} \times \frac{35}{\cancel{8}_4} = \frac{105}{4} = 26\frac{1}{4}$$

(6 ÷ 2) (8 ÷ 2)

B

(15 ÷ 5) (14 ÷ 2)

$$3\frac{3}{4} \times 2\frac{4}{5} = \frac{\overset{3}{\cancel{15}}}{\underset{2}{\cancel{4}}} \times \frac{\overset{7}{\cancel{14}}}{\underset{1}{\cancel{5}}} = \frac{21}{2} = 10\frac{1}{2}$$

(4 ÷ 2) (5 ÷ 5)

Multiply.

1. $3\frac{3}{4} \times 2\frac{2}{3}$

2. $2\frac{1}{5} \times 1\frac{1}{4}$

3. $9 \times 1\frac{2}{3}$

4. $\frac{4}{5} \times 3\frac{1}{8}$

Find the product in lowest terms.

1. $2\frac{2}{3} \times 1\frac{1}{4}$

2. $1\frac{3}{5} \times \frac{3}{5}$

3. $1\frac{1}{2} \times 2\frac{2}{3}$

4. $2\frac{1}{4} \times 5\frac{1}{3}$

5. $1\frac{3}{4} \times 1\frac{1}{2}$

6. $2\frac{2}{5} \cdot 4\frac{5}{6}$

7. $6 \times 3\frac{3}{4}$

8. $4\frac{5}{6} \times 3\frac{3}{4}$

9. $\frac{9}{10} \times 3\frac{1}{3}$

10. $2\frac{1}{4} \times 20$

11. $2\frac{3}{4} \cdot 1\frac{1}{10}$

12. $4\frac{1}{3} \times 5\frac{1}{2}$

13. $15 \cdot 4\frac{1}{6}$

14. $3\frac{1}{4} \times 2\frac{2}{3}$

15. $\frac{4}{5} \times 3\frac{3}{8}$

16. $\frac{3}{4} \times 16$

17. $15 \cdot 3\frac{1}{10}$

18. $4 \times 5\frac{3}{8}$

19. $3\frac{1}{5} \cdot 4\frac{2}{3}$

20. $3\frac{1}{4} \cdot 3\frac{1}{4}$

21. Find the product of $5\frac{1}{3}$ and $3\frac{3}{4}$.

22. What is the product when $4\frac{1}{3}$ is multiplied by 9?

23. Multiply $6\frac{1}{4}$ by $2\frac{2}{5}$.

MATH REASONING

Do not multiply. Just tell if the product is more than or less than 24.

24. $4\frac{1}{8} \times 6\frac{1}{4}$

25. $3\frac{9}{10} \times 6$

26. $8 \times 3\frac{1}{6}$

27. $1\frac{9}{10} \times 11\frac{7}{8}$

PROBLEM SOLVING

28. **Extra Data** The lumber yard has sheets of plywood that are $3\frac{3}{4}$ ft wide. Paula bought one sheet that was $5\frac{1}{2}$ ft long and another that was $4\frac{1}{5}$ ft long. What was the area of the second sheet?

29. The price was $27.75 for the large piece of plywood and $19.95 for the small piece. Paula was given a discount of $2.00 for buying 2 pieces. The tax was $2.39. After her purchase, Paula had $17.49. How much did she have before her purchase?

▶ **COMMUNICATION   Writing to Learn Math**

30. Complete this sentence:
    If the product of two different numbers is 1, then one of the numbers is greater than 1 and the other number is _____.

Dividing Fractions Using Models

EXPLORE Study the Fraction Scale

Understanding whole-number division will help you see what it means to divide by a fraction. For example, $24 \div 4$ can mean, "How many 4s are in 24?" In the same way, $3 \div \frac{1}{2}$ can mean "How many $\frac{1}{2}$s are in 3?"

Notice that the number scale below is divided into sixteenths. Think about the segments at the right to help you count on the scale. You can use the scale and counting to help you divide by a fraction. For example, you can count segments to find out how many $\frac{1}{4}$s are in $\frac{3}{2}$, or $\frac{3}{2} \div \frac{1}{4}$.

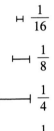

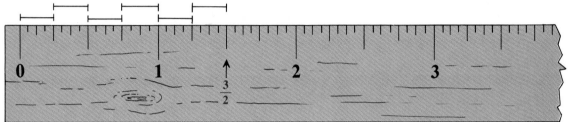

TALK ABOUT IT

1. How many $\frac{1}{4}$s are in $\frac{3}{2}$? What is $\frac{3}{2} \div \frac{1}{4}$?
2. Explain how to use the number scale to find $3 \div \frac{1}{2}$.

There are many models that help you understand dividing by a fraction.

How many $\frac{1}{2}$s are in 3?

$3 \div \frac{1}{2} = 6$

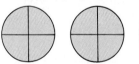

How many $\frac{1}{4}$s are in $\frac{5}{2}$?

$\frac{5}{2} \div \frac{1}{4} = 10$

Use the pictures to help you find each quotient.

1.

How many $\frac{1}{6}$s are in $\frac{2}{3}$?

$\frac{2}{3} \div \frac{1}{6}$

2.

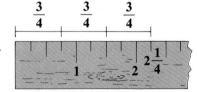

How many $\frac{3}{4}$s are in $2\frac{1}{4}$?

$2\frac{1}{4} \div \frac{3}{4}$

230

Use the number scale on the opposite page to find each quotient.

1. $2 \div \frac{1}{4}$ **2.** $\frac{3}{2} \div \frac{1}{2}$ **3.** $\frac{3}{2} \div \frac{1}{8}$ **4.** $2\frac{1}{2} \div \frac{1}{4}$ **5.** $\frac{7}{4} \div \frac{1}{8}$

Use the pictures to help you find each quotient.

6.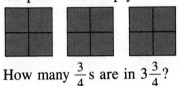

How many $\frac{3}{4}$s are in $3\frac{3}{4}$?

$3\frac{3}{4} \div \frac{3}{4}$

7.

How many $\frac{1}{8}$s are in $\frac{3}{4}$?

$\frac{3}{4} \div \frac{1}{8}$

8.

How many $\frac{1}{4}$s are in 2?

$2 \div \frac{1}{4}$

9.

How many $\frac{1}{6}$s are in $\frac{4}{3}$?

$\frac{4}{3} \div \frac{1}{6}$

APPLY

MATH REASONING

Give the number for n.

10. Since $1 \div \frac{1}{4} = 4$, we know that $7 \div \frac{1}{4} = n$.

11. Since $1 \div \frac{1}{10} = 10$, we know that $10 \div \frac{1}{10} = n$.

PROBLEM SOLVING

12. Write Your Own Problem Write a division question about this data. Nicole invited some friends over to watch a television entertainment special. She bought 5 pizzas for her party. She had them cut into eighths.

▶ **USING CRITICAL THINKING** Discover a Relationship

13. Suppose you divide a number n by a fraction between 0 and 1. Will the answer always be less than n, sometimes less than n, or never less than n? Use your answers to exercises 1–9 to help you make a decision.

Dividing Fractions

LEARN ABOUT IT

EXPLORE Analyze the Process

A director has scheduled 15 minutes of a special animal program for a roving reporter's features about the zoo. How many $\frac{3}{4}$-minute zoo features can be shown?

Since we want to find the number of $\frac{3}{4}$-minute segments in 15 minutes, we divide 15 by $\frac{3}{4}$.

Here is **how** to divide by a fraction.

Multiply the dividend by the reciprocal of the divisor.

$$15 \div \frac{3}{4} = 15 \times \frac{4}{3} = 20$$

reciprocals

Here is **why** it works.

Multiply both numbers by $\frac{4}{3}$.

$$15 \div \frac{3}{4} = (15 \times \frac{4}{3}) \div (\frac{3}{4} \times \frac{4}{3})$$

$$= (15 \times \frac{4}{3}) \div (\quad 1 \quad) = 15 \times \frac{4}{3}$$

TALK ABOUT IT

1. What is the product of $\frac{3}{4} \times \frac{4}{3}$?
2. What is the quotient when you divide a number by 1?
3. Use a complete sentence to give a reasonable answer to the story problem.

Other Examples

A $\frac{3}{5} \div \frac{2}{3} = \frac{3}{5} \times \frac{3}{2} = \frac{9}{10}$ **B** $6 \div \frac{3}{4} = \frac{6}{1} \times \frac{4}{3} = 8$ **C** $6 \div 9 = \frac{6}{1} \times \frac{1}{9} = \frac{2}{3}$

Check: $\frac{9}{10} \times \frac{2}{3} = \frac{18}{30} = \frac{3}{5}$

TRY IT OUT

Find the quotients. Check by multiplying.

1. $\frac{2}{3} \div \frac{1}{4}$ 2. $\frac{1}{2} \div \frac{2}{5}$ 3. $\frac{3}{4} \div \frac{1}{10}$ 4. $4 \div \frac{3}{8}$ 5. $3 \div 5$

Find the quotients. Check by multiplying.

1. $\frac{1}{2} \div \frac{4}{5}$ **2.** $\frac{3}{4} \div \frac{3}{5}$ **3.** $\frac{2}{3} \div \frac{3}{4}$ **4.** $\frac{1}{2} \div \frac{1}{4}$

5. $\frac{7}{8} \div \frac{7}{8}$ **6.** $5 \div \frac{2}{5}$ **7.** $\frac{5}{6} \div 10$ **8.** $3 \div 8$

9. $\frac{1}{2} \div \frac{5}{8}$ **10.** $\frac{9}{14} \div \frac{3}{7}$ **11.** $\frac{7}{8} \div \frac{3}{4}$ **12.** $\frac{1}{3} \div \frac{2}{3}$

13. $\frac{3}{10} \div \frac{3}{4}$ **14.** $\frac{4}{5} \div \frac{2}{3}$ **15.** $\frac{1}{2} \div \frac{7}{10}$ **16.** $7 \div \frac{2}{3}$

17. $\frac{9}{10} \div 3$ **18.** $4 \div 12$ **19.** $\frac{1}{10} \div \frac{3}{10}$ **20.** $\frac{3}{5} \div \frac{2}{3}$

21. Divide $\frac{5}{8}$ by $\frac{1}{3}$.   **22.** Divide 8 by $\frac{2}{5}$.   **23.** Divide $\frac{5}{12}$ by $\frac{1}{6}$.

MATH REASONING

Do not divide. Just tell if each quotient is more than or less than 8.

24. $8 \div \frac{4}{5}$ **25.** $8 \div \frac{4}{3}$ **26.** $8 \div \frac{8}{9}$ **27.** $8 \div \frac{8}{7}$

PROBLEM SOLVING

28. One TV station provides 18 free minutes each week for public service messages. How many $\frac{3}{4}$-minute messages can be broadcast in this time?

29. Language Arts Data Bank What is the total amount that the 2 largest advertisers spent on television commercials in 1988?

DATA BANK

MIXED REVIEW

Find the answers. Round decimal answers to the nearest thousandth.

30. $18\frac{3}{10} + 4\frac{1}{5}$ **31.** $0.04 \div 1.4$ **32.** $33\frac{3}{4} - 15\frac{1}{8}$

33. $8,090 \times 76$ **34.** $\frac{7}{12} + \frac{3}{8}$ **35.** 71.4×1.06

Write a decimal for each fraction. Round to the nearest thousandth.

36. $\frac{1}{4}$ **37.** $\frac{2}{3}$ **38.** $\frac{7}{8}$ **39.** $\frac{7}{10}$ **40.** $\frac{4}{7}$

Dividing Mixed Numbers

LEARN ABOUT IT

EXPLORE Analyze the Process

The signs show some distances along hiking trails at the state park. Mario walks at an average speed of $3\frac{1}{2}$ miles per hour. How long will it take him to walk Skyline trail?

To solve the problem, you will need to divide to find out how many sets of $3\frac{1}{2}$ miles are in $11\frac{9}{10}$ miles. Here's how to find the answer.

Write the numbers or whole numbers as improper fractions. $\quad 11\frac{9}{10} \div 3\frac{1}{2} = \frac{119}{10} \div \frac{7}{2}$	Divide the fractions. $\quad \frac{\overset{17}{\cancel{119}}}{\underset{5}{\cancel{10}}} \times \frac{\overset{1}{\cancel{2}}}{\cancel{7}} = \frac{17}{5} = 3\frac{2}{5}$

TALK ABOUT IT

1. Tell why you multiply $\frac{119}{10}$ by $\frac{2}{7}$ when you are dividing $\frac{119}{10}$ by $\frac{7}{2}$.
2. What did you divide the numerator 119 by to get 17? What denominator was divided by this same number?
3. How would you have estimated the answer?
4. Use a complete sentence to give a reasonable answer to the story problem.

Other Examples

A $\quad 2\frac{2}{3} \div \frac{3}{4} = \frac{8}{3} \div \frac{3}{4} = \frac{8}{3} \times \frac{4}{3} = \frac{32}{9} = 3\frac{5}{9}$

B $\quad 8 \div 3\frac{1}{5} = \frac{8}{1} \div \frac{16}{5} = \frac{\overset{1}{\cancel{8}}}{1} \times \frac{5}{\underset{2}{\cancel{16}}} = \frac{5}{2} = 2\frac{1}{2}$

TRY IT OUT

1. $2\frac{1}{2} \div 1\frac{1}{3}$ 2. $8 \div 3\frac{1}{5}$ 3. $4\frac{7}{8} \div 3$ 4. $3\frac{3}{5} \div 1\frac{1}{2}$ 5. $\frac{5}{12} \div 4\frac{3}{8}$

Divide and check.

1. $1\frac{3}{8} \div 4\frac{1}{3}$ 2. $3\frac{2}{3} \div 2$ 3. $5\frac{1}{4} \div 2\frac{1}{2}$ 4. $4 \div 1\frac{1}{3}$

5. $3\frac{1}{2} \div 2\frac{1}{3}$ 6. $8 \div 3\frac{1}{5}$ 7. $8\frac{1}{3} \div 1\frac{1}{6}$ 8. $7 \div 1\frac{1}{7}$

9. $\frac{1}{6} \div 3\frac{1}{2}$ 10. $\frac{5}{6} \div 1\frac{2}{3}$ 11. $2\frac{2}{3} \div 1\frac{1}{4}$ 12. $10 \div 1\frac{1}{4}$

13. $4\frac{3}{5} \div 2\frac{1}{5}$ 14. $8 \div 3\frac{1}{4}$ 15. $3\frac{3}{8} \div 2\frac{1}{4}$ 16. $2\frac{3}{8} \div 4$

17. $6\frac{1}{4} \div 1\frac{1}{8}$ 18. $2\frac{1}{10} \div 1\frac{1}{5}$

19. $4\frac{1}{2} \div 2\frac{7}{10}$ 20. $7\frac{1}{4} \div 3$

MATH REASONING

Do not divide. Just tell which quotient is greater.

21. $5\frac{1}{2} \div \frac{1}{4}$
     or
$5\frac{1}{2} \div 4$

22. $3\frac{7}{8} \div 2$
     or
$3\frac{7}{8} \div \frac{1}{2}$

23. $\frac{7}{8} \div \frac{1}{4}$
     or
$\frac{7}{8} \div 4$

24. $\frac{9}{10} \div \frac{3}{4}$
     or
$\frac{9}{10} \div \frac{4}{3}$

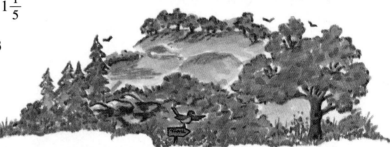

PROBLEM SOLVING

25. Ricardo's walking speed averages $2\frac{1}{3}$ miles per hour. How long would it take Ricardo to walk the Skyline Trail?

26. Suppose both Ricardo and Mario walk to Happy Hollow and back. If they each maintain their average walking speed, how much longer would it take Ricardo than Mario?

▶ **ESTIMATION**

Round each mixed number to the nearest whole number and estimate the quotient.

27. $6\frac{1}{10} \div 1\frac{7}{8} \rightarrow$ (6 ÷ 2) → ▦   28. $8\frac{9}{10} \div 2\frac{5}{6} \rightarrow$ (9 ÷ 3) ▦

29. $12\frac{1}{4} \div 3\frac{9}{10}$ 30. $24 \div 7\frac{8}{9}$ 31. $4\frac{11}{12} \div 5\frac{1}{8}$ 32. $4\frac{4}{10} \div 1\frac{9}{10}$

33. $1\frac{15}{16} \div \frac{7}{8}$ 34. $4\frac{3}{4} \div \frac{7}{8}$ 35. $6\frac{1}{5} \div 2\frac{1}{10}$ 36. $35\frac{3}{4} \div 8\frac{7}{8}$

More Practice, page 510, set E

Using a Calculator to Find Repeating Decimals

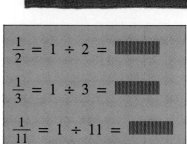

You can find a decimal for a fraction by dividing the numerator by the denominator. In this lesson you will use your calculator to find a **repeating decimal** for a fraction. You will also use it to find **terminating decimals.**

EXPLORE   Discover a Pattern

Use your calculator to find a decimal for each fraction in the table. Do not round. Use all the digits shown on your calculator.

$$\frac{1}{2} = 1 \div 2 = $$

$$\frac{1}{3} = 1 \div 3 = $$

$$\frac{1}{11} = 1 \div 11 = $$

TALK ABOUT IT

1. Which of the decimals show digits repeating? These decimals are repeating decimals.
2. The decimal for $\frac{1}{2}$ is a terminating decimal. Tell how it is different from the others.
3. Do you think that the repeating pattern for the last 2 decimals in the chart would continue beyond the digits shown on your calculator? Try dividing without the calculator and see what happens.

Below are some examples of repeating decimals. The three dots show that the repeating pattern continues. You can also use a bar to show that the digits under it continue to repeat. Check these on your calculator.

1 digit repeats	**2 digits repeat**	**3 digits repeat**
$\frac{1}{12} = 0.08333\ldots$	$\frac{5}{11} = 0.454545\ldots$	$\frac{173}{333} = 0.519519\ldots$
$\frac{1}{12} = 0.08\overline{3}$	$\frac{5}{11} = 0.\overline{45}$	$\frac{173}{333} = 0.\overline{519}$

Use your calculator to find the repeating decimal for each fraction. Give answers using the bar to show what digits repeat.

1. $\frac{7}{21}$
2. $\frac{1}{6}$
3. $\frac{17}{33}$
4. $\frac{57}{111}$
5. $\frac{34}{51}$
6. $\frac{5}{27}$

Use your calculator to find the repeating decimal for each fraction.
Give your answer using the bar to show what digits repeat.

1. $\frac{4}{12}$ **2.** $\frac{7}{9}$ **3.** $\frac{6}{11}$ **4.** $\frac{67}{99}$

5. $\frac{7}{33}$ **6.** $\frac{16}{24}$ **7.** $\frac{456}{999}$ **8.** $\frac{123}{198}$

9. $\frac{23}{66}$ **10.** $\frac{76}{37}$ **11.** $\frac{4760}{3333}$ **12.** $\frac{159}{333}$

13. Use your calculator to help you find 5 more fractions that can each be written as a repeating decimal.

14. Use your calculator to help you find 5 fractions that can be written as a terminating decimal.

MATH REASONING

15. The repeating decimal for $\frac{1}{3}$ is $0.333\ldots$ or $0.\overline{3}$. Give the repeating decimal for $\frac{2}{3}$ without using your calculator.

16. The terminating decimal for $\frac{4}{25}$ is 0.16. Give the terminating decimal for $\frac{8}{25}$ without using your calculator.

PROBLEM SOLVING

17. You can create decimals that do not repeat by developing a pattern. Try to find the pattern in this decimal:

$$0.112123123412345\ldots$$

Create your own decimal pattern so that the same digits do not repeat over and over.

▶ **MENTAL MATH**

Study the pattern.

$$\frac{1}{11} = 0.\overline{09} \qquad \frac{2}{11} = 0.\overline{18} \qquad \frac{3}{11} = 0.\overline{27}$$

Use the pattern to give repeating decimals for these fractions using mental math.

18. $\frac{4}{11}$ **19.** $\frac{5}{11}$ **20.** $\frac{6}{11}$ **21.** $\frac{7}{11}$ **22.** $\frac{8}{11}$ **23.** $\frac{9}{11}$

Problem Solving
Estimating the Answer

UNDERSTAND
ANALYZE DATA
PLAN
ESTIMATE
SOLVE
EXAMINE

LEARN ABOUT IT

Before you solve a problem, it is important to decide what would be a reasonable answer. You can begin by estimating the answer.

The table shows advertising expenditures in billions of dollars for 3 years. How much more was spent on television than on radio in 1987?

	1987	1980	1970
Newspapers	$29.4	$14.8	$5.7
Magazines	5.6	3.1	1.3
Radio	7.2	3.7	1.3
Television	23.9	11.4	3.6

Before solving the problem, estimate the answer.

I'll round 23.9 up to 24. → I'll round 7.2 down to 7. → Then, I'll subtract to estimate the answer.

$23.9 \rightarrow 24$ $7.2 \rightarrow 7$ $24 - 7 = 17$

The answer to the problem should be close to $17 billion.

Now, I'll solve the problem. → I believe that $16.7 billion is a reasonable answer since it is close to $17 billion.

$23.9 - 7.2 = 16.7$

TRY IT OUT

Before solving each problem, estimate the answer. Then solve the problem and decide if your answer is reasonable.

1. Find how much more was spent on television advertising in 1987 than in 1970.

2. Business newspapers are another medium. In 1987, advertising expenditures in business papers were about $\frac{1}{3}$ of those on radio. How much was spent on advertising in business papers?

3. Find the total advertising expenditures for the four mediums in the chart for 1980.

4. In 1987, advertising expenditures for all mediums totaled $110 billion. How much of this was for mediums other than the four in the table?

Solve. Estimate your answer first.

1. Use the table on the left page to find the total advertising expenditures in the four mediums for 1970.

2. In 1988 a disc jockey broadcasted his show for $27\frac{1}{2}$ hours each week. About how many hours did he broadcast that year?

3. Martin watches an exercise program on TV each morning. On the first day he could only do 1 curl-up. On the second day he could do 2. He did 7 curl-ups on the fourth day and 11 on the fifth day. If he continues at this rate, how many curl-ups will he be able to do on the tenth day?

5. In 1960, only about $12 billion was spent for advertising. About $\frac{1}{8}$ of that was spent on television. How much was spent on television?

6. Use the table on the left page to find how much more was spent on radio and television advertising in 1987 than in 1970.

7. During a 60-minute program, one of the advertisers has $3\frac{1}{2}$ minutes of commercial time. Each commercial lasts $\frac{1}{2}$ minute. How many commercials does the advertiser have during the program?

8. **Determining Reasonable Answers** Without solving the problem, tell which of the answers given below seems reasonable.

In 1987, a TV network company charged a record $600,000 for 30 seconds of advertising on Superbowl XXI. At this rate, how much did 10 seconds cost?
a. 10 seconds cost $60,000.
b. 10 seconds cost $200,000.
c. 10 seconds cost $20,000.

4. In 1980, total advertising expenditures were about $54 billion. Advertising expenditures for direct mail were about $8 billion. What fraction of the total expenditures were for direct mail?

Data Collection and Analysis
Group Decision Making

Doing an Investigation

Group Skill
Encourage and Respect Others

The human eye judges distance with an ability known as depth perception. For example, when you throw a ball, you rely on depth perception to help you gauge the distance between you and your target. You can do an **investigation** to test your depth perception.

Collecting Data

1. Your group will need the following materials.

   ■ two identical objects such as two small spools or two toy cars
   ■ a piece of string about 5.5 meters long
   ■ a measuring tape or stick
   ■ two pieces of masking tape

2. To do the investigation, tie the string to one of the objects. Place the objects on the floor a few centimeters apart, then move the one without the string forward one meter. Put a piece of masking tape on the floor at the front edge of the closer object. Lie on the floor three meters in front of the closer object so that your eye level is even with the two objects. Close one eye and pull on the string to try to align the objects. Once you think they are aligned, put a piece of tape on the floor at the front edge of the object on the string. Measure the distance between the two pieces of tape. This measurement reflects the error in your single-eye depth perception.

3. Find the error in single-eye depth perception for each person in your group. Keep a record.

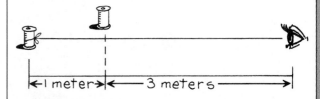

Organizing Data

4. Make a bar graph to display the depth perception abilities in your group. If necessary, adjust the scale to fit the data from your group.

5. Check your graph to be sure you have written a title and labels.

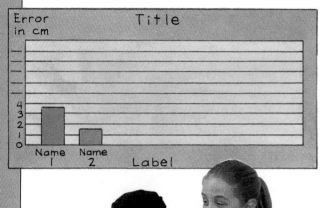

Presenting Your Analysis

6. What was the difference between the largest and smallest values, or the *range,* of the errors for your group? What was the average error for your group? You may want to use a calculator to find the average.

7. Write at least four true statements about your results.

8. Do you think you could generalize the results from the sample of students in your group to people of all ages? Why or why not?

WRAP UP

What's Happening

Choose the letter that best describes the method used to do the computing in the exercises below.

1. $\frac{1}{6}$ of 25 → $\frac{1}{6}$ of 24 → about 4

2. $\frac{3}{4} \times \frac{7}{8} = \frac{21}{32}$

3. $\frac{4}{5} \div \frac{5}{8} = \frac{4}{5} \times \frac{8}{5}$

4. $\frac{2}{3} \times \frac{9}{10} = \frac{3}{5}$

a. Multiplying by the reciprocal of the divisor

b. Reducing before multiplying

c. Using compatible numbers

d. Multiplying numerators and denominators

Sometimes, Always, Never

Decide which word goes in the blank: *sometimes*, *always*, or *never*. Explain your choices.

5. The product of two fractions less than 1 is _____ greater than either fraction.

6. If the product of two different fractions is 1, and one of the fractions is less than 1, the other is _____ greater than 1.

7. The quotient of two fractions less than 1 is _____ greater than either fraction.

8. The product of two improper fractions is _____ greater than 1.

9. The quotient of two mixed numbers is _____ less than 1.

Project

You plan to open a lunchtime restaurant specializing in soups. You can wait on about 50 customers each work day. $\frac{2}{3}$ of the customers will probably be adults, and the other $\frac{1}{3}$ will be children. Children's portions will be $\frac{1}{2}$ the size of the adult portions. Saturdays and Sundays you will probably only serve $\frac{3}{4}$ the number of weekday customers. Plan a menu and a grocery list for the first week.

CHAPTER REVIEW/TEST

Part 1   Understanding

Estimate each product using rounding.

1. $2\frac{5}{6} \times 6\frac{1}{5}$

2. $19\frac{3}{4} \cdot 4\frac{2}{3}$

3. Is the product more than or less than 25? $4\frac{7}{8} \times 6\frac{4}{5}$

4. Is the quotient more than or less than 6? $6 \div \frac{5}{6}$

5. Do not divide. Tell which quotient is greater. $6\frac{3}{4} \div 3$ or $6\frac{3}{4} \div \frac{1}{3}$

Part 2   Skills

Use mental math to find each answer.

6. $\frac{1}{6}$ of 30

7. $\frac{3}{10} \times 40$

Find the products. Write in lowest terms.

8. $\frac{1}{8} \times 40$

9. $\frac{2}{3} \times \frac{5}{6}$

10. $1\frac{1}{4} \cdot 3\frac{3}{5}$

11. $3\frac{1}{2} \times 2\frac{1}{3}$

Divide and check.

12. $3 \div \frac{2}{3}$

13. $\frac{3}{8} \div \frac{1}{4}$

14. $8 \div 2\frac{1}{2}$

15. $3\frac{3}{4} \div 1\frac{1}{4}$

Find the repeating decimal for each fraction.

16. $\frac{5}{9}$

17. $\frac{10}{11}$

Part 3   Applications

18. Arnold is on an album-buying spree. He bought 2 albums one week, 6 the next week, and 10 in the third week. If he continues this pattern, how many albums will he buy in the seventh week?

19. A radio station sold 20 minutes of air time to an advertiser. If each of the messages is $\frac{2}{3}$ minute long, how many messages did the advertiser buy?

20. **Challenge**   The department store spent a total of $21,000 on advertising. $\frac{1}{6}$ of that was spent on radio advertising. How much was spent on radio advertising? Give an estimate. Then find the exact answer. Is your exact answer reasonable?

243

ENRICHMENT
A Repeating Decimal Oddity

The idea of a decimal that repeats without end leads to an interesting result. Mathematicians have created a special name for the idea of "without end."

Idea	Name	Symbol
Without end	Infinity	∞

The following shows the idea of infinity used to write 1.

$$\frac{1}{3} \qquad = \qquad 0.333\overline{3}$$

$$+\frac{2}{3} \qquad = \qquad 0.666\overline{6}$$

$$\overline{\phantom{+\frac{2}{3}}}$$

$$1 \qquad\qquad\qquad 0.999\overline{9}$$

Use the idea of infinity to solve the following.

1. Find the repeating decimal for $\frac{1}{6}$. Find the repeating decimal for $\frac{5}{6}$. Use these two fractions and their decimals to show that $1 = 0.999\overline{9}$.

2. Find the repeating decimals for these fractions.

$$\frac{75}{99} =$$
$$\frac{87}{99} =$$
$$\frac{36}{99} =$$
$$\overline{\phantom{\frac{36}{99}}}$$
$$2$$

3. Use the repeating decimals that you found in problem 2 to show that $2 = 1.999\overline{9}$. It will help to add the decimals from right to left. Remember that you must make a trade each time you add.

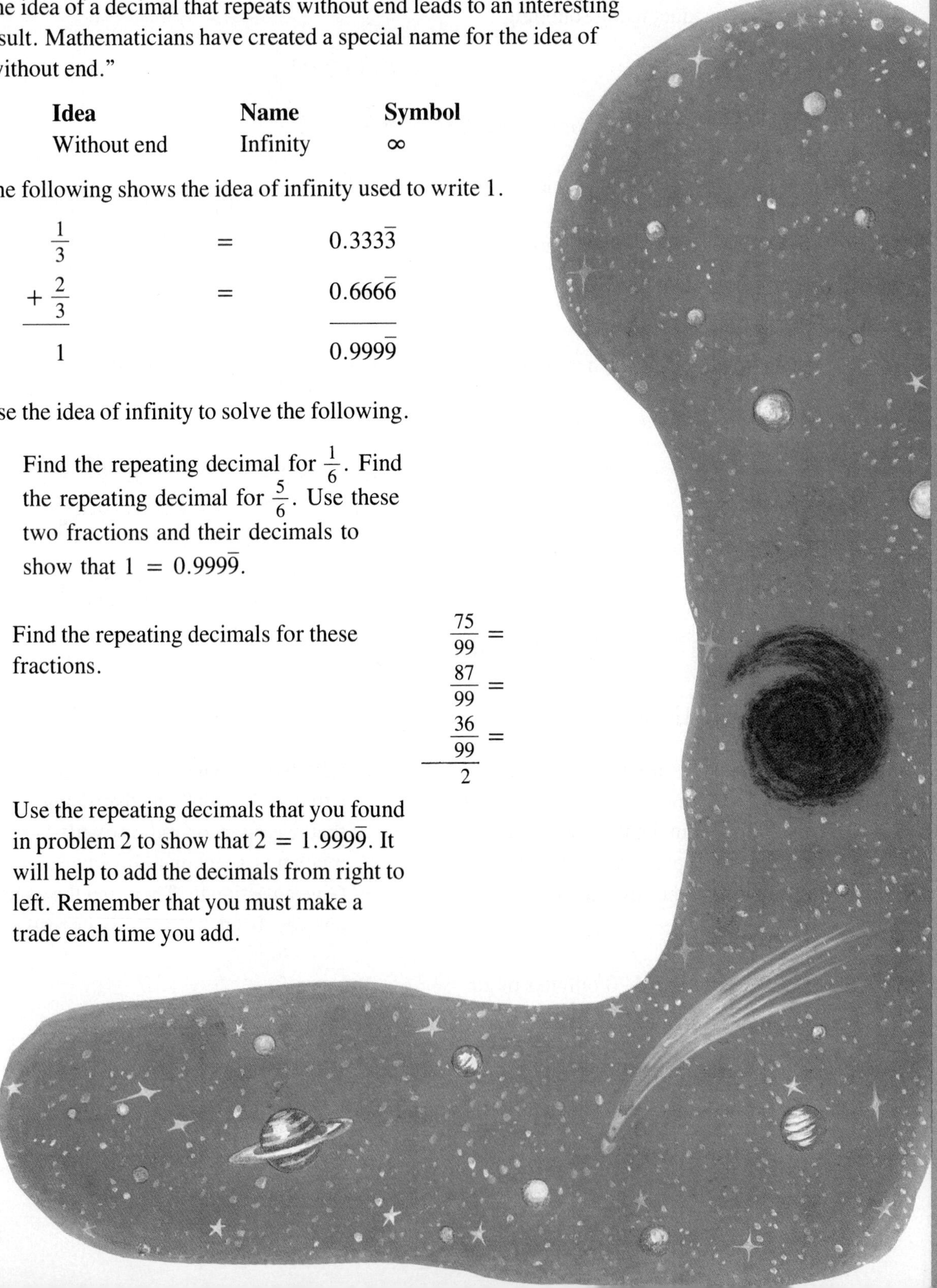

CUMULATIVE REVIEW

1. What is the sum of the parts of a circle graph?

   A. 100   B. 1

   C. 0   D. 360

2. There are 6 chess players on each of two teams. If a player plays every player on the other team once, how many games are played when the teams meet?

   A. 6   B. 12

   C. 36   D. 18

3. The snack bar serves ham, tuna, or cheese sandwiches, milk or juice, and yogurt or fruit for dessert. How many different lunches are possible for a person who wants a sandwich, a drink, and a dessert?

   A. 8   B. 7

   C. 12   D. 3

4. What do you call the number of units between spaces on the scale of a line or bar graph?

   A. mode   B. range

   C. interval   D. axes

5. Give the length in lowest terms.

   A. $4\frac{1}{3}$ B. $3\frac{2}{8}$

   C. $3\frac{1}{4}$ D. $3\frac{1}{6}$

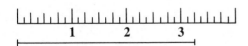

6. Write a decimal for $\frac{3}{8}$.

   A. 0.38   B. 0.375

   C. 0.625   D. 0.4

7. What is the sum of $4\frac{7}{8}$ and $3\frac{5}{8}$?

   A. $8\frac{1}{8}$ B. $7\frac{1}{4}$

   C. $8\frac{1}{2}$ D. $7\frac{1}{2}$

8. Solve. Use mental math: $6r = 42$.

   A. $r = 48$ B. $r = 7$

   C. $r = 36$ D. $r = 252$

9. Estimate the sum of $8\frac{5}{6}$ and $6\frac{1}{5}$.

   A. 13   B. 14

   C. 15   D. 3

10. Find the difference between $\frac{1}{4}$ and $\frac{5}{6}$.

    A. $\frac{5}{12}$ B. $\frac{4}{6}$

    C. $1\frac{1}{12}$ D. $\frac{7}{12}$

11. Kevin worked for $2\frac{1}{2}$ hours. Sheila worked $1\frac{3}{4}$ hours longer than Kevin. For how long did Sheila work?

    A. $\frac{3}{4}$ hour   B. $4\frac{1}{4}$ hours

    C. $1\frac{3}{4}$ hours   D. $3\frac{1}{4}$ hours

12. Jack pitched 12 innings. Mo pitched $3\frac{2}{3}$ fewer innings. How many innings did Mo pitch?

    A. $3\frac{2}{3}$ B. $15\frac{2}{3}$

    C. $8\frac{1}{3}$ D. $9\frac{1}{3}$

9

GEOMETRY

MATH AND SCIENCE

DATA BANK

Use the Science Data Bank on page 477 to answer the questions.

1 A perfect salt crystal has six flat surfaces. How many triangular surfaces does a perfect diamond crystal have?

2 If you sliced off one tip of a diamond, how many flat surfaces would you slice through?

3 What shapes are the flat surfaces of the perfect quartz crystal? How many surfaces are there?

4 **Using Critical Thinking** Describe how you could slice the perfect quartz crystal into two equal parts. How many sides would the new flat surface have?

Analyzing Space Figures

edge
face
vertex

EXPLORE **Make Space Figure Models**

Scientists use the idea of space figures to
describe crystal structures like the
formation in the picture. You can make
your own model of a space figure. Trace
or copy and enlarge this pattern. Then
cut, fold, and tape your pattern to make
the figure.

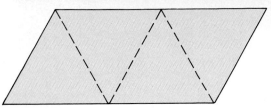

TALK ABOUT IT

1. How many flat, triangle-shaped **faces** does your model have?
2. How many corners (points), or **vertices,** does it have?
3. How many parts of lines, or **edges,** does it have?

Your model and the crystal at the top of the page are examples of
a space figure called a **polyhedron.** A polyhedron has faces that
are flat and shaped like polygons. It also has edges and vertices.
Look at the figures below. Copy and complete this table to
compare them.

Space Figure	No. of faces (F)	No. of vertices (V)	No. of edges (E)
Triangular pyramid			

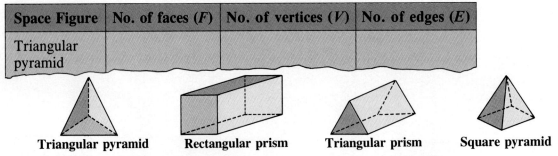

Triangular pyramid   Rectangular prism   Triangular prism   Square pyramid

Leonard Euler, a Swiss mathematician, discovered a
formula about edges, faces, and vertices of polyhedrons.

Euler's formula:
$$E = F + V - 2$$

1. Check the numbers in your table using Euler's formula.
2. Why are the space figures on the right not polyhedrons?
   Give an everyday object that suggests each figure.

Cylinder   **Sphere**   **Cone**

Give the number of faces, edges, and vertices for each space figure. Is Euler's formula true for these figures?

1.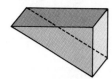

2.

3.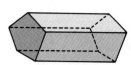

4.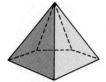

5.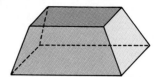

6.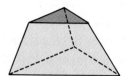

7. What space figure could you make with this pattern? How many faces, vertices, and edges would it have?

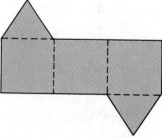

MATH REASONING

8. Salt crystals are cube-shaped. Suppose you sliced off a corner. How many more edges would your new figure have than the salt crystal?

PROBLEM SOLVING

9. Suppose you find that a polyhedron has 18 edges and 8 faces. How many vertices does it have?

10. **Science Data Bank** Describe and list the polygons shown in the crystal formations. Give names for those that you know. Compare your findings with those of the rest of the class.

11. A diamond crystal has 8 faces and 6 vertices. How many edges does it have?

▶ **USING CRITICAL THINKING** **Taking a Look**

Which of these patterns can be folded to make a cube? Copy the patterns onto large-grid graph paper. Cut them out and fold them to prove your answer.

12.

13.

14.

15.

Drawing Space Figures

EXPLORE Make Polyhedron Models

You can use what you know about faces, edges, and vertices to help you draw polyhedrons. You can use graph paper to draw models of certain types of polyhedrons. The figures show a cube and a square pyramid drawn on graph paper. First try to copy these figures on graph paper. Then see if you can create an interesting polyhedron of your own.

TALK ABOUT IT

1. Can you name the polyhedron you drew? How many faces, vertices, and edges does it have?

2. Why do you think some of the edges are shown with dotted lines?

These directions will help you draw a triangular pyramid with or without the help of graph paper.

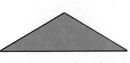

Draw a triangle.

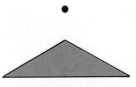

Mark a point directly above it.

Connect the points with a solid line. Show hidden edges with dotted lines.

1. Follow the directions above to draw a triangular pyramid.

2. Draw a rectangular prism that does not look like a cube. Use graph paper.

Follow the directions to draw the figures in exercises 1–3. You may want to use graph paper.

1. Draw a triangle.
Draw three segments of the
same length "straight down."
Connect the vertices.
Make the hidden edges dotted.

Triangular prism

2. Draw a "thin" pentagon, with two back
edges dotted.
Mark a point directly above it.
Connect the vertices.
Make the hidden edges dotted.

Pentagonal pyramid

3. Draw a pentagonal prism. Hint: Start
with a "thin" pentagon.

MATH REASONING

4. How many of the faces of this hexagonal prism are hidden?
How many vertices are hidden?

Hexagonal prism

PROBLEM SOLVING

5. Carlos drew a space figure that had 24 edges. It had 6 more
vertices than faces. How many faces did it have?
Hint: $E = F + V - 2$

▶ **USING CRITICAL THINKING   Taking a Look**

6. Here is a rectangular prism that is 9 units
long. How many different length
prisms could you make by using 1 or 2
cuts on the red marks only?

Space Figures
A Different Point of View

EXPLORE Visualize and Draw

If you look at space figures in different ways you can see flat, or **plane,** figures. The diagram shows different ways you might view the triangular prism. How could you draw figures to show what flat surface each person might see?

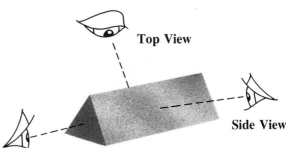

TALK ABOUT IT

1. How would the top view of the prism be different from the side view? Why?
2. What shape would you see from the front of the prism?

Look carefully at the figure of the views of a cone. The figure suggests that the front, side, top, and **cross-section** views of space figures usually show **polygons,** circles, or ovals.

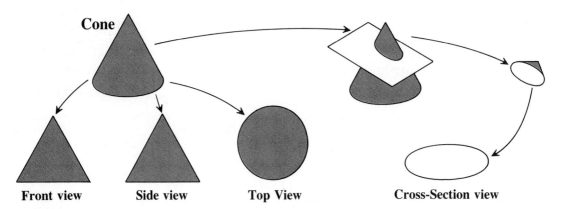

Cone

| Front view | Side view | Top View | Cross-Section view |

Here are a front, top, and side view of a figure. What figure do you think it is?

Front View　　Top View　　Side View

252

Name the space figure for the front view, top view, and side view shown.

1.

Front view · Top view · Side view

2.

Front view · Top view · Side view

3.

Front view · Top view · Side view

4.

Front view · Top view · Side view

Draw the cross-section view of a space figure "sliced" as shown.

5.

6.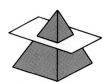

7.

MATH REASONING

8. Draw the front, top, and side views of a birdhouse.

PROBLEM SOLVING

9. The side view of a rectangular prism shows that it is 6 in. longer than it is tall. The perimeter (distance around) of the side view is 44 in. How long is the prism?

10. Science Data Bank Choose one of the perfect crystal shapes and draw a different view of it (a view from the top, bottom, or a cross-section view).

Find the answers.

11. $\frac{3}{8} \times \frac{2}{3}$ **12.** $\frac{8}{9} - \frac{1}{3}$ **13.** $4\frac{3}{8} + 7\frac{1}{2}$ **14.** $8\frac{1}{3} \div 2\frac{2}{3}$

Estimate.

15. $3{,}672 \div 5.7$ **16.** 32.145×8.6 **17.** $282.15 \div 3.87$ **18.** $7\frac{5}{6} - 2\frac{1}{7}$

More Practice, page 511, set C

From Space Figures to Plane Figures

Plane figures are unlike space figures in that they lie entirely on one flat surface.

EXPLORE **Make a Line Segment Template**

Cut a cardboard strip 12 inches long. Mark and punch holes as shown. How many different length **line segments** can you make by marking points in a pair of holes?

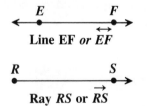

|←2 in.→|←3 in.→|←——6 in.——→|

Segment

TALK ABOUT IT

1. Could you draw a 4-in. segment with your strip? Why or why not?
2. What part of a polyhedron is a segment?

The faces, edges, and vertices of space figures suggest some basic plane figures.

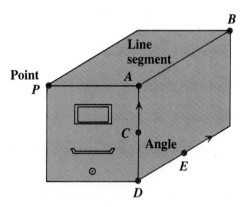

We see	We think or say	We write
a corner of a file cabinet	a **point**	P
an edge of a file cabinet	a **line segment**	$\overline{AB}$
two edges and a corner	an **angle**	$\angle CDE$, $\angle EDC$, or $\angle D$

A **line** extends without end in both directions.

A **ray** has one endpoint and extends without end in one direction.

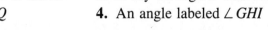

Line EF or $\overleftrightarrow{EF}$

Ray RS or $\overrightarrow{RS}$

Draw the following.

1. A line segment with endpoints G and H
2. A ray through S with endpoint R
3. A line through points P and Q
4. An angle labeled $\angle GHI$

Which geometric figure (point, line segment, ray, angle) is suggested by the object given?

1. Hands of a clock

2. A beam of light from a laser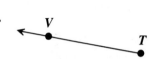

3. Tip of a straight pin

4. A straight piece of wire

Write the name and symbol for each figure.

5. • Q

6.

7.

8.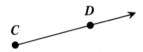

9.

10.

Draw and label a figure for each symbol.

11. $\overline{DE}$ **12.** $\angle EFG$ **13.** point G **14.** $\overrightarrow{BC}$ **15.** $\overleftrightarrow{MN}$

MATH REASONING

16. How many different length segments could you mark and draw using this strip?

A   B   C   D   E

PROBLEM SOLVING

17. Suppose the perimeter (distance around) of a 5-sided polygon is 20 cm. Each side is a whole number of centimeters. Find the length of the sides if they are all the same. If they are all different.

▶ **ESTIMATION**

18. First estimate which cylinder is the tallest. Then check by measuring to the nearest millimeter.

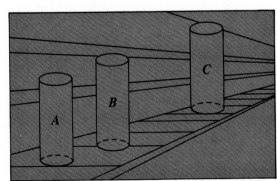

More Practice, page 511, set D

Parallel, Perpendicular, and Skew Lines

LEARN ABOUT IT

In this lesson you will study some of the
relationships two lines can have to each other.

EXPLORE Study the Figure

Think about the lines that pass through the edges of a cube. Some
of them meet, or **intersect**, each other. Some will never meet in
either direction. Find examples of each kind.

TALK ABOUT IT

1. Are there two segments on the same face that have lines that
   would never meet? Explain.
2. Are there two segments not on the same face that have lines
   that would never meet? Explain.

	We see	We think or say	We write
d c	Two streets that intersect at "square corners"	**Perpendicular lines** are lines that intersect at "square corners." c is perpendicular to d	$c \perp d$
r s	Two railroad tracks	**Parallel lines** are lines in the same plane that do not intersect. r is parallel to s	$r \parallel s$

Skew lines are lines that are not in the same plane and do not intersect.
See lines $\overleftrightarrow{AD}$ and $\overleftrightarrow{HG}$ on the cube above.

TRY IT OUT

1. Name some other everyday objects that suggest parallel and
   perpendicular lines.

2. Draw along the sides of your ruler to draw a pair of parallel lines.

3. Draw along a side and an end of a ruler to draw perpendicular lines.

1. Which edges are parallel to $\overline{TW}$?

2. Which edges are perpendicular to $\overline{TW}$?

3. Which edges are neither parallel nor perpendicular to $\overline{TW}$?

4. Give a "hidden edge" that is parallel to $\overline{SW}$.

5. Name three lines that are perpendicular to each other at point P.

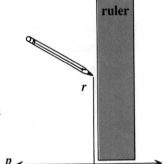

6. Draw a line p. Then use a corner of your ruler to draw two lines q and r each perpendicular to p. Label the lines. What else do you think is true about lines q and r?

7. How could you use your ruler to make a 4-sided figure with two pairs of parallel sides? (Hint: Draw a pair of parallel lines that intersect another pair of parallel lines.)

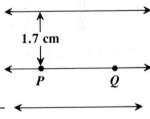

APPLY

MATH REASONING

8. The distance between parallel lines is measured using a perpendicular segment. The lines are 1.7 cm apart at P. How far apart are they at Q?

PROBLEM SOLVING

9. Four parallel lines are spaced equally. The two outside lines are 1.41 cm apart. How far apart are the two inside lines?

▶ COMMUNICATION   Writing to Learn

10. Draw several different shaped 4-sided figures. Use a red pencil or crayon to connect the midpoints of the sides of each figure. Write a sentence telling in what way all the red figures are alike.

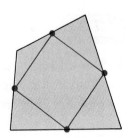

More Practice, page 511, set E

Estimating and Measuring Angles

EXPLORE Analyze the Figures

You can use a unit of angle measure to tell how big an
angle is. Suppose angle A is the unit. Estimate how many
angle As it would take side-by-side to "fill up" angle B.

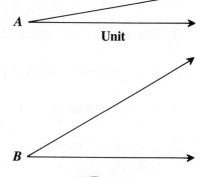

TALK ABOUT IT

1. How could you make a model to check your estimate? Try it.
2. The hands of a clock form angles. Estimate how many angle
   As it would take to fit inside the hands at 3:00.

A standard unit for measuring angles is the **degree**. Angle A
above is about 10 degrees (10°). You can use a **protractor** to
measure angles.

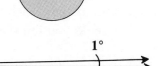

Standard unit

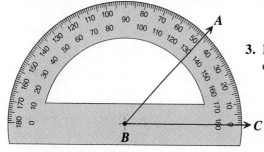

3. Read the measure
   of the angle.

1. Place the center point on
   the vertex of the angle.

2. Place the zero edge on
   one side of the angle.

The measure of
$\angle ABC$ is 47°
Read: 47 degrees

Right angle (90°)

Obtuse angle (greater than 90°)

Acute angle (less than 90°)

1. Draw a large triangle so the three angles will be easy to measure.
   Compare the angles. Which is the largest? The smallest?
   Measure each angle. Find the sum of the three measures.

2. Repeat exercise 1 with a triangle of a different shape. What
   do you notice about the two sums of the angles?

First estimate the measure of each angle. Then measure to check your estimate. Is the angle right, acute, or obtuse?

1.

angle between leg
and football

2.

angle between ground
and ramp

3.

angle of corner

Draw angles (without using a protractor) which you estimate to have the measures given below. Then measure each angle to check your estimate.

4. 90° **5.** 45° **6.** 135° **7.** 175° **8.** 15°
9. 30° **10.** 60° **11.** 120° **12.** 50° **13.** 80°

14. Draw an acute angle and an obtuse angle. Then find their measures.

MATH REASONING

15. Dan said, "I think ∠C is greater than ∠D."
Aki said, "No, they're the same size. It doesn't matter how long the rays are drawn." Who do you think is right?

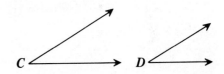

PROBLEM SOLVING

You may have discovered that the sum of the angles in any triangle is 180°. Look at these triangles. What is the measure of the third angle?

16.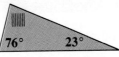

76°   23°

17.

34°   28°

▶ CALCULATOR

There are 360 degrees in a circle. How many degrees are in $\frac{1}{3}$ of a circle?

| ON/AC | 360 | × | 1 | ÷ | 3 | = |

Use your calculator to find the number of degrees in each part of a circle.

18. $\frac{1}{4}$ **19.** $\frac{5}{6}$ **20.** $\frac{5}{9}$ **21.** $\frac{11}{12}$ **22.** $\frac{2}{3}$ **23.** $\frac{3}{4}$

More Practice, page 512, set A

Exploring Polygons

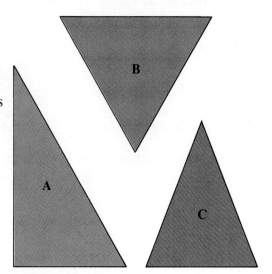

You can use relationships between sides and angles to help you describe some special polygons.

EXPLORE Make Polygon Models

Work in groups. Here are some special triangles. Make models of these shapes as needed for the activities below. What 4-sided polygon can you make with 2 *A*s? 3 *B*s? 4 *C*s?

TALK ABOUT IT

1. Did you make a rectangle? Which triangles did you use?
2. Did any of your figures have opposite sides that were parallel?
3. Did any of your figures have 2 sides equal and 2 sides not equal?

The table lists some **quadrilaterals** (4-sided figures) with descriptions and examples.

Quadrilateral	Description	Example
Square	all sides equal; 4 right angles	
Parallelogram	2 pairs of parallel sides	
Rhombus	all sides equal	
Rectangle	opposite sides equal; 4 right angles	
Trapezoid	1 pair of parallel sides	

Here are some other special polygons:

Acute triangle – all acute angles
Obtuse triangle – one obtuse angle
Right triangle – one right angle

Scalene triangle – no equal sides
Isosceles triangle – 2 equal sides
Equilateral triangle – 3 equal sides
Pentagon – 5 sides
Hexagon – 6 sides

1. Find and name an example from the real world for as many of the above polygons as you can.

1. Match the figures below with these names: rectangle, square, rhombus, trapezoid.

 A B C  D

Give all possible names for each triangle (for example *acute* and *scalene*). Choose from the following names: acute, right, obtuse, scalene, isosceles, equilateral.

2.   3.    4.   5.

APPLY

MATH REASONING

6. A diagonal is a segment that is not a side. It connects two vertices of a polygon. How many diagonals does a hexagon have?

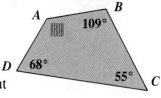

PROBLEM SOLVING

7. The sum of the angles of a 4-sided polygon is 360°. Find the measure of angle *A* in the figure on the right.

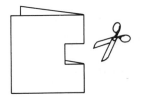

8. Use the fact given in exercise 7. What can you conclude about the measure of each angle of a rectangle?

▶ **USING CRITICAL THINKING   Take a Look**

A symmetric figure is one that can be folded in half so that the two halves match. Suppose you fold a piece of paper in half and cut out the polygons shown below. Draw and name the figure that is formed when you unfold each piece. Draw as many lines of symmetry in each figure as you can find.

9.

a square

10.

an isosceles
right triangle

11.

a trapezoid
with a right angle

More Practice, page 512, set B   **261**

Constructing and Bisecting an Angle

EXPLORE **Study the Process**

You can use a **compass** and a straightedge such as a ruler to copy an angle or to bisect an angle. When you **bisect** an angle, you divide the angle into two equal angles, or congruent angles.

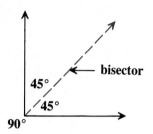

How to Copy an Angle

Step 1

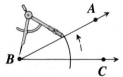

Mark an arc on the given angle.

Step 2

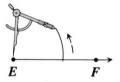

Draw$\overrightarrow{EF}$, and use the same compass opening as in step 1 to draw an arc.

Step 3

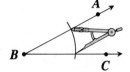

Measure the opening of the given angle with the compass.

Step 4

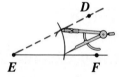

Mark the same opening for $\angle DEF$. Draw $\overrightarrow{ED}$ as shown by the dotted line.

How to Bisect an Angle

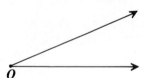

Draw an angle to be bisected.

Step 1

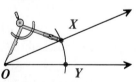

Draw any arc with center O. Label points X and Y.

Step 2

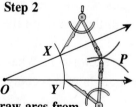

Draw arcs from points X and Y. Label the intersection P.

Step 3

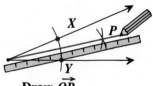

Draw $\overrightarrow{OP}$. $\overrightarrow{OP}$ bisects $\angle XOY$.

TALK ABOUT IT

1. If you bisected a 36° angle, what would be the measure of each angle?

1. Trace this angle. Use a compass and a straightedge to construct a copy of it. Then bisect your new angle.
2. Draw your own angle. Construct a copy of it. Then bisect it.

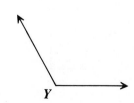

1. Carefully draw a triangular pyramid and a triangular prism. Use dotted lines to indicate hidden edges.

	showing	hidden
edges		
faces		
vertices		

2. For the triangular prism you drew, make a table to show the number of edges, faces, and vertices that are showing and that are hidden.

Use this space figure for exercises 3 through 8. In this space figure, all edges are equal and ∠EBC measures 90°.

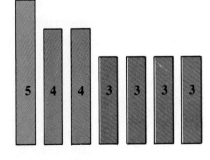

3. Draw and label the top view and the side view. Name the polygon formed by each view.

4. Draw the cross section if vertex C is sliced off.

5. Name all angles shown with vertex A.

6. Name two rays with endpoint E.

7. Name three line segments with endpoint B.

8. Name a line that is parallel to $\overleftrightarrow{BE}$, a line that is perpendicular to $\overleftrightarrow{BE}$, and a line that is skew to $\overleftrightarrow{BE}$.

Trace any of these 7 strips to make the indicated figures. Draw the figures.

9. isosceles triangle that is not equilateral

10. obtuse triangle

11. parallelogram that is not a rectangle or square

12. trapezoid

13. rhombus that is not a square

14. right triangle

PROBLEM SOLVING

15. Geoff found a crystal in the shape of a rectangular prism. How many faces, edges, and vertices did it have?

16. Catie measured two angles of a triangle to be 24° and 66°. What is the measure of the third angle? What kind of triangle is this?

Motion Geometry and Congruent Figures

EXPLORE Use Geometric Models

Work in groups. Trace Figure A. Move the tracing paper to see if it fits exactly on Figure B. Decide whether you had to only slide the tracing, slide and flip, slide and turn, or slide, flip, and turn it.

TALK ABOUT IT

1. In which box did the Figure A not fit exactly on Figure B? What motions did you have to do with the tracing to check?
2. Describe the motions you used to check on the figures in each box.

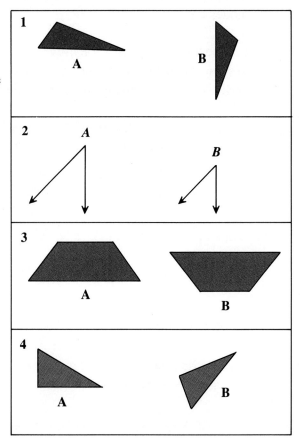

- When you only **slide** the figure, the new figure is called a **translation** image.

- When you slide and **flip** the figure, the new figure is called a **reflection** image.

- When you slide and **turn** the figure, the new figure is called a **rotation** image.

- Two figures are **congruent** if you can slide, flip, or turn one to make it fit exactly on the other.

- The symbol ≅ means "is congruent to."

Is Figure B congruent to Figure A? Use tracing paper to test. Tell what motion you used to find out. If Figure B is congruent to Figure A, name the kind of image it is.

1.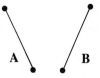

2.

3.

Is Figure B congruent to Figure A? Use tracing paper to test. Tell what motion you used to find out. If Figure B is congruent to Figure A, name the kind of image it is.

1.

2.

3.

4.

5. Two triangles are congruent if they have matching angles congruent and matching sides congruent. Trace △*ABC* and move it to fit on △*DEF*. Then copy and complete this list of congruent segments and angles.

△*ABC*	≅	△*DEF*
$\overline{AB}$	≅	
$\overline{BC}$	≅	
$\overline{AC}$	≅	
∠*A*	≅	
∠*B*	≅	
∠*C*	≅	

6. Draw a translation, reflection, and a rotation image of △*ABC*.

MATH REASONING

7. Suppose you know that Figure X is congruent to Figure Y. You also know that Figure Y is congruent to Figure Z. What conclusion can you draw?

PROBLEM SOLVING

8. The first figure Gabriella drew was a triangle, the second a pentagon, and the third had 7 sides. If Gabriella keeps up this pattern, how many sides will her 15th figure have?

▶ **USING CRITICAL THINKING Support Your Conclusion**

9. Jeri looked for times on a clock where the hands formed a 90° angle. She said that 12:15 would be such a time. Do you think Jeri is correct? Why or why not? Name some times that are correct.

More Practice, page 512, set C

Similar Figures

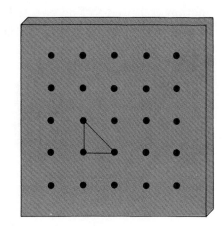

LEARN ABOUT IT

EXPLORE Use Geometric Models

Work in groups. How many different size triangles can you find on the geoboard that have the same shape as this one? Use dot paper to show each one you find.

TALK ABOUT IT

1. What special angle does each of your triangles have? What is special about the sides?
2. Did you find a triangle with matching sides twice as long as the triangle above? Three times as long? Four times as long?
3. How do you think matching angles of the triangles compare?

You have seen that congruent figures have the same size and shape. Figures that have the same shape, but not necessarily the same size, are called **similar figures**. A photo and its enlargement give an example of such figures.

When two triangles are similar, the length of the matching sides form equivalent fractions. For these figures:

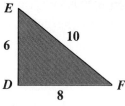

$$\frac{3}{6} = \frac{4}{8} = \frac{5}{10}$$

△**ABC** is similar to △**DEF**
We write: △**ABC** ~ △**DEF**

TRY IT OUT

1. Make a triangle on your geoboard different from the one above. Find triangles similar to it. Show them on dot paper.
2. Draw a rectangle similar to this one, but with sides two times as long. Write the equivalent fractions for the matching sides.

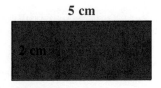

5 cm

2 cm

Each pair of figures is similar. Give the missing side lengths.

1.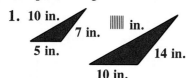

2.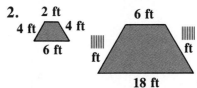

3.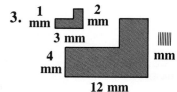

4.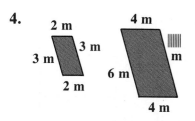

5.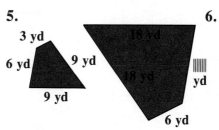

6.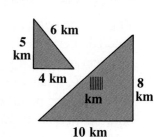

Triangle B is similar to Triangle A. The lengths of sides are represented by the lower case letters. Find

7. *e*, if *a* = 2, *d* = 6, and *b* = 4

8. *f*, if *b* = 5, *e* = 10, and *c* = 8

9. *d*, if *c* = 3, *f* = 12, and *a* = 2

10. *a*, if *f* = 25, *c* = 5, and *d* = 5

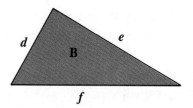

APPLY

MATH REASONING Draw pictures to support your answer.

11. Figure A is not similar to Figure B. Figure B is not similar to Figure C. Is it possible that Figure A is similar to Figure C?

PROBLEM SOLVING

12. The large triangle is similar to the small triangle. How far is it from *P* to *Q*?

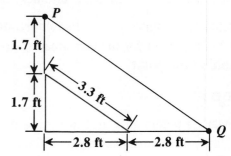

MIXED REVIEW

Find the answers.

13. 4.07 + 18.3

14. $\frac{3}{4} \times \frac{1}{8}$

15. 2,100 − 182

16. $8\frac{1}{3} - 5$

17. $8\frac{2}{3} + 3\frac{1}{4}$

18. $16\frac{1}{2} \div 4\frac{1}{4}$

19. 4.55 × 0.2

20. $14\overline{)32.407}$

More Practice, page 513, set A

Coordinate Geometry

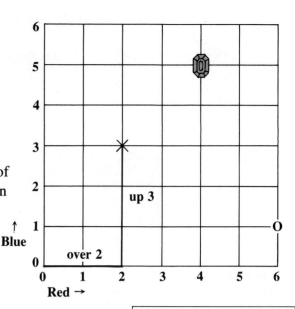

LEARN ABOUT IT

EXPLORE Play a Graphing Game

Try a game with a partner. Roll a red and a blue number cube labeled 1–6. Use the pair of numbers to mark a point on the grid as shown with an X. Then your partner rolls the cubes and marks the point with an O. If you land on a marked point, roll again. First one to land on the jewel wins.

TALK ABOUT IT

1. Does the number pair (3, 5) have the same location on the grid as (5, 3)? Explain.
2. What if you found a location for a number pair by going up first and then over? Would the location of the pair (2, 3) change? Explain.

A famous mathematician named Descartes invented a way to use pairs of numbers to show points and geometric figures on a grid. This idea has been used in mathematics and science ever since.

The pairs of numbers are called **coordinates**. When you mark a point for the coordinates, you are **graphing the point**.

TRY IT OUT

1. Mark 4 points on a grid to form a trapezoid. Name the coordinates of the points.
2. Give a partner coordinates for 3 points that form an isosceles triangle. Ask your partner to graph the points and connect them.

Your roll

To find where to mark the point, start at 0 and go over 2 and up 3.

Your partner's roll

268

Graph these points. Connect them in order and name the polygon.

1. (2, 5), (6, 5), (5, 2), (1, 2)

2. (2, 4), (5, 4), (6, 1), (0, 1)

3. (7, 5), (5, 9), (1, 7), (3, 3), (7, 5)

4. (1, 6), (5, 10), (9, 6), (7, 1), (3, 1), (1, 6)

5. (3, 4), (3, 7), (6, 9), (9, 7), (9, 4), (6, 2), (3, 4)

6. (3, 9), (6, 9), (8, 7), (8, 4), (6, 2), (3, 2), (1, 4), (1, 7), (3, 9)

These figures are symmetric. Graph them and draw their lines of symmetry.

7. (2, 1), (1, 6), (2, 9), (4, 9), (5, 6), (4, 1), (2, 1)

8. (3, 9), (8, 9), (9, 7), (8, 5), (3, 5), (4, 7), (3, 9)

Graph and connect points for each pair of figures.
Write *congruent* or *similar*.

9. Figure A: (6, 1), (2, 7), (6, 7), (10, 1), (6, 1)
Figure B: (7, 6), (5, 9), (7, 9), (9, 6), (7, 6)

10. Figure A: (2, 1), (3, 3), (6, 3), (7, 1), (2, 1)
Figure B: (3, 5), (2, 7), (7, 7), (6, 5), (3, 5)

MATH REASONING

11. Graph a square so that it has a line of symmetry through (1, 3) and (6, 3).

PROBLEM SOLVING

12. The sum of the angle measures of a triangle is 180°. What is the sum of the angle measures of a hexagon? Hint: How many triangles. . . .

▶ ALGEBRA

13. Use the numbers less than 10 and show 5 more cards this machine would output. Graph the coordinates for each card. What do you discover?

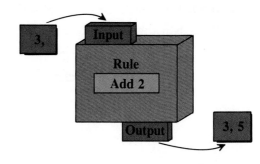

More Practice, page 513, set B

Problem Solving
Use Logical Reasoning

UNDERSTAND
ANALYZE DATA
PLAN
ESTIMATE
SOLVE
EXAMINE

LEARN ABOUT IT

Solving some problems involves more than simply deciding to add, subtract, multiply or divide. The strategy **Use Logical Reasoning** is often helpful.

Jose, Leah, and Gail are all scientists. Their fields are gemology, biology, and physics. The gemologist and Leah met in college. Jose is married to the physicist. Gail is the physicist. Who is the gemologist?

A chart is helpful to keep a record of what you know.

First, I'll write everything I know in the chart.

	Gemologist	Biologist	Physicist
Jose			No
Leah	No		
Gail			Yes

Then, I'll use what I know to find more information. Leah cannot be the physicist because Gail is. So Leah must be the biologist.

	Gemologist	Biologist	Physicist
Jose			No
Leah	No	Yes	No
Gail	No	No	Yes

Now I know that Jose must be the gemologist.

	Gemologist	Biologist	Physicist
Jose	Yes		No
Leah	No	Yes	No
Gail	No	No	Yes

TRY IT OUT

Marcie, Clark, and Karen each have different birthstones. Their birthstones are a sapphire, a ruby, and an emerald. Clark's birthstone is not an emerald. Marcie wishes hers was a sapphire. Karen's birthstone is red. Who has which birthstone?

- What are the birthstones?
- Is Marcie's birthstone a sapphire?
- What is Karen's birthstone?
- Copy and complete the chart to help you solve this problem.

	Sapphire	Ruby	Emerald
Marcie	No		
Clark			No
Karen		Yes	No

Solve using logical reasoning.

1. Nina, Madeline, Saul, and Fred are studying math, science, French, and history. None of them is studying a subject that begins with the same letter as his or her first name. Saul is measuring angles. Nina has never studied French. Fred is reading about crystals. What subject is each most likely studying?

2. Moh's scale is used to compare the hardness of different substances. Topaz is harder than both fingernail and window glass. Window glass and topaz are both softer than diamond. Fingernail is the softest. Rank each substance from hardest (1) to softest (4).

MIXED PRACTICE

Solve. Choose a strategy from the list or use another strategy that you know.

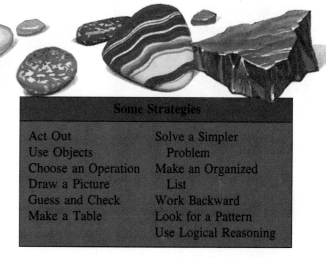

3. A faceted gemstone has 12 faces and 12 vertices. How many edges does it have? (Hint: Try Euler's formula.)

Some Strategies	
Act Out	Solve a Simpler
Use Objects	Problem
Choose an Operation	Make an Organized
Draw a Picture	List
Guess and Check	Work Backward
Make a Table	Look for a Pattern
	Use Logical Reasoning

4. Matt made a triangular box to display his crystal collection. He made one angle 45° and another 60°. How many degrees are in the third angle?

5. Mr. Abrams took the 28 students in his class to the International Gem Show. Use the table to find how much he paid for all the tickets.

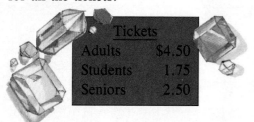

Tickets	
Adults	$4.50
Students	1.75
Seniors	2.50

6. The world's largest crystal is in the Malagasy Republic. It weighs 187 tons, is 59 ft long and 11.5 ft in diameter. How much greater is its length than its diameter?

7. Becky, Jen, Sarah, and Tara are each wearing a different color. The colors are blue, green, yellow, and red. Neither Jen nor Sarah likes yellow. Becky was going to wear red, but chose blue instead. Sarah does not have any green clothes. What color is each girl most likely wearing?

8. One of the parallel sides of a trapezoid is 12 in. longer than the other parallel side. Together, the 2 sides total 38 in. How long is each of the parallel sides?

More Practice, page 526, set A

Applied Problem Solving
Group Decision Making

UNDERSTAND
ANALYZE DATA
PLAN
ESTIMATE
SOLVE
EXAMINE

Group Skill
Listen to Others

You are helping your older brother, Dennis, and two of his friends, Julio and Martin, look for an apartment to share. All of them have jobs in the same vicinity, so they are looking for an apartment that is fairly centrally located to each of their jobs.

Facts to Consider

- Dennis can afford to pay up to $250 for a month's rent. Julio and Martin can each afford up to $300 for rent.
- None of them wants to have to walk mor than 8 blocks to work.
- None of them wants to share a bedroom, but they will consider that possibility if they find a very nice two bedroom apartment.
- None of them has a pet.
- You found 4 newspaper ads for apartments.

- The street map below shows where each of them works.

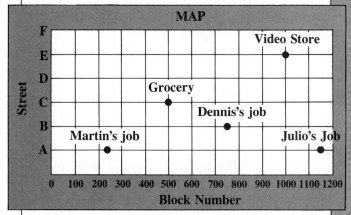

MAP

Video Store

Grocery

Dennis's job

Martin's job

Julio's Job

Street (F, E, D, C, B, A)
Block Number (0, 100, 200, 300, 400, 500, 600, 700, 800, 900, 1000, 1100, 1200)

CLASSIFIED

Apartments for Rent

3 bdr, 2 bth, spacious, deck with bay view, no pets. 330 A Street, $625, **423-3820**

1. The address where Julio works is 1132 A Street. Use the block numbers on the map to decide who works at 245 A Street.
2. Which apartment is too expensive for your brother and his friends to rent?
3. What are the disadvantages of renting the apartment at 280 D Street? What are the advantages?
4. Which apartment is closest to Dennis's job?

Make a copy of the street map and show where each job and each apartment is located. Tell which apartment you think your brother and his friends might choose and why.

2 bdr, 1 bth, jacuzzi, exercise room, pool. 780 C Street, $800, 423-8336

3 bdr, 2 bth, jacuzzi, close to bus stop. 280 D Street, $800, 425-3817

3 bdr, 2 bth, study, pool, tennis. 710 A Street, $950, 423-0351

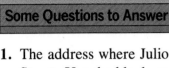

423-382(
See Ted

WRAP UP

Figuratively Speaking

Which geometric figure or figures are suggested by each?

1. textbook   **2.** dogsled tracks   **3.** can of soup   **4.** marble

In problems 5 and 6, use the words *congruent* and *similar* to describe each set of figures.

5.    **6.**

In problems 7 and 8, tell whether each figure is symmetrical.

7. 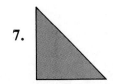   **8.**

Sometimes, Always, Never

Decide which word goes in the blank: *sometimes, always,* or *never.* Explain your choices.

9. You can _____ identify a space figure if you are shown its top and side views.

10. A triangle _____ has at least two acute angles.

11. Two figures that are similar are _____ also congruent.

12. A square is _____ also a rectangle.

13. A trapezoid is _____ also a parallelogram.

Project

Draw a large scalene triangle on heavy paper or cardboard. Construct the bisectors of each angle of your triangle. Describe what you discover about these bisectors. Cut out the triangle and balance it on your finger. Where the triangle balances is the center of gravity of the triangle. Give your conclusions about the center of gravity and the intersection of the bisectors.

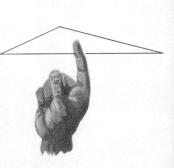

CHAPTER REVIEW/TEST

Part 1   Understanding

Fill in the blanks.

1. A rectangular prism has _____ faces, _____ vertices, and _____ edges.

2. A ray that divides an angle is called a _____ .

Write *true* or *false*.

3. Every rectangle is a parallelogram.   4. Every parallelogram is a rhombus.

5. Triangle A is congruent to triangle B. Triangle B is congruent to triangle C. What conclusions can you draw?

6. What figure is formed by connecting the following points in order? (2, 4), (5, 5), (8, 4), (8, 1), (2, 1) (2, 4)

Part 2   Skills

7. Name the cross-section view "sliced" as shown.

Name the geometric figure (*point, line, angle, ray, line segment*) that is shown.

8.   9.   10.   11. •   12.

Estimate how many degrees each angle is.   13.   14.
Then tell the kind of angle (*right, acute, obtuse*).

15. The figures are similar.
    Give the missing side length.

5 m   4 m   3 m   ▦ m   8 m   6 m

Part 3   Applications

16. **Challenge**   Four friends are deciding which television program to watch together. The choices are: a drama, comedy, mystery, or ball game. Donna will watch anything but a drama. Jack just watched two mysteries and will not watch another. Mike likes comedies, but says that the ball game is supposed to be a great one. The ball game is being delayed by rain. Which program is the best choice?

ENRICHMENT
Translation Images

Triangle B is called a **translation image** of triangle A. Each point of the triangle was moved right 2, and up 3.

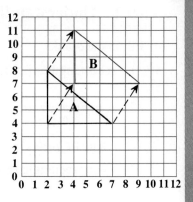

1. Give the coordinates of the points that are the vertices of triangle A. Of triangle B.

2. What can you say about the lengths of the corresponding sides of the two triangles?

Copy the figures below onto graph paper. Use the directions given to draw a translation image of each figure.

3. right 4, up 3

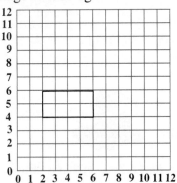

4. right 3, up 2

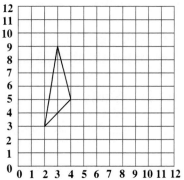

5. left 5

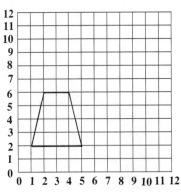

6. right 3, down 3

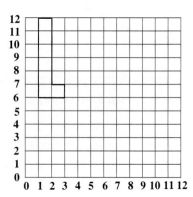

7. The coordinate of the points at the corners of rectangle C are (1, 7), (3, 7), (3, 4), and (1, 4). What are the coordinates of the corresponding points of its translation image if it is moved right 4, down 2?

8. Draw a figure of your own on graph paper. Give instructions for making the moves for a translation image of the figure. Then ask a classmate to draw the translation.

CUMULATIVE REVIEW

1. Which fraction is equivalent to $\frac{3}{5}$?

    A. $\frac{15}{20}$ B. $\frac{6}{8}$

    C. $\frac{36}{60}$ D. $\frac{5}{3}$

2. Which is the greatest common factor of 14, 42, and 28?

    A. 14   B. 84

    C. 7   D. 42

3. Which is the lowest-terms fraction for $\frac{16}{24}$?

    A. $\frac{8}{12}$ B. $\frac{2}{3}$

    C. $\frac{1}{3}$ D. $\frac{3}{4}$

4. Estimate the difference: $9\frac{1}{3} - 2\frac{7}{8}$.

    A. 7   B. 8

    C. 5   D. 6

5. Find $8 - 4\frac{1}{4}$ mentally.

    A. $4\frac{3}{4}$ B. $2\frac{3}{4}$

    C. $3\frac{3}{4}$ D. $4\frac{1}{4}$

6. Find the sum: $3\frac{5}{6} + 10\frac{2}{3}$.

    A. $13\frac{2}{3}$ B. $13\frac{1}{2}$

    C. $14\frac{1}{3}$ D. $14\frac{1}{2}$

7. Kim won the most events in the school sports contest. Josh won 5 fewer events than Kim. Ken won 2 more events than Josh. Tanya won 3 times as many events as Josh. Tanya won 6 events. How many did Kim win?

    A. 8   B. 6

    C. 7   D. 4

8. Solve. Use mental math: $\frac{3}{4} \times 16$.

    A. 48   B. 4

    C. 10   D. 12

9. Find the product of $\frac{3}{4}$ and $\frac{1}{3}$.

    A. $\frac{1}{3}$ B. $\frac{1}{4}$

    C. 3   D. $2\frac{1}{4}$

10. Divide: $56.32 \div 3.2$.

    A. 17.6   B. 1.76

    C. 0.057   D. 176

11. Estimate the product of $19\frac{2}{3}$ and $4\frac{1}{8}$.

    A. 100   B. 75

    C. 80   D. 5

12. Find the product: $3\frac{1}{3} \times 15$.

    A. $4\frac{1}{2}$ B. 50

    C. 48   D. 8

13. How many $\frac{1}{3}$-minute messages can be broadcast in 12 minutes of commercial time?

    A. 16   B. 4

    C. 12   D. 36

14. Sally is saving $5 this week. She plans to save $1 more each week than she did the week before. How many weeks will it take her to have saved a total of $160?

    A. 12   B. 14

    C. 13   D. 15

10

MATH AND FINE ARTS

DATA BANK

Use the Fine Arts Data Bank on page 481 to answer the questions.

RATIO, PROPORTION, AND PERCENT

1. Look at the pictures of some famous colossal statues. If each picture were enlarged to the actual size of the statue, which picture would be enlarged the most?

2 About how many times could the Abraham Lincoln statue be stacked to reach the same height as the Great Buddha? As the Motherland?

3 The Great Sphinx is a human-headed lion carved 4,500 years ago in Egypt. From shoulders to head, it is almost 9 meters tall. How does this compare to its total height?

4 **Using Critical Thinking** Imagine that you will create a model of any of the statues. What will you have to consider in deciding on a scale for your model?

Ratio Concepts

Favorite Fruit Snack

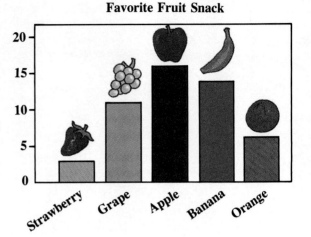

EXPLORE Study the Graph

Work in groups. The graph shows the results of a survey in which 50 students were asked to name their favorite fruit snack. Poll your class using these 5 fruits to see how their answers compare with these students' answers.

TALK ABOUT IT

1. What are the most popular fruit and the least popular fruit shown on the graph? How does this compare with your class's answers?
2. If your class had 25 students, how could you get 50 answers, as in the survey?

A **ratio** compares two numbers using a fraction. The ratio of the least popular fruit, strawberry, to the most popular fruit, apple, is 3 to 16.

We write: 3 to 16, 3:16, or $\frac{3}{16}$

We read: "three to sixteen"

Other Examples

A The ratio of grape to banana is:

11 to 14, 11:14, or $\frac{11}{14}$.

B The ratio of banana to grape is:

14 to 11, 14:11, or $\frac{14}{11}$.

Use the graph above. Write each ratio in all three forms.

1. strawberry to banana

2. grape to orange

3. banana to strawberry

4. orange to grape

5. strawberry to total votes

6. total votes to strawberry

Use this favorite fruit tally chart for exercises 1–4. Write each
ratio using all three forms.

1. apple to banana

2. banana to apple

3. plum to grape

4. orange to total votes

Pear	ЖЖ
Orange	ЖЖ ЖЖ II
Apple	ЖЖ ЖЖ ЖЖ ЖЖ III
Grape	ЖЖ ЖЖ ЖЖ I
Banana	ЖЖ ЖЖ ЖЖ ЖЖ
Plum	ЖЖ I

Use this favorite vegetable graph for exercises 5–12.
Write the ratio using all three forms.

5. cabbage to lettuce

6. lettuce to cabbage

7. least favorite to most favorite

8. most favorite to least favorite

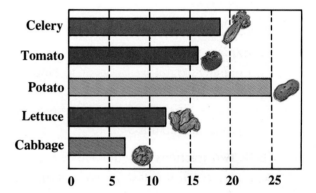

Which choice does each ratio describe?

9. 19:25

10. $\frac{25}{19}$

11. 25:7

12. $\frac{12}{16}$

MATH REASONING

13. The ratio of boys to all students in a room is 29 to 53. Are
   there more boys or more girls in the room?

PROBLEM SOLVING

14. The library's music collection has 3 albums for every
   compact disc. If there are 45 compact discs, how many
   albums are in the collection?

▶ **USING CRITICAL THINKING   Discover a Relationship**

15. The number 2 is to 3 as the number 20 is to ▥.

16. The number 40 is to 100 as the number 4 is to ▥.

17. The number 75 is to 25 as the number 3 is to ▥.

More Practice, page 513, set C

Equal Ratios

EXPLORE Solve the Problem

Brass is an alloy made by combining the metals copper
and zinc. Different kinds and colors of brass result
from changing the mix of the two metals. One kind of
brass has 7 parts of copper for every 3 parts of zinc.
Would 14 parts of copper and 6 parts of zinc make the
same brass?

TALK ABOUT IT

1. Explain why the two mixes of brass are the same type.
2. Find another ratio of copper to zinc that would give the
   same type of brass.
3. Do these ratios for the same type of brass form
   equivalent fractions?

If the two fractions are equivalent, the ratios are equal.
You may recall this test for equivalent fractions:

If the cross products are equal, the fractions are equivalent.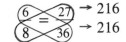

You can use the multiplication constant on your calculator to make a
ratio table to show the alloy mixes discussed above. Set up 7 as a
constant by entering $\boxed{\times}$ $\boxed{7}$ $\boxed{=}$. **Key code:** $\boxed{\text{ON/AC}}$ $\boxed{\times}$ $\boxed{7}$ $\boxed{=}$ $\boxed{1}$ $\boxed{=}$ $\boxed{2}$ $\boxed{=}$ $\boxed{3}$ $\boxed{=}$ ...

	×2	×3	×4	×5	
Copper	7	14	21	28	35
Zinc	3	6	9	12	15

The ratios $\frac{7}{3}, \frac{14}{6}, \frac{21}{9}, \frac{28}{12}, \frac{35}{15}, \ldots$
are **equal ratios.**

Write four ratios that are equal to the given ratio.

1. 2 to 3   **2.** 9 to 4   **3.** 5 to 7   **4.** 12 to 16

Are these ratios equal? Write *yes* or *no*. You may want to use
your calculator.

5. $\frac{4}{5}, \frac{28}{35}$ **6.** $\frac{7}{8}, \frac{42}{56}$ **7.** $\frac{24}{32}, \frac{9}{12}$ **8.** $\frac{34}{36}, \frac{56}{59}$

Copy and complete each ratio table. Use mental math or your calculator.

1. 3 to 2

3	6	9	▦	▦	▦
2	4	▦	▦	▦	▦

2. 9 to 5

9	▦	▦	▦	▦	▦
5	▦	▦	▦	▦	▦

Are these ratios equal? Write *yes* or *no*. You may want to use your calculator.

3. $\frac{3}{4}, \frac{5}{7}$ **4.** $\frac{3}{8}, \frac{12}{32}$ **5.** $\frac{8}{20}, \frac{6}{15}$ **6.** $\frac{3}{9}, \frac{5}{15}$

7. $\frac{6}{4}, \frac{7}{5}$ **8.** $\frac{8}{12}, \frac{6}{9}$ **9.** $\frac{78}{100}, \frac{39}{50}$ **10.** $\frac{52}{26}, \frac{4}{2}$

APPLY

MATH REASONING

11. Sort these ratios into two sets so the ratios in each set are equal. You may want to use your calculator.
35:56, 15:20, 20:32, 24:32, 36:48 45:72 72:96 75:120

PROBLEM SOLVING

12. Suppose the ratio of zinc to copper is 4 to 9. Is there more zinc or more copper in the mix?

13. If a brass alloy has half as much zinc as copper, what is the ratio of zinc to copper?

14. Bronze is made from copper, tin, and other metals. One bronze for statues is $\frac{1}{10}$ tin, $\frac{1}{4}$ lead, and the rest copper. What part of the bronze is copper?

15. Fine Arts Data Bank Compare the heights of the statues. Which pair has a ratio of about 2 to 1?

MIXED REVIEW

Find the answers.

16. $88,975 + 9,986$ **17.** $27,302 - 18,753$ **18.** 6.362×0.085 **19.** $45.365 + 389.46$ **20.** $35.23 - 29.567$

21. $67\overline{)42,547}$ **22.** $7.3\overline{)261.705}$ **23.** $27\frac{1}{8} - 12\frac{1}{6}$ **24.** $15\frac{3}{5} + 27\frac{5}{6}$

Exploring Algebra
Solving Proportions

EXPLORE Study the Information

For each 5 pounds of your body weight, about 2 pounds is muscle. About how much is the weight of the muscle for a 45-pound child?

TALK ABOUT IT

1. About how much muscle would you have for each 10 pounds of body weight?
2. How much muscle for 15 pounds of body weight?
3. Does muscle account for more body weight than other things? How can you tell?

You can solve the problem by using a ratio table.

Muscle weight →	2	4	6	8
Total body weight →	5	10	15	20

Or you can use algebra and solve a proportion.

A statement that two ratios are equal is called a **proportion.**

Let n = the unknown muscle weight. $\quad \dfrac{2}{5} = \dfrac{n}{45}$ ← muscle weight ← total weight

When two fractions are equivalent, their cross products are equal.

So: $5 \times n = 2 \times 45$

$\qquad 5 \times n = 90$ ⟨ What number times 5 equals 90? ⟩

$\qquad\quad n = 90 \div 5 = 18$ ⟨ Division undoes multiplication. ⟩

The muscles of a 45-pound child would weigh about 18 pounds.

Other Examples

A $\dfrac{3}{4} = \dfrac{n}{32}$

$\quad 4 \times n = 96$
$\qquad\quad n = 24$

B $\dfrac{4}{5} = \dfrac{n}{75}$

$\quad 5 \times n = 300$
$\qquad\quad n = 60$

C $\dfrac{7}{8} = \dfrac{n}{80}$

$\quad 8 \times n = 560$
$\qquad\quad n = 70$

Solve the proportions.

1. $\dfrac{2}{5} = \dfrac{n}{35}$
2. $\dfrac{1}{2} = \dfrac{n}{20}$
3. $\dfrac{5}{4} = \dfrac{n}{60}$
4. $\dfrac{3}{4} = \dfrac{n}{100}$
5. $\dfrac{4}{5} = \dfrac{n}{60}$

Solve the proportions.

1. $\frac{2}{3} = \frac{n}{21}$ **2.** $\frac{1}{2} = \frac{n}{12}$ **3.** $\frac{7}{8} = \frac{n}{72}$ **4.** $\frac{2}{5} = \frac{n}{40}$

5. $\frac{5}{8} = \frac{n}{80}$ **6.** $\frac{5}{6} = \frac{n}{66}$ **7.** $\frac{3}{8} = \frac{n}{56}$ **8.** $\frac{4}{3} = \frac{n}{45}$

9. $\frac{9}{10} = \frac{n}{100}$ **10.** $\frac{3}{2} = \frac{n}{50}$ **11.** $\frac{1}{5} = \frac{n}{60}$ **12.** $\frac{7}{12} = \frac{n}{120}$

13. $\frac{1}{2} = \frac{n}{16}$ **14.** $\frac{3}{5} = \frac{n}{45}$ **15.** $\frac{1}{3} = \frac{n}{36}$ **16.** $\frac{1}{8} = \frac{n}{48}$

17. $\frac{4}{5} = \frac{n}{100}$ **18.** $\frac{1}{4} = \frac{n}{32}$ **19.** $\frac{6}{5} = \frac{n}{35}$ **20.** $\frac{3}{10} = \frac{n}{60}$

MATH REASONING

Do not solve. Just tell whether n is more than or less than 50.

21. $\frac{11}{20} = \frac{n}{100}$ **22.** $\frac{12}{25} = \frac{n}{100}$ **23.** $\frac{18}{40} = \frac{n}{100}$ **24.** $\frac{22}{40} = \frac{n}{100}$ **25.** $\frac{6}{15} = \frac{n}{100}$

PROBLEM SOLVING

26. Rachel weighs 80 pounds. Using the 2 to 5 ratio, what is the weight of Rachel's muscles?

27. Bianca weighs 75 pounds. How much of Bianca's weight is not muscle?

28. Data Hunt Find your own weight. Round it to the nearest 5 pounds. Calculate the weight of your muscles.

29. You know that for two ratios to be equal, the cross products must be equal. Solve this proportion: $\frac{14}{22} = \frac{n}{165}$.

▶ **CALCULATOR**

Use your calculator to solve each proportion.

Example: $\frac{19}{61} = \frac{n}{244}$ Key code: [ON/AC] 19 [×] 244 [÷] 61 [=]

30. $\frac{26}{21} = \frac{n}{63}$ **31.** $\frac{17}{37} = \frac{n}{222}$ **32.** $\frac{17}{19} = \frac{n}{342}$ **33.** $\frac{19}{23} = \frac{n}{667}$ **34.** $\frac{41}{43} = \frac{n}{344}$

Problem Solving
Using Proportion to Find Height

UNDERSTAND
ANALYZE DATA
PLAN
ESTIMATE
SOLVE
EXAMINE

LEARN ABOUT IT

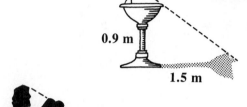

0.9 m

1.5 m

A fountain has a shadow that is 1.5 m long. A nearby statue has a 5 m shadow. If the fountain is 0.9 m tall, how tall is the statue?

Similar triangles are formed by the objects and their shadows. Since you know that the matching sides of similar triangles have equal ratios, you can estimate the statue's height. The statue's shadow is 5 ÷ 1.5, or about 3 times as long as the fountain's. So the statue height must be 3 × 0.9, or about 3 m.

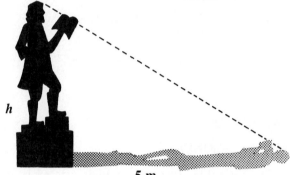

h

5 m

You can write and solve a proportion to get an exact answer.

Statue shadow → $\dfrac{5}{1.5} = \dfrac{h}{0.9}$ ← Statue height
Fountain shadow ← Fountain height

Math Point
The ratio of the shadow lengths of two objects is equal to the ratio of their heights.

$1.5 \times h = 5 \times 0.9$
$1.5 \times h = 4.5$
$h = 4.5 \div 1.5$ *Division undoes multiplication.*
$h = 3$

The statue is 3 m tall.

TRY IT OUT

Estimate each height. Then write and solve a proportion to find the exact height. Is your exact answer reasonable?

1.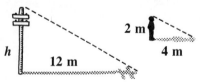

h 12 m   2 m   4 m

2.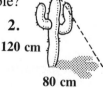

120 cm   80 cm

h 60 cm

3. A child who is 1 m tall has a shadow that is 2 m long. A tree's shadow is 9.4 m long. How tall is the tree?

Solve. Use any problem solving strategy.

1. The man is 6 ft tall and has a 2-ft shadow. The Easter Island statue has a 13.3-ft shadow. Estimate, then find the height of the statue.

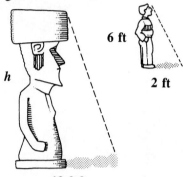

6 ft

h

2 ft

13.3 ft

2. The balloon is directly above the tree. Its shadow is 24 m from the tree. The tree is 3 m tall and has a 4-m shadow. Estimate, then find the height of the balloon.

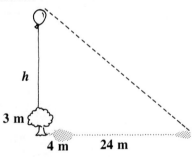

h

3 m

4 m   **24 m**

3. The Greek bronze *Charioteer of Delphi* is 5.9 ft high and has a 12-ft shadow. The post has a 4-ft shadow. Estimate, then find the height of the post. Round to the nearest hundredth of a foot.

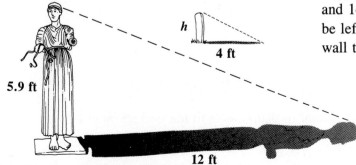

h

4 ft

5.9 ft

12 ft

4. Today there are more than 600 stone statues scattered on Easter Island. These statues were carved about 1,550 years ago. About what year were the statues carved?

5. A giraffe 3.2 m tall has a shadow 4 m long. How tall is a nearby chimpanzee that has a shadow 1 m long?

6. A street light 2.5 m tall has a shadow 3.5 m long. A nearby building has a shadow 140 m long. How tall is the building?

7. The *Charioteer of Delphi* was carved about 1,470 years ago. If an average lifetime is 75 years, about how many lifetimes ago was this?

8. **Understanding the Operation** Name the operations you need to use. Then solve the problem.

A frieze is a long, flat kind of sculpture. A certain marble frieze is 33 in. long and 14 in. wide. How much space will be left after it is placed on a 554-sq-in. wall that has the correct dimensions?

More Practice, page 526, set B

Scale Drawings

LEARN ABOUT IT

EXPLORE Study the Information

Artists often make **scale drawings** and models when they plan their work. The **scale ratio** shows the relationship between the drawing or model and the work of art.

The Italian sculptor Michelangelo created a famous statue of the Biblical hero David. In the profile drawing of *David's* head, the scale ratio is 1 cm : 0.12 m. This means that 1 cm in the drawing stands for 0.12 m in the actual statue. How tall is the actual statue's head?

TALK ABOUT IT

1. What is the height of the head in the drawing?
2. Give an estimate of the actual height of the statue's head. Explain why you think your estimate is reasonable and how you determined it.

Since *David's* head is 5 cm tall in the drawing, the actual head is:

   $5 \times 0.12 = 0.6$ m

David's head is 0.6 m tall.

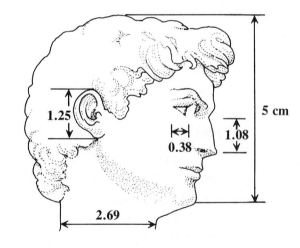

Scale   1 cm: 0.12 m

Other Example

What is the height of the actual statue's nose to the nearest hundredth m?

   $1.08 \times 0.12 = 0.13$ m

TRY IT OUT

Use the drawing of *David*. Find the actual measurements to the nearest hundredth m.

1. height of the ear   2. width of the neck   3. width of the eye

Measure to find each length. Use the scale to find the actual length to the nearest hundredth m.

1.

Alaskan brown bear
Scale 1 cm : 0.45m

2.

Polar bear
Scale 1 cm : 0.53m

APPLY

MATH REASONING

Sometimes a real object is smaller than its picture, like the ant here. For each scale, tell if the object is smaller or larger than the picture.

1 cm : 5 mm

3. 1 cm : 0.5 dm   **4.** 1 cm : 0.5 mm   **5.** 1 cm : 0.5 cm   **6.** 1 cm : 0.5 m

PROBLEM SOLVING

7. The figures of Jefferson Davis, Robert E. Lee, and Stonewall Jackson are carved into a Georgia mountain to create the Stone Mountain Confederate Memorial. The carving measures 58 m by 93 m. Could a drawing of it with a scale of 1 cm : 3 m fit on a sheet of paper 21 cm by 28 cm?

8. Consider these two scales—1 cm : 1 m and 1 cm : 1 mm. Which scale could be used for the drawing of a colossus statue? For a small statuette?

9. Fine Arts Data Bank Use the scale ratios given and a metric ruler. Calculate the head-to-toe height of the Motherland.

DATA BANK

▶ **MENTAL MATH**

Think of each segment as a scale drawing of the length of an object. Measure the segment. Use the scale to give the length of the actual object.

10. ├────────────┤
1 cm : 0.5 m

11. ├──────────────────┤
1 cm : 0.25 m

12. ├──────────────┤
1 cm : 0.2 m

13. ├────────────┤
1 cm : 0.5 m

More Practice, page 514, set A

Using Map Scales to Estimate Distances

Grand Canyon National Park

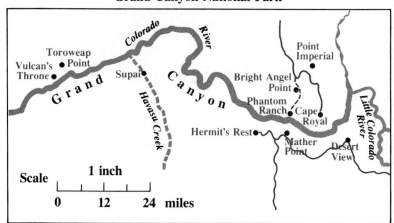

EXPLORE **Solve to Understand**

Maps have a scale so you can estimate the distances. The scale for this map of the Grand Canyon is 24 miles to the inch. About how far is it from Point Imperial to Cape Royal?

Scale 1 inch 0 12 24 miles

TALK ABOUT IT

1. What is the length on the map from Point Imperial to Cape Royal?
2. What about the problem suggests you multiply?

PRACTICE

Estimate each of these distances in the Grand Canyon National Park. Measure "crow flight" (straight) distances.

1. Hermit's Rest to Mather Point

2. Point Imperial to Phantom Ranch

3. Bright Angel Point to Toroweap Point

4. Toroweap Point to Desert View

Estimate these "curved" distances. Stay north of the river.

5. Point Imperial to Vulcan's Throne

6. Bright Angel Point to Toroweap Point

7. Cape Royal to Vulcan's Throne

8. Estimate the distance *on the river* from near Phantom Ranch to near Vulcan's Throne.

MIDCHAPTER REVIEW/QUIZ

Use the chart of eye colors for exercises 1 through 10.
Write the ratios of people with different eye colors.
Choose any form.

Eye Colors

Blue |卌 |||
Hazel	||||
Brown	卌 卌 ||

1. blue to brown

2. blue to hazel

3. hazel to blue

4. brown to hazel

Write the eye colors of people who are in the ratios.

5. There is 1 _____-eyed person for every 3 _____-eyed people.

6. There are 2 _____-eyed people for every 1 _____-eyed person.

7. The ratio of _____-eyed people to _____-eyed people is 3 to 2.

Write these ratios. Choose any form.

8. blue to total

9. brown to total

10. total to hazel

11. Copy and complete the ratio table.

5	10	▦	▦	▦	▦
4	8	▦	▦	▦	▦

Use cross products or the ratio table above
to decide which of these ratios are equal.

12. $\frac{5}{4}, \frac{15}{10}$

13. $\frac{10}{8}, \frac{25}{20}$

14. $\frac{4}{5}, \frac{20}{25}$

15. $\frac{16}{20}, \frac{15}{12}$

Solve these proportions.

16. $\frac{2}{3} = \frac{n}{9}$

17. $\frac{4}{28} = \frac{n}{7}$

18. $\frac{2}{20} = \frac{n}{30}$

19. $\frac{5}{4} = \frac{n}{20}$

20. $\frac{9}{6} = \frac{n}{4}$

PROBLEM SOLVING

21. Chelsea is 1.5 m tall and casts a 1.2 m shadow. Find the heights
of her father who casts a 1.6 m shadow and her dog who casts a
0.6 m shadow.

22. For an art project, Gabe will create a clay sculpture of his
hand. Gabe made a scale drawing of the sculpture. The scale
was 1 cm : 5 cm. If the drawing of Gabe's hand is 9.5 cm
wide, how wide will the sculpture be?

Problem Solving
Problems Without Solutions

UNDERSTAND
ANALYZE DATA
PLAN
ESTIMATE
SOLVE
EXAMINE

Most of the problems you have seen so far have had solutions. There are some problems that do not have solutions.

Discount Photo sells 120 film in 2-roll and in 4-roll packages. Ari wants exactly 19 rolls of film. He wants to buy exactly 6 packages. How many of each kind of package should he buy to get exactly 19 rolls? Is it possible?

I'll make an organized list to help me find the possibilities.

My list shows that Ari cannot buy exactly 19 rolls in 6 packages.

Pkgs. of 2 rolls	Pkgs. of 4 rolls	Total Rolls
6	0	12
5	1	14
4	2	16
3	3	18
2	4	20
1	5	22
0	6	24

PRACTICE

Solve.

1. Mercedes bought a darkroom guide for $10.75. She gave the clerk a $10-bill and 4 coins, not including a half dollar. She did not get any change back. Could she have paid the exact amount?

2. Jill wants to buy 12 rolls of 35 mm film. She found the film on sale in packages of 2 rolls and 3 rolls. She decided to buy 5 packages. Was she able to buy exactly what she wanted?

3. Bea has 5 coins in her purse. She has no coin larger than a half dollar. Bea wants to buy a magazine for $1.95. Can she pay the exact amount and use all 5 coins?

Solve. Use any strategy.

1. A 35 mm negative is 2.4 cm wide and 3.6 cm long. A print is made that is in proportion to the negative. It is 12 cm long. How wide is the print?

2. Vic belongs to a film club. He gets 2 free rolls of film for every 8 rolls he buys. Last year Vic got 26 free rolls of film. How many rolls did he buy?

3. Gia needed some darkroom supplies. She bought a $\frac{1}{2}$ gallon of developer, a gallon of fixer, and 3 large trays. Use the price list to find how much Gia spent.

Darkroom Supplies	
Paper	**Trays**
25 sheets $13.25	Small $1.80
10 sheets $7.50	Large $2.79
Developer	**Fixer**
$\frac{1}{2}$ gallon $2.98	$\frac{1}{2}$ gallon $2.45
gallon $5.08	gallon $4.76
Tongs $0.89	

4. Peter made a poster 28 in. wide and 36 in. long from a negative that was $2\frac{1}{4}$ in. long. If the negative had the same proportion as the poster, how wide was the negative?

5. Terry, Kim, Dana, and Stan are all photographers. Each has a different favorite subject—buildings, people, plants, animals. Kim thinks pictures of buildings are boring. Terry seldom photographs people, but likes to take pictures of dogs. Stan has photographed over 50 kinds of flowers. Find each photographer's favorite subject.

6. Jack bought 25 sheets of paper and 4 tongs. Use the price list to find how much each sheet of paper cost.

7. **Understanding the Question** Tell which question is another way of asking the question in this problem.

   Brian took 28 pictures one week, 35 the next week, and 13 the third week. How many fewer pictures did he take the third week than the first week?

   a. How many pictures did Brian take during the first and third weeks?
   b. How many more pictures did Brian take the first week than the third week?
   c. How many pictures did Brian take?

Understanding Percent

EXPLORE Use Percent Models

Work in groups. Outline a 10-by-10 square on graph paper. Use three colors to color all of the small squares so that you have the following ratios for the small squares:

a. The ratio of red squares to all squares is 1 to 2.

b. The ratio of blue squares to all squares is 3 to 10.

c. The ratio of orange squares to all squares is 1 to 5.

TALK ABOUT IT

1. How many squares did you color red? How did you decide?

2. How many did you color blue? Orange?

3. Did you color all of the squares?

- A special ratio that compares a number to 100 is called a **percent.**
- The word percent means *per one hundred.*
- The symbol **%** is used to show percent.

	ratio	fraction	decimal	percent
For 40 out of 100, we write:	40:100	$\frac{40}{100}$	0.40	40%
For 35¢ out of $1, we write:	35:100	$\frac{35}{100}$	0.35	35%

TRY IT OUT

Write as a percent.

1. 17:100 **2.** $\frac{87}{100}$ **3.** 3 to 100 **4.** $\frac{1}{100}$ **5.** 0.78 **6.** 75 out of 100

Write as a ratio, fraction, decimal, and percent.

7. 67 out of 100   **8.** 5 out of 100   **9.** 13¢ out of $1

Write a ratio, fraction, decimal, and percent to show what part is shaded.

1. 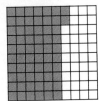   **2.** 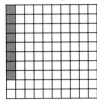   **3.** 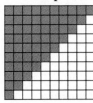   **4.**

Write each ratio as a percent.

5. $\frac{15}{100}$ **6.** 65:100   **7.** $\frac{7}{100}$ **8.** 43:100   **9.** 83 to 100

Write each percent as a ratio (use fractions).

10. 61%   **11.** 44%   **12.** 17%   **13.** 2%   **14.** 100%   **15.** 56%

APPLY

MATH REASONING

Use the square you colored in the Explore activity to answer these questions.

16. What percent is *not* blue?

17. What percent is blue *or* red?

PROBLEM SOLVING

18. Crystal's goal is to earn $100 during summer vacation. She made $28 in June and $37 in July. What percent of her goal did she achieve in two months?

19. With two weeks to go, Crystal had achieved 87% of her goal of earning $100. How much does she have to earn in the last two weeks if she is to reach her goal?

MIXED REVIEW

Find the answers.

20. $\frac{5}{7} \div \frac{3}{4}$ **21.** $0.08\overline{)0.056}$ **22.** $5 \div 2\frac{1}{2}$ **23.** $9\overline{)5218}$ **24.** $\frac{5}{6} \times 168$

Tell whether each angle below is *right, acute,* or *obtuse.*

25.   **26.**   **27.**   **28.**

Estimating a Percent of Something

EXPLORE **Discover a Relationship**

Think of each line segment as 100%. Estimate a percent for each point.

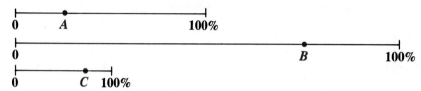

TALK ABOUT IT

1. Why would your estimate for *A* have to be less than 50%?
2. How did you decide on an estimate for *B*?
3. Is *C* more than or less than 50%? Why?

Estimating a percent of something is much the same as estimating a fraction or decimal part of something. The number line below will help you think about percents between 0 and 100%.

None		**Half**		**All**
0	$\frac{1}{4}$	$\frac{1}{2}$	$\frac{3}{4}$	1
	0.25	0.50	0.75	100%
	25%	50%	75%	

Use these percents to help you estimate percents of other things.

Estimate these percents using the graph.

1. About what percent like baseball programs best?

2. Estimate the percent who like to watch soccer.

3. What is your estimate of the total percent for football and basketball?

4. Is it possible that 25% chose golf? Why?

Favorite TV Sports Program

296

Estimate the following percents along the path.

1. About what percent of the hike will be over when hikers reach the Old Mill?

2. What is a little more than 50% of the way?

3. About what percent will be over when the hikers start the steep climb?

Estimate these percents of a set.

4. About what percent of the total vote did Josh get?

5. Who is closest to Josh's percent?

6. Who has less than 25%?

7. Which candidate is closest to 35%?

APPLY

MATH REASONING

8. Make up numbers for an audience using these percents.
A little more than 25% of the audience were girls.
A little less than 25% were boys.   About 50% were adults.

PROBLEM SOLVING

9. The 6th, 7th, and 8th graders had a party. About 30% of
the students at the party were 6th graders and 25% were
7th graders. About what percent were 8th graders?

▶ ALGEBRA

Give a percent that will fit each variable.

10. $a < 40\%$ and $a > 30\%$ 11. $b < 90\%$ and $b > 80\%$ 12. $c < 50\%$ and $c > 20\%$

Percents, Fractions, and Decimals

The Air You Breathe

LEARN ABOUT IT

In this lesson, you will work with the relations between percents, fractions, and decimals.

EXPLORE Read the Information

The air we breathe is made up of different gases. The graph shows that the two main gases are nitrogen and oxygen. The numbers that tell how the gases are divided are given in three different forms.

21% oxygen

$\frac{78}{100}$ nitrogen

0.01 other gases

TALK ABOUT IT

1. Normally a graph would use all fractions, all decimals, or all percents. Which do you think would help you best understand the graph? Why?

2. If all of the numbers were given as percents, what would they be?

The table shows the different forms for each gas.

Gas	Fraction	Decimal	Percent
Nitrogen	$\frac{78}{100}$	0.78	78%
Oxygen	$\frac{21}{100}$	0.21	21%
Other gases	$\frac{1}{100}$	0.01	1%

Sometimes you may choose to reduce the fraction to lowest terms.

Example: $40\% = 0.40 = \frac{40}{100}$ or $\frac{2}{5}$

TRY IT OUT

Write each decimal or fraction as a percent.

1. 0.35   **2.** $\frac{15}{100}$ **3.** $\frac{68}{100}$ **4.** 0.06   **5.** $\frac{2}{100}$

Write as lowest-terms fractions.   Write as decimals.

6. 75%   **7.** 60%   **8.** 6%   **9.** 35%   **10.** 99%   **11.** 50%

Write each decimal as a percent.

1. 0.75   **2.** 0.50   **3.** 0.38   **4.** 0.21   **5.** 0.05   **6.** 0.09

Write each fraction as a percent.

7. $\frac{24}{100}$ **8.** $\frac{50}{100}$ **9.** $\frac{10}{100}$ **10.** $\frac{1}{100}$ **11.** $\frac{100}{100}$

Write each percent as a decimal.

12. 43%   **13.** 20%   **14.** 17%   **15.** 8%   **16.** 42%   **17.** 2%

Write each percent as a fraction in lowest terms.

18. 90%   **19.** 2%   **20.** 45%   **21.** 30%   **22.** 23%   **23.** 65%

24. 25%   **25.** 35%   **26.** 40%   **27.** 17%   **28.** 110%   **29.** 4%

APPLY

MATH REASONING

30. Put these in order from smallest to largest.

$28\%, \frac{72}{100}, 0.46, 90\%, \frac{1}{2}$ 0.6

PROBLEM SOLVING

31. Oxygen and nitrogen together make up what percent of the air?

32. What decimal part of the air is not nitrogen?

33. What fraction of the air is not oxygen?

34. The percent of oxygen, by weight, in water is about $4\frac{1}{4}$ times the percent of oxygen in air. Estimate this percent.

▶ ESTIMATION

Some percents are very close to "easy" fractions. Choose the fraction that is the best estimate of the percent.

35. 23%: $\frac{1}{10}, \frac{1}{4}, \frac{1}{2}$ **36.** 52%: $\frac{1}{2}, \frac{5}{8}, \frac{3}{4}$ **37.** 74%: $\frac{5}{8}, \frac{3}{4}, \frac{9}{10}$

38. 33%: $\frac{1}{4}, \frac{1}{3}, \frac{1}{2}$ **39.** 19%: $\frac{1}{10}, \frac{1}{5}, \frac{1}{2}$ **40.** 91%: $\frac{3}{4}, \frac{7}{8}, \frac{9}{10}$

Writing Fractions and Decimals as Percents

LEARN ABOUT IT

Sometimes you can give information better by using a percent than if you use a fraction or a decimal.

EXPLORE Analyze the Process

Your body weight is about $\frac{2}{3}$ water. What percent of your body is water?

You divide the numerator by the denominator to find a decimal for a fraction.

First, find the decimal for $\frac{2}{3}$.

$$3\overline{)2.00} = 0.66\frac{2}{3}$$

Think: $66\frac{2}{3}$ hundredths

Then, change the decimal to a percent.

$$66\frac{2}{3}\%$$

TALK ABOUT IT

1. How can you find a decimal for a fraction?
2. How can you change a decimal to a percent?
3. If the fraction is more than $\frac{1}{2}$, will the percent be more than or less than 50%?
4. Use a complete sentence to give a reasonable answer to the story problem.

Other Examples

A Sometimes you can find an equivalent fraction with denominator 100.

$$\frac{3}{4} = \frac{75}{100} = 75\%$$

B Some percents are more than 100.

$$\frac{5}{4} = \frac{125}{100} = 125\%$$

TRY IT OUT

Find the percent for each fraction.

1. $\frac{1}{4}$ 2. $\frac{3}{5}$ 3. $\frac{1}{3}$ 4. $\frac{5}{8}$ 5. $\frac{7}{4}$ 6. $\frac{5}{6}$

Find an equivalent fraction with a denominator of 100. Then write a percent for each fraction.

1. $\frac{2}{5}$ **2.** $\frac{3}{10}$ **3.** $\frac{1}{5}$ **4.** $\frac{6}{5}$

Reduce the fraction to the lowest terms. Then find an equivalent fraction with a denominator of 100 and write the percent.

5. $\frac{6}{30}$ **6.** $\frac{9}{12}$ **7.** $\frac{8}{16}$

8. $\frac{14}{20}$ **9.** $\frac{6}{15}$ **10.** $\frac{15}{12}$

Divide to find a decimal or mixed decimal for each fraction. Then write the decimal as a percent.

11. $\frac{5}{8}$ **12.** $\frac{3}{5}$ **13.** $\frac{7}{4}$

14. $\frac{6}{5}$ **15.** $\frac{7}{8}$ **16.** $\frac{5}{3}$

APPLY

A   B

MATH REASONING

17. Which shows the better bargain, sign **A** or sign **B**?

PROBLEM SOLVING

18. Your blood is 0.9 water. What percent of your blood is not water?

19. $\frac{2}{5}$ of your body weight is muscle. What percent is $\frac{2}{5}$? About 66% of your body weight is water. Is muscle weight plus water weight more or less than 100%? What does that tell you about muscles?

▶ **MENTAL MATH**

Give each percent mentally.

20. Since $\frac{4}{8} = 50\%$ and $\frac{1}{8} = 12\frac{1}{2}\%$, we know that $\frac{5}{8} = $ ▥ %.

21. Since $\frac{2}{8} = 25\%$ and $\frac{1}{8} = 12\frac{1}{2}\%$, we know that $\frac{3}{8} = $ ▥ %.

22. Since $\frac{6}{8} = 75\%$ and $\frac{1}{8} = 12\frac{1}{2}\%$, we know that $\frac{7}{8} = $ ▥ %.

More Practice, page 515, set A

More About Percent
Using a Calculator

Class Play Ticket Sales

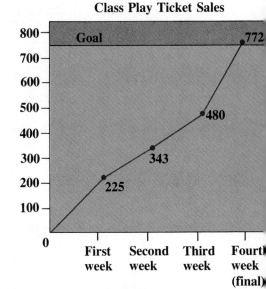

EXPLORE Analyze the Process

The play committee set a goal of selling 750 tickets. The line graph shows their progress for the four weeks. What percent (to the nearest tenth) of the goal had they reached by the end of the second week?

You can make the tickets sold and the goal a fraction that can be rewritten as a percent. You can use your calculator to find the percent.

$\frac{343}{750}$ = 343 $\boxed{\div}$ 750 $\boxed{=}$ $\boxed{\boxed{0.4573333}}$

Round to the nearest thousandth.	Think about hundredths.	Write the percent.
0.457	45.7 hundredths	45.7%

TALK ABOUT IT

1. What numbers do you use to make a fraction?
2. What about the problem suggests that you divide?
3. Use a complete sentence to give a reasonable answer to the story problem.

Other Examples

A Nearest percent

$\frac{37}{89} \rightarrow 0.416 \rightarrow 42\%$

B Nearest tenth of a percent

$\frac{356}{282} \rightarrow 1.262 \rightarrow 126.2\%$

Use your calculator to write each fraction to the nearest tenth of a percent and the nearest percent.

1. $\frac{5}{7}$
2. $\frac{11}{12}$
3. $\frac{12}{11}$
4. $\frac{45}{86}$
5. $\frac{1}{125}$
6. $\frac{789}{567}$

Use your calculator. Write each fraction to the nearest percent.

1. $\frac{6}{7}$ 2. $\frac{5}{16}$ 3. $\frac{7}{12}$ 4. $\frac{12}{7}$ 5. $\frac{3}{125}$ 6. $\frac{17}{75}$

7. $\frac{42}{43}$ 8. $\frac{43}{42}$ 9. $\frac{400}{755}$ 10. $\frac{687}{964}$ 11. $\frac{308}{572}$ 12. $\frac{762}{750}$

Write each fraction to the nearest tenth of a percent.

13. $\frac{5}{8}$ 14. $\frac{2}{7}$ 15. $\frac{5}{12}$ 16. $\frac{8}{15}$

17. $\frac{1}{250}$ 18. $\frac{9}{11}$ 19. $\frac{14}{21}$ 20. $\frac{3}{650}$

21. $\frac{38}{75}$ 22. $\frac{394}{286}$ 23. $\frac{286}{394}$ 24. $\frac{675}{801}$

APPLY

MATH REASONING

Each fraction is close to 25%, 50%, or 75%. Use mental math to tell which one.

25. $\frac{44}{87}$ 26. $\frac{15}{59}$ 27. $\frac{212}{283}$

28. $\frac{302}{407}$ 29. $\frac{217}{862}$ 30. $\frac{357}{728}$

PROBLEM SOLVING

31. What percent of the ticket sale goal was reached with one week left to go?

32. By about how many percentage points did the play committee exceed its goal?

33. A charity drive to raise $1,000 makes $\frac{3}{4}$ of its goal in three weeks. It raises $130 in the next week. What percent of its goal has been reached?

▶ **COMMUNICATION   Writing Math for Understanding.**

34. Use your calculator to find decimals for $\frac{2}{3}$ and $\frac{1}{3}$. Do these numbers added together give the same answer as $\frac{2}{3} + \frac{1}{3}$? Write a sentence telling why you think the numbers are different.

Data Collection and Analysis
Group Decision Making

UNDERSTAND
ANALYZE DATA
PLAN
ESTIMATE
SOLVE
EXAMINE

Doing a Survey

Group Skill

Check for Understanding

Most students in Canada know the name of the president of the United States. Do you think most students in the United States know who the prime minister of Canada is? Do you think adults know? Conduct a survey to find out.

Collecting Data

1. Talk with your group. Choose four countries that are regularly in the U.S. news.

2. Do some research to find out who the leaders of these countries are if you do not already know. A recent almanac is one place to look.

3. Show the list of countries to at least 15 adults and 15 young people about your age. Ask them to give the name of the leader of each country. Make a tally table to record whether or not each answer is correct.

Foreign Leaders	Adult	Young Person
England ___	Correct: ‖‖ ‖‖ Incorrect: ‖‖	Correct: ‖‖ ‖‖‖ Incorrect: ‖‖ ‖‖
Canada ___	Correct: ‖‖ ‖‖ Incorrect: ‖‖ ‖‖‖	Correct: ‖‖ ‖‖ ‖‖ Incorrect: ‖‖‖
	Correct:	Correct: orrect:

Organizing Data

4. Make a double bar graph comparing the answers of adults and young people. Show the number of correct responses for adults and for young people for each foreign leader.
5. Did you label your graph and give it a title?

Presenting Your Analysis

6. Who do you think are more informed about the leaders of the world—adults or young people? Tell how you came to your conclusion.
7. Write at least three true statements about the information in your graph.
8. Why is it a good idea to include about the same number of adults and young people in your sample? What other things should you consider to make sure you have fair representation in your sample?

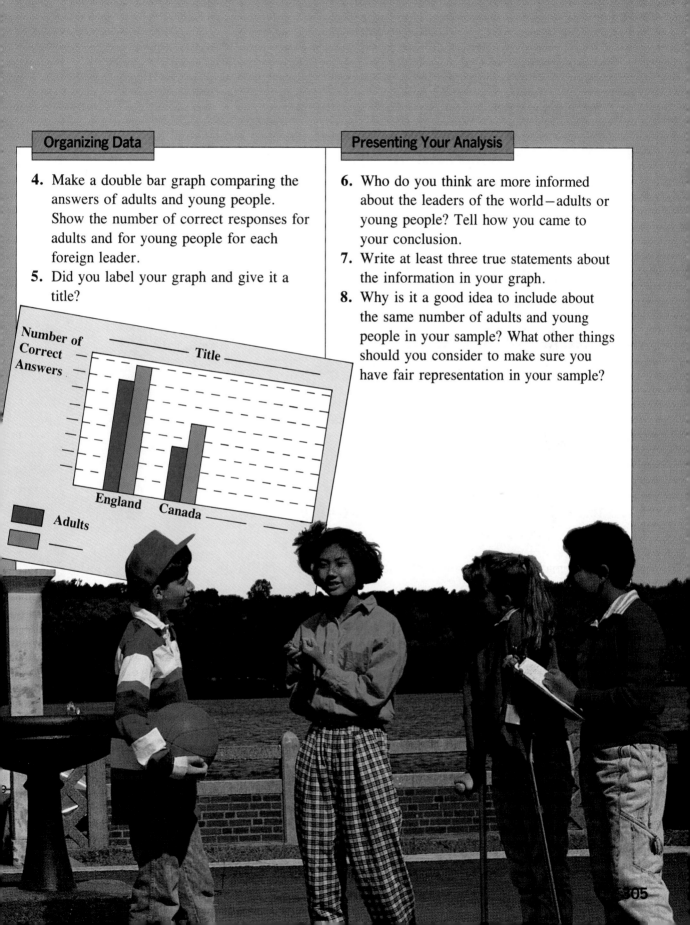

Number of Correct Answers

Title

England   Canada

Adults

305

WRAP UP

Percent or Ratio?

Give the percent or ratio for each description.

1. ratio of weekdays to days of week

2. ratio of states to state capitals

3. percent equal to $\frac{1}{2}$

4. percent equal to $\frac{1}{4}$

5. ratio of states to United States senators

6. percent score for 40 correct answers on a 100-question test

7. percent score for 35 correct answers on a 50-question test

Sometimes, Always, Never

Decide which word goes in the blank: *sometimes*, *always*, or *never*. Explain your choices.

8. If two ratios are equal, their fractions are _____ equivalent.

9. If the cross-products of two ratios are unequal, the ratios are _____ equal.

10. If a person casts a shadow of 12 feet, a 6-foot pole nearby _____ casts a 12-foot shadow.

11. A map scale of 100 miles to 1 inch is _____ appropriate to use when making a map.

12. A candidate can _____ win an election with 30% of the popular vote.

13. If a team has won more than 50% of its games, it _____ has won more often than it has lost.

Project

Make a floor plan of a section of your classroom. Decide on a reasonable scale for the area you choose. Place objects within the area. Objects with regular geometric shapes will be easiest to work with. Use a centimeter ruler and graph paper to make accurate scale drawings of the objects and to measure the distances between them. Make up problems about your floor plan for classmates to solve.

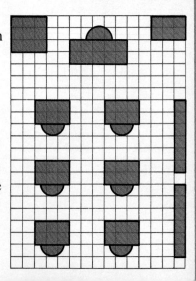

CHAPTER REVIEW/TEST

Part 1 Understanding

In a fruit bowl there are 5 apples, 2 bananas, and 3 pears.

1. What is the ratio of pears to apples?

2. What is the ratio of bananas to pears?

3. Consider these two scales: 1 cm : 2 mm and 1 cm : 2 m. Which would most likely be used for a drawing of the Statue of Liberty?

4. Put in order from least to greatest: 23%, $\frac{32}{100}$, 0.21.

5. Which fraction is the best estimate of 36%: $\frac{3}{5}$, $\frac{3}{8}$, or $\frac{1}{4}$?

6. Estimate a percent for point A. For point B.

Part 2 Skills

```
  |------+-------•---------•-------|
 0%          A         B      100%
```

Are the ratios equal? Write *yes* or *no*.

7. $\frac{2}{3}$, $\frac{6}{8}$

8. $\frac{7}{20}$, $\frac{35}{100}$

Solve the proportion.

9. $\frac{4}{5} = \frac{n}{30}$

10. $\frac{7}{6} = \frac{n}{48}$

11. Write as a ratio, fraction, decimal, and percent: 37 out of 100.

Write as a percent.

12. $\frac{7}{50}$

13. $\frac{3}{8}$

Write each fraction as a percent to the nearest tenth of a percent.

14. $\frac{3}{16}$

15. $\frac{7}{11}$

Part 3 Applications

16. The map of a region is drawn to the scale 1 in. : 22.5 mi. About how far apart are two towns that are about $3\frac{3}{4}$ in. apart on the map?

17. A tree casts a 6-m shadow. A nearby post is 1.5 m tall and casts a 3-m shadow. How tall is the tree?

18. **Challenge** Donna has 6 coins. She wants to buy an item that now costs $\frac{2}{3}$ of what it used to cost. If the original price was $1.50, is it possible for Donna to pay the exact amount using all 6 coins?

ENRICHMENT
Scale Drawing

Make a map of Mammal County. You will need a ruler and centimeter graph paper. Use a scale of 1 cm : 15 km.

First make an outline of the county. It is a square, 225 km on each side. Assign the coordinates (0, 0) to the southwest, or bottom left corner. Place the town of Pig at point (2, 13).

Now, use the information below to place the towns on the map.

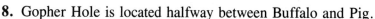

1. Porcupine is 60 km south of Pig.

2. Whalebone is 45 km south, and 75 km east of Porcupine.

3. Kangaroo Pouch is 112.5 km north of Whalebone.

4. Lambchop is 135 km east of Porcupine.

5. Buffalo is 60 km north, and 22.5 km east of Lambchop.

6. Horseradish is 97.5 km south, and 37.5 km east of Lambchop.

7. Moosenose is 90 km west of Horseradish.

8. Gopher Hole is located halfway between Buffalo and Pig.

CUMULATIVE REVIEW

1. Solve for t. Use mental math:
   $t - 40 = 50$.
   - A. $t = 2,000$
   - B. $t = 10$
   - C. $t = \frac{4}{5}$
   - D. $t = 90$

2. Subtract: $5\frac{2}{3} - 3\frac{1}{4}$.
   - A. $2\frac{1}{12}$
   - B. $2\frac{5}{12}$
   - C. $3\frac{11}{12}$
   - D. $2\frac{1}{4}$

3. Divide: $5 \div 1\frac{2}{3}$.
   - A. 3
   - B. $3\frac{1}{3}$
   - C. 4
   - D. $6\frac{2}{3}$

4. Find the repeating decimal for $\frac{8}{24}$.
   - A. $0.\overline{16}$
   - B. $0.\overline{3}$
   - C. $\overline{3}$
   - D. $0.\overline{6}$

5. Choose the most reasonable answer: An athlete signed a contract paying him a total of $12.5 million for 5 years. Each year he receives a pay increase. What could his first year's salary be?
   - A. $150,000,000
   - B. $1,500,000
   - C. $3,000,000
   - D. $2,500,000

6. Solve. Use mental math: $\frac{3}{4} \times 60$.
   - A. 40
   - B. 80
   - C. 45
   - D. 15

7. How many faces does a square pyramid have?
   - A. 3
   - B. 4
   - C. 5
   - D. 6

8. Name the space figure.
   - A. triangular pyramid
   - B. cube
   - C. square pyramid
   - D. square

Front view   Top view   Side view

9. What figure is represented by the edge of a shoe box?
   - A. point
   - B. line
   - C. line segment
   - D. ray

10. What do you call lines that intersect at square corners?
    - A. planes
    - B. parallel
    - C. skew
    - D. perpendicular

11. Dana's dance instructor had her place her feet at an angle of about 120°. What kind of angle was formed?
    - A. right
    - B. obtuse
    - C. straight
    - D. acute

12. Carl's sketch of the side of a building is a trapezoid. How many pairs of parallel sides does it have?
    - A. 1
    - B. 4
    - C. 0
    - D. 2

11

USING PERCENT

MATH AND
SOCIAL STUDIES

DATA BANK

Use the Social Studies Data Bank on page 471 to answer the questions.

1. According to predictions, the United States will have about twice as many people as Japan in the year 2000. How will the percentage of people in each age group compare? How will the number of people in each age group compare?

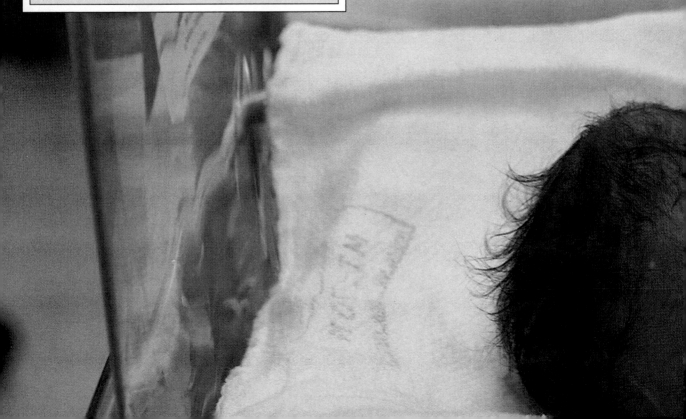

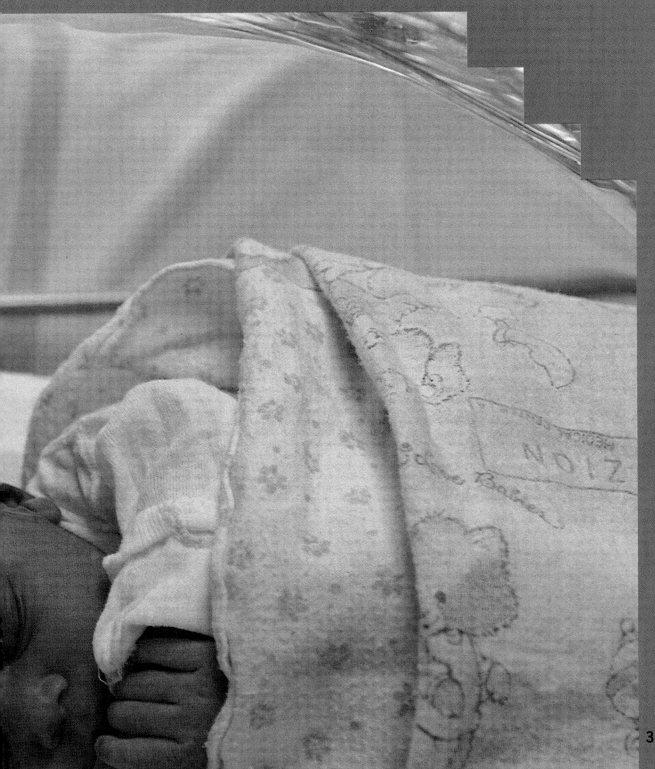

2 The world population is increasing at different rates in various parts of the world. Which countries are expected to double their population by the year 2000?

3 The work force of a country is made up of people 15 to 64 years of age. Which countries now have about two thirds of their population in the work force? Which have more than one third under the age of 15?

4 **Using Critical Thinking** Compare the percentages of each country's population that is 65 or older now and by the year 2000. In industrialized nations, this population is ___. In developing nations, it is ___. Give some reasons for this.

Finding A Percent Of A Number

EXPLORE Analyze the Process

Social scientists predict that in 1995, about 0.13 of the United States population will be age 65 or older; $\frac{4}{13}$ of the population will be men from 18 through 64 years old; and 25% of the population will be under age 18. If the population is 260 million, how many people will be in each group?

TALK ABOUT IT

1. What is 0.13 of 260?
2. How can you find $\frac{4}{13}$ of 260? What is it?
3. Can you write 25% as a fraction or decimal? What is 25% of 260?

- To find a percent of a number, change the percent to a fraction or a decimal. Then multiply the number by the fraction or decimal.

Examples

A 75% of 24

$\frac{3}{4} \times 24 = 18$

$0.75 \times 24 = 18$

B $33\frac{1}{3}$% of 24

$\frac{1}{3} \times 24 = 8$

C 45% of 24

$0.45 \times 24 = 10.8$

Find the percent of each number. Use fractions.

1. 25% of 32   **2.** 10% of 32   **3.** $33\frac{1}{3}$% of 12   **4.** 50% of 48   **5.** 75% of 48

Find the percent of each number. Use decimals.

6. 24% of 30   **7.** 18% of 25   **8.** 72% of 15   **9.** 64% of 50   **10.** 94% of 64

Find the percent of each number. Use fractions.

1. 75% of 92   **2.** 40% of 40   **3.** $33\frac{1}{3}$% of 78   **4.** 50% of 98

5. $66\frac{2}{3}$% of 51   **6.** 10% of 250   **7.** 25% of 52   **8.** 90% of 80

Find the percent of each number. Use decimals.

9. 19% of 26   **10.** 43% of 85   **11.** 76% of 95   **12.** 3% of 32

13. 87% of 24   **14.** $12\frac{1}{2}$% of 72   **15.** 24% of 36   **16.** 11% of 20

Find the percent of each number. Choose your own method.

17. 31% of 90   **18.** 75% of 240   **19.** $12\frac{1}{2}$% of 64   **20.** 50% of 68

21. 20% of 35   **22.** 45% of 180   **23.** 25% of 60   **24.** 67% of 320

APPLY

MATH REASONING Write each percent without multiplying.

$\boxed{32 \times 24 = 768}$ **25.** 32% of 24   **26.** 24% of 32   **27.** 24% of 320

PROBLEM SOLVING

28. Extra Data Of the estimated 305 million people in the United States in the year 2030, about 65 million will be 65 years old or older. About 60% of these will be women. About how many men will be 65 or older in the year 2030?

29. Social Studies Data Bank Calculate numbers to the nearest million to complete these statements: In the year 2000, there will be _____ more children under the age of 15 living in Nigeria than there were in 1975. And, there will be _____ more Nigerian children than Japanese children.

DATA BANK

▶ **CALCULATOR**

You can use the percent key $\boxed{\%}$ on your calculator to find the percent of a number.

Example: 46% of 75   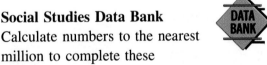

Use your percent key to find each of these.

30. 78% of 127   **31.** 34% of 96   **32.** 83% of 834   **33.** 7% of 975

More Practice, page 515, set C

Mentral Math
Percent of a Number

When a percent can be replaced by an "easy" fraction, you may be able to find the percent of the number mentally.

EXPLORE Study the Information

Meat is an important source of protein. In addition to protein, meat contains many essential vitamins and minerals. Meat also contains an abundance of fat. For example, lean hamburger is approximately 20% fat. How many ounces of fat would there be in a 15-ounce package of hamburger?

Some Percents That Have "Easy" Fractions	
$50\% = \frac{1}{2}$	
$33\frac{1}{3}\% = \frac{1}{3}$	
$25\% = \frac{1}{4}$	
$20\% = \frac{1}{5}$	
$12\frac{1}{2}\% = \frac{1}{8}$	
$10\% = \frac{1}{10}$	

TALK ABOUT IT

1. Is there a simple fraction for 20%? What is it?
2. Can you find $\frac{1}{5}$ of 15 mentally? How?
3. Solve the story problem.

Other Examples

A $33\frac{1}{3}\%$ of 27

$\frac{1}{3} \times 27 = 9$

B 25% of 48

$\frac{1}{4} \times 48 = 12$

Find the percent of each number mentally.

1. 10% of 40
2. 50% of 40
3. 25% of 40
4. $12\frac{1}{2}\%$ of 240
5. $33\frac{1}{3}\%$ of 90
6. 25% of 240

Find the percent of each number mentally.

1. 25% of 32

2. 10% of 90

3. 50% of 18

4. $33\frac{1}{3}$% of 60

5. $12\frac{1}{2}$% of 40

6. $33\frac{1}{3}$% of 24

7. $12\frac{1}{2}$% of 160

8. 10% of 30

9. $33\frac{1}{3}$% of 270

10. 20% of 450

11. 25% of 240

12. 50% of 160

Find the savings on each item. Use mental math.

13. **14.** **15.**

SALE
save 25%
ON EACH ITEM

$28 $24 $32

APPLY

MATH REASONING

16. Is it true that 20% of 25 is the same as 25% of 20?

Use your discovery in exercise 16 to find these mentally:

17. 32% of 25

18. 35% of 20

19. 16% of $12\frac{1}{2}$

20. 21% of $33\frac{1}{3}$

PROBLEM SOLVING

Solve using mental math.

21. A pound is 16 ounces. How many ounces of fat are in 2 pounds of corned beef that is 25% fat?

22. A beef rib roast is $33\frac{1}{3}$% fat. How many pounds of fat are in a 15-pound rib roast? A 12-ounce serving?

23. **Write Your Own Problem** Write a question about this data that can be answered using mental math: Lean ground beef is 20% fat.

▶ **ALGEBRA**

Find the missing percent.

24. *a*% of 12 is 6

25. *b*% of 12 is 3

26. *c*% of 12 is 4

More Practice, page 515, set D

Estimation
Percent of a Number

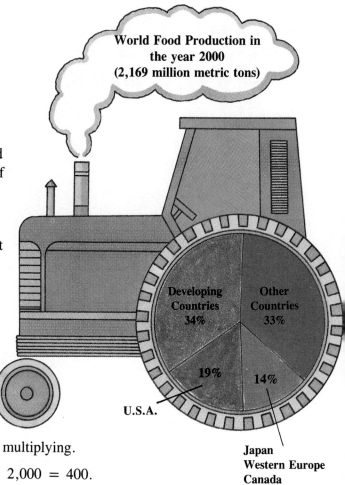

World Food Production in
the year 2000
(2,169 million metric tons)

You can sometimes use "easy" fractions and
compatible numbers to estimate a percent of
a number.

EXPLORE Interpret a Graph

The graph shows a prediction of the percent
of the world food supply produced by
certain countries in the year 2000. About
how many million metric tons are
developing countries expected to produce?

TALK ABOUT IT

1. What "easy" fraction is close to 34%?
2. Explain how to estimate $\frac{1}{3}$ of 2,169.

Developing
Countries
34%

Other
Countries
33%

19%

14%

U.S.A.

Japan
Western Europe
Canada
Australia

You can choose compatible numbers before multiplying.

To estimate 19% of 2,169, think about $\frac{1}{5} \times 2,000 = 400$.

To estimate 33% of 2,169, think about $\frac{1}{3} \times 2,100 = 700$.

Estimate the percent of the number.

1. 32% of 24
2. 49% of 140
3. 21% of 37
4. 27% of 199

Estimate the percent of each number.

1. 12% of 24   **2.** 51% of 60   **3.** 24% of 60   **4.** 33% of 60

5. 48% of 120   **6.** 21% of 45   **7.** 9% of 80   **8.** 13% of 80

9. 19% of 150   **10.** 11% of 120   **11.** 34% of 120   **12.** 21% of 350

13. 26% of 23   **14.** 33% of 28   **15.** 12% of 63   **16.** 49% of 151

17. 9% of 140   **18.** 13% of 49   **19.** 67% of 152   **20.** 11% of 49

APPLY

MATH REASONING

First estimate the percent of the number. Then tell if the estimate
is an overestimate or an underestimate.

21. 33% of 11   **22.** 26% of 33   **23.** 48% of 19   **24.** 21% of 31

PROBLEM SOLVING

This graph shows the percent of the world food
supply that may be consumed by certain countries
in the year 2000.

25. By the year 2000, about 4% of the
population may live in the United
States. About what percent of the world
food supply will they consume?

26. To the nearest million, how many tons
less will the United States consume
than it produces?

27. Social Studies Data Bank Which group of
countries may increase in population from 1975 to 2000:
a. close to 25%   **b.** close to 100%

World Food Consumption in the Year 2000
(2,169 million metric tons)

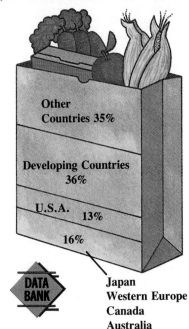

Other Countries 35%

Developing Countries 36%

U.S.A. 13%

16%

DATA BANK

Japan
Western Europe
Canada
Australia

▶ CALCULATOR

First estimate the percent of each number. Then use your
calculator to check to see how close your estimate is.

28. 49% of 179   **29.** 24% of 319   **30.** 19% of 354   **31.** 34% of 175

More Practice, page 515, set E

Using Critical Thinking

There are 24 students in Jenny's class. The chart shows some of their activities and the percent of students in each one.

Percent of Class in Each Club			
Science Club	$33\frac{1}{3}\%$	Drama Club	50%
Math Club	25%	Sports Club	75%

Maria looked at the chart and said, "Something is wrong. Those percents add up to well over 100."

Tony declared, "I figured the number of students in each club and the total is way over 24."

Jeno exclaimed, "Something is wrong. I know 2 students who are not in Drama or Sports."

TALK ABOUT IT

1. Why does Maria think the total percents should not be over 100?
2. How would you figure the total club membership? What is it? How can it be over 24?
3. Is it possible that some of the students are not in any of the clubs?
4. What can you conclude about the club membership of the students in Jenny's class?

Use the chart above to answer these questions.

1. What is the greatest number of students who could be in both the Science and the Math club? What is the least? Explain.

2. What is the greatest number of students who could be in both the Drama and the Sports club? What is the least?

3. What is the greatest number of students who could be in all four clubs? What is the least?

4. Make up a question of your own about club membership in Jenny's class. Ask a classmate to answer it.

318

MIDCHAPTER REVIEW/QUIZ

Estimate the percent of each number.

1. 24% of 59

2. 35% of 147

3. 19% of 250

4. 13% of 55

Find the percent of each number. Hint: Try mental math first.

5. 50% of 150

6. 75% of 88

7. $33\frac{1}{3}$% of 57

8. $66\frac{2}{3}$% of 63

9. 40% of 65

10. 5% of 80

11. 64% of 50

12. 92% of 25

13. 25% of 92

14. $12\frac{1}{2}$% of 24

15. 20% of 55

16. 10% of 250

17. $12\frac{1}{2}$% of 250

18. 15% of 64

19. 90% of 125

20. 4% of 125

21. 25% of 74

22. 30% of 12

23. $66\frac{2}{3}$% of 105

24. 48 % of 36

PROBLEM SOLVING

25. The graph shows survey results for Julie's sixth grade class. If these results are typical for the whole school, about how many bike spaces are needed for 350 students?

How Students Get to School

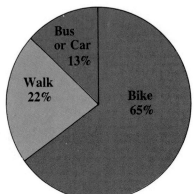

26. In 1980, about 227 million people lived in the United States and about 32% were under age 20. If 51% of those people were males, about how many males were under age 20 in 1980? (Hint: First find out about how many people were under age 20.)

27. In 1890, about 63 million people lived in the United States. About 12% were under age 5, 34% were aged 5 through 19, and only 4% were age 65 or older. Estimate how many people were in each of those age groups.

Problem Solving
Choosing a Calculation Method

UNDERSTAND
ANALYZE DATA
PLAN
ESTIMATE
SOLVE
EXAMINE

When you solve a problem, you often will need to decide on a calculation method.

Calculation Methods
- Mental Math
- Pencil and Paper
- Calculator

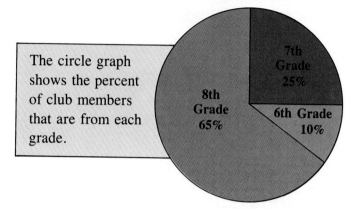

**Science Club
40 Members**

The circle graph shows the percent of club members that are from each grade.

8th Grade 65%

7th Grade 25%

6th Grade 10%

How many 6th graders are in the Science Club?

> 10% is the same as 0.10, or 0.1. I can find 0.1 of 40 easily using mental math.

How many 7th graders are in the club?

> 25% is the same as $\frac{1}{4}$. I can find $\frac{1}{4}$ of 40 easily, too, using mental math.

How many 8th graders are in the club?

> 65% is the same as $\frac{65}{100}$, or 0.65. I cannot find 65% of 40 easily using mental math. So, I should use pencil and paper or a calculator.

When you have to choose a calculation method

- First try mental math.
- If you can't use mental math, choose between pencil and paper and a calculator.

TRY IT OUT

Tell what calculation method you choose and why. Then solve.

1. 50% of 24   **2.** 50% of 296   **3.** 50% of 3,758   **4.** 25% of 36

5. $12\frac{1}{2}$% of 48   **6.** $12\frac{1}{2}$% of 456   **7.** $37\frac{1}{2}$% of 2,208   **8.** 40% of 200

Choose an appropriate calculation method and tell why. Then solve.

1. 10% of 80

2. 10% of 85

3. 25% of 80

4. 25% of 85

5. $33\frac{1}{3}$% of 6

6. $33\frac{1}{3}$% of 27

7. $33\frac{1}{3}$% of 75

8. $33\frac{1}{3}$% of 861

9. 75% of 100

10. 75% of 24

11. $12\frac{1}{2}$% of 16

12. $12\frac{1}{2}$% of 386

13. 20% of 15

14. 20% of 625

15. 68% of 54

16. 34% of 2,006

Solve. Choose an appropriate calculation method.

17. There are 24 students in Karen's class. 50% of them have a brother or sister in the school. What fraction of the students have a brother or sister in the school? What is the number of students that have a brother or sister in the school?

18. Edward is in a class of 13 boys and 12 girls. 40% of the class ride their bicycles to school. How many is that? Can you tell how many girls ride bicycles to school?

19. In Devin's class, 14 students are taller than Devin and 13 students are shorter than Devin. If 25% of the class ride the bus to school, how many do not ride the bus to school?

20. Valerie's class has 2 more students than Ashley's class. There are 50 students in the two classes. How many are in each class?

21. Scott asked 50 students what their favorite color was. $\frac{1}{5}$ chose red and 36% chose blue. What percentage of the students chose a color other than red or blue?

22. 90% of the students in Trevor's class have some kind of pet at home. 3 of the students do not have pets. How many are in the class?

23. Courtney's class has 27 students. $\frac{5}{9}$ of them are girls. How many are boys?

24. **Missing Data** Make up missing data so you can solve the problem. 40% of the students in Mark's class are in the band. How many are not in the band?

Finding Interest

EXPLORE Think About the Situation

Danielle charged $79.95 on her credit card.
When she paid off the credit card, she found
that she had to pay $81.15. Why do you think
she had to pay back more than she charged?

TALK ABOUT IT

1. How much more did Danielle have to pay
   back than she charged?
2. How is charging something on a credit
   card like borrowing money?

Interest is a fee paid for the use of money. If you use someone
else's money, you pay the person interest. If someone else uses
your money, the person pays you interest.

The amount of interest you pay (or collect) as a fee depends on
three things:

- The **amount** of money loaned or borrowed
- The **rate** of interest
- The length of **time** before repayment

Examples

A You loan $400   at   8% per year   for   1 year

You collect interest ⟶ $400 × 0.08 × 1 = $32

B You borrow $400   at   15% per year   for   2 years

You pay interest ⟶ $400 × 0.15 × 2 = $120

Find the interest.

1. Borrow: $320
   Interest Rate:
   $12\frac{1}{2}$% per year
   Time: 1 year

2. Loan: $250
   Interest Rate:
   6% per year
   Time: 6 months

3. Borrow: $1,000
   Interest Rate:
   16% per year
   Time: 3 years

Find the interest.

1. Borrow: $240
   Rate: 20% per year
   Time: 1 year

2. Borrow: $175
   Rate: 10% per year
   Time: 2 years

3. Borrow: $456
   Rate: $12\frac{1}{2}$% per year
   Time: 1 year

4. Loan: $400
   Rate: 8% per year
   Time: 2 years

5. Loan: $58
   Rate: 10% per year
   Time: 9 months

6. Loan: $1,000
   Rate: $12\frac{1}{2}$% per year
   Time: 2 years

Estimate and then find the interest.

7. Borrow: $44.95   Rate: 20% per year   Time: 2 years

APPLY

MATH REASONING

8. Suppose you borrowed $100. What interest rate did you pay if the interest was $20 for 1 year? $20 for 2 years?

PROBLEM SOLVING

9. Mallory has $450 in a savings account that pays 6% per year. Her club dues are $2.50 a month. Does she make enough interest to pay her club dues?

10. **Write Your Own Problem** Ask a question about this data. Then solve the problem.

    Nathan put $250 in an account that paid interest at a rate of 7% per year. At the end of a year he withdrew $65.50 for clothes.

MIXED REVIEW

Solve the proportions.

11. $\frac{4}{5} = \frac{n}{15}$ 12. $\frac{7}{10} = \frac{n}{40}$ 13. $\frac{1}{2} = \frac{n}{12}$ 14. $\frac{3}{8} = \frac{n}{48}$ 15. $\frac{7}{3} = \frac{n}{9}$

Write each decimal or fraction as a percent.

16. 0.83   17. $\frac{1}{2}$ 18. 0.12   19. 0.05   20. $\frac{2}{5}$ 21. $\frac{3}{20}$

Evaluate each algebraic expression for $a = 7.2$, $b = 5.3$, and $c = 2.1$.

22. $(a + b) + c$ 23. $a + (b + c)$ 24. $3 \times (a + b)$ 25. $(3 \times a) + (3 \times b)$

Sale Prices and Discounts

EXPLORE **Think About the Situation**

Stores often run sales where they sell their merchandise at prices below the regular marked price. Here are some typical sale ads that you might see in a newspaper or storefront.

TALK ABOUT IT

1. Why do you think store managers have sales?
2. Do you think you save much money by shopping at sales?
3. Which of these sales looks most attractive to you? Why?
4. What are some of the key words that suggest you subtract from the regular price?

- To find the **sale price,** you subtract the **discount** from the regular price.

Examples

A $20 at 25% off
   $0.25 \times \$20 = \$5$ discount
   $\$20 - \$5 = \$15$ sale price

B $75 at 40% off
   $0.40 \times \$75 = \$30$ discount
   $\$75 - \$30 = \$45$ sale price

Find the discount and sale price.

1. $125 at 25% off

2. $24 at 10% discount

3. $36 at $\frac{1}{3}$ off

4. $6.95 at 20% off

5. $12.50 at 30% off

6. $12.88 at 25% off

Find the discount and sale price.

1. $100 at 20% off

2. $49.90 at 10% discount

3. $24.50 at 25% discount

4. $340 at 50% off

5. $7.99 at $12\frac{1}{2}$% off

6. $25 at $\frac{1}{4}$ off

7. $32.50 at 20% discount

8. $375 at $33\frac{1}{3}$% discount

9. $15.75 at 15% off

10. $19.80 at 5% discount

Estimate and then find the sale price.

11. $39.95 at 25% discount

12. $58.98 at $33\frac{1}{3}$% off

APPLY

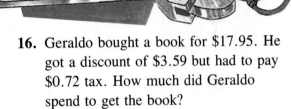

MATH REASONING

13. Without calculating, what can you say about each pair of discounts?
$20 at 25% off; $25 at 20% off
$25 at 50% off; $50 at 25% off

PROBLEM SOLVING

14. Mei was in a store where she could get a 10% discount if her purchases were over $20. The items she bought cost $4.95, $12.49, and $1.98. Did Mei qualify for the discount?

15. Ryan went into a hardware store that had a 20% off sale. His two purchases had prices of $38.75 and $7.90. How much did Ryan save because of the sale?

16. Geraldo bought a book for $17.95. He got a discount of $3.59 but had to pay $0.72 tax. How much did Geraldo spend to get the book?

17. Jessica bought a $14.96 game. She got a discount of 25%. The sales tax was $0.67. What was the total that Jessica spent for the game?

▶ **COMMUNICATION Writing to Learn Math**

18. Fill in the blanks with numbers in the form asked for.

$0.25 is the same as _____ of $1.00, _____ of $1.00, and _____ of $1.00.
(decimal)   (percent)   (fraction)

Problem Solving
Data from a Tax Table

UNDERSTAND
ANALYZE DATA
PLAN
ESTIMATE
SOLVE
EXAMINE

Sales Tax Table ($6\frac{1}{2}$%)

Transaction	Tax	Transaction	Tax	Transactio
5.31–5.46	.35	10.70–10.84	.70	16.08–16.23
5.47–5.61	.36	10.85–10.99	.71	16.24–16.3
5.62–5.76	.37	11.00–11.15	.72	16.39–16.5
5.77–5.92	.38	11.16–11.30	.73	16.54–16.6
5.93–6.07	.39	11.31–11.46	.74	16.70–16.8
6.08–6.23	.40	11.47–11.61	.75	16.85–16.9
6.24–6.38	.41	11.62–11.76	.76	17.00–17.1
6.39–6.53	.42	11.77–11.92	.77	17.16–17.3
6.54–6.69	.43	11.93–12.07	.78	17.31–17.4
6.70–6.84	.44	12.08–12.23	.79	17.47–17.6
6.85–6.99	.45	12.24–12.38	.80	17.62–17.
7.00–7.15	.46	12.39–12.53	.81	17.77–17.9
7.16–7.30	.47	12.54–12.69	.82	17.93–18.
7.31–7.46	.48	12.70–12.84	.83	18.08–18.
7.47–7.61	.49	12.85–12.99	.84	18.24–18.
7.62–7.76	.50	13.00–13.15	.85	18.39–18.
7.77–7.92	.51	13.16–13.30	.86	18.54–18.
7.93–8.07	.52	13.31–13.46	.87	18.70–18.8
8.23	.53	13.47–13.61	.88	18.85–18.9
	.54	13.6		00–19

LEARN ABOUT IT

To find the sales tax on a purchase, you find a percent of the purchase price. The figure shows part of a sales tax table for a tax rate of $6\frac{1}{2}$%. When you don't have a table, you may have to calculate the tax.

> Dawn lives in an area where sales are taxed at $6\frac{1}{2}$%. How much did she spend at each store if she bought items that cost $12.95 at the first store and $25.49 at the second store.

First, I'll use the tax table to find the tax on $12.95.
Then I'll add that to $12.95.

Now I'll find the tax on $25.49.
I can't find $25.49 on the table, so I'll use my calculator.
Then I'll add the tax to $25.49.

12.85–12.99	.84

$12.95 + $0.84 = $13.79

$25.49 × 0.065 = 1.65685
Rounding to the nearest cent, the tax is $1.66.
$25.49 + $1.66 = $27.15

`1.65685`

Dawn spent $13.79 at the first store and $27.15 at the second.

TRY IT OUT

Find the total cost for each purchase. Use the tax table when you can. Use your calculator for the others.

1. Purchase: $6.49
   Tax Rate: $6\frac{1}{2}$%

2. Purchase: $6.49
   Tax Rate: 5.4%

3. Purchase: $14.95
   Tax Rate: $6\frac{1}{2}$%

4. Purchase: $11.39
   Tax Rate: 6.5%

Solve the problems. Use the tax table when you can. Use your calculator when you cannot.

1. Irene bought a pair of jeans that cost $13.49. How much tax must be added to the cost if the rate is $6\frac{1}{2}\%$? What is the total cost?

2. Miguel bought a $12.98 game at a discount of 25%. He paid a sales tax of $0.54. What was his total cost?

3. Anthony bought a T-shirt for $3.95 and a pair of walking shorts for $8.98. What is the total for these items if the tax rate is $6\frac{1}{2}\%$?

4. Chad had to pay 73 cents tax when he bought 6 pairs of socks. Estimate the cost of each pair if the tax rate was $6\frac{1}{2}\%$.

5. Mr. Lu operates a clothing store. He multiplied the cost of a pair of shoes by 1.75 and then added a sales tax of $2.96. The cost to Genna, the buyer, was $48.46. What was Mr. Lu's original cost?

6. Anna spent $6.70, including a tax of $0.41, for a scarf. The tax rate was $6\frac{1}{2}\%$. How much was the scarf before the tax?

7. Carolyn saw a blouse on sale for $13.49. How much tax will be charged if the rate is $5\frac{1}{2}\%$? What will be the total cost?

8. Crystal gave the clerk a $20 bill when she purchased a sweater for $18.95. Was that enough money if the sales tax rate was 6%?

9. Tyne bought a scarf that was on sale for $9.95. How much change will she get back from a $20 bill if the tax rate is $4\frac{1}{2}\%$?

10. **Thinking About Your Solution** You want to buy a boxcar and a name sticker to put on the car for your model train set. Boxcars come in silver ($18.98), red ($17.39), and blue ($19.49). There are name stickers for Mule Train R.R. ($3.19) and Overland R.R. ($1.59). How many different choices do you have? Which combination of boxcar and sticker is the least expensive? What is its total cost if the sales tax is 5.5%?
    a. Show the steps you took to solve the problem.
    b. Use complete sentences to write your answer.
    c. Name the strategy you used to solve the problem.

Applied Problem Solving
Group Decision Making

UNDERSTAND
ANALYZE DATA
PLAN
ESTIMATE
SOLVE
EXAMINE

Group Skill
Explain and Summarize

You have earned and saved $50 to spend toward redecorating your bedroom.

Facts to Consider

- Your room is painted a dark color, so you want to brighten up your room.
- Supplies needed to hang one unframed poster cost $0.25. Supplies needed to hang one framed poster cost $0.45.
- The sales tax in your state is 6%. You don't have to pay tax on items bought from a newspaper ad.

Some Questions to Answer

1. What different lamps do you have to choose from? How much is the most expensive? The least expensive?

2. Suppose you bought a large frame at Bailey's for a large poster at Pack's. What else would you need to buy in order to hang the framed poster?

   What would the total cost be with tax?

   How much would you have left to spend?

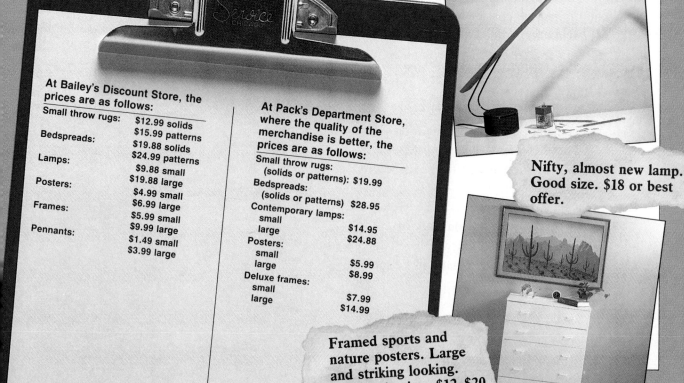

At Bailey's Discount Store, the prices are as follows:

Small throw rugs:	$12.99 solids
	$15.99 patterns
Bedspreads:	$19.88 solids
	$24.99 patterns
Lamps:	$9.88 small
	$19.88 large
Posters:	$4.99 small
	$6.99 large
Frames:	$5.99 small
	$9.99 large
Pennants:	$1.49 small
	$3.99 large

At Pack's Department Store, where the quality of the merchandise is better, the prices are as follows:

Small throw rugs: (solids or patterns):	$19.99
Bedspreads: (solids or patterns)	$28.95
Contemporary lamps: small	
large	$14.95
	$24.88
Posters: small	
large	$5.99
	$8.99
Deluxe frames: small	
large	$7.99
	$14.99

Nifty, almost new lamp. Good size. $18 or best offer.

Framed sports and nature posters. Large and striking looking. Good selection. $12–$20.

3. Suppose you bought the lamp in the newspaper ad and a patterned bedspread at Bailey's. How much would they cost, including tax?

Make a list to show which items you would buy. Show the cost for each and the total cost including tax. Would you have any money left over?

WRAP UP

What's the New Price?

Match the item description with the new price. Use mental math or estimation when it makes sense to do so.

1. a $250 tape deck reduced by 50%

2. a $79.95 poster increased by 5%

3. a $61.95 radio on sale at $\frac{1}{3}$ off

4. a $120 dress on sale for $\frac{2}{5}$ of its listed price

5. an $80 jacket with a price increase of 25%

   a. $125
   b. $48
   c. $40
   d. $100
   e. $84

Sometimes, Always, Never

Decide which word goes in the blank: *sometimes, always,* or *never.* Explain your choices.

6. To find a percent of a number, _____ multiply the number by the fraction or decimal for that percent.

7. Fifty percent of a number is _____ half that number.

8. The rate of interest is _____ the only thing that determines the amount of interest.

9. When you deposit money in a bank, the bank is _____ borrowing the money from you.

10. When an item is reduced in price, the amount of sales tax _____ decreases.

Project

You want to open an exotic pet store. Start by naming the store and stocking it with unusual and silly pets. Make up price lists for the pets. Analyze your stock to help you decide at which time of year to increase your prices and when to have sales. Use percents and fractions to show price changes. Purchase pets from others and sell some of your pets. Mark these changes on your stock list. (Be sure to add on the local sales tax.)

CHAPTER REVIEW/TEST

Part 1   Understanding

Tell if the estimate is an overestimate or an underestimate.

1. 27% of 16 is 3.

2. 47% of 60 is 31.

3. Suppose you borrowed $100. What interest rate did you pay if the interest was $15 for 1 year?

Part 2   Skills

Use decimals or fractions to find the percent of each number.

4. 75% of 64

5. $66\frac{2}{3}$% of 54

Find the percent of each number mentally.

6. 50% of 140

7. 20% of 250

Estimate the percent of each number.

8. 11% of 80

9. 24% of 200

Tell which calculation method you choose. Then solve.

10. $33\frac{1}{3}$% of 75

11. 48% of 40

12. 75% of 400

Part 3   Applications

13. Miguel bought a record with a list price of $12.50 at 30% off. How much was the discount? What was the sale price?

14. Gail bought a $12 shirt and an $18.90 pair of pants. If both items were on sale for $33\frac{1}{3}$% off the list price, and the sales tax was 8%, how much did she spend?

15. Janice borrowed $300 for 6 months at an interest rate of 10% per year. What is the interest she pays?

16. Challenge   Together, Meg and John spent 50% of the treasury money on supplies. Then Alex spent 50% of what remained on food. If there was still $8 left over, how much money was in the treasury to begin with?

ENRICHMENT
Area Percents

The area inside the red square represents 100% for the activities on this page. Do you see why the blue square encloses 25% of the total area?

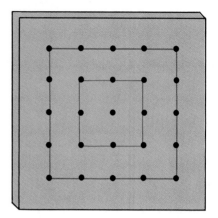

You can use your calculator to find the percent. There are 16 small squares inside the red square. Each small square is $\frac{1}{16}$, or 0.0625, of the large square.

$$\frac{1}{16} = 1 \div 16 = 0.0625 = 6\frac{1}{4}\%$$

Since the blue square has 4 small squares, the area is $4 \times 6\frac{1}{4}$, or 25%.

Is there another way to show that the blue square is 25%?

Give the percent for the area inside each blue outline.

1.

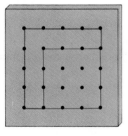

2.

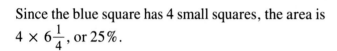

3.

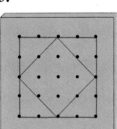

4.

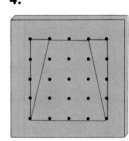

5. The blue triangle has an area of $12\frac{1}{2}\%$ of the large square. How many different triangle shapes can you find that have an area of $12\frac{1}{2}\%$? Show your answers on dot or graph paper.

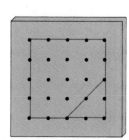

332

CUMULATIVE REVIEW

1. Use mental math to solve: $\frac{7}{8} \times 32$.
   - A. 36
   - B. 28
   - C. 30
   - D. 24

2. Find the product: $\frac{3}{8} \times \frac{2}{9}$.
   - A. $\frac{5}{17}$
   - B. $\frac{16}{27}$
   - C. $\frac{5}{72}$
   - D. $\frac{1}{12}$

3. Estimate the product: $4\frac{5}{6} \times 3\frac{1}{8}$.
   - A. 10
   - B. 12
   - C. 15
   - D. 20

4. A pole is 12 feet tall and has a shadow 4.5 feet long. A nearby bush has a shadow 1.5 feet long. How tall is the bush?
   - A. 4 feet
   - B. 9 feet
   - C. 18 feet
   - D. 6.75 feet

5. A reflection image is formed when you:
   - A. turn a figure
   - B. flip a figure
   - C. slide a figure
   - D. rotate a figure

6. Name the polygon formed by graphing the following points: (3, 6), (7, 6), (6, 3), and (2, 3).
   - A. parallelogram
   - B. square
   - C. trapezoid
   - D. rectangle

7. The figures are similar. Which is the missing length?
   - A. 5
   - B. 8
   - C. 15
   - D. 10

8. What is the ratio of months that have 31 days to months in a year?
   - A. 5:12
   - B. 5:7
   - C. 7:12
   - D. 7:5

9. Which ratio is equal to 12:25?
   - A. 60:100
   - B. 48:100
   - C. 24:75
   - D. 3:5

10. Which is the solution to the proportion: $\frac{2}{3} = \frac{n}{45}$?
    - A. $n = 7.5$
    - B. $n = 125$
    - C. $n = 45$
    - D. $n = 30$

11. Using a scale ratio of 1 in. = 24 mi, what distance does 5 in. represent?
    - A. 29 mi
    - B. 120 mi
    - C. 100 mi
    - D. 5 mi

12. A magazine costs $.75. Is it possible to form that exact amount with 5 coins?
    - A. sometimes
    - B. yes
    - C. cannot tell
    - D. no

13. The scale ratio is 1 cm : 5 m. How tall is the actual statue if the picture of it is 7 cm high?
    - A. 7 m
    - B. 5 m
    - C. 35 m
    - D. 12 m

14. The numbers along the bottom of a bar graph with horizontal bars are called the
    - A. numbers
    - B. scale
    - C. title
    - D. range

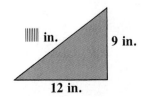

12

INTEGERS

MATH AND SCIENCE

DATA BANK

Use the Science Data Bank on page 477 to answer the questions.

1 When do you think each of these things was invented? Within the last 10, 25, 50, 100, or 200 years? Check to see if you guessed correctly.

television, airplane, automobile, computer, bicycle, digital watch

List in order the inventions that were introduced within 25 years of 1900.

 Color TV began in 1953. How many years before or after color TV were black and white TV and the compact disc player introduced?

 Using Critical Thinking Examine the data for the years before 1700, for the 1700s, for the 1800s, and for the 1900s. What can you say about inventions that seems certain? What seems *almost* certain? What is not certain at all?

335

Positive and Negative Integers

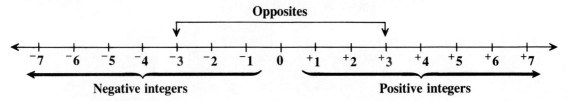

LEARN ABOUT IT

EXPLORE **Study the Information**

In 1714, Gabriel Fahrenheit invented the mercury thermometer. On his scale, zero represented the lowest temperature then attainable (using a freezing mixture of ice and salt). Today's Fahrenheit thermometers record temperatures well below zero.

The figure shows how the integers $^+70$ and $^-70$ are used to measure the opposites 70° *above zero* and 70° *below zero*. **Integers** are whole numbers that can describe opposites.

Degrees Fahrenheit

TALK ABOUT IT

1. What is the opposite of 10° below zero? What two integers would you use for these two temperatures?
2. What would the integer $^-15$ describe on the temperature scale? What would $^+15$ describe?

The number line below shows **positive integers** and **negative integers.**

- The integer 0 is neither positive nor negative.
  $^+3$ is read "positive three." $^-8$ is read "negative eight."

- Each integer has an opposite.
  The opposite of $^+3$ is $^-3$.
  The opposite of 0 is 0.

- Integers can describe opposite ideas.
  The opposite of *lose* 8 lb is *gain* 8 lb.
  The opposite of 0 km *west* is 0 km *east*.

TRY IT OUT

Give the opposite idea and the opposite integer.

1. 3 miles north, $^+3$ 2. Spent $5, $^-5$ 3. 5 steps forward, $^+5$

Give the opposite idea and the opposite of the integer.

1. Increase 7 kg, $^+7$

2. 18 km east, $^+18$

3. 4 flights up, $^+4$

4. 6 s before blastoff, $^-6$

5. Spent $10, $^-10$

6. 7 steps forward, $^+7$

7. Lose 5 points, $^-5$

8. Gain 6 yards, $^+6$

9. $2 profit, $^+2$

Give the opposite of each integer.

10. $^+61$ **11.** $^-6$ **12.** $^+56$ **13.** $^-75$ **14.** $^-167$ **15.** $^+732$

Complete the following statements.

16. If $^-8$ means 8 km below sea level, then $^+8$ means _____.

17. If $^+4$ means 4° above zero, then _____ means 4° below zero.

18. The opposite of a negative integer is a _____ integer.

19. The opposite of a positive integer is a _____ integer.

MATH REASONING

20. On the number line, $^-375$ is to the _____ of $^-374$.

21. On the number line, $^-599$ is to the _____ of $^-600$.

PROBLEM SOLVING

22. Science Data Bank Look at this time line for inventions. 1980 is at the zero point. What inventions would you place at $^-10$ and at $^+2$?

▶ **ALGEBRA**

Find the integers. Use a number line if you need help.

23. The integer a is 8 units to the right of integer b. If $b = {}^-2$, what is integer a?

24. The integer c is 12 units to the left of integer d. If $d = {}^+4$, what is integer c?

More Practice, page 516, set C

Comparing and Ordering Integers

EXPLORE Study the Information

Using positive and negative integers, we can compare distances above and below sea level. In 1783, a hot-air balloon flew 1,500 ft above sea level. In 1797, Fulton's submarine reached a depth of 10 ft below sea level. The Nautilus atomic submarine reached 720 ft below sea level in 1954.

TALK ABOUT IT

1. What integer tells the distance that the hot-air balloon traveled above sea level?
2. What integer tells the distance that the atomic submarine traveled below sea level?
3. Which submarine went to a lower (greater) depth? Explain how you decided.

- You can compare two integers by thinking about a number line. The integer that is farther to the right is the greater of the two integers.

Which is greater, $^+2$ or $^-3$?	Compare $^-10$ and $^-720$.
$^+2 > {}^-3$ or $^-3 < {}^+2$	$^-10 > {}^-720$ or $^-720 < {}^-10$

- You can order a set of integers by comparing them two at a time.

Order $^-3, {}^+5, {}^-2, {}^+1, 0, {}^-6$

greatest → $^+5, {}^+1, 0, {}^-2, {}^-3, {}^-6$ ← least

Write > or < for each ⫿⫿⫿ .

1. $^-8$ ⫿⫿⫿ $^+1$ 2. 0 ⫿⫿⫿ $^-2$ 3. $^-6$ ⫿⫿⫿ $^-3$ 4. $^-4$ ⫿⫿⫿ 0

5. Order from greatest to least.
   $^-2, {}^+3, {}^+2, {}^-9, 0$

6. Order from least to greatest.
   $^-4, {}^-8, 0, {}^+1, {}^-6, {}^-2$

Write > or < for each ⫿⫿⫿.

1. $^+4$ ⫿⫿⫿ $^-3$
2. $^+7$ ⫿⫿⫿ $^+9$
3. $^+6$ ⫿⫿⫿ $^-15$
4. $^+4$ ⫿⫿⫿ 0

5. $^-5$ ⫿⫿⫿ $^-2$
6. $^+3$ ⫿⫿⫿ $^-3$
7. $^+1$ ⫿⫿⫿ $^-4$
8. $^-12$ ⫿⫿⫿ $^-35$

9. 0 ⫿⫿⫿ $^-6$
10. $^+2$ ⫿⫿⫿ $^-4$
11. $^-8$ ⫿⫿⫿ $^+3$
12. $^-5$ ⫿⫿⫿ $^+5$

Order from greatest to least.

13. $^-4$, $^+3$, 0, $^-2$, $^-6$, $^+7$

14. $^-2$, $^+7$, $^-1$, $^+1$, $^-4$, $^+3$

Order from least to greatest.

15. $^-15$, $^+6$, $^+10$, 0, $^-8$, $^-3$

16. $^+8$, 0, $^-1$, $^+1$, $^-4$, $^+14$

APPLY

MATH REASONING

17. The three points marked on the number line represent the integers $^-80$, $^-70$, and $^-90$. Which integer is at point *A? B? C?*

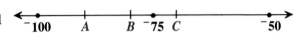

PROBLEM SOLVING

18. In 1742, Anders Celsius invented a thermometer scale in which 0° was the temperature at which water froze and $^+100°$ was the temperature at which water boiled. Today, scientists have determined that no heat is present at 373°C below the boiling point of water. What temperature is this Celsius?

19. **Science Data Bank** About what percent of the inventions listed were invented in this century?

DATA BANK

▶ USING CRITICAL THINKING   Discover a Rule

The **absolute value** of a number is its positive distance from 0 on the number line. We use the symbol $|x|$. We read $|5|$ as "the absolute value of 5." Look at the examples. Look for patterns.

$$|^+4| = {}^+4, \quad |^-6| = {}^+6, \quad |^-12| = {}^+12, \quad |0| = 0$$

20. Is the absolute value of a positive integer positive or negative?

21. Is the absolute value of a negative integer positive or negative?

22. If you know $|x| = 5$, what are the possible values for *x?*

More Practice, page 516, set D

Using a Calculator to Check Addition and Subtraction Patterns for Integers

EXPLORE **Think About the Process**

You know how to enter positive integers on your calculator. To enter negative numbers, you can use the ┃ +⟲– ┃ key. Negative 7 was entered on this calculator by first pressing 7 and then ┃ +⟲– ┃. Try it.

Push the keys shown to check these examples.

$8 + {}^-5 = 3$

8 ┃ + ┃ 5 ┃ +⟲– ┃ = ┃

$6 - {}^-2 = 8$

6 ┃ – ┃ 2 ┃ +⟲– ┃ = ┃

Copy each column of equations. Follow the pattern from top to bottom to give each sum or difference without your calculator. Then use your calculator to check the ones that involve negative integers.

1. $5 + 4 = $ ▥
    $5 + 3 = $ ▥
    $5 + 2 = $ ▥
    $5 + 1 = $ ▥
    $5 + 0 = $ ▥
    $5 + {}^-1 = $ ▥
    $5 + {}^-2 = $ ▥
    $5 + {}^-3 = $ ▥
    $5 + {}^-4 = $ ▥

2. $3 + 3 = $ ▥
    $3 + 2 = $ ▥
    $3 + 1 = $ ▥
    $3 + 0 = $ ▥
    $3 + {}^-1 = $ ▥
    $3 + {}^-2 = $ ▥
    $3 + {}^-3 = $ ▥
    $3 + {}^-4 = $ ▥
    $3 + {}^-5 = $ ▥

3. $5 - 4 = $ ▥
    $5 - 3 = $ ▥
    $5 - 2 = $ ▥
    $5 - 1 = $ ▥
    $5 - 0 = $ ▥
    $5 - {}^-1 = $ ▥
    $5 - {}^-2 = $ ▥
    $5 - {}^-3 = $ ▥
    $5 - {}^-4 = $ ▥

4. $3 - 3 = $ ▥
    $3 - 2 = $ ▥
    $3 - 1 = $ ▥
    $3 - 0 = $ ▥
    $3 - {}^-1 = $ ▥
    $3 - {}^-2 = $ ▥
    $3 - {}^-3 = $ ▥
    $3 - {}^-4 = $ ▥
    $3 - {}^-5 = $ ▥

5. Explain how you can use your calculator to check on this rule: The sum of any integer and its opposite is 0.

More Practice, page 516, set E

Give the opposite idea and the opposite integer.

1. 10 s after blastoff, $^+10$

2. Spend $15, $^-15$

3. 1 m below sea level, $^-1$

Give the opposite of each integer.

4. $^-17$　　　　**5.** $^+25$　　　　**6.** $^+1$　　　　**7.** 0　　　　**8.** $^-45$

9. If 3 years from now is $^+3$, then
   a. 3 years ago is _____　　**b.** 10 years from now is _____　　**c.** $^-15$ means _____

Use the number line. Name the integers described.

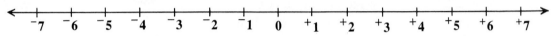

10. An integer that is:　　**a.** 3 units to the right of 0　　**b.** 6 units to the left of 0

11. Two integers that are:　　**a.** 2 units from 0　　**b.** 3 units from $^-1$

12. All integers that are:　　**a.** positive and less than $^+4$　　**b.** negative and greater than $^-6$

Write < or > for each ▧.

13. $^-7$ ▧ $^-8$　　　　**14.** 0 ▧ $^-3$　　　　**15.** $^-12$ ▧ $^+1$　　　　**16.** $^-46$ ▧ $^-45$

17. Order from greatest to least: $^-5, ^+7, ^-1, 0, ^-15, ^+2$

18. Order from least to greatest: $^-3, ^-13, ^+13, ^+23, ^-31, ^+32$

PROBLEM SOLVING

19. Two integers are opposites of each other. One of the integers is 5 units to the left of $^+3$ on the number line. What are the integers?

The chart shows the daily average temperatures for 5 winter days.

20. Which day had the coldest average temperature?

21. Which day had the warmest average temperature?

22. What was the median (middle) temperature?

Monday	$^+3°$
Tuesday	$^-2°$
Wednesday	$^+5°$
Thursday	$^-3°$
Friday	$^-4°$

Adding Integers

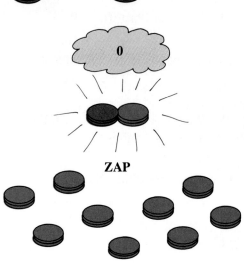

EXPLORE Use Counters

Work in groups. Use counters of two different colors, such as red and yellow. Let the red counters represent negative numbers and the yellow counters represent positive numbers. You know that the sum of any integer and its opposite is 0. So you can think of a red counter and a yellow counter as disappearing (making 0) when they meet. Use your counters to find these sums.

$$^{+}8 + {}^{-}5 \qquad {}^{-}4 + {}^{-}5 \qquad {}^{-}7 + {}^{+}4$$

TALK ABOUT IT

1. How can you show $^{+}8$ with your counters? How can you show $^{-}5$?
2. How many counters disappear (make 0) if you put 8 yellow counters with 5 red ones? What is left over?

These examples show how to use counters to find sums.

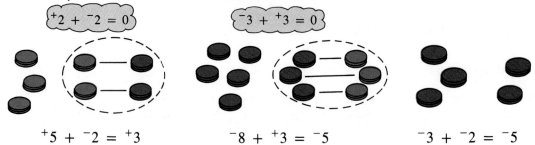

$$^{+}5 + {}^{-}2 = {}^{+}3 \qquad\qquad {}^{-}8 + {}^{+}3 = {}^{-}5 \qquad\qquad {}^{-}3 + {}^{-}2 = {}^{-}5$$

Other Examples

A $^{-}9 + {}^{+}6 = {}^{-}3$ **B** $^{+}12 + {}^{-}8 = {}^{+}4$ **C** $^{-}7 + {}^{-}8 = {}^{-}15$ **D** $^{+}5 + {}^{+}7 = {}^{+}12$

Find the sums. Use counters if you need help.

1. $^{+}9 + {}^{-}2$ 2. $^{-}8 + {}^{+}7$ 3. $^{-}6 + {}^{-}2$ 4. $^{-}4 + {}^{+}6$ 5. $^{+}4 + {}^{+}1$

Find the sums. It may help to think about counters.

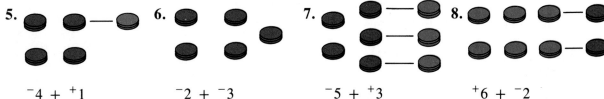

1. $^+3 + {}^-2$

2. $^-3 + {}^+5$

3. $^-4 + {}^+2$

4. $^+5 + {}^-4$

5. $^-4 + {}^+1$

6. $^-2 + {}^-3$

7. $^-5 + {}^+3$

8. $^+6 + {}^-2$

Find the sums. Use counters if you need help.

9. $^+6 + {}^-2$ 10. $^+3 + {}^+8$ 11. $^-6 + {}^+13$ 12. $^-6 + {}^-4$ 13. $^-6 + {}^+3$

14. $^+10 + {}^-8$ 15. $^+12 + {}^-4$ 16. $^-5 + {}^+1$ 17. $^+4 + {}^-4$ 18. $^-8 + {}^+1$

19. $^-11 + {}^+7$ 20. $^-3 + {}^+7$ 21. $^-9 + {}^-8$ 22. $^+3 + {}^-13$ 23. $^+9 + {}^-4$

MATH REASONING

Without adding, tell if each sum is positive or negative.

24. $^+57 + {}^-49$ 25. $^-78 + {}^+64$ 26. $^-83 + {}^-79$ 27. $^-28 + {}^+92$ 28. $^+83 + {}^-84$

PROBLEM SOLVING

29. Kristen was playing a game where she could make both positive and negative scores. On her first try, she scored $^-7$. Then she scored $^+5$. What was her total score?

30. Patrick received a check for $50 ($^+50$). At the same time, he received a bill for club dues of $10 ($^-10$). Write the money amount and an integer to show Patrick's standing after cashing the check and paying his dues.

▶ **USING CRITICAL THINKING   Analyzing the Statement**

31. Jorge said, "If the sum of two integers is negative, the greater of the two addends is negative." Give examples to show that Jorge's statement is sometimes, but not always, true.

Subtracting Integers

LEARN ABOUT IT

EXPLORE

Mallory had $30 in the bank. She deposited $7 ($^+7$) in her account. The bank made a mistake. Instead of depositing $7, it withdrew $5 ($^-5$).

TALK ABOUT IT

1. How much does Mallory think she has in the bank?
2. Because of the mistake, how much does Mallory actually have in the bank?
3. What is the difference between what Mallory thinks she has and the amount the bank thinks she has?

As with whole numbers, you can think of subtracting integers as finding a missing addend.

sum addend addend
$^+7 -$ $^-5$ =   ?

What integer adds to $^-5$ to give $^+7$?

$^+7 - {}^-5 = {}^+12$

because

$^+12 + {}^-5 = {}^+7$

Other Examples

A $^-6 - {}^-4 = {}^-2$ because $^-2 + {}^-4 = {}^-6$ **B** $^-6 - {}^+4 = {}^-10$ because $^-10 + {}^+4 = {}^-6$

C $^+4 - {}^-6 = {}^+10$ because $^+10 + {}^-6 = {}^+4$ **D** $^-4 - {}^-6 = {}^+2$ because $^+2 + {}^-6 = {}^-4$

TRY IT OUT

Subtract. Check by adding.

What integer adds to $^-3$ to give $^-5$?

What integer adds to $^-8$ to give $^-5$?

What integer adds to $^-3$ to give $^+1$?

1. $^-5 - {}^-3 = n$ 2. $^-5 - {}^-8 = n$ 3. $^+1 - {}^-3 = n$

What integer adds to $^+3$ to give $^-5$?

What integer adds to $^-2$ to give $^+4$?

What integer adds to $^+5$ to give $^-4$?

4. $^-5 - {}^+3 = n$ 5. $^+4 - {}^-2 = n$ 6. $^-4 - {}^+5 = n$

344

Find the differences. Thinking of addends and a sum may help you.

1. $^+3 - {}^-5 = n$

2. $^-2 - {}^+6 = n$

3. $^-2 - {}^-4 = n$

4. $^+5 - {}^-3 = n$

5. $^-3 - {}^+8 = n$

6. $^+8 - {}^-6 = n$

7. $^-8 - {}^-5 = n$

8. $^+2 - {}^+9 = n$

9. $^-5 - {}^-4 = n$

10. $^+5 - {}^-1 = n$

11. $^+2 - {}^-3 = n$

12. $^+6 - {}^-1 = n$

13. $^-8 - {}^-8 = n$

14. $^+6 - {}^-3 = n$

15. $^-9 - {}^-8 = n$

16. $^-5 - 0 = n$

17. $^+6 - {}^+9 = n$

18. $^+2 - {}^-4 = n$

APPLY

MATH REASONING

Use the pattern to subtract the negative integers. Give each difference.

19. $8 - 2 = n$
    $8 - 1 = n$
    $8 - 0 = n$
    $8 - {}^-1 = n$
    $8 - {}^-2 = n$

20. $10 - 2 = n$
    $10 - 1 = n$
    $10 - 0 = n$
    $10 - {}^-1 = n$
    $10 - {}^-2 = n$

21. $7 - 4 = n$
    $7 - 2 = n$
    $7 - 0 = n$
    $7 - {}^-2 = n$
    $7 - {}^-4 = n$

22. $9 - 4 = n$
    $9 - 2 = n$
    $9 - 0 = n$
    $9 - {}^-2 = n$
    $9 - {}^-4 = n$

PROBLEM SOLVING

23. Ken got a letter from the crafts store. He thought it was a refund of $8. Instead, it was a bill for $7. After paying the bill, how much less money does Ken have than he thought he was going to have?

▶ **COMMUNICATION   Write Math for Understanding**

24. Copy and complete this sentence.

    Subtracting a negative 3 is the same as adding _____ .

Exploring Algebra
Integer Equations

EXPLORE Study the Chart

The chart shows the high and low temperature for two days during a January cold spell.

	High	*Low*
Mon.	$^+7°$	$^-5°$
Tues.	$^+9°$	$^-3°$

TALK ABOUT IT

1. How much did the temperature change from Monday's high to Monday's low?
2. What was the change from Monday's low to Tuesday's high? From Tuesday's high to Tuesday's low?

You can think about movements on the number line just as you think about rising and falling temperatures.

- Positive integers represent movements to the right.
- Negative integers represent movements to the left.

The examples below show how to use these movements on the number line to solve addition equations.

Examples

A — How do you get from $^+4$ to $^-1$?

$^+4 + n = ^-1$

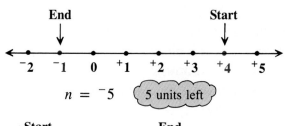

$n = ^-5$ — 5 units left

B — How do you get from $^-6$ to $^-2$?

$^-6 + m = ^-2$

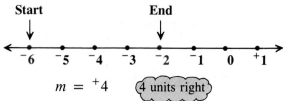

$m = ^+4$ — 4 units right

Draw and use a number line to solve the equations.

1. $^-2 + y = ^-4$ 2. $^-7 + a = 0$ 3. $^+3 + r = ^-4$ 4. $^-6 + r = ^+2$

346

Solve. Use a number line if you need help.

1. $^-3 + c = ^-7$ **2.** $^+5 + m = ^-2$ **3.** $^+2 + e = ^-6$ **4.** $^-4 + g = ^+5$

5. $^+6 + k = ^+2$ **6.** $^-4 + h = 0$ **7.** $0 + b = ^+4$ **8.** $^+1 + i = ^-1$

9. $^-4 + d = ^-10$ **10.** $^+2 + f = ^-5$ **11.** $^-7 + j = ^-2$ **12.** $0 + a = ^-3$

Write an integer equation for each jump on the number line.

Example:
$^-3 + n = ^+2$ $n = ^+5$

13.

14.

15.

16.

MATH REASONING

17. Give an example of an integer equation that has a solution of 0.

PROBLEM SOLVING

18. The low temperature for Thursday night was $^-5°$. On Friday the temperature rose $12°$ during the day. Then it fell $9°$ on Friday night. What was the low temperature Friday night?

19. From the daytime high the temperature plunged $20°$ to a low of $^-12°$ that night. What was the daytime high before the sharp fall in the temperature?

▶ **CALCULATOR**

Use your calculator to solve each equation.

20. $(^-4 + ^+7) - ^+3 = n$

21. $^-12 + (^-7 - ^+8) = p$

22. $^+6 + (^-10 + ^-10) = k$

23. $(^+14 - ^-5) + ^+11 = r$

Positive and Negative Coordinates

EXPLORE

Lines that intersect at Lebanon, Kansas are used as number lines. These number lines can help you give locations on the map.

TALK ABOUT IT

1. How can you tell someone what vertical line (↕) passes through Salt Lake City? What horizontal (↔) line?
2. Describe two lines that would help someone locate Phoenix.
3. Describe two lines that would help someone locate Atlanta. Estimate using fractions. Estimate using decimals.

The center of the map, Lebanon, is the **origin** (0,0) of the graph. Ordered pairs of numbers can be used to give locations of some other cities. These ordered pairs are **coordinates** of the points they locate.

- The first coordinate tells the number of spaces right (+) or left (−).
- The second coordinate tells the number of spaces up (+) or down (−).

Examples

A Knoxville: coordinates ($^{+}10$, $^{-}3$)
right 10, down 3

B Boston: coordinates ($^{+}16.4$, $^{+}4$)
right 16.4, up 4

Give the coordinates for these cities.

1. New York   2. Seattle   3. Dayton   4. Miami (estimate)

What cities are at these coordinates?

5. ($^{+}14$, 0)   6. ($^{-}13$, $^{+}7$)   7. ($^{-}12$, $^{-}4$)   8. ($^{+}12$, $^{-}7$)

Give the coordinates for each of these cities.

1. Los Angeles   **2.** Albuquerque   **3.** New Orleans

What cities are at the points named by these coordinates?

4. $(^-8, {}^+2)$ **5.** $(^+1, {}^-6)$ **6.** $(^-15, {}^+1)$ **7.** $(^+2, {}^-8)$ **8.** $(^+5, {}^-1)$

Give the coordinates for each point.

9. B   **10.** D   **11.** G

12. F   **13.** I   **14.** P

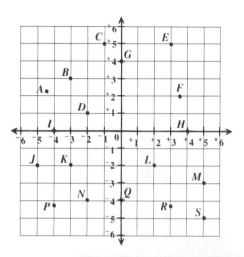

Give the point for each set of coordinates.

15. $(^-2, {}^-4)$ **16.** $(^-4, 0)$ **17.** $(^+5, {}^-3)$

18. $(^+5, {}^-5)$ **19.** $(^+3, {}^-4\frac{1}{4})$ **20.** $(0, {}^+4)$

21. $(^-4.5, {}^+2.25)$ **22.** $(^+3.5, {}^+2)$ **23.** $(^-4, {}^-4\frac{1}{4})$

MATH REASONING

Write *horizontal* or *vertical* to complete each statement.

24. All the points with first coordinate 0 lie on a _____ line.

25. All the points with second coordinate 0 lie on a _____ line.

PROBLEM SOLVING

26. Start with the coordinates for Salt Lake City. Subtract $^-4$ from the first coordinate. Add $^-2$ to the second coordinate. What city is located at the resulting coordinates?

Find the percent of each number.

27. 25% of 80   **28.** 60% of 75   **29.** 24% of 88   **30.** 32% of 100   **31.** 16% of 102

Solve the proportions.

32. $\frac{3}{5} = \frac{n}{15}$ **33.** $\frac{7}{20} = \frac{n}{40}$ **34.** $\frac{1}{2} = \frac{n}{12}$ **35.** $\frac{5}{8} = \frac{n}{16}$ **36.** $\frac{11}{3} = \frac{n}{9}$

Problem Solving
Developing a Plan

UNDERSTAND
ANALYZE DATA
PLAN
ESTIMATE
SOLVE
EXAMINE

LEARN ABOUT IT

Sometimes there is more than one strategy that you can use to solve a problem. It is helpful to develop a plan before you start to solve the problem.

> I think I could solve this problem by **guessing and checking.**

> I might also be able to solve the problem by **making an organized list.**

> I think I'll try an organized list.

Ms. Ardito said to her class of 29 students, "This week you will be working on science and geography projects at 8 stations. Some stations are set up for groups of 3, and some are set up for groups of 4. The stations are set up so that all the students in the class can work at the same time. How many stations did I set up for groups of 3, and how many for groups of 4?"

Ms. Ardito set up 3 stations for groups of 3, and she set up 5 stations for groups of 4.

Groups of 3	Groups of 4	Total People
0	8	32
1	7	31
2	6	30
3	5	29

TRY IT OUT

List at least 2 strategies that you think might help you solve each problem. Then solve the problem.

1. Kenji's class is taking a field trip to the Museum of Natural Science. There are 27 students in the class. If 4 students can ride in each car and 7 in each van, find the least number of cars and vans needed so that every seat is taken.

2. Mrs. Thomas gave her class a list of countries and capitals to memorize. Jed's group memorized 5 the first day and twice as many the second day. Now they have 12 left to learn. How long was the list?

3. Roberto's group has this model. Their task is to find out how many blocks they would need to put in the bottom row to make the model 12 rows high. How many blocks do they need in the bottom row?

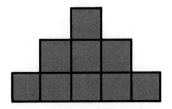

Solve. Use any problem solving strategy.

1. Mr. Jacobson bought a world map for each of the 6 groups in his class. How much did the maps cost, including tax?

Maps	
North America	$2.80
South America	$2.95
Europe and Asia	$4.25
World	$5.20
(+ 5% tax)	

2. The Nile is the longest river in the world. The Yukon is shorter than the Mississippi. The Amazon is longer than both the Yukon and the Mississippi. Which river is the shortest?

3. Calipatria, California lies 184 feet below sea level. Find the elevation of the top of a 57-foot building located in Calipatria.

4. The world's lowest recorded temperature was ⁻128.6°F in Antarctica. The highest recorded temperature there was 56°F. Find the difference between the two temperatures.

5. Summer in Antarctica begins in December and lasts for 4 months. During one summer 2,732 tourists visited Antarctica. About how many tourists came each month?

6. Antarctica covers 5.4 million square miles. Ice up to 3 miles thick covers almost 98% of the continent. How many square miles of Antarctica are covered by ice?

7. **Determining Reasonable Answers**
   Without solving the problem, tell which of the answers given below seems reasonable.

   The highest point in the United States is Mt. McKinley in Alaska at 20,320 feet. The lowest point is 282 feet below sea level at Death Valley, California. How much higher is Mt. McKinley than Death Valley?
   a. Mt. McKinley is 20,038 feet higher.
   b. Mt. McKinley is 20,162 feet higher.
   c. Mt. McKinley is 20,602 feet higher.

Data Collection and Analysis
Group Decision Making

UNDERSTAND
ANALYZE DATA
PLAN
ESTIMATE
SOLVE
EXAMINE

Doing a Questionnaire
Group Skill
Encourage and Respect Others

You know that living things, including people, cannot live without water. You want to find out if people are using water carefully or if they are wasting it. You will make a questionnaire to find out.

Collecting Data

1. With your group, brainstorm ways people can conserve water. Make a list of at least five ways.

Ways to Save Water
1. Take showers rather than baths.
2. Shut the water off when you brush your teeth.
3. —
4. —
5. —

2. Use your list of ideas to help you write a questionnaire about water conservation. Write at least four multiple choice questions and give three or four choices for each question. Below is a sample.

Water Conservation Questionnaire
Choose one answer for each question.
1. Do you run the water while you brush your teeth?
   a) usually   c) not very often
   b) sometimes   d) never
2. How careful are you about saving water?
   a) not very careful   c) careful
   b) somewhat careful   d) very careful

3. Test your questionnaire by having two or three people answer it. That way you can find out if any of the questions need to be revised.

4. Decide who you want your sample to represent. Do you want it to represent all students, all adults, or a mixture? Do you want the sample to represent all boys, all girls, or a mixture? Select 25 people for your sample.

5. Have each person in your sample fill out a questionnaire. Do you think people should put their names on the questionnaires? Why or why not?

6. Count the number of responses for each multiple choice answer. Make a multiple bar graph to show the responses for each question in your survey. Use this graph as an example.

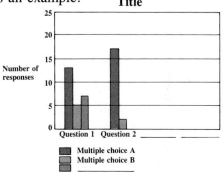

Title

Number of responses

25
20
15
10
5
0

Question 1   Question 2 _____ _____

■ Multiple choice A
■ Multiple choice B

7. What did you find out about water conservation and wasting? Write a short paragraph to describe the results of your questionnaire. Be sure to tell how many were in your sample and who your sample represents. Do you think your results would be the same for your whole city? Whole state? Whole country?

WRAP UP

Just the Opposite

Write an expression that is the opposite.

1. six seconds after blast-off

2. a gain of 12 pounds

3. forty paces to the right

4. thirty feet below sea level

5. a discount of 20%

6. a withdrawal of $300 from the bank

Sometimes, Always, Never

Decide which word goes in the blank: *sometimes*, *always*, or *never*.
Explain your choices.

7. Integers _____ increase in value as you move from left to right on a number line.

8. The opposite of a positive integer is _____ a positive integer.

9. Adding a negative integer is _____ equivalent to subtracting a positive integer.

10. The sum of a negative integer and a positive integer is _____ a positive integer.

11. The sum of two negative integers is _____ a positive integer.

12. The difference of two negative integers is _____ a positive integer.

Project

Use an atlas or a state map to trace or copy a map of a state onto centimeter grid paper. Choose a spot that appears to be in the center of the state. Mark the spot as the origin, or (0, 0). Make a grid. Write on a piece of paper the approximate coordinates of towns and cities in the state. Then challenge classmates to use the coordinates to find the towns and cities on your map.

CHAPTER REVIEW/TEST

Part 1   Understanding

Give the opposite of each.

1. 3 steps up

2. 5 km west

3. lose 0 points

4. Order from least to greatest: $^+6$, $^-5$, $^+2$, $^-1$, 0

5. Use the pattern to subtract the negative integers. Give each difference.

$6 - 2 = n$
$6 - 1 = n$
$6 - 0 = n$
$6 - {}^-1 = n$
$6 - {}^-2 = n$

Give the point for each set of coordinates.

6. $(^+2, {}^-5)$

7. $(^-2\frac{1}{2}, {}^+2)$

8. $(^-3, {}^-4)$

9. $(^+2, {}^+5)$

10. $(^+3, {}^+4)$

11. $(^+4.75, {}^-1.5)$

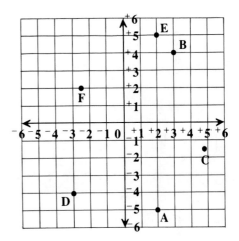

Part 2   Skills

Find the sum or difference.

12. $^-4 + {}^+6$

13. $^+12 + {}^-5$

14. $^+7 - {}^-4$

15. $^-10 - {}^-6$

Solve. Draw and use a number line if you need help.

16. $^-4 + n = {}^-9$

17. $^-6 + m = {}^+3$

Part 3   Applications

18. An archaeological dig is located 85 feet above sea level. If the workers dig a hole to find ruins that lie 52 feet below sea level, how deep is the hole?

19. From the daytime high, the temperature dropped 14° to a low of $^-4°$. What was the daytime high?

20. Challenge   Dana memorized 15 state capitals one day, which was 3 times as many as she memorized on the previous day. If Kevin has memorized 5 more capitals than Dana, how many has he memorized?

ENRICHMENT
Integer Multiplication Patterns

You can use your calculator to check some amazing multiplication patterns.

Push the keys shown to check these examples.

$^+5 \times {}^-4 = {}^-20$ 5 ☐× 4 ☐+↻− ☐=

$^-5 \times {}^-4 = {}^+20$ 5 ☐+↻− ☐× 4 ☐+↻− ☐=

Copy each column of equations. Follow the pattern from top to bottom to give each product **without using your calculator**. Then use your calculator to check the problems that involve negative integers.

1. $4 \times 4 = $ ▥

    $4 \times 3 = $ ▥

    $4 \times 2 = $ ▥

    $4 \times 1 = $ ▥

    $4 \times 0 = $ ▥

    $4 \times {}^-1 = $ ▥

    $4 \times {}^-2 = $ ▥

    $4 \times {}^-3 = $ ▥

    $4 \times {}^-4 = $ ▥

2. $3 \times 4 = $ ▥

    $3 \times 3 = $ ▥

    $3 \times 2 = $ ▥

    $3 \times 1 = $ ▥

    $3 \times 0 = $ ▥

    $3 \times {}^-1 = $ ▥

    $3 \times {}^-2 = $ ▥

    $3 \times {}^-3 = $ ▥

    $3 \times {}^-4 = $ ▥

3. $4 \times {}^-4 = $ ▥

    $3 \times {}^-4 = $ ▥

    $2 \times {}^-4 = $ ▥

    $1 \times {}^-4 = $ ▥

    $0 \times {}^-4 = $ ▥

    $^-1 \times {}^-4 = $ ▥

    $^-2 \times {}^-4 = $ ▥

    $^-3 \times {}^-4 = $ ▥

    $^-4 \times {}^-4 = $ ▥

4. $4 \times {}^-3 = $ ▥

    $3 \times {}^-3 = $ ▥

    $2 \times {}^-3 = $ ▥

    $1 \times {}^-3 = $ ▥

    $0 \times {}^-3 = $ ▥

    $^-1 \times {}^-3 = $ ▥

    $^-2 \times {}^-3 = $ ▥

    $^-3 \times {}^-3 = $ ▥

    $^-4 \times {}^-3 = $ ▥

5. How could you use adding to show that $3 \times {}^-4 = {}^-12$?

6. What do you believe to be true about the product of any two negative integers?

CUMULATIVE REVIEW

1. Which figure has exactly 1 endpoint?
   - A. triangle
   - B. line
   - C. ray
   - D. line segment

2. Which triangle has 1 obtuse angle?
   - A. acute
   - B. equilateral
   - C. right
   - D. obtuse

3. One of the parallel sides of a trapezoid is 8 in. shorter than the other. Together the 2 sides total 20 in. How long is each of the parallel sides?
   - A. 13 in., 7 in.
   - B. 6 in., 14 in.
   - C. 12 in., 6 in.
   - D. 8 in., 6 in.

4. Write as a percent: 9:100.
   - A. 90%
   - B. 9%
   - C. 0.09%
   - D. 0.9%

5. Of the 200 votes cast, Dennis got 53. About what percent of the votes did he get?
   - A. 106%
   - B. 50%
   - C. 25%
   - D. 75%

6. Write 0.87 as a percent.
   - A. 870%
   - B. 87%
   - C. 8.7%
   - D. 0.87%

7. Write as a percent: $\frac{7}{20}$.
   - A. 140%
   - B. 7%
   - C. 35%
   - D. 20%

8. Find 35% of 300.
   - A. 10.5
   - B. 105
   - C. 335
   - D. 35

9. Find $33\frac{1}{3}$% of 90 mentally.
   - A. 30
   - B. 60
   - C. $33\frac{1}{3}$
   - D. 120

10. Estimate 12% of 150.
    - A. 30
    - B. 40
    - C. 10
    - D. 20

11. Which calculation method would most likely be the fastest to use to find 25% of 40?
    - A. mental math
    - B. computer
    - C. pencil and paper
    - D. calculator

12. Find the interest on $300 borrowed at a rate of 15% per year for 2 years.
    - A. $30
    - B. $60
    - C. $45
    - D. $90

13. Claudia bought a $45 radio at a 20% discount. She paid $1.80 in sales tax. What was the total cost?
    - A. $10.80
    - B. $36
    - C. $37.80
    - D. $46.80

14. Carmen bought a hat for $12.95. The sales tax rate is $5\frac{1}{2}$%. What is the total cost of her purchase?
    - A. $13.66
    - B. $.71
    - C. $12.24
    - D. $12.95

13

MEASUREMENT

MATH AND
LANGUAGE ARTS

DATA BANK

Use the Language Arts Data
Bank on page 480 to answer
the questions.

1 Use the prefixes to help you
find the difference when you
subtract a decigram from a
kilogram. Find the difference when
you subtract a decigram from a
hectogram.

2 In 46 B.C., Julius Caesar designed a calendar. In it, the last month of the year was called December. How many months were in a year in this Julian calendar?

3 Using the prefixes, give another word for the units of time in **A** and **B**.
A In *one billionth of a second*, a beam of light travels the length of a notebook.
B *One billion seconds* from now, you will be more than 40 years old.

4 **Using Critical Thinking**
Use the prefixes to group these words. Explain your classifications. *Decathlon, centigram, percent, decimal, centipede, decade, century, decagon, centennial, decimeter.*

Changing Units

EXPLORE Discover a Relationship

One of the great advantages of the metric system is the ease of changing from one unit to another. This is because the metric system is based on 10 just like our place-value system. The cubit is a unit of length used by many early civilizations. It was based on the length of a man's arm from the elbow to the tip of the middle finger. How would you express the English cubit in millimeters and in meters?

CUBIT	
Egyptian	53 cm
Roman	44.5 cm
Hebrew	44.7 cm
English	46 cm

TALK ABOUT IT

1. Think about how you can use a place-value chart to examine the relationship of metric units. Describe what you would do to change meters (ones) to decimeters (tenths).

ones	tenths	hundredths	thousandths
m	dm	cm	mm

2. Describe what you would do to change decimeters (tenths) to meters (ones).

3. Describe what you would do to express the English cubit in millimeters.

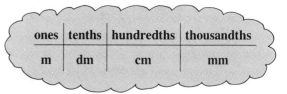

4. Describe what you would do to express the English cubit in meters.

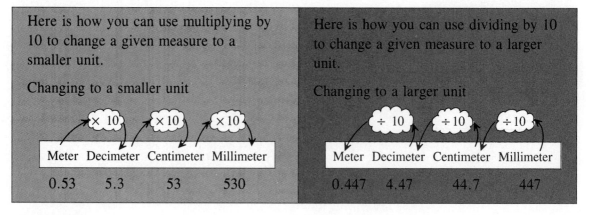

Here is how you can use multiplying by 10 to change a given measure to a smaller unit.

Changing to a smaller unit

× 10 × 10 × 10

Meter	Decimeter	Centimeter	Millimeter
0.53	5.3	53	530

Here is how you can use dividing by 10 to change a given measure to a larger unit.

Changing to a larger unit

÷ 10 ÷ 10 ÷ 10

Meter	Decimeter	Centimeter	Millimeter
0.447	4.47	44.7	447

Use multiplying by 10 or dividing by 10 to find each answer.

1. Change 327 mm to cm.
2. Change 286 cm to m.
3. Change 5.3 dm to cm.

Give the number for each changed unit.

1. 3.6 m = ▧ dm

2. 3.64 m = ▧ cm

3. 743 mm = ▧ m

4. 3.662 m = ▧ mm

5. 147 dm = ▧ m

6. 4.3 m = ▧ dm

7. 9.68 m = ▧ cm

8. 48 cm = ▧ m

9. 2.75 m = ▧ mm

10. 56 mm = ▧ m

11. 0.86 m = ▧ cm

12. 47 mm = ▧ dm

13. 4.9 dm = ▧ cm

14. 376 cm = ▧ m

15. 8.04 m = ▧ cm

16. 9,467 mm = ▧ m

17. 157 dm = ▧ m

18. 4.65 dm = ▧ mm

19. 12.2 m = ▧ cm

20. 137 mm = ▧ dm

21. 8.4 cm = ▧ mm

This diagram shows the relation
between the kilometer (km) and the
meter (m). Give the number for each
changed unit.

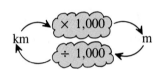

22. 0.32 km = ▧ m

23. 1,264 m = ▧ km

24. 846 m = ▧ km

MATH REASONING

Which of the numbers is greater? Tell how you know.

25. Lindsay's height was x cm or x m.

26. Bryan's height was x mm or x dm.

PROBLEM SOLVING

27. The length of the Roman cubit is
44.5 cm. Express the length in m.

28. Data Hunt Measure your own cubit
in cm. Express it in mm and in m.

29. The length of Joel's arm from the tip of his shoulder to the
tip of his finger is 60 cm. His cubit is 12 cm longer than his
upper arm. How long is his cubit?

▶ **ALGEBRA**

Amber is y centimeters tall. Tell which of the following
expressions show Amber's height in other units. Write *yes* or *no*.

30. $\frac{y}{10}$ dm

31. $10y$ dm

32. $10y$ mm

33. $\frac{y}{10}$ mm

More Practice, page 517, set D

361

Estimating Length
Metric Units

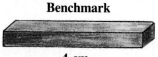

4 cm

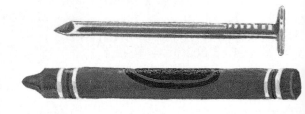

EXPLORE Use Metric Benchmarks

If you know the length of one object, sometimes you can use that to help you estimate the length of another object. The object of known length is called a **benchmark.**

Use the benchmark to estimate the length in centimeters of each of these objects. Then measure to see how close your estimates were.

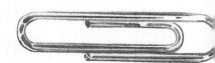

TALK ABOUT IT

1. Tell how the benchmark makes it easier to estimate the length of the other objects.
2. Did your estimates tend to be more or less than the actual length?
3. Which was easier to estimate—the objects closer to the benchmark or the ones farther away? Tell why.

The rod below is 1 decimeter (dm) long.

To estimate greater lengths than those above, you might want to use a benchmark such as the decimeter (10 cm). For even greater lengths, it would be helpful to think of a meter stick (100 cm) as the benchmark.

TRY IT OUT

Estimate. Then measure to see how close your estimates are.

1. Estimate the length and width of your math book in centimeters.
2. Estimate the height from the floor to your chair seat in decimeters.
3. Estimate the height from the floor to your desktop in decimeters.

Estimate. Then measure to see how close your estimate is.

1. **Your pencil**
   Your estimate: cm
   Actual measure: ||||| cm
   (nearest cm)

2. **Your armspan**
   Your estimate: ||||| dm
   Actual measure: ||||| dm
   (nearest dm)

3. **Your height**
   Your estimate: ||||| cm
   Actual measure: ||||| cm
   (nearest cm)

4. **Width of your desktop**
   Your estimate: ||||| cm
   Actual measure: ||||| cm
   (nearest cm)

5. **Length of your normal step**
   Your estimate: ||||| dm
   Actual measure: ||||| dm
   (nearest dm)

6. **Length of your classroom**
   Your estimate: ||||| m
   Actual measure: ||||| m
   (nearest m)

MATH REASONING

7. Suppose your normal walking step is about 60 cm. Your little brother's normal step is 31 cm. If you take 170 steps to cross a small park, estimate about how many you would expect your little brother to take.

PROBLEM SOLVING

8. Marti estimated the width of the classroom would be about 100 m. Is this estimate reasonable? Explain how you know.

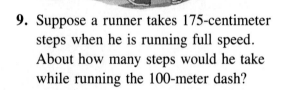

9. Suppose a runner takes 175-centimeter steps when he is running full speed. About how many steps would he take while running the 100-meter dash?

Write >, <, or = for each ||||| .

10. $^+2$ ||||| $^-8$

11. $^-6$ ||||| $^-7$

12. $^-7$ ||||| 0

13. $^-10$ ||||| 12

14. $\frac{5}{7}$ ||||| $\frac{2}{3}$

15. $\frac{1}{2}$ ||||| $\frac{5}{8}$

16. $\frac{10}{15}$ ||||| $\frac{2}{5}$

17. $\frac{7}{11}$ ||||| $\frac{3}{4}$

Find the quotients to the nearest tenth.

18. $61\overline{)3162}$

19. $18\overline{)186.2}$

20. $27\overline{)1205}$

21. $82\overline{)29.017}$

Problem Solving
Deciding When to Estimate

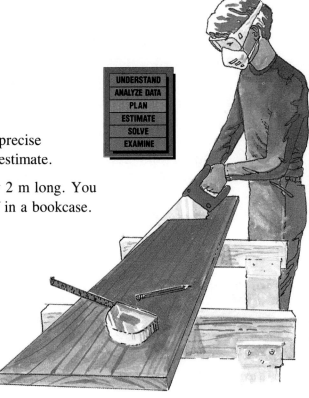

LEARN ABOUT IT

UNDERSTAND
ANALYZE DATA
PLAN
ESTIMATE
SOLVE
EXAMINE

In some real-world situations you need to make precise measurements while in others you need only an estimate.

Suppose you have a board that is 25 cm wide by 2 m long. You are going to saw the board to use as a bookshelf in a bookcase. How do you decide where to cut the board?

I want the shelf to fit exactly into the space in my bookcase. I'd better make a precise measurement.

Suppose you decide instead to cut the board to use as a sign to advertise a garage sale. Now, how do you decide where to cut the board?

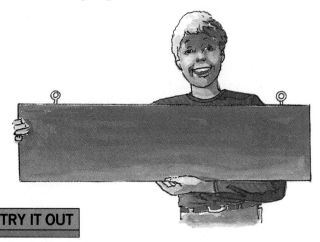

I can easily guess how large to make my sign. I'll need only to make an estimate to decide where to cut the board.

TRY IT OUT

Decide if you need an estimate or a precise measure. Tell why.

1. Suppose you decide to cut the board to make a runway for your model car.

2. Suppose you decide to cut the board to use as part of the floor of a doghouse you are making.

Decide if you need an estimate or a precise measure. Tell why.

1. Cutting a stake for a small tree

2. The amount of flour in a recipe

3. The time it would take you to walk to school

4. The time a runner takes for the 100-meter dash

5. Installing draperies

6. The water needed for your houseplant

7. The distance you live from school

8. The amount of cheese in a package at the grocery store

9. Making a leg for a table

10. Some milk to drink

Tell if you need a precise answer or if an estimate will do.
Then solve the problems that need precise answers.

11. Frank weighs 96 lb, Erin weighs 89 lb, Andy weighs 79 lb, and Molly weighs 99 lb. In a tug-of-war contest, will they weigh more or less than the students on the other side whose combined weight is 400 lb?

12. Stacy has a board that is 5 ft $2\frac{1}{2}$ in. long. She needs a piece that measures 4 ft $6\frac{1}{4}$ in. long for a chest of drawers. How much will she cut off to get the board she wants?

13. Casey is 4 ft $10\frac{1}{4}$ in. tall. Carlos is 5 ft $2\frac{1}{2}$ in. tall. Is Casey taller than Carlos?

14. Kyle is baking bread. The recipe calls for $2\frac{1}{2}$ cups of whole wheat flour and $1\frac{3}{4}$ cups of white flour. How much flour does he need in all?

15. **Write Your Own Problem** Make up one situation where you would measure precisely before sawing a board and another situation where you would only estimate.

Volume, Capacity, and Mass
Metric Units

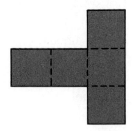

LEARN ABOUT IT

In the metric system, volume, capacity, and
mass are all related to each other.

EXPLORE Use a Pattern

Work in groups to build an open-top box that is 10 cm on
each edge. Imagine that your box can be filled with water.

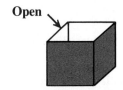

Open

TALK ABOUT IT

1. What in your room do you think would have about
the same mass as your box of water?

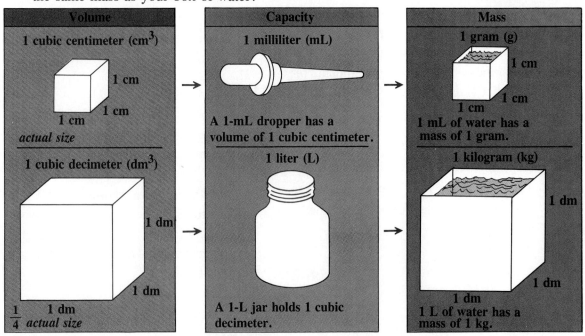

Volume	Capacity	Mass
1 cubic centimeter (cm³)	**1 milliliter (mL)**	**1 gram (g)**
1 cm, 1 cm, 1 cm — *actual size*	A 1-mL dropper has a volume of 1 cubic centimeter.	1 cm, 1 cm — 1 mL of water has a mass of 1 gram.
1 cubic decimeter (dm³)	**1 liter (L)**	**1 kilogram (kg)**
1 dm, 1 dm, 1 dm — ¼ *actual size*	A 1-L jar holds 1 cubic decimeter.	1 dm, 1 dm, 1 dm — 1 L of water has a mass of 1 kg.

A **milligram (mg)** is a very tiny unit of mass. It is 1 thousandth of a gram.
A **kiloliter (kL)** is a very large unit of capacity. It is 1,000 liters.

TRY IT OUT

Choose the best estimate.

1. can of juice
825 mL   825 L   825 kL

2. bowling ball
7 mg   7 g   7 kg

3. bathtub
225 mL 225 L 225 kL

Choose the best estimate for the capacity of each container.

1. tablespoon
15 mL   15 L   15 kL

2. home aquarium
40 mL   40 L   40 kL

3. city water tank
2,000 mL   2,000 L
2,000 kL

Choose the best estimate for the mass of each item.

4. bear
90 mg   90 g   90 kg

5. paper clip
1 mg   1 g   1 kg

6. ball point pen
15 mg   15 g   15 kg

Give the number for each changed unit.

7. 3 kL = ▥ L

8. 7 L = ▥ mL

9. 0.250 kL = ▥ L

10. 0.750 L = ▥ mL

11. 1,435 L = ▥ kL

12. 2,374 mL = ▥ L

13. 476 L = ▥ kL

14. 375 mL = ▥ L

15. 5 kg = ▥ g

16. 12 g = ▥ mg

17. 0.250 kg = ▥ g

18. 0.500 g = ▥ mg

19. 8,346 g = ▥ kg

20. 1,765 mg = ▥ g

MATH REASONING

21. Erica said, "I think it has a mass of 5 g." Is Erica thinking about a book, a nickel, or a feather?

22. Adam said, "I think it holds about 2 L." Is Adam thinking about a drinking glass, a large pitcher, or a bathtub?

PROBLEM SOLVING

23. How many 5-mL teaspoons does it take to fill a 250-mL cup?

24. Language Arts Data Bank Use the prefixes *mega-* and *micro-* to complete these sentences. There are a million _____ in a meter. A _____ is one million grams.

▶ USING CRITICAL THINKING   Use Careful Reasoning

25. Here are two pails. There are no marks on either pail. How can you use the pails to get 4 L of water in the larger pail?

3 L   8 L

Using Critical Thinking

Five Common Types of Measurement	
Length	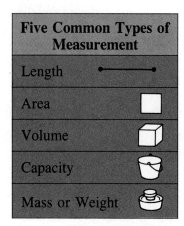
Area	
Volume	
Capacity	
Mass or Weight	

LEARN ABOUT IT

Shigeo works in a home improvement store. The things he sells are measured in many different ways and with many different units. The table shows some of the more common types of measurement. Each type may have several different units.

One customer asked Shigeo for enough lawn fertilizer to cover 10,000 sq ft. Another customer asked for one hundred pounds of lawn fertilizer. Shigeo told his friend Keith that he sold both customers the same size bag. Keith asked, "Did your boss get angry about your mistake?"

Shigeo countered, "No. My boss thought I did very well."

Is that possible?

TALK ABOUT IT

1. Do you think a bag of fertilizer might have the weight printed on it?
2. Is it possible that directions on the bag might tell the area of lawn that can be covered?
3. How could Shigeo have been correct?

TRY IT OUT

For each item, give the likely type of measurement and a likely unit. If you aren't sure, try to find out.

1. Electrical Cord

2. Carpeting

3. Refrigerator

4. Nails

5. Paint

6. TV Set

MIDCHAPTER REVIEW/QUIZ

First estimate using each of the given units. Then measure to check.

1. your forearm from elbow to wrist in decimeters and in centimeters

2. your teacher's height in meters, in decimeters, and in centimeters

For each situation, decide if you would need an estimate or a precise measure.

3. fixing cheese and crackers for an after-school snack

4. adding liquid soap to a bucket of water

5. finishing half of your homework before dinner

6. making a wooden frame for a picture

7. building a clubhouse floor

Choose the best unit of measure to estimate the capacity, weight, or distance.

8. A child's mass is about 45 (g, mg, or kg).

9. A small glass of juice contains about 250 (kL, L, or ml).

10. A box of 100 paper clips has a mass of about 100 (kg, g, or mg).

11. A 1-hour bike ride is about 15 (m, km, mm).

Give the number for each changed unit.

12. $3 \text{ m} = $ ▦ cm

13. $32 \text{ mm} = $ ▦ cm

14. $1.59 \text{ m} = $ ▦ dm

15. $5.2 \text{ cm} = $ ▦ m

16. $525 \text{ mm} = $ ▦ m

17. $5.7 \text{ km} = $ ▦ m

18. $8 \text{ L} = $ ▦ mL

19. $0.25 \text{ kg} = $ ▦ g

20. $1,426 \text{ L} = $ ▦ kL

21. $5 \text{ g} = $ ▦ mg

22. $750 \text{ mL} = $ ▦ L

23. $3,010 \text{ g} = $ ▦ kg

PROBLEM SOLVING

24. Melanie estimates that a car seat is about 2 m wide. How would you use a benchmark to decide if her estimate is reasonable?

25. Elizabeth is making fruit salad for the school picnic. Describe when she might need a precise measurement and when she might estimate.

Time

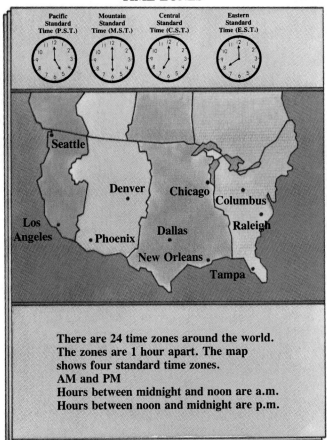

TIME ZONES

Pacific Standard Time (P.S.T.) Mountain Standard Time (M.S.T.) Central Standard Time (C.S.T.) Eastern Standard Time (E.S.T.)

Seattle
Denver Chicago
Columbus
Los Angeles Raleigh
Phoenix Dallas
New Orleans
Tampa

There are 24 time zones around the world. The zones are 1 hour apart. The map shows four standard time zones.
AM and PM
Hours between midnight and noon are a.m.
Hours between noon and midnight are p.m.

LEARN ABOUT IT

EXPLORE Study the Data

The picture at the right shows some important facts about time.

TALK ABOUT IT

1. What is the difference in time between Pacific time and Eastern time?
2. Is Central time earlier or later than Mountain time?
3. If a game begins at 8:00 p.m. in Columbus, what time can it be seen on TV in Los Angeles?

Sometimes you may need to add or subtract time. When you add or subtract time, you may need to trade just as you do with whole numbers.

$$\begin{array}{r} 3 \text{ h } 25 \text{ min} \\ + 2 \text{ h } 45 \text{ min} \\ \hline 5 \text{ h } 70 \text{ min} \end{array}$$

70 min = 1 h 10 min
→ 6 h 10 min

$$\begin{array}{r} 4 \text{ h } 25 \text{ min} \\ - 2 \text{ h } 45 \text{ min} \end{array}$$

Trade 1 h for 60 min →

$$\begin{array}{r} 3 \text{ h } 85 \text{ min} \\ 4 \text{ h } 25 \text{ min} \\ - 2 \text{ h } 45 \text{ min} \\ \hline 1 \text{ h } 40 \text{ min} \end{array}$$

TRY IT OUT

Find each answer. Remember, 1 min = 60 s.

1. $\begin{array}{r} 4 \text{ h } 55 \text{ min} \\ + 2 \text{ h } 35 \text{ min} \end{array}$

2. $\begin{array}{r} 8 \text{ h } 20 \text{ min} \\ - 3 \text{ h } 45 \text{ min} \end{array}$

3. $\begin{array}{r} 4 \text{ min } 29 \text{ s} \\ + 8 \text{ min } 46 \text{ s} \end{array}$

4. $\begin{array}{r} 9 \text{ min } 12 \text{ s} \\ - 3 \text{ min } 20 \text{ s} \end{array}$

5. A game starts in Seattle at 1:00 p.m. and ends at 4:10 p.m. If it is shown live on TV in Tampa, what time does the game begin? What time does it end?

Find the sums and differences.

1.   8 h 50 min
  + 7 h 40 min
	2. 10 h 30 min
	  − 1 h 45 min
		3. 8 min 45 s
		  + 5 min 45 s
			4. 9 min 15 s
			  − 2 min 30 s

5.   15 h 30 min
  − 8 h 17 min
	6. 7 h 25 min
	  + 9 h 30 min
		7. 6 h 57 min
		  + 4 h 49 min
			8. 7 h 24 min
			  − 2 h 56 min

Give the times.

9. When it is 9 p.m. in Dallas, what time is it in Los Angeles?

10. When it is 12:00 noon in Los Angeles, what time is it in Columbus?

APPLY

MATH REASONING

11. A game started in Chicago at 7:30 p.m. It was shown in Seattle on a 1-hour delay. What time should people in that city tune into the game?

PROBLEM SOLVING

12. April finished soccer practice at 4:15 p.m. She needs to be home at 6:00 p.m. How much time does she have?

13. The flight left Denver at 11:00 a.m. and arrived in Tampa at 4:15 p.m. How long was the flight? Don't forget the time change.

14. Language Arts Data Bank
Complete the following statement.

If   1 kilosecond = 1,000 seconds, or 16.67 minutes

then   1 megasecond = ▓▓▓ minutes

      1 gigasecond = ▓▓▓ minutes, and

      1 terasecond = ▓▓▓ minutes.

▶ MENTAL MATH

Solve mentally.

15. Jim started work at 1:30 p.m. Rosario started 1 h 20 min earlier. When did Rosario start?

16. Marie planned to finish the project at 4:30 p.m. She finished 2 h 25 min earlier. What time did she finish?

Estimating Length
Customary Units

Benchmark

2 inches

EXPLORE Use Customary Benchmarks

Use the benchmark to estimate the length in inches of each of these objects. Then measure to see how close your estimates were.

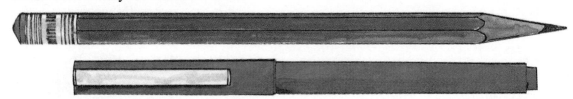

TALK ABOUT IT

1. Explain how you used the benchmark to make your estimates.
2. Did your estimates tend to be more than or less than the actual length?
3. Which was easier to estimate, the shorter objects or the longer objects? Why?

This bar is 6 inches long.

To estimate greater lengths than those above, you might want to use a larger benchmark such as this 6-inch bar. For even larger objects, you might want to use the foot (12 inches) or the yard (3 feet) as your benchmark.

TRY IT OUT

1. Estimate the length and width of your math book in inches.
2. Estimate the height from the floor to your chair seat in inches.
3. Estimate the height from the floor to your desktop in inches.

First estimate. Then measure.

1. **Your pencil**
   Your estimate: ▦ in.
   Actual measure: ▦ in.
   (nearest in.)

2. **Your arm span**
   Your estimate: ▦ in.
   Actual measure: ▦ in.
   (nearest in.)

3. **Your normal step**
   Your estimate: ▦ in.
   Actual measure: ▦ in.
   (nearest in.)

4. **Height of classroom door**
   Your estimate: ▦ ft
   Actual measure: ▦ ft
   (nearest ft)

5. **Width of your room**
   Your estimate: ▦ ft
   Actual measure: ▦ ft
   (nearest ft)

6. **Length of your room**
   Your estimate: ▦ yd
   Actual measure: ▦ yd
   (nearest yd)

7. Estimate a distance of 50 ft by using your normal walking step as a measuring unit. Measure to see how close your estimate is to the actual distance.

APPLY

MATH REASONING

8. Candice asked, "How far is it to Chicago?" Phillip replied, "About an hour and a half." How can Phillip give a distance using time? What do you think he meant?

PROBLEM SOLVING

9. Rachel estimates that the length of the classroom is about 30 feet. Is this estimate reasonable? Explain how you know.

10. Manuel estimates the length of a rectangle to be about twice its width. The actual perimeter is 18 inches. About how long is the rectangle if Manuel's estimate is right?

MIXED REVIEW

Solve.

11. $a + {}^-8 = {}^-7$

12. $n + {}^+3 = {}^+1$

13. ${}^+6 + n = {}^-2$

14. ${}^-5 + b = {}^-7$

Write the base and the exponent. Then write the number in standard form.

15. 9×9

16. $3 \times 3 \times 3 \times 3$

17. $10 \times 10 \times 10 \times 10 \times 10 \times 10$

Capacity and Weight
Customary Units

Small
49¢ each

Large
79¢ each

EXPLORE Study the Information

The picture at the right shows some things priced according to weight and capacity.

TALK ABOUT IT

1. Which apple would you buy? Why?
2. How many of the small cups would the large cup need to hold for it to be a good buy? Do you think it does? Why?

Small

Medium

Large

39¢

69¢

99¢

Capacity

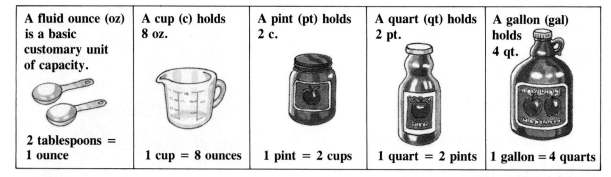

A fluid ounce (oz) is a basic customary unit of capacity.	A cup (c) holds 8 oz.	A pint (pt) holds 2 c.	A quart (qt) holds 2 pt.	A gallon (gal) holds 4 qt.
2 tablespoons = 1 ounce	1 cup = 8 ounces	1 pint = 2 cups	1 quart = 2 pints	1 gallon = 4 quarts

Weight

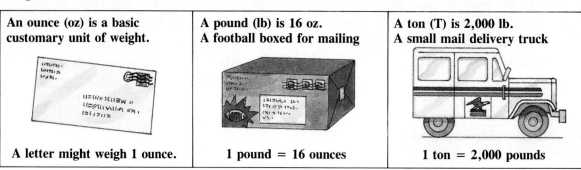

An ounce (oz) is a basic customary unit of weight.	A pound (lb) is 16 oz. A football boxed for mailing	A ton (T) is 2,000 lb. A small mail delivery truck
A letter might weigh 1 ounce.	1 pound = 16 ounces	1 ton = 2,000 pounds

1. How many tablespoons are in a cup? Pint? Quart? Gallon?
2. How many ounces are in a quarter pound? Half pound? Ton?

Give the missing numbers.

1. 2 c = oz

2. 3 pt = c

3. 3 T = lb

4. 10 lb = oz

5. $\frac{3}{4}$ lb = oz

6. $\frac{1}{2}$ T = lb

7. 1 gal = pt

8. 8 qt = gal

9. A gallon and 2 pints of lemonade can fill cups.

10. A pint of cough syrup can fill tablespoons.

11. A quart and a half of milk can fill cups.

Write *oz*, *lb*, or *T*.

12. A tennis ball weighs about 2 .

13. An automobile might weigh $1\frac{1}{2}$.

14. A person might weigh 140 .

15. A book might weigh 28 .

16. A large whale might weigh 160 .

17. A loaf of bread might weigh 1 .

APPLY

MATH REASONING

18. Container A holds more than D but less than C. Container B holds less than D. Which is the cup, the pint, the quart, and the gallon?

PROBLEM SOLVING

19. Karen noticed that tomato juice was six 6-oz cans for $1.89 or 59¢ for a 12-oz can. Which is the better buy?

20. A pint of water weighs about 1 lb. How many gallons of water are there in a ton?

▶ **CALCULATOR**

Solve this problem using | M + | on your calculator.

21. Suppose a rich king gave his daughter 1 oz of gold the first day, 2 oz the second, 4 oz the third, 8 oz the fourth, and so on. If the gold was worth $489 an oz, what was the value of her gold after 10 days? Hint:

| ON/AC | 1 | M+ | × | 2 | = | M+ | × | 2 | = | M+ |

... | × | 2 | = | M+ | MR | × | 489 | = |

More Practice, page 518, set B

Computing with Customary Units

EXPLORE **Analyze the Process**

Marlo's Yorkshire terrier weighs 6 lb 8 oz.
Miranda's Chihuahua weighs 2 lb 13 oz. How
much more does the Yorkshire terrier weigh than
the Chihuahua? How much do they weigh
altogether?

You can find the difference like this.

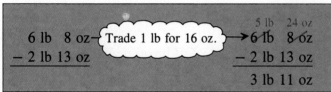

You can find the sum like this.

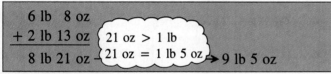

TALK ABOUT IT

1. What trade was made in the subtraction problem? Explain why
   it was made.
2. What trade was made in the addition problem? Explain why it
   was made.
3. How would you have estimated the difference in weight? The
   total weight of both dogs?
4. Use a complete sentence to answer each question of the story
   problem.

TRY IT OUT

Find the sum, the difference, or the product.

1.   6 ft 7 in.
    + 6 ft 10 in.

2.   12 ft 3 in.
    − 8 ft 6 in.

3.   6 lb 3 oz
    − 1 lb 8 oz

4.   2 lb 9 oz
    ×   4

Find the sum, the difference, or the product.

1.   3 ft 4 in.
     + 5 ft 10 in.

2.   7 ft 2 in.
     − 1 ft 3 in.

3.   9 ft 6 in.
     + 8 ft 4 in.

4.   12 ft 10 in.
     − 6 ft 5 in.

5.   8 ft 0 in.
     − 2 ft 3 in.

6.   2 ft 7 in.
     ×   4

7.   6 lb 9 oz
     +   8 oz

8.   2 lb 6 oz
     ×   3

9.   7 lb 2 oz
     + 1 lb 15 oz

10.   9 lb 0 oz
      − 2 lb 10 oz

11.   1 ft 3 in.
      ×   6

12.   7 ft 11 in.
      + 2 ft 2 in.

APPLY

MATH REASONING Which is greater?

13. 1 ft 15 in. or 20 in.

14. 2 lb or 1 lb 10 oz

15. 3 ft 1 in. or 2 ft 15 in.

PROBLEM SOLVING

16. Ian is taller than Kara. Ian is shorter than Shinji but taller than Federico. Kara is shorter than Federico. List the students in order from shortest to tallest.

17. When Anthony entered high school, he weighed 98 lb 4 oz. When he graduated 3 years 9 months later, he weighed 147 lb 13 oz. How much had he gained?

18. Language Arts Data Bank Complete the following statement. Remember, 1 mile = 5,280 feet. Round answers to the nearest thousandth.

If light travels 186,200 miles in 1 second,
then it travels ▓▓▓▓ miles in 1 millisecond,
                 ▓▓▓▓ miles in 1 microsecond,
                 ▓▓▓▓ foot in 1 nanosecond, and
                 ▓▓▓▓ inch in 1 picosecond.

▶ ESTIMATION

Round to the nearest larger unit. Then estimate each answer.

19.   6 lb 14 oz —(Closer to 7 lb)→ 7 lb
      + 8 lb 5 oz —(Closer to 8 lb)→ + 8 lb
                                         ▓▓▓▓ lb

20.   9 lb 3 oz
      − 2 lb 15 oz

21.   7 ft 11 in.
      + 6 ft 4 in.

22.   5 ft 11 in.
      ×   6

23.   9 ft 2 in.
      ×   5

Problem Solving
Problems with More than One Answer

UNDERSTAND
ANALYZE DATA
PLAN
ESTIMATE
SOLVE
EXAMINE

LEARN ABOUT IT

Some problems have more than one answer. When you find an answer to a problem, do not stop. Ask yourself if there may be other answers.

I could use guess and check to find an answer.

But I should check for other answers. I'll make an organized list of the different possibilities.

The list shows there are 4 possible answers.

- ten 2-point and one 3-point goals
- seven 2-point and three 3-point goals
- four 2-point and five 3-point goals
- one 2-point and seven 3-point field goals

The Bengals scored several field goals totaling 23 points during the first half of a basketball game. The score for a field goal is either 2 points or 3 points. How many of each kind of field goal did they score?

Try six 2-point and three 3-point goals.
$12 + 9 = 21$ Too low!

Try seven 2-point and three 3-point goals.
$14 + 9 = 23$ Correct!

2-point		3-point		Total	
12	24	0		24	Won't work
11	22				Won't work
10	20	1	3	23 ✓	
9	18				Won't work
8	16				Won't work
7	14	3	9	23 ✓	
6	12				Won't work
5	10				Won't work
4	8	5	15	23 ✓	
3	6				Won't work
2	2				Won't work
1	2	7	21	23 ✓	
0	0				Won't work

TRY IT OUT

Solve.

1. A football team scored 38 points during one game. They scored 3 points for each field goal and 7 points for each touchdown and its successful conversion. How many of each did they make?

2. Aaron bought a basketball. The clerk gave him dimes and quarters totaling $1.35 in change. How many dimes and how many quarters did Aaron get?

Solve. Use any strategy.

1. A regulation basketball must weigh between 1 lb 6 oz and 1 lb 8 oz. If each of 4 balls weighs 1 lb 7 oz, what will their total combined weight be?

2. A football field is 120 yards long and 53 yards 1 foot wide. How much longer is the length of the field than the width?

3. The diagram shows the measurements for football goal posts. Find the distance between the uprights if each upright is 4″ in diameter.

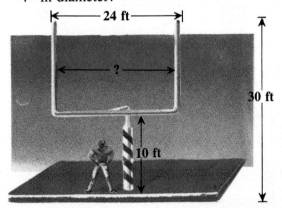

4. Julie, Ann, Bev, and Kay play on a basketball team. Their positions are center, forward, point guard, and off guard. Ann is the shortest member of the team. The center is taller than the forward. Kay does not play point guard or center. Bev plays off guard. What position does Ann play?

5. Laurent bought some golf balls in boxes of 4 and some tennis balls in cans of 3. Altogether he bought 31 balls. How many of each kind did he buy?

Some Strategies

Act Out	Solve a Simpler Problem
Use Objects	Make an Organized List
Choose an Operation	Work Backward
Draw a Picture	Look for a Pattern
Guess and Check	Use Logical Reasoning
Make a Table	

6. A famous football player attempted 3,276 passes during his first 9 years with his team. He completed almost 64%. About how many passes did he complete? Tell whether you need an exact answer or an estimate. Then answer the question.

7. An approved football must have between 12.5 lb and 13.5 lb of air pressure. In checking a ball, the referee measured 9.7 lb. How many pounds must be added to bring the air pressure up to 13.5 lb?

8. **Thinking About Your Solution**
Suppose Bing has quarters, dimes, and nickels in his pocket. At the game, he bought a box of popcorn for $0.75. He gave the clerk exact change using 3 nickels and other coins. What other coins did he use?

   a. Show the steps you took to solve the problem.

   b. Write your answer in a complete sentence.

   c. Name the strategy you used to solve the problem.

More Practice, page 527, set A

379

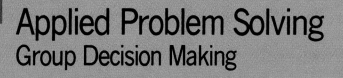

Applied Problem Solving
Group Decision Making

UNDERSTA
ANALYZE DA
PLAN
ESTIMATE
SOLVE
EXAMINE

Group Skill
Disagree in an Agreeable Way

Your class has been asked to help the cafeteria plan a lunch menu for one day each month. Begin by planning a healthy menu for yourself for one day.

Facts to Consider

1. You need to fulfill your daily nutritional needs. Try to get as close as possible to the average number of calories you require, and always be sure you fulfill your daily needs for protein.

2. Choose at least 4 servings from the milk group, 4 servings from the bread and cereals group, 2 servings from the meat group, and 4 servings from the fruits and vegetables group.

Average Daily Nutritional Needs

Females Age (years)	Calories	Protein (grams)
1–3	1300	23
4–6	1700	30
7–10	2400	36
11–14	2200	44
15–18	2100	48
19–22	2100	46
23–50	2000	46
51 on	1800	46

Males Age (years)	Calories	Protein (grams)
1–3	1300	23
4–6	1700	30
7–10	2400	36
11–14	2700	44
15–18	2800	54
19–22	2900	54
23–50	2700	56
51 on	2400	56

BASIC FOOD GROUPS

Bread and Cereals

	Quantity	Calories	Protein(g)
bread, white	1 slice	55	2
whole wheat	1 slice	60	3
cereal, dry	$\frac{3}{4}$ cup	110	1
macaroni	1 cup	155	5
noodles	1 cup	200	7
pancake, plain	1	60	2
rice, white	1 cup	225	4
spaghetti	1 cup	155	5

Meat and Related Foods

	Quantity	Calories	Protein(g)
beans, red kid	1 cup	230	15
beef, lean	1 portion	208	23
chicken drum	1	90	12
egg	1	80	6
hamburger	1 (2.9 oz)	235	20
lamb chop	1 (3.1 oz)	360	18
peanut butter	1 tbsp.	95	4
peanuts	1 cup	840	37
shrimp	1 portion	100	21
steak, lean	1 portion	172	27
tuna	$\frac{1}{2}$ can	170	24

Milk and Milk Products

	Quantity	Calories	Protein(g)
cheese, cheddar	1 slice	115	7
ice cream	1 cup	270	5
milk, lowfat	1 cup	140	8
milk, whole	1 cup	150	8
yogurt	$\frac{1}{2}$ cup	200	7

Fruits and Vegetables

	Quantity	Calories	Protein(g)
apple	1	80	trace
banana	1	100	1
broccoli	1 cup	40	5
corn	1 ear	70	2
cucumber	6 slices	5	trace
lettuce	1 head	70	5
mushrooms	1 cup	20	2
orange	1	65	1
orange juice	1 cup	120	2
pear	1	100	1
peas, green	cup	110	8
potato	1	105	3
strawberries	1 cup	55	1
tomato	1	25	1

Some Questions to Answer

1. Suppose you are an 11-year-old female. How many calories per day do you require on the average? How much protein? Tell how you know.

2. In what ways are the nutritional needs different for a 12-year-old boy than for a 12-year-old girl? How will this affect your daily menu? Do you think this will affect your recommendations to the cafeteria for a school lunch menu? Explain your answer.

3. Which food group appears to have the most protein? The least?

4. Which food group appears to have the least number of calories?

5. How would a table help you keep track of the number of calories, the number of grams of protein, and your choices from the four food groups?

What Is Your Decision?

Share your one-day menu with your classmates. Based on this menu, what foods would you recommend that the cafeteria serve for lunch?

WRAP UP

Measure for Measure

Match each measure on the left with a description on the right.

1. about a kilogram
2. about 4 meters
3. about 1 liter
4. about a kilometer
5. about 200 liters
6. about 2 centimeters
7. about 100 grams
8. about 5:30 p.m.

a. height of a classroom
b. diameter of a nickel
c. capacity of a bathtub
d. weight of a math textbook
e. capacity of a juice bottle
f. weight of a math workbook
g. the time in New York when it is about 2:30 p.m. in Los Angeles
h. twelve city blocks

Sometimes, Always, Never

Decide which word should go in the blank: *sometimes*, *always*, or *never*. Explain your choices.

9. A millimeter is _____ an appropriate unit for measuring a very long time.

10. A meter is _____ an appropriate unit for measuring distance.

11. The gram and kilogram are _____ used as units of mass in the metric system.

12. When converting from a larger unit of measure to a smaller unit, the number of units _____ increases.

Project

Invent your own benchmark for measuring distance, weight, and capacity. Make them humorous, but practical. Guess, and then estimate the measures of several classroom objects or features using your measuring system. Record your results. Have a contest with classmates to see who is the best guesser in the group.

CHAPTER REVIEW/TEST

Part 1 Understanding

Decide if each estimate is reasonable. Write *yes* or *no*.

1. Maria estimated the height of a 2-story building to be about 100 m.

2. Willis estimated the length of the classroom to be about 75 feet.

Tell whether an estimate or a precise answer is needed.

3. the amount of yogurt in a package at the grocery store

4. the number of cut logs needed for a fireplace

Choose the best estimate for the weight of each.

5. dog: **a.** 30 mg **b.** 30 g **c.** 30 kg

6. tack: **a.** 1 mg **b.** 1 g **c.** 1 kg

7. child: **a.** 60 oz **b.** 60 lb **c.** 60 T

8. elephant: **a.** 5 oz **b.** 5 lb **c.** 5 T

Part 2 Skills

Give the missing number.

9. $2.8 \text{ m} = \text{▥} \text{ dm}$

10. $342 \text{ cm} = \text{▥} \text{ m}$

11. $7.9 \text{ cm} = \text{▥} \text{ mm}$

12. $4 \text{ kL} = \text{▥} \text{ L}$

13. $3{,}986 \text{ mL} = \text{▥} \text{ L}$

14. $2 \text{ gal} = \text{▥} \text{ pt}$

15. $3 \text{ c} = \text{▥} \text{ oz}$

16. $12 \text{ qt} = \text{▥} \text{ gal}$

17. $\frac{1}{2} \text{ gal} = \text{▥} \text{ qt}$

Find the sum, difference, or product.

18.
$$\begin{array}{r} 6 \text{ h } 40 \text{ min} \\ + \ 5 \text{ h } 30 \text{ min} \\ \hline \end{array}$$

19.
$$\begin{array}{r} 4 \text{ ft } 2 \text{ in.} \\ + \ 5 \text{ ft } 9 \text{ in.} \\ \hline \end{array}$$

20.
$$\begin{array}{r} 8 \text{ lb } 4 \text{ oz} \\ - \ 3 \text{ lb } 7 \text{ oz} \\ \hline \end{array}$$

21.
$$\begin{array}{r} 2 \text{ ft } 5 \text{ in.} \\ \times \qquad 4 \\ \hline \end{array}$$

Part 3 Applications

22. Shane found that the movie started at 2:45 p.m. and ended at 5:10 p.m. How long did the show last?

23. **Challenge** A basketball team scored 27 points. They scored at least four 3-point field goals, at least six 2-point field goals, and at least one 1-point free throw. How many of each did they score?

383

ENRICHMENT
Degree of Accuracy in Measurement

You have used very small and very large units to measure length, capacity, weight, and time. You have also learned how to measure to the nearest unit, nearest tenth of a unit, nearest hundredth of a unit, and so on. There are times when you will need to determine not only what unit to use, but how accurate the measurement must be, depending on the purpose.

Examples for Time

Baking time for muffins	**Time for a fast race**
Unit: minutes	Unit: seconds
Accuracy: nearest whole number	Accuracy: nearest tenth, hundredth, or thousandth

For each measurement situation, give a unit of measure and the degree of accuracy you think would most likely be used.

Weight

1. your body weight

2. package of hamburger

3. box of cereal

4. bag of apples

Length

5. shelf for a bookcase

6. diameter of a bike gear

7. perimeter of the school yard

8. distance to nearest town

Capacity

9. car gas tank

10. dose of cough syrup

11. small carton of juice

12. flour for a muffin recipe

Your choice

13. Create some examples of your own about time.

14. Create some examples of your own about two other measurement situations.

CUMULATIVE REVIEW

1. Which pair of ratios is equal?

   A. $\dfrac{5}{12}, \dfrac{1}{3}$ B. $\dfrac{2}{3}, \dfrac{6}{9}$

   C. $\dfrac{7}{4}, \dfrac{4}{1}$ D. $\dfrac{4}{5}, \dfrac{8}{9}$

2. Solve the proportion: $\dfrac{4}{5} = \dfrac{n}{30}$.

   A. $n = 24$ B. $n = 10$

   C. $n = 20$ D. $n = 6$

3. Write the fraction $\dfrac{5}{6}$ to the nearest percent.

   A. 88%   B. 84%

   C. 83%   D. 17%

4. Which is 18% of 25?

   A. 2.25   B. 18

   C. 4.5   D. 9

5. Which is 20% of 60?

   A. 48   B. 20

   C. 3   D. 12

6. Which is the reasonable estimate for 52% of 300?

   A. 104   B. 208

   C. 140   D. 155

7. Nearly 50% of the 250 students in the school ride bikes to school. How many bike slots is a sensible amount for the school to have?

   A. 75   B. 120

   C. 200   D. 50

8. Which is the opposite of 6 steps up?

   A. 12 steps up   B. 6 steps down

   C. 9 steps down   D. 0 steps up

9. Which set is in order from least to greatest?

   A. $^+4, ^+3, ^-6, ^-2$ B. $^-5, 0, ^-1, ^+4$

   C. $^-2, 0, ^+4, ^+5$ D. $^-8, ^-3, ^+7, 0$

10. Which is the sum of $^+5$ and $^-5$?

    A. $^-10$ B. $^+10$

    C. $^+25$ D. 0

11. Find the sum: $^-7 + {}^+4$.

    A. $^-11$ B. $^-3$

    C. 11   D. 3

12. Find the difference: $^+4 - {}^-6$.

    A. $^+2$ B. $^-2$

    C. $^+10$ D. $^-10$

13. The temperature rose 8° from a low of $^-3$° to reach the present temperature. What is the present temperature?

    A. $^+11$°   B. $^-11$°

    C. $^+5$°   D. $^-5$°

14. Students are going on a trip to the museum. Nine have never been there before. Twelve have been there once, half as many as that have been there twice, and none has been there more than that. How many students are on the trip?

    A. 33   B. 27

    C. 36   D. 18

14

MATH AND SOCIAL STUDIES

DATA BANK

Use the Social Studies Data Bank on page 472 to answer the questions.

1 Sherborne Castle is surrounded by a high wall that protected it from attack. If a guard walked along this wall the shorter way from the tower to the East Gate, about how many meters did he walk?

PERIMETER, AREA, AND VOLUME

2 In the hall, the knights ate their meals and slept. What is an advantage of the location of the hall? What is a disadvantage?

3 Castles were built more like fortresses than palaces. What shape is made by the outer walls of Sherborne Castle? Is it a regular or irregular polygon?

4 **Using Critical Thinking** Give a reason why each of the following might be an advantage in defending a castle: long narrow windows, moats, outer walls taller than rooftops of inner buildings, constructing the castle on a hilltop, shape of castle walls.

Problem Solving
Using Perimeter Formulas

UNDERSTAND
ANALYZE DATA
PLAN
ESTIMATE
SOLVE
EXAMINE

The distance around a figure is called the **perimeter** of the figure. The Pentagon building has 5 equal sides. We can use a **formula** to find its perimeter.

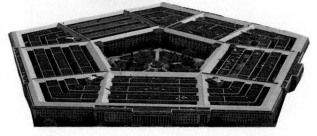

$p = s + s + s + s + s$
or
$p = 5s$

s = length of a side
p = perimeter

The Pentagon is one of the largest office buildings in the world. It has the shape of a regular pentagon with 5 equal sides. Each side is 276.3 m. What is the perimeter of the Pentagon?

Using the formula, we can find the perimeter like this:

$p = 5 \times 276.3 \text{ m} = 1,381.5 \text{ m}$

Here are some other examples of finding perimeter with and without formulas.

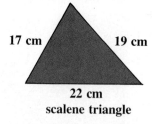

17 cm   19 cm

22 cm
scalene triangle

$p = 17 + 19 + 22$
$\quad = 58 \text{ cm}$

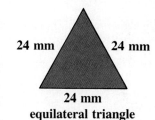

24 mm   24 mm

24 mm
equilateral triangle

$p = 3s$
$\quad = 3 \bullet 24$
$\quad = 72 \text{ mm}$

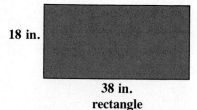

18 in.

38 in.
rectangle

$p = 2l + 2w$
$\quad = (2 \times 18) + (2 \times 38)$
$\quad = 36 + 76$
$\quad = 112 \text{ in.}$

l means *length*
w means *width*

Solve.

1. Find the perimeter of the equilateral triangle. Use the formula above.

$s = 6.8 \text{ cm}$

2. What is the formula for the perimeter of a regular octagon? Find its perimeter.

$s = 9.23 \text{ ft}$

388

Solve. Use any strategy.

1. A rectangular field has sides of 87.3 m and 39.4 m. What is the formula for the perimeter? What is the perimeter?

2. A triangular lot has sides of 37.2 yd, 48.3 yd, and 54.1 yd. How much shorter is the shortest side than the longest side?

3. Suppose the sides of all the following figures are the same length. List the figures in order from smallest perimeter to largest perimeter.

   square, regular hexagon, regular octagon, equilateral triangle

4. The state of Colorado is one of the states that is nearly rectangular. It is approximately 589 km by 456 km. What is the perimeter of Colorado?

5. A picture frame is twice as long as it is wide. The perimeter of the frame is 228 in. What is the length and width of the picture frame?

6. A pennant is shaped like an isosceles triangle. The short side is 24 cm and is half as long as a longer side. What is the perimeter of the pennant?

7. Renee drove 385 km in 4 h. If she drives at this same rate without stopping, how far will she travel in 10 h?

Some Strategies	
Act Out	Solve a Simpler Problem
Use Objects	Make an Organized List
Choose an Operation	Work Backward
Draw a Picture	Look for a Pattern
Guess and Check	Use Logical Reasoning
Make a Table	

8. A sail for windsurfing is shaped like a right triangle. The longest side is 9 yd. The next-longest side is 3 yd shorter than this. The third side is $\frac{1}{3}$ the sum of the other two. What is the perimeter?

9. **Talk About Your Solution** Leslie is buying a fence for a square field that is 96 m on a side. He needs two gates that are 3 m each. How much fence does he need to buy? Explain to a classmate how you reached your solution. Did you and your classmate get the same answer?

Area of Rectangles and Parallelograms

LEARN ABOUT IT

EXPLORE Discover a Relationship

Motion geometry can help you understand the
relationship between the area of a rectangle and
the area of a parallelogram. The figure suggests
how you can think about moving the triangle to
change the parallelogram (shaded) into a rectangle.

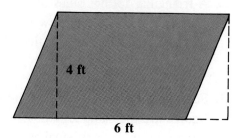

TALK ABOUT IT

1. Describe the motion of the triangle. Is it a
   translation, a rotation, or a reflection?
2. How does the area of the parallelogram compare to the
   area of the "new" rectangle formed by the motion?
3. What is the area of the rectangle? Of the parallelogram?

The base and height of both figures below are the same. The
triangle helps you see that the two figures have the same area.

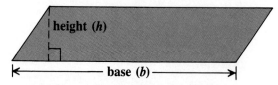

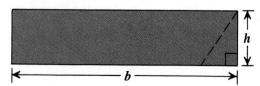

The area of the parallelogram = the area of the rectangle.

- Area of a rectangle = base × height $A = bh$
- Area of a parallelogram = base × height $A = bh$

TRY IT OUT

Find the area of each figure.

1.

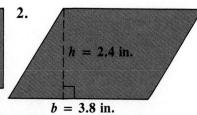

$h = 2.1$ cm

$b = 4.8$ cm

2.

$h = 2.4$ in.

$b = 3.8$ in.

3.

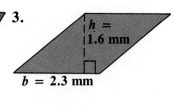

$h = 1.6$ mm

$b = 2.3$ mm

390

Find the area of each figure.

1.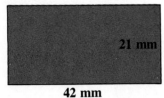

21 mm

42 mm

2.

15 m

43 m

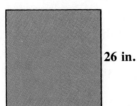

3.

22 ft

50 ft

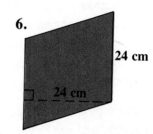

4.

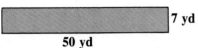

7 yd

50 yd

5.

26 in.

26 in.

6.

24 cm

24 cm

MATH REASONING

7. Suppose the length of side *a* is doubled. What will happen to the area? Suppose it is tripled? Give examples to support your answer. (Hint: You might let *a* = 3 and *b* = 5.) What would you predict will happen if the length of side *b* is doubled or tripled?

a

b

a

b

PROBLEM SOLVING

8. The height of a rectangular-shaped castle wall is 8 m less than the base. What is the area of the wall if the base is 17 m?

9. Social Studies Data Bank
Suppose the square court area of Sherborne Castle measures 132.25 m². What is the length of each side?

DATA BANK

Give the missing numbers.

10. 100 cm = ▓ m **11.** 245 cm = ▓ m **12.** 500 mm = ▓ m **13.** 50 dm = ▓ m

14. 1 gal = ▓ pt **15.** 4 c = ▓ pt **16.** 5,000 lb = ▓ T **17.** 64 oz = ▓ lb

Estimate.

18. 38.84 − 19.2 **19.** 8.2 × 19.78 **20.** $8\frac{3}{5} \times 7\frac{1}{4}$ **21.** 25% of 104

More Practice, page 519, set A

Area of Triangles and Trapezoids

EXPLORE **Make Area Models**

Work in groups. Emily said she could
take any two congruent triangles and fit them
together to form a parallelogram. Julio said
he could take any two congruent trapezoids
and fit them together to form a parallelogram.

Cut out a pair of congruent triangles or
trapezoids and see if you can show whether
or not they are right.

TALK ABOUT IT

1. How does the area of the parallelogram you made
   compare to the area of the figures used to make it?
2. If you know the area of the parallelogram, how can
   you find the area of each figure used to make it?

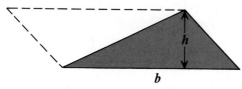

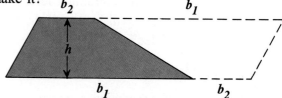

Area of this parallelogram $= bh$

Area of the triangle $= \frac{1}{2} bh$

$$A = \frac{1}{2} bh$$

Area of this parallelogram $= (b_1 + b_2)h$

Area of the trapezoid $= \frac{1}{2}(b_1 + b_2)h$

$$A = \frac{1}{2}(b_1 + b_2)h$$

TRY IT OUT

Find the area of each figure.

1.

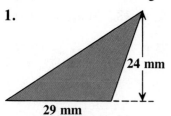

24 mm

29 mm

2.

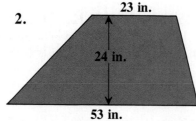

23 in.

24 in.

53 in.

3.

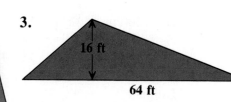

16 ft

64 ft

Find the area of each figure.

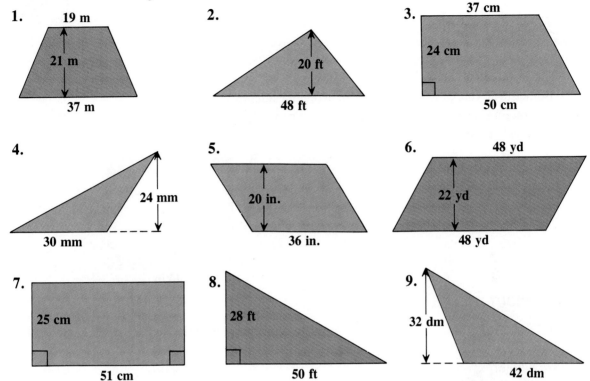

1.
19 m
21 m
37 m

2.
20 ft
48 ft

3.
37 cm
24 cm
50 cm

4.
24 mm
30 mm

5.
20 in.
36 in.

6.
48 yd
22 yd
48 yd

7.
25 cm
51 cm

8.
28 ft
50 ft

9.
32 dm
42 dm

MATH REASONING

10. A triangle and a rectangle have the same area and the same base. What can you say about their heights?

PROBLEM SOLVING

11. A rectangular medieval banner is 2 yd long and has an area of 18 sq ft. How many inches wide is it?

12. **Social Studies Data Bank** What is the perimeter of the side view of the White Tower shown?

▶ **USING CRITICAL THINKING   Visualize the Process**

13. Suppose there were 7 lookout posts on each side of a triangular castle. How many knights (1 to a post) would be needed to stand at all of the posts?

More Practice, page 519, set B

Area of Irregular Shapes

EXPLORE Analyze the Situation

Sometimes you can find the area of irregular shapes by adding or subtracting the areas of familiar shapes. Try to find the area of the shaded parts of each of these figures.

A
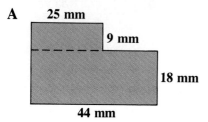

B
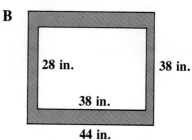

TALK ABOUT IT

1. Which figure, A or B, is made up of two shaded rectangles? Does this suggest adding or subtracting to find the area of the whole?
2. Which figure is made up of one rectangle with a rectangular hole cut in it? Does this suggest adding or subtracting to find the area of the shaded part?

You can use a calculator to find the area of an irregular shape by using the $\boxed{\text{M+}}$ or $\boxed{\text{M-}}$ keys or by writing down partial areas. Example:

$\boxed{\text{ON/AC}}$ $\boxed{44}$ $\boxed{\times}$ $\boxed{38}$ $\boxed{=}$ $\boxed{\text{M+}}$ $\boxed{38}$ $\boxed{\times}$ $\boxed{28}$ $\boxed{=}$ $\boxed{\text{M-}}$ $\boxed{\text{MR}}$ $\boxed{\quad 608 \quad}$

Estimate the area of each shaded figure. Then check your estimate. You may want to use your calculator.

1.
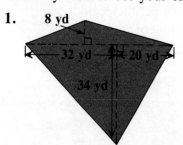

2.
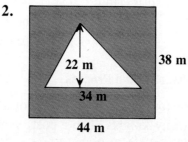

3.
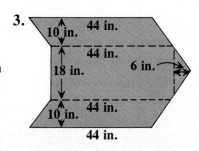

More Practice, page 519, set C

MIDCHAPTER REVIEW/QUIZ

Try to find the perimeter and the area for each figure. If there is not enough data, tell what necessary information is missing.

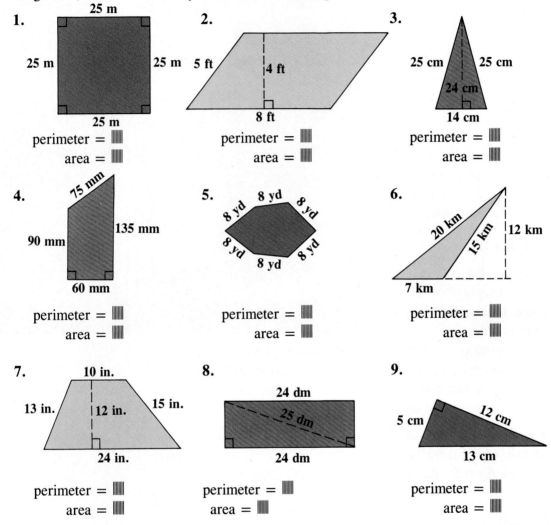

1.
25 m
25 m   25 m
25 m

perimeter = ▓
area = ▓

2.
5 ft   4 ft
8 ft

perimeter = ▓
area = ▓

3.
25 cm   25 cm
24 cm
14 cm

perimeter = ▓
area = ▓

4.
75 mm
135 mm
90 mm
60 mm

perimeter = ▓
area = ▓

5.
8 yd   8 yd
8 yd   8 yd
8 yd   8 yd

perimeter = ▓
area = ▓

6.
20 km   15 km   12 km
7 km

perimeter = ▓
area = ▓

7.
10 in.
13 in.   12 in.   15 in.
24 in.

perimeter = ▓
area = ▓

8.
24 dm
25 dm
24 dm

perimeter = ▓
area = ▓

9.
5 cm   12 cm
13 cm

perimeter = ▓
area = ▓

PROBLEM SOLVING

10. Four students each used 40 yd of fencing to surround their rectangular gardens. Each garden had a different width and length than the other gardens. What whole-number dimensions were possible?

11. A rectangular field is 3 times as long as it is wide. What are its width and length if the perimeter is 600 m?

Estimating Area

EXPLORE **Make a Decision**

Work in groups. This shaded region is 1 square decimeter, or 100 square centimeters. Try to use the region as a benchmark to estimate the area of your math book cover and the top of your desk or table.

TALK ABOUT IT

1. Did you estimate in square centimeters or square decimeters? How did you decide?
2. Why would you be more likely to estimate the area of a table top in square decimeters than in square centimeters?
3. Choose another flat surface in your classroom and estimate its area in square centimeters or square decimeters.

When you use a benchmark to estimate measure, you mentally try to decide what part or how many of the benchmarks it would take to "be the same as" the object under consideration.

TRY IT OUT

Use this 4 cm^2 benchmark to estimate the area of each of these regions. Then measure and calculate to check your estimate.

4 cm^2

1.

2.

Estimate the area. Use the 4 cm² benchmark. Measure and calculate to check your estimate.

1.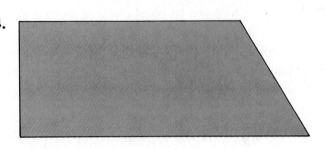

2.

3.

4.

MATH REASONING

5. Each small square is 1 square unit. Estimate the area of the shaded part by counting whole squares and parts of squares.

6. Try to find a way to get the exact area. According to your estimate, is your exact answer reasonable?

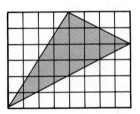

PROBLEM SOLVING

7. Data Hunt Suppose each small square represents an area of 125,000 square kilometers. Estimate the total area of the continental United States. Check your estimate with an encyclopedia.

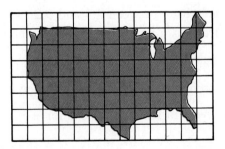

▶ **ALGEBRA**

Sometimes you may want to give estimates that are between certain numbers. You can do this with algebraic notation. If your estimate is between 30 cm² and 40 cm² you could write $30 \text{ cm}^2 < x < 40 \text{ cm}^2$.

Give possible whole-number estimates for x.

8. $55 \text{ m}^2 < x < 60 \text{ m}^2$ **9.** $24 \text{ cm}^2 < x < 28 \text{ cm}^2$ **10.** $360 \text{ dm}^2 < x < 364 \text{ dm}^2$

More Practice, page 519, set D

Circles and Circumference

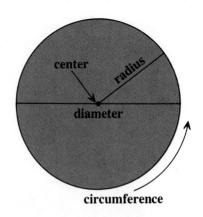

center
radius
diameter

circumference

EXPLORE Use String and a Ruler

Work in groups. A **circle** is a special closed curve, all points of which are an equal distance from a given point called the **center.** The **radius** is the distance from the center to the circle. The **diameter** (twice the radius) is the distance across the interior of the circle through the center. The **circumference** is the length of the closed curve.

Choose several different-sized circular objects and measure both the circumference and the diameter of each. Calculate the ratio of the circumference to the diameter to the nearest tenth for each of your circles.

You can use a calculator: circumference 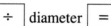 diameter [=]

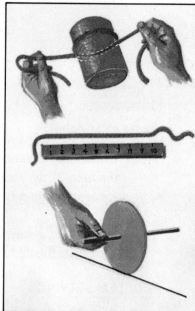

TALK ABOUT IT

1. What method did you use to measure the circumference of your circles?
2. Were the ratios for your different circles all about the same?

If your measurements were accurate, each of the ratios should have been between 3.1 and 3.2. This special ratio for all circles is a number called π (pronounced "pi").

C = circumference d = diameter

$$\pi = \frac{C}{d} = 3.1415927 \text{ (rounded to seven places)}$$

(We will use 3.14 or $3\frac{1}{7}$ for π.)

Since $\pi = \frac{C}{d}$, we know that $C = \pi \times d$

Find the circumference. Use 3.14 or $3\frac{1}{7}$ for π. You may want to use a calculator.

1. $d = 15$ in.   2. $d = 14$ cm   3. $d = 50$ mm   4. $d = 49$ ft

Find the circumference. You may want to use a calculator.

1. Record

$d = 30.5$ cm
Use 3.14 for π.

2. Bike gear

$d = 21$ cm
Use $3\frac{1}{7}$ for π.

3. Flower bed

$d = 2.5$ yd
Use 3.14 for π.

4. Clock face

$d = 14$ in.
Use $3\frac{1}{7}$ for π.

5. Mower wheel

$d = 15.24$ cm
Use 3.14 for π.

6. Earth

$d = 12{,}766$ km
Use 3.14 for π.

APPLY

MATH REASONING

Do not solve. Just tell if the circumference is more than or less than 100 cm.

7. $d = 35$ cm, $C =$ **8.** $d = 25$ cm, $C =$ **9.** $d = 30$ cm, $C =$

PROBLEM SOLVING

10. Suppose the diameter of your bicycle wheel is 63 cm. How far will you go in one turn of your wheel? How many times will your wheel turn in riding 1 km?

▶ ESTIMATION

Use the fact that the circumference is about 3 times the diameter to help you estimate the following. Find a way to check your estimate.

11. The diameter of an orange or grapefruit   **12.** The diameter of a solid rubber ball

Area of Circles

EXPLORE Make a Model of Circle Area

Work in groups. Draw and cut out a 10-cm
circle. Fold the circle through the center
4 times so you divide it into sixteenths.
Cut out the pieces and make a "crooked"
parallelogram as in the figure.

TALK ABOUT IT

1. How does the area of the crooked
   parallelogram compare to the area of
   the circle?
2. How does the height of the
   parallelogram compare to the radius
   of the circle?
3. How does the base of the parallelogram
   compare to the circumference of the
   circle?
4. What is the area of the parallelogram
   to the nearest tenth? What is the area
   of the circle to the nearest tenth?

|← ——————— 10 cm ——————— →|

A "Crooked" Parallelogram

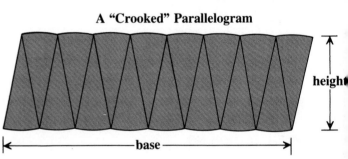

height

|← —————————— base —————————— →|

The crooked parallelogram above will help you understand the
formula for the area of a circle. The parallelogram and the circle
have the same area.

$C = \pi \times$ diameter,
so $\frac{1}{2}C = \pi \times$ radius

$$A = bh = \frac{1}{2}C \times r$$

$$A = \pi \times r \times r = \pi r^2$$

$$A = 3.14 \times (0.5)^2$$
$$= 3.14 \times 0.25$$
$$= 0.785 \text{ m}^2$$

0.5 m

TRY IT OUT

Find the area of each circle. Use 3.14 for π. Round to the nearest
hundredth when necessary. You may want to use a calculator.

1. $r = 12$ in.   2. $r = 5$ mm   3. $d = 7.2$ yd   4. $d = 25$ cm

Find the area.

1. Plate

$r = 28$ cm
Use $3\frac{1}{7}$ for π.

2. Pizza

$r = 20$ cm
Use 3.14 for π.

3. Dried fruit

$r = 14$ in.
Use $3\frac{1}{7}$ for π.

4. Tomato slice

$d = 10$ cm
Use 3.14 for π.

5. Button

$d = 21$ mm
Use $3\frac{1}{7}$ for π.

6. Ribbon spool

$d = 5$ in.
Use 3.14 for π.

APPLY

MATH REASONING

7. Suppose the area of a circle is about 3.14 cm². About what is the length of the radius of the circle?

PROBLEM SOLVING

8. A rotating lawn sprinkler sprays water over the area of a circle whose radius is 8 m. What is the area of the lawn watered?

MIXED REVIEW

Add or subtract.

9.   4 min 29 s
    + 8 min 46 s

10.   5 yd 1 ft
    + 4 yd 2 ft

11.   8 h 20 min
    − 3 h 45 min

12.   7 ft 8 in.
    − 3 ft 11 in.

More Practice, page 520, set B

Volume and Surface Area of a Rectangular Prism

EXPLORE Make a Rectangular Prism Model

Work in groups. Copy this pattern on heavy paper or cardboard. Fold your pattern on the dashed lines to make a rectangular prism. Tape the edges so you have a box with a lid you can open.

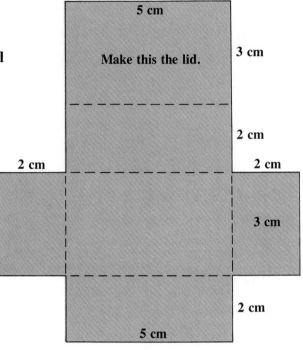

TALK ABOUT IT

1. How can you find out how many 1-cm cubes your box will hold?
2. What is the area of the irregular shape that you used as a pattern?

- The **surface area** of a rectangular prism is the sum of the areas of all its faces.
- The **volume** of a rectangular prism is the number of cubic units it will hold. Here is the formula for this volume.

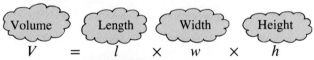

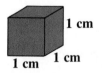

Example

Volume = 6 × 3 × 2 = 36 cubic units (36 unit^3)

Top	=	18 sq units
Bottom	=	18 sq units
Face Front side	=	12 sq units
Areas Back side	=	12 sq units
Left end	=	6 sq units
Right end	=	6 sq units
Surface Area	=	72 sq units

Find the volume and the surface area. You may want to use a calculator.

1.

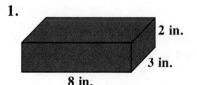

2.

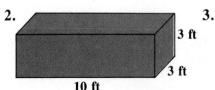

3.

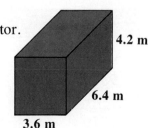

Find the volume and the surface area. You may want to use a calculator.

1. Tool box

95 cm

56 cm

42 cm

2. Record box

8 cm

3 cm

14 cm

3. Coin box

28 cm

7 cm

16 cm

4. Shoe box

14 in.

5 in.

6 in.

5. Cedar chest

1.2 m

0.5 m

0.45 m

6. Small refrigerator

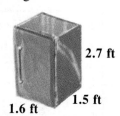

2.7 ft

1.5 ft

1.6 ft

APPLY

MATH REASONING

7. Estimate the cost of a box of soap that has edges that are twice the size of these. Check your estimate by finding the volume of each box.

14 cm

10 cm 4 cm

$1.39

PROBLEM SOLVING

8. A room is 4.2 m long, 3 m wide, and 2.8 m high. What is the volume of the room in cubic meters (m³)?

9. A fish tank is 60 cm long, 25 cm wide, and 20 cm high. What is the area of the 4 sides that are glass?

10. Data Hunt A cubic meter of air weighs about 1.29 kg. About how much does the air in your classroom weigh? (Assume that the room is empty except for air.)

▶ **ESTIMATION**

Estimate the volume of each box by first rounding each decimal to the nearest whole number.

11.

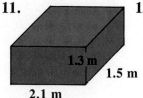

1.3 m

1.5 m

2.1 m

12.

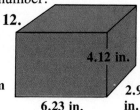

4.12 in.

2.9 in.

6.23 in.

13.

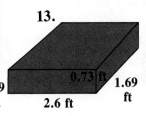

0.73 ft

1.69 ft

2.6 ft

14.

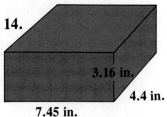

3.16 in.

4.4 in.

7.45 in.

More Practice, page 520, set C

Problem Solving
Finding a Related Problem

UNDERSTAND
ANALYZE DATA
PLAN
ESTIMATE
SOLVE
EXAMINE

LEARN ABOUT IT

Many problems are related. They can be solved using the same strategies. When you have a problem to solve, thinking of a related problem may be helpful. Here are two related problems.

> Karen's family needs to choose the exterior paint for their new house. The wall colors are white, green, and beige. The trim colors are white, green, blue, and cocoa. How many combinations of wall color and trim are possible?

> Eric bought some brass house numbers to put on the front of his house. He has these 3 numbers: 3, 5, 8. What house numbers can he make using all 3 numbers?

I could solve both of these problems by drawing a picture, making an organized list, or by using objects.

```
ww   gw   bw
wg   gg   bg
wb   gb   bb
wc   gc   bc
```

There are 12 possible combinations.

I think I'll try making an organized list.

```
358   538   835
385   583   853
```

There are 6 possible combinations.

TRY IT OUT

Read all the problems first. Tell which two problems are related.
Then solve each problem.

1. Nina bought some bricks to build a wall. She laid 45 bricks the first day and 3 times as many the second day. She then bought 25 more to be sure she had enough. Now she has 70 bricks. How many did she have when she started?

2. The telephone company is installing telephone lines for 10 buildings. Each building is to be connected to each of the other buildings with one line. How many telephone lines are needed?

3. Fred wrote a check for some building supplies. He bought a sack of cement for $9, some 2-by-4s for $34, and 2 gallons of paint for $12 each. He got $10 back. What was the amount of the check?

404

Solve. Use any strategy.

1. The blueprint shows the floor plan for an apartment. How many square meters of vinyl tile are needed to cover the kitchen floor?

2. Michael wants to put some molding around the top edge of the walls in the bedroom. Use the blueprint to find how many meters of molding he needs.

3. Use the blueprint to estimate the total area of the apartment. Then find the exact area. According to your estimate, is your answer reasonable?

4. Gerry has a 2-by-4 that is 12 ft long. He wants to cut it into pieces that are 8 in. long. How many cuts will he have to make?

5. Cathy made a hexagonal table. She wants to put wood trim around the outside edge. Use the diagram to decide if 125 cm of trim will be enough.

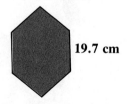
19.7 cm

6. Mr. Valdez spent $64.75 for 5 light fixtures and $12.50 for 4 light switches. The light fixtures are all the same. How much did each light fixture cost?

7. Mara built a fence around a rectangular pool area that is 18 m long and 14 m wide. She put a post at each corner and one every 2 m in between. How many posts did Mara use?

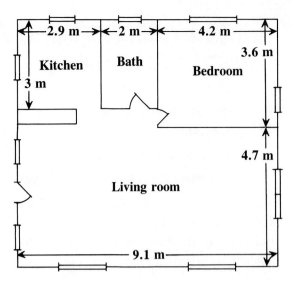

8. **Suppose** . . . Carpet costs $18.75 per m². Pad costs $1.75 per m². The installation runs $40 for a 20-m² room. Find the total cost for carpet, pad, and installation for a 20-m² room.

Tell which of the following pieces of information would change the solution to the problem above.
   a. The carpet just went on sale for 25% off.
   b. Installation costs $2 per m².
   c. The room has an area of 24 m².

Data Collection and Analysis
Group Decision Making

UNDERSTAND
ANALYZE DATA
PLAN
ESTIMATE
SOLVE
EXAMINE

Doing an Investigation

Group Skill

Explain and Summarize

Is there a pattern in the way that geometric shapes such as squares "grow?" Do you think they grow at an even rate? You can conduct an investigation to find out.

Collecting Data

1. Work with your group to cut out squares from one-inch grid paper. You will need about 100 squares.

2. What is the smallest square you can build? Build the next largest square and the next. Keep building until you run out of squares.

3. Record the length of one side of each square you build and the number of paper squares used to build it.

Length of side	Number of squares to build
_____	_____
_____	_____
_____	_____
_____	_____
_____	_____

Organizing Data

4. Make a line graph to show the relationship between the length of a side of a square and the number of squares needed to build it. Adjust the scales to fit your data. Plot the points and draw a line through them.

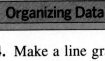

Presenting Your Analysis

5. Is the line on your graph straight or curved? Do the squares grow at an even rate? Explain.

6. Predict how many squares would be in a square that is 7 units long. How could you use the graph to help you make a prediction?

7. What patterns do you notice in the way squares grow? Predict how many squares it would take to build a square 10 units on a side.

8. What is the rule for the number of squares when you know the length of the sides?

WRAP UP

Language Match

Match each description on the left with the geometric term on the right that best describes it.

1. the boundaries of a basketball court   **a.** radius

2. space in a storage bin   **b.** area

    c. perimeter

3. a spoke on a bicycle wheel   **d.** diameter

4. paper needed to wrap a package   **e.** surface area

    f. circumference

5. distance run around a circular track   **g.** volume

6. floor space covered by a rug

7. a 14-inch pizza

Sometimes, Always, Never

Decide which word should go in the blank: *sometimes, always,* or *never.* Explain your choices.

8. Figures with the same area _____ have the same perimeter.

9. If a triangle and a parallelogram have the same base and height, the area of the parallelogram is _____ twice that of the triangle.

10. If a triangle and a rectangle have the same area, they _____ have the same height.

11. If a triangle and a trapezoid have the same base and area, they _____ have the same height.

12. Rectangular prisms with the same height _____ have the same volume.

Project

Ms. Herrera needs to build a corral for her horse. She has 60 meters of fencing material. Using whole numbers only, decide on the dimension of the rectangle that will enclose the greatest area. Describe the strategy you used to solve the problem.

CHAPTER REVIEW/TEST

Part 1 Understanding

1. Each small square is 1 square unit. Estimate the area of the shaded part by counting whole squares and parts of squares.

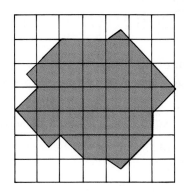

Part 2 Skills

Write the formula for the area of each figure. Then use the formula to find the area.

2.
14 m
26 m

3.

9 in.
32 in.

4.
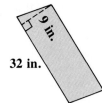
10.5 mm
12.4 mm

5.
10 ft.
12 ft.
16 ft.

6. Write the formula for the area of a circle. Then use the formula to find the area of this circle. Use 3.14 for π.

12 in.

7. Estimate the area of the irregular figure. Then find the area.

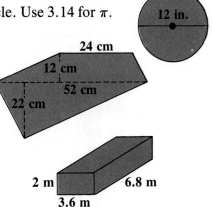
24 cm
12 cm
52 cm
22 cm

8. Write the formula for the volume of this figure. Use the formula to find the volume. Then find the surface area of the figure.

2 m
3.6 m
6.8 m

Part 3 Applications

9. If the diameter of a bicycle wheel is 60 cm, how far will it go in one complete turn?

10. **Challenge** Don had $80. He spent $5 on cement, spent 4 times as much as that on bricks, and bought 3 gallons of paint for $11 each. How much money did he have left?

ENRICHMENT
Pentominoes and Hexominoes

Each of the six figures below is made with five congruent squares that meet along at least one edge. This type of figure is called a **pentominoe.** Figure F can be folded to make an open-top box, as shown.

1. Which other pentominoes can be folded to make an open-top box?

2. Altogether, there are 12 possible arrangements of squares that form pentominoes. Use graph paper to draw as many of the other six as you can.

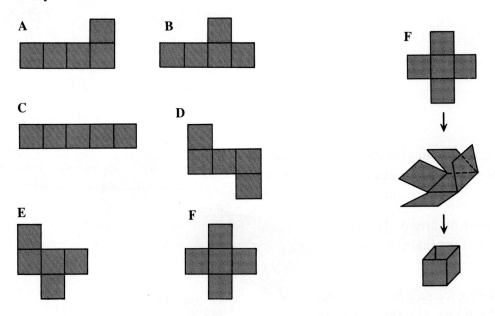

The figures at the right are **hexominoes.** There are 35 possible arrangements that form hexominoes. Some of those shown can be folded to make a closed box.

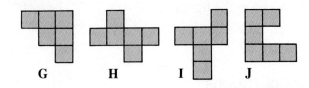

3. Which of the hexominoes can be folded to make a closed box?

4. Altogether, 11 hexaminoes can be folded to make closed boxes. Use graph paper to draw as many of them as you can.

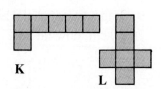

CUMULATIVE REVIEW

1. Choose a calculation method and solve: $12\frac{1}{2}\%$ of 48.

   A. 12.5   B. 6

   C. 4   D. 8

2. Find the interest: borrow \$200 at a rate of 12% for 2 years.

   A. \$2.40   B. \$24

   C. \$480   D. \$48

3. Find the sale price: \$120 at 10% off.

   A. \$12   B. \$108

   C. \$112   D. \$8

4. Without adding, tell which sum is positive.

   A. $^-8 + {}^+5$ B. $^+6 + {}^-2$

   C. $^+4 + {}^-7$ D. $^-3 + {}^-4$

5. Solve the equation $^-4 + y = {}^+2$.

   A. $y = {}^+6$ B. $y = {}^-6$

   C. $y = {}^+2$ D. $y = {}^-2$

6. Find the difference: $^+3 - {}^-5$.

   A. $^+8$ B. $^+2$

   C. $^-8$ D. $^-2$

7. Which type of graph would you use to show what parts of your diet are fat, protein, or carbohydrate?

   A. circle graph   B. line graph

   C. pictograph   D. bar graph

8. 4.7 m = ▦ cm.

   A. 4,700   B. 47

   C. 470   D. 0.47

9. Which is a reasonable estimate for the length of a baseball bat?

   A. 1 mm   B. 1 m

   C. 1 cm   D. 1 dm

10. For which would you need a precise measure?

    A. some tea to drink   B. capacity of car trunk

    C. trees in forest   D. flour in recipe

11. Choose the best estimate for the weight of a math textbook.

    A. 10 g   B. 1 g

    C. 1 mg   D. 1 kg

12. If it is 3 p.m. in Washington, D.C., what time is it in San Diego, CA?

    A. 5 p.m.   B. noon

    C. 6 p.m.   D. midnight

13. What is a reasonable estimate for the height of a classroom?

    A. 11 yards   B. 6 feet

    C. 11 feet   D. 36 feet

14. You draw a triangle, place a dot directly above it, and connect each vertex to the point. Of what figure have you drawn a picture?

    A. triangle   B. triangular pyramid

    C. prism   D. triangular prism

15

MATH AND HEALTH AND FITNESS

DATA BANK

Use the Health and Fitness Data Bank on page 474 to answer the questions.

PROBABILITY

1 Of the four major types of human blood, which is the most common? The least common?

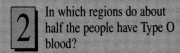

2 In which regions do about half the people have Type O blood?

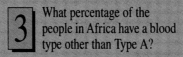

3 What percentage of the people in Africa have a blood type other than Type A?

4 **Using Critical Thinking**
Long ago, many people died from transfusions because the blood did not match their type. Suppose you had lived in Western Europe. Do you think your chances of surviving a transfusion would have been high or low? Explain.

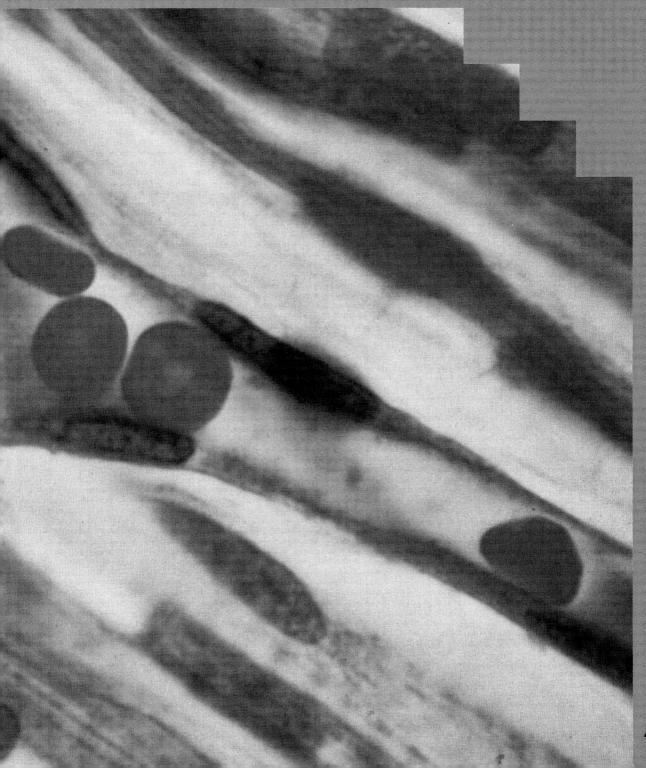

Fair and Unfair Games

EXPLORE **Use Number Cubes**

Play a game of Square-4-Times with a classmate.

> ### Square-4-Times Rules
>
> - Decide who will be the Square Player and who will be the 4-Times Player.
> - One player tosses a number cube with the numbers 1 through 6 on its faces.
> - The 4-Times Player multiplies the top number by 4 to get his or her score.
> - The Square Player squares the top number (multiplies the number by itself) to get his or her score.
> - The highest score wins.

Square Player   4-Times Player
$3 \times 3 = 9$ $4 \times 3 = 12$
The 4-Times Player wins!

TALK ABOUT IT

1. Suppose a player tosses a 5. Who will be the winner?
2. Who wins if a player tosses a 4? Explain your answer.
3. Do you feel this game is fair to both players? Why or why not?

A game is a **fair game** if each player has the same chance of winning. You can see from the table that the 4-Times Player has 3 chances to win (when 1, 2, or 3 is tossed). The Square Player has only 2 chances to win (when 5 or 6 is tossed). Since the 4-Times Player has more chances to win, the Square-4-Times game is not a fair game.

Toss	1	2	3	4	5	6
Square Score	1	4	9	16	25	36
4-Times Score	4	8	12	16	20	24

TRY IT OUT

Suppose the numbers on the cube are 2, 3, 4, 5, 6, and 7.

1. Does one player have more chances of winning? If yes, tell which player and why.

2. Does the Square-4-Times game now become a fair game? Tell how you know.

414

Work in a small group or with a classmate. Decide whether each game is fair or unfair. Give reasons for your answers.

1. Play a Square-3-Times game. Use a number cube with the numbers 1–6. The Square Player squares the top number, and the 3-Times Player multiplies the top number by 3. The highest score wins.

2. Toss a coin. If it comes up heads, you win. If it comes up tails, your opponent wins.

3. Toss 2 coins. If both coins come up heads or both coins come up tails, you win. If not, your opponent wins.

4. Toss 3 coins. If all 3 coins come up heads or all 3 coins come up tails, you win. If not, your opponent wins.

APPLY

MATH REASONING

Suppose you and two classmates are playing a game with this spinner. Each player picks a different letter. A player scores one point if the spinner points to the letter he or she picks.

5. Is the game fair? Tell how you know.

6. Which letter do you prefer? Tell why.

7. Which letter would you least prefer? Why?

PROBLEM SOLVING

8. Suppose you played the Square-4-Times game and you were the Square Player. What is your average score if you toss a 3, a 5, a 2, a 4, a 3, a 1, a 6, and a 2?

9. Is your average score for the game in Exercise 8 greater than or less than the average score of the 4-Times Player? By how much?

▶ **COMMUNICATION   Write to Learn Math**

Complete each sentence.

10. A game is unfair if one player _____ .

11. A game is fair if _____ .

Equally Likely Outcomes

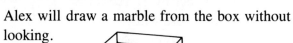

EXPLORE Think about the Situations

The result of a single trial of an experiment is called an **outcome**.

Eduardo will spin the spinner.

Alex will draw a marble from the box without looking.

TALK ABOUT IT

1. Give the possible outcomes Eduardo might get. Do you think these outcomes have the same chance of occurring? Tell how you know.
2. Do you think Alex is just as likely to draw a red marble as a blue one if he doesn't look? Explain your answer.

If each outcome of an experiment has the same chance of occurring, the outcomes are **equally likely**.

Other Examples

Flip a coin.
Outcomes: Heads or tails
Equally likely

Roll a cube numbered 1–6.
Outcomes: Odd or even
Equally likely

Spin this spinner.
Outcomes: Red or blue
Not equally likely

1. Which situation at the top of the page has equally likely outcomes?

2. Which outcome is more likely for the other situation?

3. Why are you equally likely to roll an odd or even number when you roll a number cube with sides numbered 1–6?

4. Which outcome, red or blue, is more likely for the spinner in the examples? Tell how you know.

For each experiment, tell if the outcomes are equally likely. If they are not equally likely, tell which outcome is more likely.

1. Spin the spinner.
Outcomes: Yellow, Green

2. Draw a marble without looking.
Outcomes: Red, Green, Blue

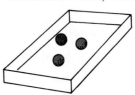

For each experiment, list the possible outcomes. Then tell if they are equally likely. If they are not equally likely, tell which outcome is more likely.

3. Draw a name without looking.

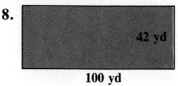

4. Spin the spinner.

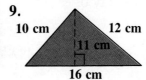

5. Roll a cube with sides lettered A, B, C, D, E, F.

MATH REASONING

6. Suppose you roll a number cube with sides numbered 1, 2, 3, 4, 5, 6. Is it possible to roll four 3s in a row? Is it likely?

PROBLEM SOLVING

7. A spinner is divided into three parts labeled A, B, and C. The table shows the result of 24 spins. Draw a picture to show what you think the spinner looks like.

A	ⵏⵀⵜ		
B	ⵏⵀⵜ	ⵏⵀⵜ	IIII
C	ⵏⵀⵜ		

MIXED REVIEW

Find the area and perimeter of each figure.

8.

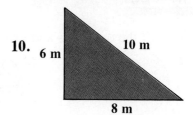

42 yd
100 yd

9.

10 cm   12 cm
11 cm
16 cm

10.

6 m   10 m
8 m

Chances and Probability

A

B

EXPLORE Analyze the Situation

There are 3 treasure chests labeled A, B, and C and 3 keys labeled 1, 2, and 3. Each key opens a different chest. What are your chances of choosing a key and chest that match?

C

TALK ABOUT IT

1. How many choices do you have of keys? Of chests?
2. Make an organized list that shows all the outcomes.
3. How many of the pairings are matches?

When the equally likely outcomes are known, we can find the **probability** of those outcomes.

1   2   3

We know: There are 3 **chances** in 9 of matching.

We say: The **probability** (P) of matching is $\frac{3}{9}$, or $\frac{1}{3}$.

We write: $P(\text{matching}) = \frac{1}{3}$.

> 3 matching outcomes
> 9 equally likely outcomes

Other Examples

$P(2) = \frac{1}{6}$ $\qquad P(\text{green}) = \frac{1}{4}$ $\qquad P(n < 7) = \frac{6}{6} = 1$

$\qquad\qquad\qquad P(\text{red}) \ \ = \frac{2}{4} = \frac{1}{2}$ $\qquad P(n > 6) = \frac{0}{6} = 0$

Math Point
The probability of any outcome is always a number from 0 to 1.

List all the outcomes and give the probability of each.

1.

2.

3.

4.

418

List all the outcomes and give the probability of each.

1. Flip a coin.

2. Spin a spinner.

3. Toss a cube with + on all its faces.

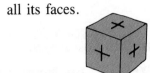

4. Toss a cube with these faces.

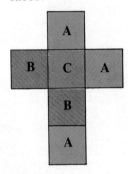

5. Sketch a cube pattern and show how to label the faces with X, Y, and Z so that:

$$P(X) = \frac{2}{3}$$

$$P(Y) = \frac{1}{6}$$

$$P(Z) = \frac{1}{6}$$

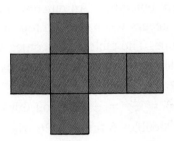

APPLY

MATH REASONING

6. Suppose that $P(A) = \frac{1}{2}$ and $P(B) = \frac{2}{10}$. What is $P(C)$?

7. Suppose you have a jar of 100 beads. You know that $P(\text{red}) = \frac{2}{5}$ and $P(\text{blue}) = \frac{3}{5}$. What can you say about the jar of beads?

PROBLEM SOLVING

8. Becky's little brother took the labels off a can of beans, a can of corn, 2 cans of peas, and a can of beets. If Becky chooses a can for supper, what is the probability that she will choose peas?

▶ **USING CRITICAL THINKING** Analyzing the Situation

9. Danny said, "Whenever I shoot a basketball, it will either go in the goal or it won't. There are just 2 outcomes. Therefore, the probability that I will make the basket is $\frac{1}{2}$." Is Danny's reasoning sound? Why or why not?

More Practice, page 520, set D

Experimental Probability

EXPLORE Use Number Cubes

Work with a partner. When two number cubes with faces numbered 1–6 are tossed, there are 36 different outcomes. An outcome of "doubles" occurs when the two top numbers are the same. The table of outcomes shows that doubles have 6 out of 36 chances of happening.

$P(\text{doubles}) = \frac{6}{36} = \frac{1}{6}$. Do you think you would get doubles 6 times in 36 trials? Try the experiment. Record your results.

Outcomes

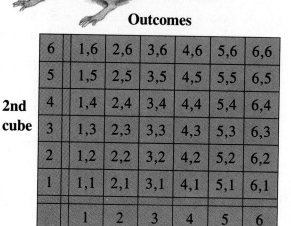

6	1,6	2,6	3,6	4,6	5,6	6,6
5	1,5	2,5	3,5	4,5	5,5	6,5
4	1,4	2,4	3,4	4,4	5,4	6,4
3	1,3	2,3	3,3	4,3	5,3	6,3
2	1,2	2,2	3,2	4,2	5,2	6,2
1	1,1	2,1	3,1	4,1	5,1	6,1
	1	2	3	4	5	6

2nd cube (rows), 1st cube (columns)

1st cube

TALK ABOUT IT

1. How close did you get to 6 doubles?
2. Why do you think some teams will get more than or less than 6 doubles?
3. Combine your results with the results of classmates. Is the average of these results closer to 6? Is the probability any closer to $\frac{1}{6}$? Explain your answer.

The **experimental probability** of doubles is the number of times you got doubles divided by the number of trials. The experimental probability will almost always come close to but not match exactly the mathematical (or theoretical) probability.

Experimental $P(\text{doubles}) = \dfrac{\text{doubles}}{\text{trials}}$

In problems 1–3, find the experimental and mathematical probability of all outcomes of each experiment.

1. Toss a coin 100 times.

2. Spin a spinner 100 times.

3. Toss a number cube labeled 1–6 100 times.

MIDCHAPTER REVIEW/TEST

Decide whether each game is fair or unfair. Give reasons for your answers.

1. Toss three coins. If there are more heads than tails, you win. Otherwise, your opponent wins.

2. Toss four coins. If there are more heads than tails, you win. Otherwise, your opponent wins.

3. Toss a 1–6 number cube. Square the top number and divide by 2. Your opponent doubles the top number. The higher score wins.

List all possible outcomes for each situation. Tell if the outcomes are equally likely.

4. Choose a marble without looking.

5. Toss a nickel, a dime, and a quarter.

6. Spin the spinner.

List all possible outcomes for each situation. Give the probability of each outcome.

7. Spin the spinner.

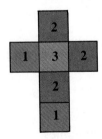

8. Toss the cube.

9. Spin the spinner.

PROBLEM SOLVING

10. Draw a four-colored spinner of red, blue, yellow, and green so that $P(\text{red}) = \frac{1}{3}$, $P(\text{blue}) = \frac{1}{6}$, and $P(\text{yellow}) = \frac{1}{4}$. What is $P(\text{green})$?

11. Draw a 6-sided letter cube that might give these outcomes: A, B, A, A, B, B, C, A, B, C, B, B, A, B, B, C, A, B.

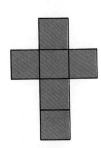

Using Tree Diagrams

LEARN ABOUT IT

EXPLORE **Play a Probability Game**

Work in groups. Play Martin's game several times. Try to determine who will win most often—a player or the person who draws from the sack.

TALK ABOUT IT

1. How many different outcomes are possible in the 2-3 Draw game? Tell how you know.
2. What is the probability of guessing the 2 numbers in the right order in 2-3 Draw? Explain your answer.
3. Is 2-3 Draw a fair game? Why or why not?

Martin invented a game called 2-3 Draw. He wrote 1, 2, and 3 on separate cards. Then he put the three cards in a sack.

Rules: Martin will draw two cards from the sack, one at a time. Before the drawing, players will write the two numbers in the order they guess Martin will draw them.

Scoring: If players have written the numbers in the correct order in which they are drawn, they get 3 points. Otherwise, they get nothing, and Martin gets 1 point.

The **tree diagram** at the right can help you understand the 2-3 Draw game. The tree diagram shows that there are 6 equally likely outcomes. Each outcome has 1 out of 6 chances of happening. So the probability of each outcome is $\frac{1}{6}$.

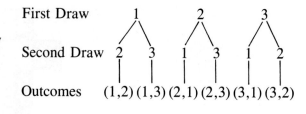

Notice that (1,2) and (2,1) are different outcomes.

TRY IT OUT

Suppose you are playing 2-3 Draw. Give each probability.

1. $P(3,1) = $ ▦   2. $P(2,3) = $ ▦   3. $P(\text{both numbers odd}) = $ ▦

4. $P(\text{both numbers even}) = $ ▦

5. To make the game of 2-3 Draw a fair game, how many points do you think players should get for guessing the two numbers correctly?

Use the tree diagram for spinning Spinner 1 and then Spinner 2 to help you answer these questions.

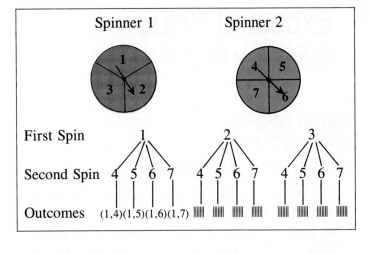

Spinner 1   Spinner 2

First Spin

Second Spin

Outcomes

1. How many possible outcomes does the tree show? Give each outcome.

2. What is $P(1,4)$?

3. What is $P(3,7)$?

4. What is the probability that the sum of the two numbers on the spinners is 6?

5. What is the probability that the sum of the numbers is 8?

APPLY

MATH REASONING

6. Suppose you have a choice between two games to play. In each game, only one of the possible outcomes will be a winner. Tree diagrams show 15 possible outcomes for one game and 20 possible outcomes for the other. Which game gives you a better chance to win? Explain your answer.

PROBLEM SOLVING

7. There are 4 cards labeled 1, 2, 3, 4 in a sack and 2 are drawn one at a time and replaced. To win, you must guess the 2 numbers in the right order. What is the probability of winning this game? Make a tree diagram to help you solve the problem.

▶ **ESTIMATION**

Estimate the probability of each outcome on the spinner.

8. $P(\text{red}) = $

9. $P(\text{green}) = $

10. $P(\text{blue}) = $

11. $P(\text{yellow}) = $

Expected Value
Estimating Outcomes

EXPLORE Study the Information

The table below shows the probability of choosing at random a person with Type O, Type A, Type B, or Type AB blood in three countries. For example, the probability of choosing a person with Type A blood in the United Kingdom is 0.37.

TALK ABOUT IT

1. In which of the countries listed would you have the highest probability of choosing a person at random that has Type O blood? Type AB blood?
2. In which countries does about 1 person out of 5 have Type B blood?
3. In a group of 320 people in Japan, would you expect about 10 people, 32 people, or 100 people to have Type AB blood? Explain how you decided.

You can use probability to predict the number of outcomes when the number of trials is known.

	United Kingdom	U.S.S.R.	Japan
Type O	0.49	0.35	0.29
Type A	0.37	0.37	0.38
Type B	0.11	0.2	0.23
Type AB	0.03	0.08	0.10

To estimate how many people in Japan have Type O blood, multiply the number of people in the group (320) by the probability of a person having that type of blood (0.29)

Trials	Probability	Expected value
320 ×	0.29 =	92.8

About 93 people in a group of 320 could be expected to have Type O blood. The **expected value** is 93.

Find the expected value.

1. Trials: 500
   Probability: 0.3
2. Trials: 1,250
   Probability: 0.04
3. Trials: 100
   Probability: $\frac{3}{5}$
4. Trials: 80
   Probability: $\frac{1}{4}$

Find the expected value.

1. Trials: 280
   Probability: $\frac{1}{3}$

2. Trials: 125
   Probability: $\frac{4}{5}$

3. Trials: 66
   Probability: $\frac{1}{2}$

4. Trials: 12,500
   Probability: 0.18

5. Trials: 338
   Probability: 0.2

6. Trials: 960
   Probability: $\frac{1}{12}$

7. Trials: 25,000
   Probability: 0.13

8. Trials: 1,616
   Probability: 0.004

Suppose the spinner is spun 80 times.
Give the expected value of each outcome.

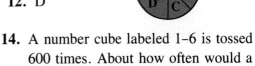

9. A   **10.** B   **11.** C   **12.** D

13. A coin is tossed 100 times. What is the expected value for heads?

14. A number cube labeled 1–6 is tossed 600 times. About how often would a number greater than 4 be expected?

MATH REASONING

15. Suppose a classmate told you that in 100 tosses, heads came up 71 times. Is that possible? Is it likely?

PROBLEM SOLVING

16. In a group of 500 people from the United Kingdom, what is the expected number of people having each type of blood?

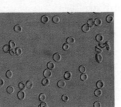

17. Health and Fitness Data Bank Suppose that during a United Nations blood drive, 250 people from each region donate 1 pint of blood. Should the U.N. expect more than or less than 100 pints of Type AB blood? Explain.

DATA BANK

▶ **CALCULATOR**

Write *even* or *odd* to complete these facts about products of whole numbers.

18. Even × Even =   **19.** Even × Odd =   **20.** Odd × Even =   **21.** Odd × Odd =

22. If you did 12 trials, each time choosing two whole numbers at random and multiplying them, how many even products would you expect? How many odd products? Try the experiment. Use some small and some large numbers. Compare your results with the expected results.

More Practice, page 521, set A

Using Samples to Predict

EXPLORE Do an Experiment

Work in groups. To make predictions about a large group of objects too large to count easily, small sets of the objects, called **samples,** can be taken. By analyzing the samples, some predictions about the large group can be made.

Try this experiment. How many beans do you predict are in the sack?

> **Experiment:**
> **Predict the number of beans.**
>
> - Start with a large sack full of white beans. Count out 50 of the beans. Mark them with a felt pen.
> - Mix the marked beans in with the others thoroughly.
> - Draw a sample of 25 beans from the sack without looking.
> - Count the number of marked beans in the sample.
> - Use the data to predict the total number of beans.

TALK ABOUT IT

1. Why should you mix the marked beans and unmarked beans thoroughly?
2. How do you think you can use the number of marked beans in a sample to estimate the total number of beans?
3. Suppose a classmate did the experiment with two different sizes of full sacks. The classmate told you there were more marked beans in the sample from the first sack than in the sample from the second sack. Which sack would probably hold a greater number of beans? Explain your answer.

When you take a sample, you can use a proportion to help you estimate the number of beans in a sack. Suppose your group found that 5 out of 25 beans in a sample were marked. Remember, there are 50 marked beans in all. Let n stand for the total number of beans in the sack.

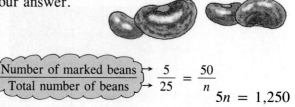

$$\text{Number of marked beans} \rightarrow \frac{5}{25} = \frac{50}{n} \leftarrow \text{Total number of beans}$$

$$5n = 1{,}250$$
$$n = 250$$

There are an estimated 250 beans in the sack.

Use these samples to predict about how many in all. Let n stand for the total number.

1. Sample: 6 out of 24 are marked.
   Sack: 50 out of n are marked.

2. Sample: 3 out of 40 are marked.
   Sack: 30 out of n are marked.

Use these samples to predict about how many in all. Let n stand for the total number.

1. Sample: 4 out of 36 are marked.
   Sack: 50 out of n are marked.

2. Sample: 2 out of 30 are marked.
   Sack: 60 out of n are marked.

3. Sample: 8 out of 32 are marked.
   Sack: 40 out of n are marked.

4. Sample: 10 out of 100 are marked.
   Sack: 250 out of n are marked.

5. Sample: 6 out of 120 are marked.
   Sack: 50 out of n are marked.

6. Sample: 20 out of 25 are marked.
   Sack: 80 out of n are marked.

APPLY

MATH REASONING

7. Three groups of students took samples of beans from a sack containing 48 marked beans. What can you find out from these samples? Could you improve the estimates by combining samples? Explain your answers.

Sample 1	Sample 2	Sample 3
60 beans	40 beans	54 beans
4 marked	2 marked	3 marked

PROBLEM SOLVING

8. In a sack containing 50 marked beans, a sample of 20 beans contains only 1 marked bean. Predict the total number of beans in the sack.

9. A sack has 3 colors of marbles in it. There are 500 marbles in all. A sample of 20 marbles contains 4 red, 10 blue, and 6 yellow marbles. How many marbles of each color do you predict are in the sack?

10. In a sack of colored markers, 1 out of every 3 markers is red. Other colors are green, yellow, black, and brown. In a sample of 33 markers, how many of the red markers would you expect to find?

▶ ALGEBRA

11. The sum of the probabilities of all outcomes must be 1. If A is an outcome and $P(A) = \frac{1}{3}$, then the probability of A not happening, $P(\text{not A})$, is $\frac{2}{3}$. Copy and complete the function table.

$P(A)$	$\frac{1}{4}$	$\frac{2}{5}$		0.9	
$P(\text{not A})$			0.3		0.99

Problem Solving
Data from a Map

UNDERSTAND
ANALYZE DATA
PLAN
ESTIMATE
SOLVE
EXAMINE

You often need data from a table, a graph, or some other source in order to solve a problem. To solve this problem, you need data from a map.

Dennis flew from San Francisco to Moscow with stops in Washington, D.C. and Paris on the way. He then flew directly home from Moscow. How much shorter was his flight home?

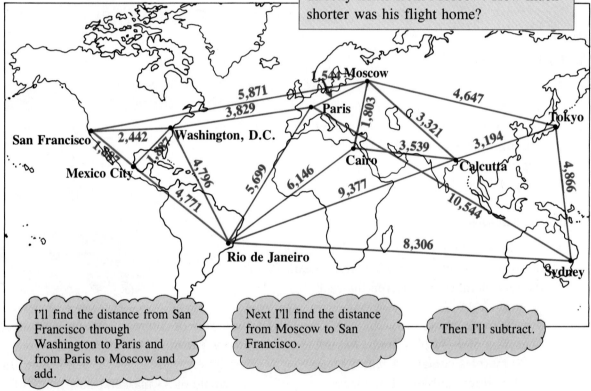

I'll find the distance from San Francisco through Washington to Paris and from Paris to Moscow and add.

Next I'll find the distance from Moscow to San Francisco.

Then I'll subtract.

$$2,442 + 3,892 + 1,544 = 7,878 \qquad 7,878 - 5,871 = 2,007$$

The flight home was 2,007 miles shorter.

TRY IT OUT

You can use data from the map to help you solve these problems.

1. Last year, Maria made 3 round-trip flights between San Francisco and Mexico City. How many miles did she fly?

2. A flight from Rio de Janeiro to Sydney took 14 hours and 53 min. About how many miles per hour did the plane fly?

Solve.

1. Leah's family flew from Washington, D.C. to Mexico City for a vacation. The trip took 4 hours. How many miles by air had they traveled when they returned home?

2. Alfredo belongs to a frequent flyer program. Last month he flew 49,168 miles on trips between Cairo and Rio de Janeiro. How many trips did he make?

3. Wendall, Karla, Rosalie, and Lee are each traveling to a different city this summer. The cities are Paris, Sydney, Tokyo, and Mexico City. Karla is staying in North America, and Lee is going to Europe. Rosalie can hardly wait to see kangaroos in their natural habitat. Who is going to what city?

4. The probability of rain in Tokyo for March, April, and May is 0.33. If you are in Tokyo for 12 days, about how many days of rain would you expect?

5. If a jet averages 535 miles per hour, can it fly from Paris to Sydney in less than 20 hours?

6. Rob's company is giving away 5 free trips to Paris. There are 85 employees in Rob's company. What is the probability that Rob will win a trip to Paris?

7. Nancy withdrew some money from her savings account to spend during her trip. She spent $15 for a T-shirt, $29 for cassette tapes, $59 for clothing, and $7 for miscellaneous items. At the end of her trip, she had $36 left. How much money did she withdraw from her savings account?

8. **Finding Another Way** Karna just finished packing for her trip to Mexico. She packed 2 skirts—navy and tan, 3 tops—white, yellow, and pink, and 2 pairs of shoes— brown and black. How many different outfits can she wear? Karna solved this problem by drawing a picture. Find another way to solve it.

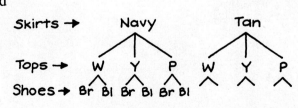

Skirts → Navy   Tan

Tops → W Y P   W Y P

Shoes → Br Bl Br Bl Br Bl

She can wear 12 outfits.

More Practice, page 527, set C

Applied Problem Solving
Group Decision Making

UNDERSTAND
ANALYZE DATA
PLAN
ESTIMATE
SOLVE
EXAMINE

Group Skill
Check for Understanding

Students from your school are going on a field trip to Sea Life Learning Labs. Your group is in charge of scheduling the Learning Labs for all the different groups of students. One advantage of this job is that your group gets to pick the labs your group members most want to attend.

Facts to Consider

1. You can choose to put groups of students in four Sea Life Learning Labs. The number of students that can be placed in each lab at one time is given below.

   Octopus Lab – 20 students
   Shark Lab – 30 students
   Whale Lab – 30 students
   Tide Pool Lab – 40 students

2. The same four labs can be scheduled at three different times: 9 a.m., 10 a.m., and 11 a.m.

3. Each group of students should be scheduled for three different labs.

4. These are the groups of students and their adult leaders. Students remain with their leader for all three labs.

Adult Leader	Number of Students
Ms. Doyle	8
Mr. Katz	10
Ms. Ely	10
Mr. Smith	9
Ms. Shock	8
Mr. Kyle	15
Ms. Hanson	9
Ms. Mechling	10
Mr. Wong	8
Ms. Pei	9

5. You are in Mr. Wong's group.

1. Can you arrange the schedule so that you can attend all four labs? Why or why not?
2. How many groups can usually be scheduled into the Shark Lab?
3. Could Ms. Ely's group, Mr. Smith's group, and Mr. Kyle's group all be scheduled in the Shark Lab together?
4. What labs do you want to be sure to schedule for your group?
5. Which two groups do you think you should schedule first?

6. Can you think of more than one plan you could use to create your schedule? Explain.

What Is Your Decision?

Your schedule must show the name of the labs, the times, and the names of the group leaders. What labs will you be attending? Compare your schedule with those made by other groups and see how many chose the same labs for Mr. Wong's class.

431

WRAP UP

What's the Probability?

Think of number cubes labeled 1 through 6. Decide whether the outcome is *likely* or *not likely*.

1. You will roll a sum of 2 when tossing two number cubes.

2. You will get a sum of 4 or greater when tossing three number cubes.

3. You will roll a 1 or a 6 when tossing one cube.

4. When rolling 2 cubes, you will roll the same number on both cubes.

5. The double of the number you roll with 1 cube is less than 10.

6. You will roll a cube 20 times and never get a 6.

Sometimes, Always, Never

Decide which word should go in the blank: *sometimes*, *always*, or *never*. Explain your choices.

7. If there are 10 equally likely outcomes possible, the probability of any of the outcomes occuring is _____ $\frac{1}{10}$.

8. The probability of an event occuring is _____ expressed as a number less than 1.

9. If an event cannot happen, its probability is _____ a number greater than zero.

Project

Suppose all students in your school are asked to vote on this question: *Would you like to see each school day shortened by 1 hour if it meant the school year had to be lengthened by 1 month?* You want to know how your schoolmates will vote, but it is not possible for you to ask every student. Decide on a method for finding out how students in each grade will vote and for predicting the final outcome.

CHAPTER REVIEW/TEST

Part 1 Understanding

Decide whether the game is fair or unfair.

1. Roll a number cube with the numbers 1–6 on its faces. If it lands on an even number, you win. If not, your opponent wins.

2. Toss 2 coins. If both coins come up heads, you win. Otherwise your opponent wins.

Tell if the outcomes are equally likely. If not, tell which is more likely.

3. Roll a cube with faces numbered 1–6.

4. Spin the spinner.

5. There are 12 equally likely outcomes and 3 winning outcomes. Give the probability of winning.

6. If you tossed a coin 200 times, what is the mathematical probability of getting a head each time?

If you spun the two spinners shown, what is

7. P (A, F)?   **8.** P (B, D)?   **9.** P (C, C)?

Part 2 Skills

Find the expected value.

10. Trials: 1,000
Probability: 0.4

11. Trials: 60
Probability: $\frac{1}{5}$

Use the samples to predict how many in all. Let n stand for the total number.

12. Sample: 4 out of 15 are marked.
Sack: 48 out of n are marked.

13. Sample: 30 out of 45 are marked.
Sack: 90 out of n are marked.

Part 3 Applications

Use the map to help you solve the problem.

14. Challenge Beth is bicycling from Dallas to Arlington. She rode 8 miles in one hour. If she continues to ride at that rate, about how many hours will it take her?

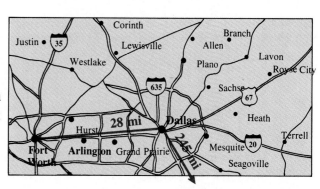

ENRICHMENT
Networks

A
B
C
D

All of the diagrams shown above are called **networks.** In some of them, you can trace over all of the lines without ever following any path more than once or lifting your pencil from the paper. The 18th-century mathematician Leonhard Euler proved that a network can be traced if

■ it has *exactly* 2 odd vertices, or
■ it has *no* odd vertices

1. Which of the networks above can you trace without lifting your pencil or going over any path more than once?

A vertex is odd if an odd number of paths meet there. Look at the following odd vertices:

3 paths

5 paths

7 paths

Use Euler's rule to decide which of the networks can be traced. Tell why.

2.

3.

4.

5.

6. Draw some networks of your own. Make some that can be traced and some that cannot.

CUMULATIVE REVIEW

1. What is the opposite of a gain of $5?

   A. profit of $5   B. loss of $5

   C. gain of $0   D. $5 found

2. Without adding, tell which sum is positive.

   A. $^-8 + {}^+6$ B. $^-12 + {}^-18$

   C. $^+65 + {}^-66$ D. $^+32 + {}^-26$

3. A textbook might weigh about 30 ___ .

   A. qt   B. T

   C. lb   D. oz

4. Which is greater than 1 lb 12 oz?

   A. 25 oz   B. 20 oz

   C. 15 oz   D. 30 oz

5. When it is 2 p.m. in California, what time is in in New York?

   A. 5 p.m.   B. 4 p.m.

   C. 12 noon   D. 11 a.m.

6. What is the perimeter of a regular octagon with sides of 9.5 cm?

   A. 19 cm   B. 38 cm

   C. 76 cm   D. 90.25 cm

7. What is the area of the shaded figure?

   A. 45 in.^{2} B. 36 in.^{2}

   C. 9 in.^{2} D. 27 in.^{2}

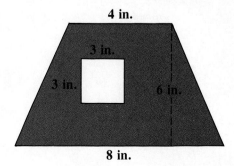

4 in.

3 in.

3 in.

6 in.

8 in.

8. What is the area of a parallelogram with a base of 12 m and a height that is 3 m less than the base?

   A. 180 m^2 B. 108 m^2

   C. 21 m^2 D. 45 m^2

9. The area of a trapezoid is 32 cm^2. The bases are 9.5 cm and 6.5 cm. What is the height?

   A. 3 cm   B. 4 cm

   C. 16 cm   D. 8 cm

10. The diameter of a circular pool is 22 feet. What is the area of the pool? Use 3.14 for π.

    A. 379.94 ft^2 B. 69.08 ft^2

    C. 34.54 ft^2 D. 1,519.76 ft^2

11. A terrarium with a screen top is 60 cm long, 20 cm wide, and 30 cm high. What is the surface area of its 5 glass sides?

    A. 3,600 cm^2 B. 4,800 cm^2

    C. 6,000 cm^2 D. 7,200 cm^2

12. Give the point for the set of coordinates $(3, {}^-2)$.

    A. A   B. B

    C. C   D. D

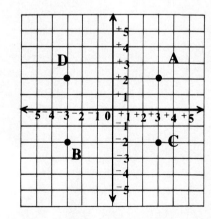

16

INTRODUCTION TO ALGEBRA

MATH AND
FINE ARTS

DATA BANK

Use the Fine Arts Data
Bank on page 482 to answer
the questions.

1 Complete this statement:
In a horizontally balanced
mobile, the length of
the rod between the heavier object
and the suspension wire is
(*greater*/*less*) than the length of
the rod between the lighter object
and the suspension wire.

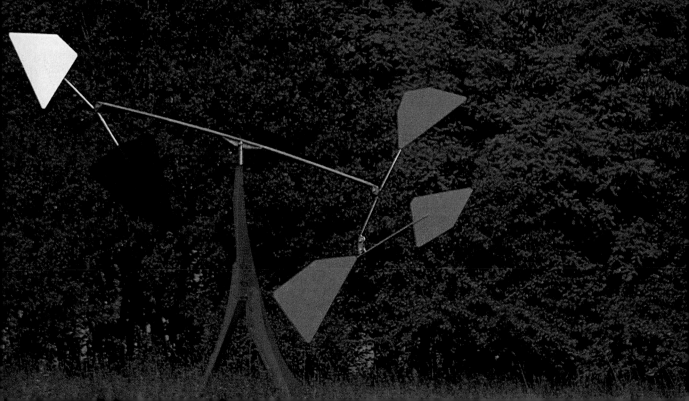

2 Find the missing weight suspended by wire C. What is the total weight suspended by each of the wires: A, B, C, D, and E?

3 Suppose wires A and B are 10 inches apart. Is suspension wire D attached closer to A or to B? How much closer?

4 Using Critical Thinking
What distances between wires D and E and between wires E and C make the mobile balance? What other ways can you find?

437

Solving Equations
Using Manipulatives

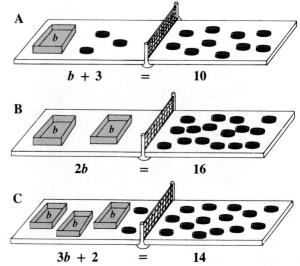

A

$b + 3 \quad = \quad 10$

EXPLORE Use an Equation Model

Work in groups. An equation uses an equal
sign to state that the two sides name the same
number. Think of the net as an equal sign.
Use counters to decide how many to put in
each box (*b*) so there are the same number on
each side. When there is more than 1 box,
put the same number of counters in each box.

B

$2b \quad = \quad 16$

TALK ABOUT IT

1. How many counters did you need for
   table A?
2. How many did you put in each box on
   table B?
3. How did you decide on the number for
   each box on table C?

C

$3b + 2 \quad = \quad 14$

You can use counters to help you solve
equations such as $b + 5 = 11$.

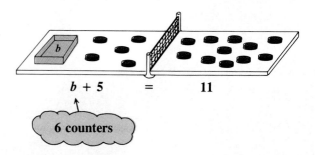

$b + 5 \quad = \quad 11$

6 counters

Other Examples

$2b + 3 = 17 \longrightarrow \boxed{b}\,\boxed{b} + 3 = 17$
$b = 7$

$4b = 24 \longrightarrow \boxed{b}\,\boxed{b}\,\boxed{b}\,\boxed{b} = 24$
$b = 6$

Solve. Use counters.

1. $3n + 1 = 7$

2. $6a = 18$

3. $5r + 2 = 17$

4. $4t + 3 = 11$

438

Solve. Use counters if you need help.

1. $w + 7 = 12$ **2.** $15 \times n = 30$ **3.** $b + 2 = 14$ **4.** $25 + y = 30$

5. $9 + c = 9$ **6.** $m + 1 = 20$ **7.** $5 + a = 16$ **8.** $x + 0 = 17$

9. $f \times 8 = 24$ **10.** $7 \cdot r = 0$ **11.** $6s = 42$ **12.** $10 \times t = 120$

13. $p \cdot 9 = 81$ **14.** $s \times 11 = 22$ **15.** $1 \times y = 19$ **16.** $b \cdot 7 = 28$

17. $3d + 4 = 28$ **18.** $5n + 2 = 52$ **19.** $7x + 1 = 50$ **20.** $3 + 4t = 39$

APPLY

MATH REASONING

21. Do not solve. Just tell which is greatest, a, b, or c.
    $3a = 171$ $3b + 6 = 171$ $3c + 36 = 171$

PROBLEM SOLVING

22. Suppose a, b, c, and d are numbers. b is less than d and more than c. a is between b and d. What is the order of these numbers starting with the smallest?

23. Two times a number plus 7 is 23. What is the number? Use counters if you need help.

▶ ESTIMATION

Use rounding and compatible numbers to help you estimate the solution to each equation.

24. $2n + 3 = 1{,}997$

25. $4a + 5 = 7{,}985$

26. $3x + 2 = 3{,}017$

Solving Equations
Using Guess and Check or Mental Math

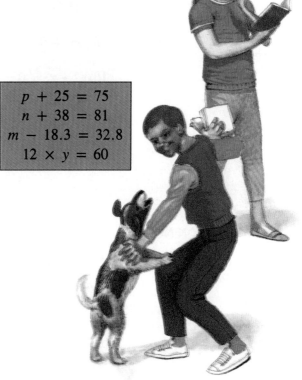

LEARN ABOUT IT

You have solved simple equations using mental math. Another way to solve equations is to guess and check.

$$p + 25 = 75$$
$$n + 38 = 81$$
$$m - 18.3 = 32.8$$
$$12 \times y = 60$$

EXPLORE Analyze the Situation

Try to solve the equations in the box. If you cannot solve them by using mental math, solve them by guessing and checking. Keep guessing until you find the solution.

TALK ABOUT IT

1. Which equations did you solve by using mental math? By guessing and checking?
2. Which equation required the most guesses?

Problems with one operation that involve compatible numbers can often be solved using mental math. When the numbers are not compatible, try guessing and checking. Use results from incorrect guesses to help you revise your next guess. You can use a calculator to make your guessing and checking easier.

Example

Solve: $n + 76 = 182$

Try 96. → $96 + 76 = 172$ Too low. Guess higher.
Try 116. → $116 + 76 = 192$ Too high. Guess lower.
Try 106. → $106 + 76 = 182$ Correct.
        The solution is $n = 106$.

TRY IT OUT

Solve by using mental math or by guessing and checking. You may want to use a calculator.

1. $h + 68 = 145$ **2.** $34 \times n = 408$ **3.** $k - 35 = 65$ **4.** $17 \cdot d = 306$

Solve by using mental math or by guessing and checking.
You may want to use a calculator.

1. $c + 13 = 71$ 2. $14 \times n = 98$ 3. $a \cdot 25 = 100$ 4. $r - 38 = 95$

5. $78 + x = 104$ 6. $p - 50 = 50$ 7. $y \times 7 = 364$ 8. $d - 7.5 = 8.7$

9. $q + 67 = 70$ 10. $211 - s = 174$ 11. $n \cdot 38 = 114$ 12. $r + 25 = 100$

13. $y - 1.9 = 3.7$ 14. $50 \cdot b = 100$ 15. $f + 26 = 71$ 16. $h \times 9 = 99$

17. $38 + k = 46.5$ 18. $j - 1.8 = 7.3$ 19. $m \times 6 = 480$ 20. $27 \times g = 162$

MATH REASONING

Estimate to tell which number would be a good first
guess to solve the equation.

21. $m - 54 = 112$ **a.** 60   **b.** 250   **c.** 160

22. $28 \cdot r = 532$ **a.** 10   **b.** 20   **c.** 30

23. $n + 287 = 402$ **a.** 25   **b.** 225   **c.** 125

PROBLEM SOLVING

Understanding the Operation   Tell which equation you would
use to solve each problem below.

24. Mike bought 6 boxes of crayons. There
were the same number in each box. He
bought 96 crayons. How many were in
each box?

    a. $6 + n = 96$ **b.** $6 \times n = 96$
    c. $6 - n = 96$ **d.** $6 \div n = 96$

25. Pina had 34 colored pencils in a box.
She took all but 18 of them to school.
How many did she take to school?

    a. $34 + n = 18$ **b.** $34 \times n = 18$
    c. $34 - n = 18$ **d.** $34 \div n = 18$

▶ CALCULATOR

Use a calculator to help you solve this problem by guessing and checking.

26. Arrange the digits 1, 2, 7, 8, 9 to make this equation true:
    ABCDE $\times$ 4 = EDCBA.

Solving Equations
Addition and Subtraction

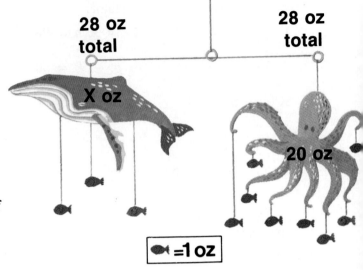

28 oz total

28 oz total

X oz

20 oz

◄ =1 oz

LEARN ABOUT IT

EXPLORE· Study the Picture

This mobile is balanced when the total weights on each side (28 oz) are equal. The mobile will stay balanced if you add or take away the same amount on both sides. Since there are the same number of ounces on both sides, you can think of the mobile as showing an equation. Can you write and solve the equation?

TALK ABOUT IT

1. What expression can you write for the left side?
2. How many ounces are on each side?
3. If you remove 3 ounces from each side, will the mobile still be balanced? What does the whale weigh?

You can solve addition and subtraction equations by adding or subtracting the same number on both sides of the equal sign. The idea is to use **inverse operations** so you get the variable alone on one side of the equation.

■ Two operations are inverses if they "undo" each other. Subtracting 28 is the inverse of adding 28. Adding 19 is the inverse of subtracting 19.

> Undo subtracting 19.

> Do the same to both sides.

Solve: $x - 19 = 84 \rightarrow x - 19 + 19 = 84 + 19$
$$x = 103$$
Check: $103 - 19 = 84$

TRY IT OUT

Solve and check.

1. $h + 123 = 309$ 2. $34 = j - 18$ 3. $23.8 = f + 9.08$ 4. $m - 45.1 = 29.7$

Write what you would do to both sides of the equation to solve it. Do not solve.

1. $x + 19 = 56$ **2.** $a - 56 = 128$ **3.** $7.8 + f = 12.3$ **4.** $n - 3\frac{5}{8} = 6\frac{1}{2}$

Solve and check.

5. $c - 75 = 128$ **6.** $29 + s = 46$ **7.** $r + 92 = 92$ **8.** $z - 128 = 27$

9. $156 + n = 200$ **10.** $d - 85 = 34$ **11.** $p + 26 = 43$ **12.** $g + 0 = 47$

13. $y + 7.5 = 10.5$ **14.** $d - 3.8 = 1.2$ **15.** $j + \frac{1}{8} = \frac{3}{4}$ **16.** $9 - k = \frac{1}{2}$

APPLY

MATH REASONING

Do not solve. Just tell whether the solution is greater than, less than, or equal to 278.

17. $a + 19 = 278$ **18.** $b - 19 = 278$ **19.** $0 + r = 278$

PROBLEM SOLVING

Use the **Fine Arts Data Bank** to solve these problems.

20. Look at the fish mobile. Fill in the number to complete each equation.

$y = $ ▥ x $z = $ ▥ $y + $ ▥ x

21. If the smallest fish in the fish mobile weighs 10 oz, how much does the largest fish weigh?

22. Design a three-fish mobile that uses only a 5-oz fish, a 10-oz fish, and a 20-oz fish. Be sure to label the weights and the rod lengths.

DATA BANK

MIXED REVIEW

Find the circumference and area for a circle with the given diameter. Use 3.14 for π.

23. $d = 12$ cm   **24.** $d = 20$ in.   **25.** $d = 100$ ft   **26.** $d = 15$ mm

Find the sale price.

27. $28.98 at 10% off   **28.** $25.99 at 30% discount   **29.** $18.99 at $\frac{1}{3}$ off

More Practice, page 521, set D

Using Critical Thinking

LEARN ABOUT IT

Courtney said, "My vegetable garden is a rectangle and one side is 6 yards longer than the other side." Darren claimed that if she would tell him the length of any side, he could find the other side and the perimeter. Do you agree?

$w + 6$

TALK ABOUT IT

1. If Courtney tells the length of the short side, how can Darren find the long side? What if she tells the long side instead?
2. Could Darren find the sides if Courtney tells the perimeter? How?

TRY IT OUT

w

Solve.

1. The shortest side of the isosceles triangle is 9 units. How long are the other two sides?

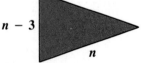

2. What is the perimeter of this triangle if the longest side is 12 units?

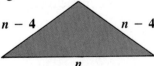

3. The shortest side of this triangle is 7 units. What is the length of each other side?

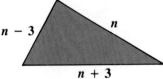

4. The longer sides of this rectangle are 15 units. What is the perimeter?

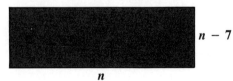

5. The longest side of this triangle is 15 units. How long are the other sides?

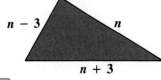

6. The longest side of this hexagon is 8 units. What is the perimeter?

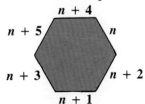

MIDCHAPTER REVIEW/QUIZ

Both sides of the net are equal. How many counters are in each box?

1.

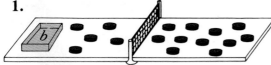

2.

$$b + 5 = 11$$
$$b = \text{▓}$$

$$3b + 4 = 13$$
$$b = \text{▓}$$

Solve. Use mental math.

3. $7 \times n = 21$ **4.** $c + 5 = 30$ **5.** $9 - m = 3$ **6.** $j \cdot 8 = 64$

7. $14f = 140$ **8.** $y - 17 = 27$ **9.** $12 + n = 24$ **10.** $k \times 25 = 100$

Write what you would do to both sides of the equation to solve. Do not solve.

11. $17 + x = 75$ **12.** $14 + j = 87$ **13.** $g - 8 = 154$ **14.** $6.3 + h = 14.67$

Solve and check.

15. $x + 27 = 106$ **16.** $125 - f = 48$ **17.** $p - 485 = 587$ **18.** $y - \dfrac{1}{2} = \dfrac{2}{3}$

19. $18.75 + j = 46.1$ **20.** $85 - h = 44$ **21.** $z - \dfrac{2}{5} = \dfrac{1}{5}$ **22.** $n + 13 = 48$

PROBLEM SOLVING

23. A bag of apples and 2 oranges weigh the same as 10 oranges. If each orange weighs 5 ounces, how much does the bag of apples weigh?

24. After depositing $5 into her savings account, Melanie has $172 in the account. How much was in the account before this deposit?

25. Larry jogged 10 miles in 3 days. If he jogged 3.6 miles the first day and 2.4 miles the second day, how far did he jog the third day?

Problem Solving
Using Addition and Subtraction Equations

UNDERSTAND
ANALYZE DATA
PLAN
ESTIMATE
SOLVE
EXAMINE

LEARN ABOUT IT

Many real-world situations can be translated into an equation. Tala bought a compact disc set on sale for $6 less than the regular price. She paid $18 for the set. What was the regular price?

To translate this situation into an equation, think about the meaning of each phrase. Next decide what the variable will stand for. Then, write and solve an equation and check.

Step 1: Select the variable.

Let p be the regular price of the compact disc set.

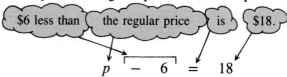

$6 less than   the regular price   is $18.

Step 2: Translate to an equation.

$$p - 6 = 18$$

Step 3: Solve the equation and check.

$$p - 6 = 18$$
$$(p - 6) + 6 = (18) + 6$$
$$p = 24$$

Check: $24 - 6 = 18$, $18 = 18$

TRY IT OUT

The cost of a ticket was $3.00 more than what Jared expected. A ticket cost $11.50. What did Jared expect to pay for a ticket?

Let t be the amount Jared expected to pay for the ticket.

1. Write an expression using t that shows how much he paid.

2. How much did he pay for a ticket?

3. Write an equation for this situation.

4. Solve the equation and the problem.

5. Check your answer.

446

Solve.

Tax on a rock group sweat shirt was $0.77. The total cost, including tax, was $13.52. What was the cost of the shirt without tax?

Let *c* be the cost before tax.

1. Write an expression using *c* that shows the price including tax.
2. What was the price including tax?
3. Write an equation for this situation.
4. Solve the equation and the problem.
5. Check your answer.

Eighteen sixth graders go home for lunch and the rest eat in the cafeteria. There are a total of 107 sixth graders. How many eat in the cafeteria?

Let *c* be the number of sixth graders that eat in the cafeteria.

6. Write an expression using *c* that shows the total number of sixth graders.
7. What is the total number of sixth graders?
8. Write an equation for this situation.
9. Solve the equation and the problem.
10. Check your answer.

Five books were taken from the school's Sweet Valley Twins set for recovering. There were 12 left on the shelf. How many books are in the school set altogether?

Let *n* be the total number of books.

11. Write an expression using *n* that shows the number of books left on the shelf.
12. How many were left on the shelf?
13. Write an equation for this situation.
14. Solve the equation and the problem.
15. Check your answer.

16. The art supply store held a 20%-off sale. Meryl bought some colored pens, regularly $6.95, and some art paper, regularly $4.35. The clerk gave her $0.96 in change. How much money did Meryl give the clerk?

17. A tree casts a shadow that is 10 m long. A nearby post that is 1.5 m high casts a shadow that is 4 m long. How tall is the tree?

18. **Write Your Own Problem** Let *c* = cost of a record. Write a question that can be answered by writing and solving the equation *c* − $2 = $12.

More Practice, page 527, set D

Solving Equations
Multiplication and Division

EXPLORE Study the Picture

The technique you used to solve addition and subtraction equations will work for multiplication and division equations. The mobile is balanced. The weights on each side are equal. The mobile will stay balanced if what is done on one side is also done on the other side.

TALK ABOUT IT

1. What algebraic expression can you write for the weight on the left side?
2. To have only one large bird on the left side, would you double the number of large birds or take half (divide by 2) the number of large birds?
3. If you removed half of the number of small birds on the right, what would be the weight of the remaining group of small birds?

You can solve multiplication and division equations by multiplying or dividing by the same number on both sides of the equal sign. The idea is to use inverse operations so you get the variable alone on one side of the equation. Multiplying by 12 is the inverse of dividing by 12. Dividing by 4 is the inverse of multiplying by 4.

> Undo multiplying 4.

> Do the same to both sides.

Solve: $4n = 96 \rightarrow 4n \div 4 = 96 \div 4$ OR $\dfrac{4n}{4} = \dfrac{96}{4}$

Check: $n = 24$
$4 \times 24 = 24$

TRY IT OUT

Solve and check.

1. $7 \cdot x = 87.5$ **2.** $a \div 8 = 2.5$ **3.** $5.8d = 21.46$ **4.** $\dfrac{k}{14} = 336$

 = 1 oz

448

Write what you would do to both sides of the equation to solve it.
Do not solve.

1. $8y = 520$

2. $\frac{n}{6} = 17$

3. $r \div 5 = 28$

4. $9 \cdot z = 207$

5. $\frac{b}{2.3} = 8.6$

6. $5.4x = 32.4$

7. $m \times 8 = 728$

8. $\frac{s}{57} = 2$

Solve and check.

9. $d \times 9 = 108$

10. $\frac{n}{3} = 48$

11. $\frac{t}{7} = 128$

12. $7b = 245$

13. $3g = 282$

14. $\frac{w}{4} = 72$

15. $4 \cdot f = 724$

16. $\frac{y}{8} = 39$

17. $0.5e = 45.4$

18. $\frac{u}{3.7} = 2$

19. $s \div 4 = 27$

20. $c \times 8 = 504$

APPLY

MATH REASONING

Do not solve. Just tell if solutions are getting larger or smaller.

21. $\frac{t}{2} = 87, \frac{t}{3} = 87, \frac{t}{4} = 87, \frac{t}{5} = 87, \ldots$

22. $2r = 60, 3r = 60, 4r = 60, 5r = 60, \ldots$

PROBLEM SOLVING

Use the **Fine Arts Data Bank** to solve these problems.

23. Look at the bird mobile. Fill in the numbers to complete each equation.

$2g = \text{▥} \, r$ $\qquad$ $\text{▥} \, y = 2g + \text{▥} \, r$ $\qquad$ $\text{▥} \, b = \text{▥} \, g + \text{▥} \, r + \text{▥} \, y$

24. Design a five-bird mobile that uses only two 5-oz birds, two 10-oz birds, and one 20-oz bird. Be sure to label the weight and the rod lengths.

DATA BANK

▶ **USING CRITICAL THINKING** Analyze the Situation

In a magic square, the sum of each row, column, and diagonal is the same.

25. Write and solve equations as needed to find x, y, and z.

x	7	19
17	14	y
z	21	12

Problem Solving
Using Multiplication and Division Equations

LEARN ABOUT IT

You have translated real-world situations into equations involving addition or subtraction. Others can be translated into equations involving multiplication or division.

Gary was able to sell twice as many tickets to the school play as the old record for number of tickets sold. He sold 210 tickets. What was the previous record?

To translate this situation into an equation, think about the meaning of each phrase. Next, decide what the variable will stand for. Then, write and solve an equation and check.

Step 1: Select the variable.

Let r be the number of tickets for the old record.

2 times more than) the old record) is) 210.

Step 2: Translate to an equation.

$$2 \times r = 210$$

Step 3: Solve the equation and check.

$$2 \times r = 210$$
$$(2 \times r) \div 2 = (210) \div 2 \quad OR \quad \frac{2 \times r}{2} = \frac{210}{2}$$
$$r = 105$$

Check: $2 \times 105 = 210$, $210 = 210$

TRY IT OUT

The sixth graders were divided into 7 homerooms. Each had 27 students. What is the total number of sixth graders?

Let t be the total number of sixth graders.

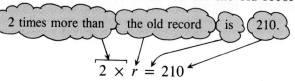

1. Write an expression using t that shows the number in each homeroom.

2. How many were in each homeroom?

3. Write an equation for this situation.

4. Solve the equation and the problem.

5. Check your answer.

Solve.

Willie decorated 3 times more eggs than Keiko in the egg-decorating contest. Willie decorated 54 eggs. How many did Keiko decorate?

Let *n* be the number of eggs Keiko decorated.

1. Write an expression using *n* that shows the number of eggs Willie decorated.
2. How many eggs did Willie decorate?
3. Write an equation for this situation.
4. Solve the equation and the problem.
5. Check your answer.

The length of a rectangular flower garden is 5 times the width. The length is 62.5 ft. What is the width?

Let *w* be the width of the garden.

6. Write an expression using *w* for the length of the garden.
7. What is the length of the garden?
8. Write an equation for this situation.
9. Solve the equation and the problem.
10. Check your answer.

A full pot of popcorn was divided into 12 boxes. Each box holds 8 oz. How many ounces does the full pot hold?

Let *p* be the number of ounces of popcorn the full pot holds.

11. Write an expression using *p* that shows how many ounces were put in each box.
12. How many ounces were put in each box?
13. Write an equation for this situation.
14. Solve the equation and the problem.
15. Check your answer.

16. A snail traveled in this order: 3 dm east, 1 dm south, 2 dm east, 3 dm south, 5 dm west, and 4 dm north. Draw the figure outlined by its path. What is the perimeter of the figure? What is the area enclosed by the path?

17. A shell mobile contains 40 shells. About how many of each kind of shell are in the mobile?

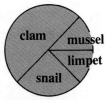

18. **Finding a Related Problem** Write an equation that can be used to solve the problem below. Tell which of the problems on this page can be solved in the same way as this one.

    Problem: Juana put all of her animal stickers on 12 pages of an album. Each page had 15 stickers. How many stickers did she have altogether?

Data Collection and Analysis
Group Decision Making

UNDERSTAND
ANALYZE DATA
PLAN
ESTIMATE
SOLVE
EXAMINE

Doing a Simulation
Group Skill
Disagree in an Agreeable Way

This maze of tunnels leads to two caverns, one of which holds a giant ruby and the other, a worthless rock. You will be allowed one trip through the tunnels. If you reach the ruby, you get to keep it. At each intersection in the tunnels, you will use a random method to decide which way to go. If you could choose the room to put the ruby in, which would you choose? Conduct a simulation to find out if it makes any difference.

Collecting Data

1. Draw a maze like this one on a piece of paper. Choose three cubes, each a different color. (Or write the names of three different colors on blank number cubes). Color the tunnels to match the cubes as shown.

452

2. Put a marker at the entrance. Since there are three ways to go, you will decide which way by choosing from the three cubes. Put the cubes in a bag. Choose a cube without looking and go down the tunnel of the same color to the next intersection. Put the cube back into the bag. At each intersection choose a cube to show you which way to go. Remember to choose from only two cubes if the intersection has two choices. When you reach cavern A or B, make a tally on a chart. Then start over at the entrance. Do this at least 100 times.

Cavern A
++++ ++++
++++ ++++

Cavern B
++++ ++++
++++ //

3. Count the number of times you reached cavern A and cavern B. What percent of the total number of times did you reach each room?

4. Make a bar graph to show the percent of times you reached each cavern.

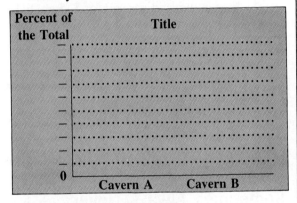

Percent of the Total — Title — Cavern A — Cavern B

Presenting Your Analysis

5. Are your chances of getting the ruby better in one cavern than the other? Explain why you think so.

453

WRAP UP

Using Algebraic Language

Write each statement as an equation or an algebraic expression. Use the variable n.

1. Dawn scored 15 points more than she did last week.

2. The price is six times what it was in 1950.

3. Four students moved away, shrinking the class size to 18.

4. Five compact discs sell for $35 at Dick's Discount Discs.

5. The number of tapes Joel has left after returning three is 2.

6. Suzanne has 25 more sit-ups to do to reach her goal of 60.

7. Tanya ran for 12 minutes longer than she did on Monday.

8. The ticket line is one third as long as it was on Saturday.

Sometimes, Always, Never

Decide which word should go in the blank: *sometimes, always,* or *never.* Explain your choices.

9. You can _____ multiply both sides of an equation by the same number.

10. If n is a whole number, then $n + 8$ is _____ greater than n.

11. If x is an integer, then $x + 4$ is _____ greater than 4.

12. If n is a negative integer, and p is a positive integer, then $n + p$ is _____ 0.

Project

Make up a crossnumber puzzle, a puzzle that uses numbers instead of letters. Answers should be whole numbers. Each clue should be in the form of an equation to be solved. For example, a clue might be $n + 6 = 20$. The answer 14 would be written in the puzzle squares. Give your puzzle to a classmate to solve.

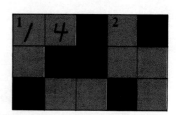

Crossnumber Puzzle

Across	Down
1. $n + 6 = 20$	1. $3 \times n = 45$
2. $7 - n = 4$	2.

CHAPTER REVIEW/TEST

Part 1   Understanding

Do not solve. Just tell which is greatest, *a, b,* or *c*.

1. $2a + 60 = 100$ $2b + 40 = 100$ $2c = 100$

Do not solve. Just tell whether *n* is greater than, less than, or equal to 216.

2. $n + 12 = 216$ **3.** $n + 0 = 216$

Part 2   Skills

Solve by using mental math or by guessing and checking.

4. $24 + w = 36$ **5.** $k \times 5 = 350$ **6.** $47r = 188$ **7.** $p - 12 = 12$

Solve and check.

8. $142 + p = 300$ **9.** $d - 6.8 = 4.2$ **10.** $7 - j = \frac{3}{4}$

11. $m \div 4 = 3.6$ **12.** $8 \cdot f = 352$ **13.** $\frac{d}{16} = 7.6$

Part 3   Applications

The cost of a T-shirt was $4.00 more than Kay expected. The T-shirt cost $14.98. Let *t* be the amount Kay expected to pay for the shirt.

14. Write an expression using *t* that shows how much she paid.

15. How much did she pay for the shirt?

16. Write an equation for this situation.

17. Solve the equation and the problem.

18. Check your answer.

19. Three times a number plus 4 is 40. What is the number?

20. Challenge   This year Kara sold 420 tickets, which was 3 times as many as she sold last year. How many tickets did she sell last year? Solve the problem by writing and solving an algebraic equation.

ENRICHMENT
Modular Arithmetic

Here is a riddle: When does 9 + 5 = 2 and 4 − 9 = 7?
Answer: On a clock. These are clock sums and differences. Five hours after 9 o'clock is 2 o'clock; and 9 hours before 4 o'clock is 7 o'clock.

Find the following sums or differences using clock arithmetic. You may use your watch.

1. 8 + 5   **2.** 5 − 8   **3.** 9 + 6   **4.** 6 − 9

5. 7 − 4   **6.** 8 + 8   **7.** 9 − 3   **8.** 3 − 9

9. What do you notice about your answers to exercises 7 and 8?

10. In this system, which number can be added to or subtracted from any number without changing that number?

On our planet we use a 12-hour clock. On the planet Pentune, there are 5 hours in the day.

You can use the picture to find the sum 4 + 3 on this clock.

When we compute with a 5-hour clock, we use the phrase **mod 5.** The *mod 5* sum of 4 and 3 is 2.

4 + 3 = 2

The *mod 5* sum of 4 and 3 is 2. We write (4 + 3) *mod 5* = 2. Here are other examples:

   (3 + 3) *mod 5* = 1   (1 − 2) *mod 5* = 4   (0 − 4) *mod 5* = 1

Use the 5-hour clock to solve these problems. Run the clock each number of hours to find the answers.

Solve.

11. (2 + 2) mod 5   **12.** (4 + 2) *mod 5*   **13.** (0 − 1) *mod 5*   **14.** (2 + 4) *mod 5*

15. (3 + 4) *mod 5*   **16.** (2 − 2) *mod 5*   **17.** (0 + 4) *mod 5*   **18.** (3 − 4) *mod 5*

19. Make up some addition and subtraction problems using the 5-hour clock.

CUMULATIVE REVIEW

1. Which is a reasonable estimate for the height of a classroom ceiling?

   A. 25 m　　　　B. 5 m

   C. 15 cm　　　D. 15 m

2. The diameter of a circular serving tray is 30 cm. What is the circumference?

   A. 33.14 cm　　B. 94.2 cm

   C. 9.5 cm　　　D. 47.1 cm

3. How many different 4-digit mailbox numbers can be made by using all 4 of these numbers: 2, 4, 7 and 9? Assume that each digit is used exactly once.

   A. 16　　　　　B. 24

   C. 6　　　　　D. 4

4. You and an opponent are playing a game in which you toss 3 coins. If you get 3 tails, you win. If not, your opponent wins. Who has the better chance of winning this game?

   A. neither　　　　B. you

   C. your opponent　　D. cannot tell

5. You toss a penny twice. What is $P(H, T)$?

   A. $\dfrac{1}{2}$　　　　B. $\dfrac{1}{4}$

   C. $\dfrac{0}{4}$　　　　D. $\dfrac{3}{4}$

6. Find the expected value: 250 trials with a probability of $\dfrac{2}{5}$.

   A. 200　　　　B. 50

   C. 100　　　　D. 150

7. What is P(winning) when there are 15 equally likely outcomes and 5 winning outcomes?

   A. $\dfrac{3}{1}$　　　　B. $\dfrac{1}{5}$

   C. $\dfrac{1}{3}$　　　　D. $\dfrac{10}{15}$

8. What is the mathematical probability of getting a 4 or a 6 when rolling a cube with the numbers 1–6 on its faces?

   A. $\dfrac{1}{6}$　　　　B. $\dfrac{2}{3}$

   C. $\dfrac{3}{2}$　　　　D. $\dfrac{1}{3}$

9. A sample of 35 beans drawn from a sack had 4 marked beans. Predict the total number of beans in the sack if the number of marked beans is 28.

   A. 195　　　　B. 5

   C. 245　　　　D. 140

10. Solve: $\dfrac{y}{4.5} = 6$.

    A. $y = 30$　　　B. $y = 27$

    C. $y = 1.5$　　　D. $y = 10.5$

11. The tax on a meal was $1.28. The total cost, including tax, was $26.88. What was the cost of the meal without tax?

    A. $24.34　　　B. $28.16

    C. $26.88　　　D. $25.60

12. The length of a rectangular garden is 4 times the width. The length is 50 feet. What is the width?

    A. 12.5 feet　　B. 200 feet

    C. 10 feet　　　D. 46 feet

RESOURCE BANK AND APPENDIX

APPENDIX

Adding Whole Numbers

Lynda Novachek is running for president of La Entrada School. In order to make badges for everyone, she asks the school secretary how many students there are in the school. She is told that there are 128 sixth grade students, 94 seventh grade students, and 102 eighth grade students. How many badges should Lynda make?

Lynda adds 128 + 94 + 102.

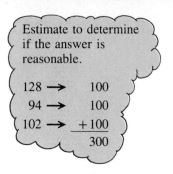

Add the ones. Trade if necessary.	Add the tens. Trade if necessary.	Add the hundreds.
$\overset{1}{1}28$ 94 + 102 —— 4 *Look for compatible numbers. 8 + 2 = 10*	$\overset{11}{1}28$ 94 + 102 —— 24	$\overset{11}{1}28$ 94 + 102 —— 324

There are a total of 324 students at La Entrada School. This is reasonable since the estimated total is 300 students.

Estimate to determine if the answer is reasonable.

$$128 \rightarrow 100$$
$$94 \rightarrow 100$$
$$102 \rightarrow +100$$
$$300$$

TRY IT OUT

Add.

1. 975
    + 76

2. 1,497
    + 7,108

3. 56,387
    + 90,783

4. 6,874 + 876

460

Subtracting Whole Numbers

Lake Michigan, the largest body of fresh water in the United States, has an area of 22,300 square miles. Lake Winnebago, the largest lake in Wisconsin, has an area of 215 square miles. How much larger is Lake Michigan?

Since we want to know how much more area Lake Michigan covers than Lake Winnebago, we subtract.

$$22,300 - 215$$

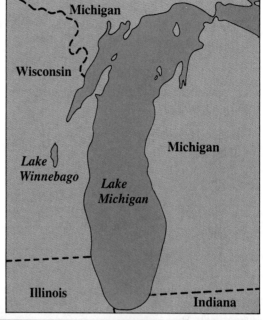

Subtract the ones, regrouping if needed.	Subtract the tens, regrouping if needed.	Subtract the hundreds, regrouping if needed.	Subtract the thousands, etc. regrouping if needed.
$\begin{array}{r} {}^{2\ 9\ 10} \\ 22,3\not0\not0 \\ -\quad 215 \\ \hline 5 \end{array}$	$\begin{array}{r} {}^{2\ 9\ 10} \\ 22,3\not0\not0 \\ -\quad 215 \\ \hline 85 \end{array}$	$\begin{array}{r} {}^{2\ 9\ 10} \\ 22,3\not0\not0 \\ -\quad 215 \\ \hline 085 \end{array}$	$\begin{array}{r} {}^{2\ 9\ 10} \\ 22,3\not0\not0 \\ -\quad 215 \\ \hline 22,085 \end{array}$

Lake Michigan is 22,085 square miles larger than Lake Winnebago. The answer is reasonable since the estimated answer is 22,000 square miles.

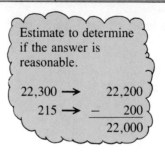

Estimate to determine if the answer is reasonable.

$$\begin{array}{r} 22,300 \rightarrow \quad 22,200 \\ 215 \rightarrow -\quad\ \ 200 \\ \hline 22,000 \end{array}$$

TRY IT OUT

Subtract.

1.	$\begin{array}{r} 607 \\ -\ 348 \end{array}$	**2.**	$\begin{array}{r} 800 \\ -\ 416 \end{array}$	**3.**	$\begin{array}{r} 7,008 \\ -\ 4,209 \end{array}$	**4.**	$\begin{array}{r} 45,000 \\ -\ 26,327 \end{array}$	**5.**	$\begin{array}{r} 10,000 \\ -\quad 842 \end{array}$

Multiplying Whole Numbers

Brandon takes his pulse and finds that his heart beats 72 times per minute. How many times does his heart beat in one day?

Brandon must first determine how many minutes there are in a day by multiplying 60 minutes per hour times 24 hours per day.

$$60 \times 24$$

$$
\begin{array}{r}
\overset{2}{24} \\
\times\ 60 \\
\hline
00 \\
1\ 440 \\
\hline
1{,}440
\end{array}
$$

← Multiply by the ones, regrouping if needed.
← Multiply by the tens, regrouping if needed.
← Add the products.

After determing that there are 1,440 minutes in a day, Brandon then multiplies this number by 72 to determine how many times his heart beats in one day.

$$
\begin{array}{r}
\overset{3\ 2}{1{,}440} \\
\times\ \ \ \ \ 72 \\
\hline
2\ 880 \\
100\ 800 \\
\hline
103{,}680
\end{array}
$$

← Multiply by the ones, regrouping if needed.
← Multiply by the tens, regrouping if needed.
← Add the products.

Brandon's heart beats 103,680 times per day.

TRY IT OUT

1. $\begin{array}{r} 721 \\ \times\ 38 \\ \hline \end{array}$

2. $\begin{array}{r} 506 \\ \times\ 41 \\ \hline \end{array}$

3. $\begin{array}{r} 2{,}004 \\ \times\ 421 \\ \hline \end{array}$

4. $\begin{array}{r} 278 \\ \times\ 360 \\ \hline \end{array}$

5. $\begin{array}{r} 7{,}291 \\ \times\ 109 \\ \hline \end{array}$

Adding and Subtracting Decimals

Keiko noted that the color TV, a light bulb, and the oven were on for one hour. She used the chart below to determine how many kilowatts of electricity were used during the hour.

Appliance	Kilowatts used per hour
Clock radio	0.5
Light bulb	0.075
Color TV	0.33
Microwave oven	0.6
Toaster	1.5
Electric oven	2.4

Keiko adds $0.075 + 0.33 + 2.4$

Write the problem with the decimal points in line.	Add (or subtract) as with whole numbers.	Place the decimal point in line with the others.
0.075 0.33 + 2.4	0.075 0.330 + 2.400 2 805	0.075 0.330 + 2.400 2.805

The total kilowatts of electricity used is 2.805. This is reasonable since the estimated total is 2.8 kilowatts.

Determine if your answer is reasonable.
0.075 → 0.1
0.33 → 0.3
$2.4 + 0.1 + 0.3 = 2.8$

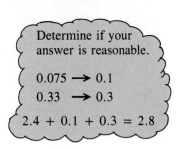

TRY IT OUT

1. $10.2 + 8.6$

2. $25.38 - 14.1$

3. $\$2.41 + \$8.92 + \$3$

4. $\$15 - \$2.45$

5. $13 + 2.56 + 0.01$

6. $241.5 - 180.72$

Multiplying and Dividing by Powers of Ten

While using his calculator, Luis notices the following patterns.

$34.12 \times 10 = 341.2$
$34.12 \times 100 = 3{,}412$
$34.12 \times 1{,}000 = 34{,}120$
$34.12 \div 10 = 3.412$
$34.12 \div 100 = 0.3412$
$34.12 \div 1{,}000 = 0.03412$

Luis sees that he can find these products and quotients mentally.

To **multiply** by a power of ten	Count the number of zeros.	Move the decimal point 1 place to the **right** for each zero.
	$67.21 \times 10 =$	672.1
	$13.147 \times 100 =$	$1{,}314.7$
	$8.12 \times 1{,}000 =$	$8{,}120.$ ← Add a zero to get 3 places.
	14×100	1400

The decimal point is always to the right of the ones place.

To **divide** by a power of ten	Count the number of zeros.	Move the decimal point 1 place to the **left** for each zero.
	$67.21 \div 10 =$	6.721
	$13.147 \div 100 =$	0.13147
	$8.12 \div 100 =$	0.0812 ← Add a zero to get 2 places.
	$14 \div 10 =$	1.4
	$1{,}500 \div 100 =$	$15.00 = 15$

TRY IT OUT

1. 5.12×10
2. $5.12 \div 10$
3. 172.8×100
4. $172.8 \div 100$

5. $23.18 \times 1{,}000$
6. $23.16 \div 1{,}000$
7. $32 \div 100$
8. $410 \div 10$

Dividing Whole Numbers
1 Digit-Divisors

Playing on the sixth grade basketball team, Marissa made a total of 135 points in 9 games. She wants to compute the average number of points she made per game.

She divides the total number of points by the number of games.

$$135 \div 9$$

Decide where to start.

$$
\begin{array}{r}
1 \\
9{\overline{\smash{\big)}\,135}}
\end{array}
$$ ← Divide.

Estimate: $13 \div 9$ is about 1.

$$
\begin{array}{r}
1 \\
9{\overline{\smash{\big)}\,135}} \\
\underline{9} \\
4
\end{array}
$$ ← Multiply.
← Subtract and compare.
$4 < 9$?

$$
\begin{array}{r}
15 \\
9{\overline{\smash{\big)}\,135}} \\
\underline{9} \\
45 \\
\underline{45} \\
0
\end{array}
$$ ← Divide.
← Multiply.
← Subtract and compare.

$$135 \div 9 = 15$$

Marissa made an average of 15 points per game. This is reasonable since the estimate is 10.

Estimate to determine if the answer is reasonable.

$135 \longrightarrow 100$

$9 \longrightarrow 10$

$100 \div 10 = 10$

TRY IT OUT

1. $5{\overline{\smash{\big)}\,325}}$ **2.** $8{\overline{\smash{\big)}\,3{,}322}}$ **3.** $6{\overline{\smash{\big)}\,628}}$ **4.** $9{\overline{\smash{\big)}\,6{,}319}}$

Dividing Whole Numbers
2-Digit Divisors

Rosalie's family is driving to Redwood Forest for a family campout. Rosalie spots a sign that says Redwood Forest—136 miles. They are traveling at 45 miles an hour on the mountain roads. Rosalie wants to know how much longer they will have to ride in the car.

Rosalie can divide the number of miles, 136 miles, by the speed, 45 miles per hour, to find the time it will take them to arrive at Redwood Forest.

$$136 \div 45$$

Decide where to start.

$$\begin{array}{r} 3 \leftarrow \text{Divide.} \\ 45\overline{)136} \\ 135 \leftarrow \text{Multiply.} \\ 1 \leftarrow \text{Subtract} \\ \text{and compare.} \end{array}$$

Round the divisor and quotient, and estimate.

Estimate: $\dfrac{140}{50} = \dfrac{14}{5} \rightarrow 3$

Divide.
Multiply.
Subtract and compare.

$136 \div 45 = 3 \text{ R1}$

After Rosalie's family has traveled for 3 hours, they will have 1 mile left to travel.

TRY IT OUT

1. $47\overline{)2,447}$ 2. $22\overline{)9,102}$ 3. $36\overline{)3,782}$ 4. $81\overline{)40,651}$ 5. $68\overline{)46,517}$

6. $68\overline{)9,658}$ 7. $29\overline{)7,016}$ 8. $23\overline{)488}$ 9. $58\overline{)2,700}$ 10. $27\overline{)1,975}$

Dividing Whole Numbers
3-Digit Divisors

The school band in which Eric plays has been invited to perform in the Parade of Roses in Los Angeles. A chartered flight to Los Angeles for the 113 band members costs $9,831. Eric wants to know how much he will have to pay.

To determine the cost per person, Eric can divide the total cost by the number of band members.

$$\$9,831 \div 113$$

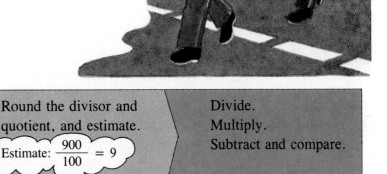

Decide where to start.	Round the divisor and quotient, and estimate.	Divide. Multiply. Subtract and compare.
$9 \leftarrow$ Divide. $113\overline{)9,831}$ $10\ 17 \leftarrow$ Multiply.	Estimate: $\dfrac{900}{100} = 9$	

Eric's first estimate is too large. He can try a number smaller than 9, say 8.

$$\begin{array}{r} 8 \leftarrow \text{Divide.} \\ 113\overline{)9,831} \\ \underline{9\ 04} \leftarrow \text{Multiply.} \\ 79 \leftarrow \text{Subtract and compare.} \end{array}$$

$$\begin{array}{r} 87 \leftarrow \text{Divide.} \\ 113\overline{)9,831} \\ \underline{9\ 04} \\ 791 \\ \underline{791} \leftarrow \text{Multiply.} \\ 0 \leftarrow \text{Subtract and compare.} \end{array}$$

Estimate: $\dfrac{800}{100} = 8$; try 7

$9,831 \div 113 = 87$

Each of the band members will pay $87.

TRY IT OUT

1. $402\overline{)2,412}$ **2.** $764\overline{)767,896}$ **3.** $215\overline{)38,724}$ **4.** $688\overline{)53,714}$ **5.** $365\overline{)74,095}$

Math and Social Studies Data Bank

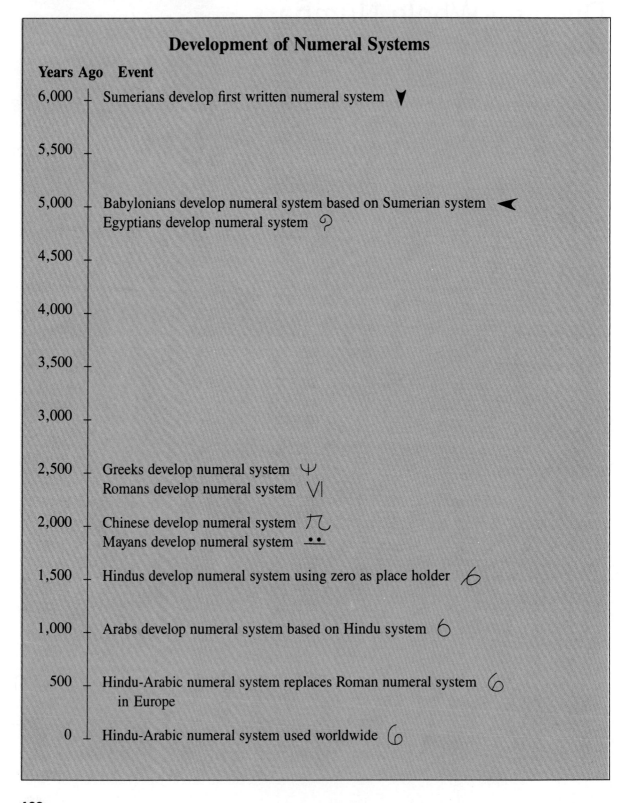

Development of Numeral Systems

Years Ago	Event
6,000	Sumerians develop first written numeral system
5,500	
5,000	Babylonians develop numeral system based on Sumerian system
	Egyptians develop numeral system
4,500	
4,000	
3,500	
3,000	
2,500	Greeks develop numeral system
	Romans develop numeral system
2,000	Chinese develop numeral system
	Mayans develop numeral system
1,500	Hindus develop numeral system using zero as place holder
1,000	Arabs develop numeral system based on Hindu system
500	Hindu-Arabic numeral system replaces Roman numeral system in Europe
0	Hindu-Arabic numeral system used worldwide

Math and Social Studies Data Bank

Ancient Egyptian Numeral System

Ancient Egyptians had a tally system for writing their numbers. Their numerals could be written in any order and then added up to determine the number. Egyptians used a system based on 10, but there was no place value or zero. Egyptians used the following hieroglyphic symbols in their numeral system.

1 *(stroke)*: |

10 *(heelmark)*: ∩

100 *(rope coil)*: ୧

1,000 *(lotus flower)*: ⚘

10,000 *(bent finger)*: 𓆼

100,000 *(fish)*: ⌒○

1,000,000 *(astonished man)*: 𓁨

Examples: 11: ∩|

209: ୧୧ ||| ||| |||

Ancient Hindu Numeral System

Ancient Hindus (in India) had a code system for writing their numbers. They also used place value and eventually a zero as a place holder. Their system was based on 10 and used 10 numerals. Symbols could be put in certain places to form numbers. It was the value of the numeral and the place it was located that determined the number. A zero was used to tell where a place was empty. Hindus used the following numerals.

— = ≡ ⸕ Γ ᕗ 7 ᢺ ◇

Examples: 1,600: — ᕗ ◇ ◇

41: ⸕ —

209: = ◇ ᢺ

Longest Texas Rivers

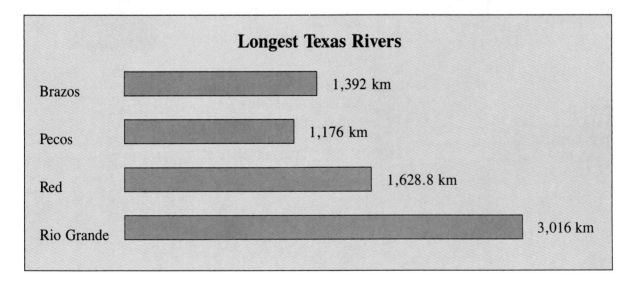

River	Length
Brazos	1,392 km
Pecos	1,176 km
Red	1,628.8 km
Rio Grande	3,016 km

Math and Social Studies Data Bank

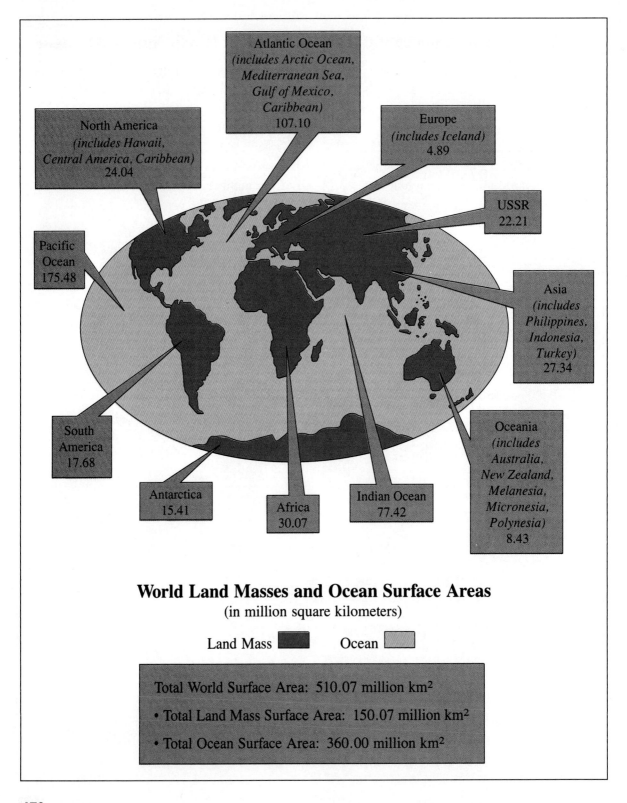

North America
*(includes Hawaii,
Central America, Caribbean)*
24.04

Atlantic Ocean
*(includes Arctic Ocean,
Mediterranean Sea,
Gulf of Mexico,
Caribbean)*
107.10

Europe
(includes Iceland)
4.89

USSR
22.21

Pacific
Ocean
175.48

Asia
*(includes
Philippines,
Indonesia,
Turkey)*
27.34

South
America
17.68

Antarctica
15.41

Africa
30.07

Indian Ocean
77.42

Oceania
*(includes
Australia,
New Zealand,
Melanesia,
Micronesia,
Polynesia)*
8.43

World Land Masses and Ocean Surface Areas
(in million square kilometers)

Land Mass   Ocean

Total World Surface Area: 510.07 million km²

• Total Land Mass Surface Area: 150.07 million km²

• Total Ocean Surface Area: 360.00 million km²

Math and Social Studies Data Bank

Population and Age Groups of Selected Countries

0–14 years old   15–64 years old   65 years and older

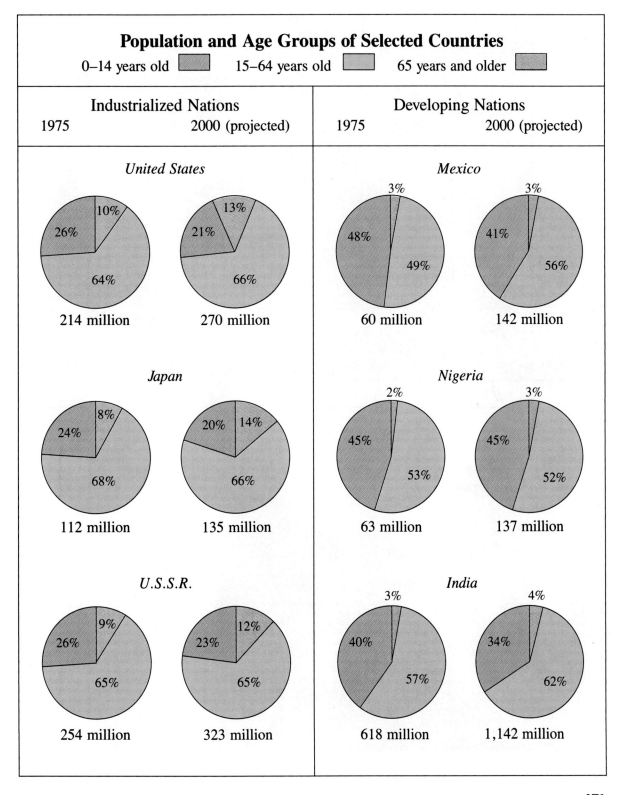

Industrialized Nations

| 1975 | 2000 (projected) |

United States

10%
26%
64%
214 million

13%
21%
66%
270 million

Japan

8%
24%
68%
112 million

20% 14%
66%
135 million

U.S.S.R.

9%
26%
65%
254 million

12%
23%
65%
323 million

Developing Nations

| 1975 | 2000 (projected) |

Mexico

3%
48%
49%
60 million

3%
41%
56%
142 million

Nigeria

2%
45%
53%
63 million

3%
45%
52%
137 million

India

3%
40%
57%
618 million

4%
34%
62%
1,142 million

Math and Social Studies Data Bank

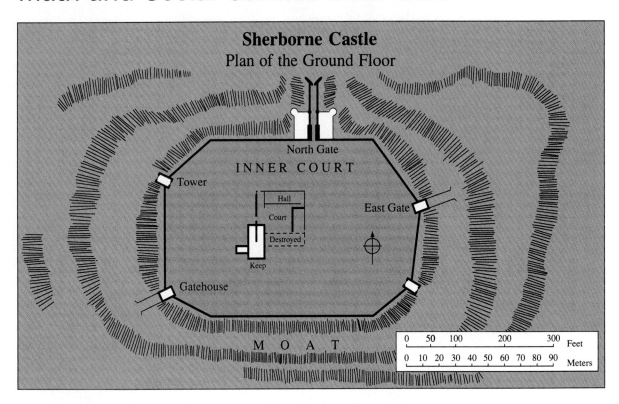

Sherborne Castle
Plan of the Ground Floor

North Gate

INNER COURT

Tower

East Gate

Hall

Court

Destroyed

Keep

Gatehouse

M O A T

| 0 | 50 | 100 | 200 | 300 | Feet |
| 0 | 10 20 30 40 50 60 70 80 90 | | | | Meters |

Tower of London
Plan of the White
Tower Wall

3 m

28 m   28 m

5 m

Math and Health and Fitness Data Bank

Popular Team Sports

Sport	Maximum Number of Players on the Field	Equipment	Maximum Circumference	Maximum Weight
Baseball	9	Ball	23.5 cm	160 g
Basketball	5	Ball	78.0 cm	650 g
Field Hockey	11	Ball	23.5 cm	163 g
Football	11	Ball	(long) 72.4 cm (short) 54.6 cm	425 g
Ice Hockey	6	Puck	(circum) 23.9 cm (width) 2.5 cm	650 g
Soccer	11	Ball	71.1 cm	454 g
Softball	9	Ball	30.8 cm	198 g
Volleyball	6	Ball	67.0 cm	280 g
Water Polo	7	Ball	71.1 cm	450 g

Stan Musial's Championship Batting Averages

Year	Average
1943	0.357
1946	0.365
1948	0.376
1950	0.346
1951	0.355
1952	0.336
1957	0.351

Math and Health and Fitness Data Bank

Approximate Number of Calories Used in One Hour of Certain Activities*

sleeping	60	basketball	300
sitting	80	racquetball	300
standing	100	hockey	300
baseball	130	soccer	400
skateboarding	150	slow running	400
table tennis	180	minitrampoline	400
badminton	200	mountain climbing	420
volleyball	200	swimming	450
walking	220	squash	450
skating	250	skiing	500
dancing	250	jumping rope	600
tennis	250	running	650
brisk walking	300	competitive swimming	650
bicycling	300	water polo	650
gentle jogging	300	climbing (up) stairs	1,200

*Actual number of calories used depends on age, sex, size, and the intensity of active participation.

Blood Groups of Selected World Regions
(Estimated fraction of total population to the nearest hundredth)

	O	A	B	AB
United States	0.46	0.39	0.11	0.04
Western Europe	0.45	0.40	0.11	0.04
India	0.33	0.23	0.38	0.06
Africa	0.51	0.25	0.20	0.04
Asia	0.33	0.36	0.22	0.09
South America	0.50	0.37	0.10	0.03

The chart shows the fraction of a population that is estimated to have each of the four major blood groups.

Math and Science Data Bank

Planet	Surface area	Distance from Sun (AU)*	Speed of planet around Sun (km per s)	Amount of time to revolve around Sun
Mercury	75 million km²	0.39	48	90.0 Earth days
Venus	460 million km²	0.72	35	225 Earth days
Earth	510 million km²	1.00	30	365.25 Earth days
Mars	145 million km²	1.52	24	687.0 Earth days
Jupiter	64,017 million km²	5.20	13	11.9 Earth years
Saturn	45,281 million km²	9.54	10	29.5 Earth years
Uranus	8,436 million km²	19.18	7	84.0 Earth years
Neptune	7,719 million km²	30.06	6	164.8 Earth years
Pluto	111 million km²	39.79	5	248.5 Earth years

*AU stands for astronomical unit. An astronomical unit is approximately 150,000,000 km, which is the distance from the Sun to the Earth.

Math and Science Data Bank

Average Weather Conditions for Miami, Florida

	Spring (Mar., April, May)	Summer (June, July, Aug.)	Autumn (Sept., Oct., Nov.)	Winter (Dec., Jan., Feb.)
Cloud Cover				
clear days	23	8	16	28
partly cloudy days	44	49	43	36
cloudy days	25	35	32	26
Temperature	74.8° F	82.0° F	77.4° F	67.8° F
Precipitation	11.95 in.	22.49 in.	18.52 in.	5.94 in.

Average Rainfall in the Continental United States

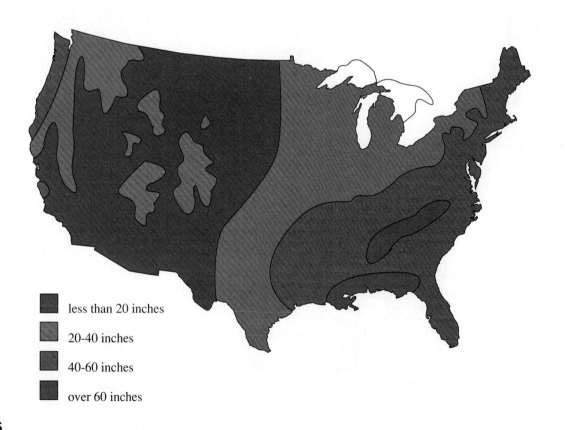

- less than 20 inches
- 20-40 inches
- 40-60 inches
- over 60 inches

Math and Science Data Bank

Crystals

Crystals are structures that occur in many forms in nature. Crystal structures have flat faces that meet in edges. They can be described and classified using geometric ideas and terms. Below are pictures of some mineral crystal shapes.

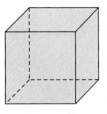

Perfect Salt
Crystal

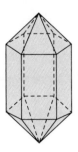

Perfect Quartz
Crystal

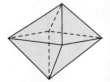

Perfect Diamond
Crystal

Dates of Selected Important Inventions

Instruments: compass (1101); eyeglasses (1286); mechanical clock (1300); telescope (1590); microscope (1590); thermometer (1593); pendulum clock (1657); sea clock (1761); computer (1946); digital watch (1970)

Communications: telegraph (1838); telephone (1876); phonograph (1877); radio (1895); magnetic tape recorder (1898); television (1923); videotape recording (1956); artificial satellite (1957); videocassette recorder (1961); compact disc player (1982)

Transportation: submarine (1776); hot-air balloon (1783); steamship (1807); steam railroad (1830); bicycle (1839); automobile (1885); electric car (1898); airplane (1903); jet airplane (1939); nuclear-powered ship (1950)

477

Math and Language Arts Data Bank

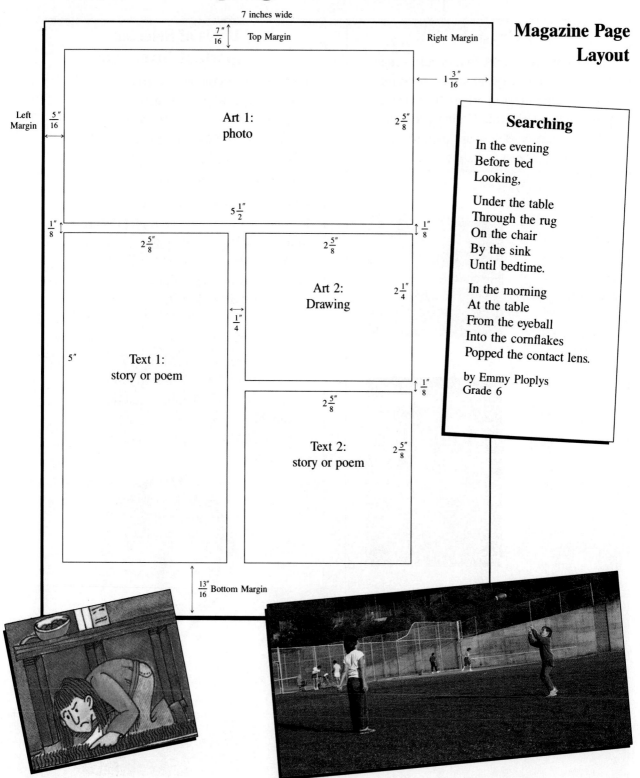

Magazine Page Layout

7 inches wide

$\frac{7''}{16}$ Top Margin

Right Margin

Left Margin $\frac{5''}{16}$

$1\frac{3''}{16}$

Art 1:
photo

$2\frac{5''}{8}$

$5\frac{1''}{2}$

$\frac{1''}{8}$

$\frac{1''}{8}$

$2\frac{5''}{8}$

$2\frac{5''}{8}$

Art 2:
Drawing

$2\frac{1''}{4}$

$\frac{1''}{4}$

5"

Text 1:
story or poem

$\frac{1''}{8}$

$2\frac{5''}{8}$

Text 2:
story or poem

$2\frac{5''}{8}$

$\frac{13''}{16}$ Bottom Margin

Searching

In the evening
Before bed
Looking,

Under the table
Through the rug
On the chair
By the sink
Until bedtime.

In the morning
At the table
From the eyeball
Into the cornflakes
Popped the contact lens.

by Emmy Ploplys
Grade 6

478

Math and Language Arts Data Bank

Storyboard for a 30-Second Commercial

Client: Yummy Soup

Title: It's Mine

Time: 30 Seconds

Lorem ipsum dolor sit amet, consectetuer adipiscing elit, sed diam nonummy. nibh euismod tincidunt ut laoreet dolore magna aliquam erat volutpat. Ut wisi

Duis autem vel eum iriure dolor in hendrerit in vulputate velit esse molestie consequat.

Blandit praesent luptatum zzril delenit augue duis dolore te feugait nulla facilisi. Duis autem vel eum iriure dolor in consequat.

Vel illum dolore eu feugiat nulla facilisis at vero eros accumsan et iusto odio.

Dolore eu feugiat nulla facilisis at vero eros et accumsan et iusto odio.

Autem vel eum iriure dolor in hendrerit in vulputate velit esse molestie consequat, vel illum.

Ut wisi enim ad minim veniam, quis nostrud exercitation ullamcorper suscipit.

Nonummy nibh euismod tincidunt ut laoreet dolore magna aliquam erat volutpa. Blandit praesent luptatum zzril delenit augue duis dolore te feugait nulla.

Ut wisi enim ad minim veniam, quis nostrud exercitation ullamcorper suscipit lobortis.

Feugiat nulla facilisis at vero eros et accumsan et iusto odio dignissim qui. Ut wisi enim ad minim veniam, quis nostrud exercitation ullamcorper suscipit.

Duis autem vel eum iriure dolor in hendrerit in vulputate velit esse molestie consequat.

Blandit praesent luptatum zzril delenit augue duis dolore te feugait nulla.

Math and Language Arts Data Bank

Television Viewing in the United States

- 98 percent of all households own at least one television set.
- An average household has a television set on about 50 hours per week.
- A child may see as many as 20,000 commercials in one year, researchers estimate.

Television Advertising in the United States

- In 1988, the two largest advertisers spent their advertising dollars as follows:

	Total Dollars for Advertising	Dollars for TV Advertising
Company 1	$1,435,000,000	$717,929
Company 2	$1,399,999,000	$508,512

- Generally, networks and stations allow 10 to 12 minutes of a prime-time program hour to be devoted to commercials.
- Three-fourths of all commercials are a half minute long (30 seconds).
- One-fifth of all commercials are $\frac{1}{4}$ minute long (15 seconds).
- The rest of all commercials are divided among lengths of $\frac{1}{3}$ minute, $\frac{3}{4}$ minute, 1 minute, and $1\frac{1}{2}$ minutes (20 seconds, 45 seconds, 60 seconds, or 90 seconds).

Origins of Selected Numerical Prefixes

Prefix	Description		Origin/Meaning
tera-	trillion	(10^{12})	Greek: ''monster''
giga-	billion	(10^{9})	Greek: ''giant''
mega-	million	(10^{6})	Greek: ''great''
kilo-	thousand	(10^{3})	Greek: ''thousand''
hecto-	hundred	(10^{2})	Greek: ''hundred''
deca-	ten	(10^{1})	Greek: ''ten''
deci-	tenth	$\frac{1}{10}$	Latin: ''ten''
centi-	hundredth	$\frac{1}{10^{2}}$	Latin: ''hundred''
milli-	thousandth	$\frac{1}{10^{3}}$	Latin: ''thousand''
micro-	millionth	$\frac{1}{10^{6}}$	Latin: ''small''
nano-	billionth	$\frac{1}{10^{9}}$	Greek: ''dwarf''
pico-	trillionth	$\frac{1}{10^{12}}$	Spanish: ''small''

Math and Fine Arts Data Bank

Colossal Statues of the World

Great Sphinx
2550 B.C., Giza, Egypt
Limestone, 20.1 m tall

1 cm : 3.35 m

Lincoln Memorial
1922, Washington, D.C., U.S.A.
Marble, 5.8 m tall

1 cm : 0.967 m

*Liberty Enlightening
the World*
1886, New York City, U.S.A.
Repoussé copper,
46.1 m tall

1 cm : 7.675 m

Great Buddha
1252, Kamakura, Japan
Bronze, 12.8 m tall

1 cm : 2.13 m

Motherland
1967, Volgograd, Russia
Reinforced concrete,
82.3 m tall

1 cm : 13.72 m

Math and Fine Arts Data Bank

Mobiles

The word *mobile* means "moveable." Mobile sculptures are designed so that parts are moved by currents of air. This form of modern art was begun by the American artist Alexander Calder. It was first exhibited in Paris in 1932.

When a mobile sculpture balances horizontally, a special relationship exists.

(weight of object *X*) × (length *x*) = (weight of object *Y*) × (length *y*)

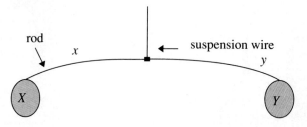

Four ways to balance weights totaling 18 ounces:

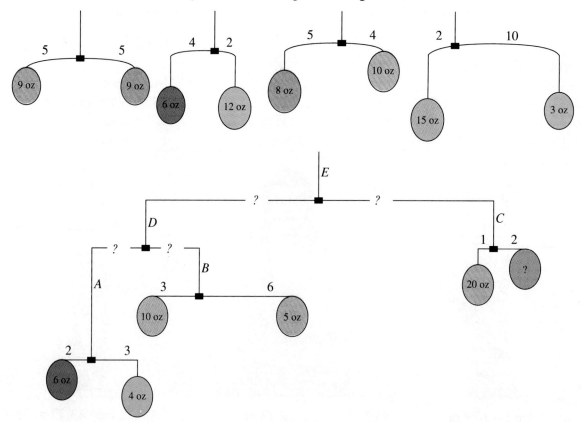

Math and Fine Arts Data Bank

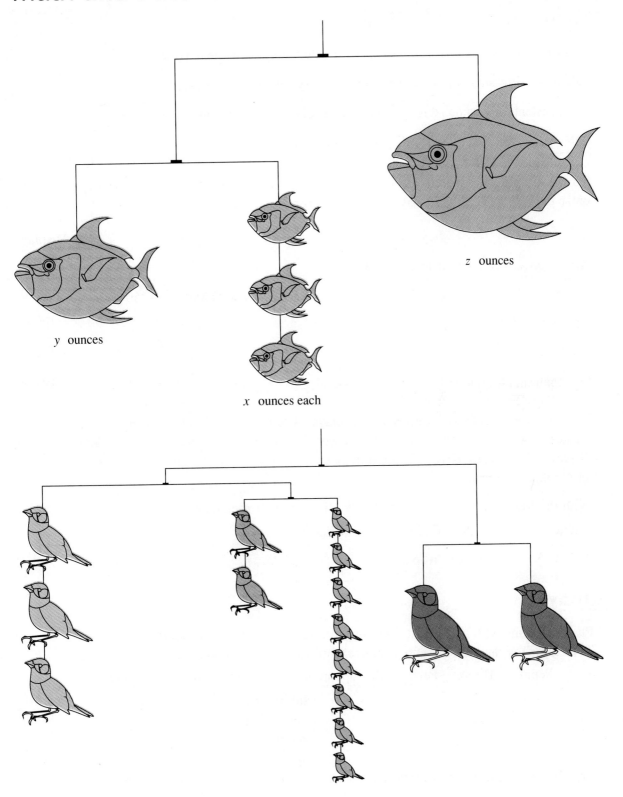

y ounces

x ounces each

z ounces

Basic Operations

Enter the largest number you can on your calculator. Now clear your calculator. Pressing CE/C clears the last entry, error conditions, and constants. Pressing CE/C clears the display and operation. ON/AC clears the memory, display, and operation.

To work problems involving basic operations ($+$, $-$, $\times$, and $\div$), enter the key code just the way you say the problem.

Say	Enter	Display
Nine thousand times four tenths equals	9000 $\times$ .4 $=$	3600
Twelve million divided by 250 equals	12000000 $\div$ 250 $=$	48000
Nine divided by zero equals	9 $\div$ 0 $=$	Error
Five million times one hundred equals	5000000 $\times$ 100	Error
One thousandth divided by five million equals	.001 $\div$ 5000000 $=$	Error

The last three problems create **Error** displays. Attempting to divide by zero creates a **Logic** or **Arithmetic Error.** When a number is too large, many calculators display an **Overflow Error.** When a number is too small for the calculator, there is an **Underflow Error.**

With the Math Explorer, you can also do division with remainders.

Problem	Key Code	Display
$172 \div 5$	172 INT $\div$ 5 $=$	34 2
		└Q┘ └R┘

Activity

Play this game with a partner. Each player enters 4 million on a calculator. Take turns tossing a penny and a dime according to the following rules:

Penny	Dime	Perform this operation on the number in your display
H	T	Multiply by 5
H	H	Divide by 2
T	T	Add 5000
T	H	Subtract 1000

The first person to get an overflow error is the winner. (H = heads, T = tails)

Counting and Patterns

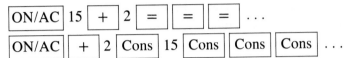

Use your calculator to count by twos starting at 15.

| ON/AC | 15 | + | 2 | = | = | = | ... |

| ON/AC | | + | 2 | Cons | 15 | Cons | Cons | Cons | ... |

Your display should show 17, 19, 21, 23, and so on.

Entering ⟨ + ⟩ 2 or ⟨ + ⟩ 2 ⟨ Cons ⟩ sets up a **constant.**

Each time you press ⟨ = ⟩ or ⟨ Cons ⟩ the calculator adds 2 to the number in the display.

Now count backward by 2.5, starting from 76.

| ON/AC | 76 | − | 2.5 | = | = | = | ... |

| ON/AC | | − | 2.5 | Cons | 76 | Cons | Cons | Cons | ... |

Your display should show 73.5, 71, 68.5, 66, and so on.

Use the **multiplication constant** to multiply 11 by 4, 7, 11, 14, and 22. Enter these key codes:

| ON/AC | × | 11 | Cons | 4 | Cons | 7 | Cons | 11 | Cons | 14 | Cons | 22 | Cons |

or | ON/AC | 4 | × | 11 | = | 7 | = | 11 | = | 14 | = | 22 | = |

Your calculator should display 44, 77, 121, 154, and 242.

Use the **division constant** to divide 81, 72, 45, and 36 by 9.

Enter | ON/AC | ÷ | 9 | Cons | 81 | Cons | 72 | Cons | 45 | Cons | 36 | Cons |

or | ON/AC | 81 | ÷ | 9 | = | 72 | = | 45 | = | 36 | = | .

Your display should show 9, 8, 5, and 4.

Activity

Match each pattern with its description.

1. Divide 192, 96, 64, 48, and 24 by 8.   **a.** 24, 12, 8, 6, 3

2. Multiply 24 by 1, 0.5, 0.25, 0.75, and 0.875.   **b.** 24, 19, 14, 9, 4

3. Start at 24 and count backward by 5s.   **c.** 24, 12, 6, 18, 21

Order of Operations

To do a problem involving more than one operation, do operations inside parentheses first. Next multiply and divide from left to right. Then add and subtract from left to right. The Math Explorer calculator follows order of operations. Enter the key code for each problem.

Problem	Key Code	Display
$6 + 4 \times 7$	6 $+$ 4 $\times$ 7 $=$	34
$(6 + 4) \times 7$	$($ 6 $+$ 4 $)$ $\times$ 7 $=$	70
$124 \div 4 - 2 \times 15$	124 $\div$ 4 $-$ 2 $\times$ 15 $=$	1
$124 \div (4 - 2) \times 15$	124 $\div$ $($ 4 $-$ 2 $)$ $\times$ 15 $=$	930

The **memory keys** on your calculator allow you to remember the result of one calculation while you do another calculation.

M+	Adds the display to the calculator's memory	MR	Recalls the total in memory
M−	Subtracts the display from the calculator's memory	ON/AC	Clears memory and the display

If $20 \div 4 + 72 \div 6 = a$, find a. Then evaluate $(83 + a) \times (a - 2)$.

Enter	Display
ON/AC 20 $\div$ 4 $+$ 72 $\div$ 6 $=$ M+	17
$($ 83 $+$ MR $)$ $\times$ $($ MR $-$ 2 $)$ $=$	1500

Activity

Use only these numerals and symbols: 12 6 $+$ $-$ 4 3 $\times$ $\div$ ( )

Place numbers in the squares and place signs in the circles. Can you find at least one true equation for each total?

TOTALS: 21, 14 30, 33, and 15

Computing with Integers

The [+/−] key changes the sign of the number in the display. Try these.

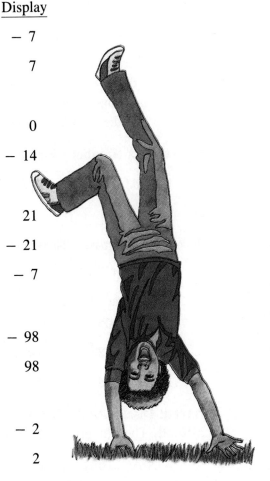

Enter	Display
ON/AC 7 [+/−]	− 7
Press [+/−] again.	7

Adding a negative number and a positive number.

7 + ⁻7   7 [+] 7 [+/−] [=]   0

⁻7 + ⁻7   7 [+/−] [+] 7 [+/−] [=]   − 14

Subtracting positive and negative numbers.

14 − ⁻7   14 [−] 7 [+/−] [=]   21

⁻14 − 7   14 [+/−] [−] 7 [=]   − 21

⁻14 − ⁻7   14 [+/−] [−] 7 [+/−] [=]   − 7

Multiplying positive and negative numbers.

⁻14 × 7   14 [+/−] [×] 7 [=]   − 98

⁻14 × ⁻7   14 [+/−] [×] 7 [+/−] [=]   98

Dividing positive and negative numbers.

14 ÷ ⁻7   14 [÷] 7 [+/−] [=]   − 2

⁻14 ÷ ⁻7   14 [+/−] [÷] 7 [+/−] [=]   2

Activity

Find the sum, difference, product, or quotient. Then plot the points on graph paper and connect the points in order.

	Horizontal	Vertical		Horizontal	Vertical
1.	⁻8 + 3	5 − 7	**6.**	25 ÷ ⁻5	17 + ⁻19
2.	⁻12 ÷ ⁻3	⁻5 − ⁻4	**7.**	2 × ⁻2	⁻15 ÷ ⁻5
3.	⁻6 ÷ ⁻2	⁻55 + 53	**8.**	⁻25 + 22	13 + ⁻9
4.	⁻32 ÷ ⁻16	84 ÷ ⁻21	**9.**	⁻14 − ⁻12	28 ÷ 4
5.	⁻2 × 2	⁻16 − ⁻12	**10.**	⁻80 ÷ ⁻20	0 + ⁻1

Percent

The percent key $\boxed{\%}$ converts the number in the display to a decimal by dividing it by 100. Try this.

Enter $\boxed{\text{ON/AC}}$ 25 $\boxed{\%}$. The display will show 0.25.

Try these percent calculations on your calculator. Does your display match the display shown? If not, what changes can you make to the key codes so that they work for your calculator?

Percent of a Number   Find 6% of 20.

Display

$\boxed{\text{ON/AC}}$ 6 $\boxed{\%}$ $\boxed{\times}$ 20 $\boxed{=}$ 1.2

or   20 $\boxed{\times}$ 6 $\boxed{\%}$ $\boxed{=}$ 1.2

Percent of Increase   The value of a $48 stock rose 25%. The new value is $48 plus 25% of $48.

$\boxed{\text{ON/AC}}$ 48 $\boxed{+}$ 25 $\boxed{\%}$ $\boxed{=}$ 60

or   48 $\boxed{\times}$ 25 $\boxed{\%}$ $\boxed{=}$ $\boxed{+}$ 48 $\boxed{=}$ 60

or   48 $\boxed{\text{M}+}$ $\boxed{\times}$ 25 $\boxed{\%}$ $\boxed{=}$ $\boxed{\text{M}+}$ $\boxed{\text{MR}}$ 60

or   48 $\boxed{\times}$ 125 $\boxed{\%}$ $\boxed{=}$ 60

Percent Discount   A $168 camera is on sale for 20% off. The sale price is $168 minus 20% of $168.

$\boxed{\text{ON/AC}}$ 168 $\boxed{-}$ 20 $\boxed{\%}$ $\boxed{=}$ 134.4

or   168 $\boxed{\times}$ 20 $\boxed{\%}$ $\boxed{=}$ $\boxed{\leftrightarrows}$ $\boxed{+}$ 168 $\boxed{=}$ 134.4

or   168 $\boxed{\times}$ 80 $\boxed{\%}$ $\boxed{=}$ 134.4

Activity

Play this game with a partner. Each person enters 100 on a calculator. Take turns rolling 2 number cubes following the rules below. The first person to reach 500 wins. After each turn, you may want to record your total.

If you roll: Do this:
4, 7, or 11   Increase the number in your display by 40%.
5, 6, 8, or 9   Discount the number in your display by 15%.
2, 3, 10, or 12   The number in your display is 50% of what?

488

Exponents, Powers, and Roots

Here are some ways you can find the value of 4^5, that is, the number 4 raised to the **power** of 5. In each case, the display will show 1024.

| CE/C | 4 | × | 4 | × | 4 | × | 4 | × | 4 | = |

| CE/C | 4 | × | 4 | = | = | = | = |

Use the **power key** | y^x |. | ON/AC | 4 | y^x | 5 | = |

Find 16^2.

			Display
ON/AC	16	×	16	=		256
ON/AC	16	x^2			256

The **square root** key | $\sqrt{}$ | finds a number that can be multiplied by itself to equal the number entered.

The | $\sqrt{}$ | key "undoes" the work of the | x^2 | key.

| ON/AC | 256 | $\sqrt{}$ | 16

Count the number of times you divide by 9 to figure out the power in the equation $9^e = 531441$.

| ON/AC | 531441 | ÷ | 9 | = | = | = | = | = | = |

Activity

Find the values to complete the table. Use the table to help you figure out how to multiply numbers with exponents.

$5^2 =$	$5^5 =$	$6^2 =$	$6^5 =$	$7^2 =$	$7^5 =$
$5^3 =$	$5^6 =$	$6^3 =$	$6^6 =$	$7^3 =$	$7^6 =$
$5^4 =$	$5^7 =$	$6^4 =$	$6^7 =$	$7^4 =$	$7^7 =$

1. $5^2 \times 5^3 =$ $6^2 \times 6^3 =$ $7^2 \times 7^3 =$

2. $5^4 \times 5^2 =$ $6^4 \times 6^2 =$ $7^4 \times 7^2 =$

3. $5^6 \times 5^3 = 5^{\blacksquare}$ $6^6 \times 6^3 = 6^{\blacksquare}$ $7^6 \times 7^3 = 7^{\blacksquare}$

489

Fractions and Decimals

To find the decimal equivalent of a fraction, divide the numerator by the denominator. Find the decimal for $\frac{3}{4}$.

Enter $\boxed{\text{ON/AC}}$ 3 $\boxed{\div}$ 4 $\boxed{=}$. The display shows 0.75.

Find the decimals for $\frac{5}{8}$, $\frac{27}{12}$, $\frac{5}{11}$, and $\frac{4}{3}$. Your display should show 0.625, 2.25, 0.4545455, and 1.3333333.

You can add or subtract fractions by adding or subtracting their decimal equivalents. Add $\frac{5}{8} + \frac{3}{4}$.

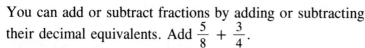

Display

$\boxed{\text{ON/AC}}$ 5 $\boxed{\div}$ 8 $\boxed{=}$ $\boxed{\text{M+}}$ 3 $\boxed{\div}$ 4 $\boxed{=}$ $\boxed{\text{M+}}$ $\boxed{\text{MR}}$ 1.375

Use this key code to subtract $\frac{6}{5} - \frac{1}{2}$.

$\boxed{\text{ON/AC}}$ 6 $\boxed{\div}$ 5 $\boxed{=}$ $\boxed{\text{M+}}$ 1 $\boxed{\div}$ 2 $\boxed{=}$ $\boxed{\text{M−}}$ $\boxed{\text{MR}}$ 0.7

You can multiply fractions by multiplying their decimal equivalents. To multiply $\frac{1}{4} \times \frac{5}{8}$, use this key code.

$\boxed{\text{ON/AC}}$ 1 $\boxed{\div}$ 4 $\boxed{=}$ $\boxed{\text{M+}}$ 5 $\boxed{\div}$ 8 $\boxed{=}$ $\boxed{\times}$ $\boxed{\text{MR}}$ $\boxed{=}$ 0.15625

Multiply $\frac{9}{8} \times \frac{1}{2}$. Your display should show 0.5625.

You can divide fractions by dividing their decimal equivalents. Try this key code for $\frac{7}{8} \div \frac{1}{5}$.

$\boxed{\text{ON/AC}}$ 1 $\boxed{\div}$ 5 $\boxed{=}$ $\boxed{\text{M+}}$ 7 $\boxed{\div}$ 8 $\boxed{=}$ $\boxed{\div}$ $\boxed{\text{MR}}$ $\boxed{=}$ 4.375

Divide $\frac{9}{10}$ by $\frac{1}{4}$. Your display should show 3.6.

Activity

Use your calculator to do these problems. Give your answers in decimal form.

1. $\frac{7}{10} \div \frac{4}{5} =$ **2.** $\frac{2}{10} \div \frac{2}{5} =$ **3.** $\frac{2}{5} \div \frac{1}{4} =$

4. $\frac{3}{8} \div \frac{1}{2} =$ **5.** $\frac{14}{5} \times \frac{6}{8} =$ **6.** $\frac{3}{2} \times \frac{3}{8} =$

7. $\frac{9}{10} \times \frac{3}{2} =$ **8.** $\frac{5}{16} + \frac{6}{8} =$ **9.** $\frac{1}{2} + \frac{5}{8} =$

10. $\frac{15}{16} - \frac{1}{2} =$ **11.** $\frac{1}{4} - \frac{1}{8} =$ **12.** $\frac{5}{7} \div \frac{5}{7} =$

Computing with Fractions

Use the fraction/decimal change key $\boxed{F\!\rightleftharpoons\!D}$ on your
Math Explorer calculator to change 0.75 to a fraction.

Enter	Display
$\boxed{\text{ON/AC}}\ \boxed{.}\ 75\ \boxed{F\!\rightleftharpoons\!D}$	75/100

N/D $\rightarrow$ n/d in the display means that the fraction is not in
simplest form. To simplify the fraction, enter $\boxed{\text{Simp}}\ \boxed{=}$ until
N/D $\rightarrow$ n/d disappears from the display. You can also simplify
the numerator and denominator by a number you choose. For
instance, find the simplest form fraction for 1.35.

$1\ \boxed{.}\ 35\ \boxed{F\!\rightleftharpoons\!D}\ 1\ u\ 35/100$ $\boxed{\text{Simp}}\ 5\ \boxed{=}\ 1\ u\ 7/20$

The u in the display shows that 1 is the whole number or unit
part of a mixed number.

To solve the problems on the Math Explorer, enter the key code
just the way you write the problem. The $\boxed{\text{Ab/c}}$ key changes
fractions to mixed numbers. Try these problems below.

Problem	Key Code	Display
$\dfrac{7}{12} - \dfrac{1}{3}$	$7\ \boxed{/}\ 12\ \boxed{-}\ 1\ \boxed{/}\ 3\ \boxed{=}$	3/12
$\dfrac{7}{8} \div \dfrac{1}{3}$	$7\ \boxed{/}\ 8\ \boxed{\div}\ 1\ \boxed{/}\ 3\ \boxed{=}$	21/8
	$\boxed{\text{Ab/c}}$	2 u 5/8
$1\dfrac{5}{8} \times 2\dfrac{1}{2}$	$1\ \boxed{\text{Unit}}\ 5\ \boxed{/}\ 8\ \boxed{\times}\ 2\ \boxed{\text{Unit}}\ 1\ \boxed{/}\ 2\ \boxed{=}$	65/16
	$\boxed{\text{Ab/c}}$	4 u 1/16

Activity

Write each of the four numbers in a box, and an operation sign in
the triangle. Make a true equation.

1. Use 5, 4, 3, and 2. $A = \dfrac{5}{6}$

2. Use 3, 4, 8, and 15. $A = 4\dfrac{1}{8}$

$$\frac{\square}{\square}\ \triangle\ \frac{\square}{\square} = A$$

Star Count

You are aboard the space ship Commander and are traveling at $\frac{1}{4}$ the speed of light. Stars seem to speed past you. You try to estimate when you think 50 stars have whizzed by. Do you think you can do it? How many stars do you estimate are in the cluster at the right? More than 50 or less than 50?

The computer program below simulates the space ship passing by stars. You must estimate when you think 50 stars have passed. The computer will tell you how close your estimate was to the actual number of stars.

```
10 G = 0
20 PRINT:PRINT:PRINT"STAR COUNT": PRINT "TRY TO ESTIMATE
   THE NUMBER OF STARS YOU":PRINT"SEE GO BY. TO START,
   TYPE 'GO' AND "
30 INPUT "PRESS <RETURN>. ";G$
40 N = 0:PRINT:PRINT
50 Z = INT (10000*RND (1) + 1)
60 K = INT (70*RND (1) + 1)
70 PRINT TAB(K)"*":N = N + 1
80 IF N >SQR (Z) THEN 100
90 GOTO 60
100 PRINT:PRINT:PRINT:INPUT"ESTIMATE THE NUMBER OF
    STARS.";E
110 PRINT "THERE WERE"; N;"STARS."
120 IF N = E THEN GOSUB 180:GOTO 140
130 PRINT "YOU WERE OFF BY";ABS (N − E);"STARS.":G = G + 1
140 PRINT:PRINT"END OF GAME"
150 INPUT "DO YOU WANT TO TRY AGAIN?";Y$
160 IF LEFT$ (Y$,1) = "Y" THEN GOTO 20
170 END
180 PRINT:PRINT"YOU WIN 100 STARS FOR GUESSING THE":
    PRINT"CORRECT NUMBER.":PRINT
190 FOR P = 1 TO 5
200 FOR N = 1 TO 20:PRINT"*";:NEXT N
210 PRINT:NEXT P
220 RETURN
```

Estimating Averages

Which state in the United States is closest to the average in area? Since there are 50 states, this is not an easy question. The list shows the areas of the first 8 states in alphabetical order. What is your estimate of the average area of these 8 states? Which state is nearest to the average in size?

It would be a long task for you to find the average area of all 50 states in the United States using pencil and paper. Using the computer program below and data you can find for the sizes of the states, you can find the solution to the problem quickly.

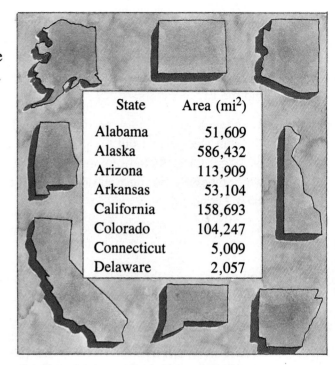

State	Area (mi^2)
Alabama	51,609
Alaska	586,432
Arizona	113,909
Arkansas	53,104
California	158,693
Colorado	104,247
Connecticut	5,009
Delaware	2,057

```
10 GOSUB 110
20 PRINT:PRINT"HOW MANY NUMBERS DO YOU WANT TO":INPUT"AVERAGE?";N
30 PRINT"TYPE EACH NUMBER AND PRESS <RETURN>>"
40 T = 0:C = 0
50 FOR X = 1 TO N:INPUT E:T + E:NEXT X
55 PRINT:INPUT"ESTIMATED AVERAGE?";A:PRINT
60 PRINT"ESTIMATE";TAB( 12)"AVERAGE"; TAB( 24)"DIFFERENCE"
65 PRINT A; TAB( 12)T/N; TAB( 24) ABS (T/N − A)
70 PRINT:INPUT"MORE NUMBERS TO AVERAGE?";Y$
80 IF LEFT$(Y$,1) = "Y" THEN 20
100 END
110 PRINT"ESTIMATING AVERAGES"
120 PRINT"TYPE IN HOW MANY NUMBERS YOU WISH TO":PRINT"AVERAGE. THEN
    TYPE EACH NUMBER. THE":PRINT"COMPUTER WILL CALCULATE THE
    AVERAGE."
130 RETURN
```

Guess and Check

Roxie thought of two numbers. She told Larry the sum of the two numbers was 21 and the product of the two numbers was 108. Larry tried to use the strategy of Guess and Check to find the two numbers.

He thought: $10 + 11 = 21$, but $10 \times 11 = 110$. The sum was correct but the product was a little too large. Larry thought he must be close to the two numbers so he must guess again and then check his guess.

What do you think Roxie's two numbers were?

You can practice the Guess and Check strategy using the computer program below.

```
10 PRINT:PRINT:PRINT"GUESS AND CHECK STRATEGY"
20 A = INT (10*RND(1) + 1):B = INT(20*RND(1) + 1)
30 PRINT"THE SUM OF TWO NUMBERS IS";A + B;"."
40 PRINT"THE PRODUCT OF THE TWO NUMBERS IS ";A*B;"."
50 PRINT"USE THE GUESS AND CHECK STRATEGY TO":PRINT"FIND THE TWO
   NUMBERS."
60 PRINT:INPUT"FIRST NUMBER =";F:INPUT"SECOND NUMBER =";S
70 PRINT:PRINT"SUM =";F + S,"PRODUCT =";F*S
80 IF A = F AND B = S OR A = S AND B = F THEN GOTO 110
90 PRINT:PRINT"NOT CORRECT.":INPUT"DO YOU WANT TO TRY AGAIN?";Y$:IF
   LEFT$(Y$,1) = "Y" THEN PRINT:PRINT:GOTO 30
100 GOTO 120
110 PRINT:PRINT"YOU HAVE FOUND THE TWO NUMBERS."
120 INPUT"DO YOU WANT ANOTHER PROBLEM?";Y$
130 IF LEFT$(Y$,1) = "Y" THEN 10
140 END
```

Estimating Length

Estimate the length and the width of your classroom in feet. Measure the length and width to get the actual measurements. Are your estimates close?

It is important to develop good estimation skills. In the computer program below you can practice estimating the lengths of unmarked segments using a unit measure.

```
10 U = INT (6*RND(1) + 3)
20 S = INT (78*RND(1) + 1)
30 IF S < U THEN 10
40 L = INT (S/U*10)/10
50 PRINT:PRINT:FOR N = 1 TO U:PRINT " – ";:NEXT N:PRINT"1
   UNIT":PRINT:PRINT:FOR N = 1 TO S:PRINT " – ";:NEXT N
60 PRINT:PRINT:GOSUB 150:PRINT:INPUT"WHAT IS YOUR ESTIMATE?";E
70 PRINT:PRINT"LENGTH","EST.","DIFF."
80 PRINT L,E,ABS (L – E)
90 PRINT:INPUT "TRY AGAIN? (Y/N)";Y$
100 IF LEFT$ (Y$,1) = "Y" THEN 10
130 END
150 PRINT "ESTIMATING LENGTH":PRINT "USE THE UNIT SEGMENT SHOWN TO
   ESTIMATE"
160 PRINT "THE LENGTH OF THE UNMARKED SEGMENT TO":PRINT"THE
   NEAREST TENTH OF A UNIT."
170 RETURN
```

Lowest Terms

There were 93,279 people at the stadium to see a football game. There were 186 free passes given out to some of the people who attended the game. What part of the total number of people were given free passes?

Estimate a simple fraction to show what part of the total number of people received free passes to the game. Then try to find the lowest-terms fraction.

To find the lowest-terms fraction, you can divide a numerator and denominator by their greatest common factor (GCF). For large numbers, the GCF may be hard to find. You may have to divide repeatedly by smaller factors. The computer program below will do this for you quickly and accurately.

```
10 GOSUB 200
20 PRINT:INPUT"ENTER NUMERATOR";N
30 PRINT:INPUT"ENTER DENOMINATOR";D
40 PRINT:PRINT "WHAT NUMBER CAN DIVIDE BOTH "N:PRINT"AND"D
   "EVENLY?":INPUT X
50 A = N/X:IF INT (A) < > N/X THEN PRINT X" WILL NOT DIVIDE "N" EVENLY.":PRINT
   "TRY AGAIN.":GOTO 40
60 B = D/X: IF INT (B) < > D/X THEN PRINT X" WILL NOT DIVIDE "D" EVENLY.":PRINT
   "TRY AGAIN.":GOTO 40
70 PRINT:PRINT:PRINT"THE NEW FRACTION IS "A"/"B"."
80 PRINT"REDUCE"A"/"B" AGAIN?":INPUT Y$
90 N = A:D = B: IF LEFT$ (Y$,1) = "Y" THEN 40
100 PRINT:INPUT"REDUCE A NEW FRACTION? (Y/N) ";Y$
110 IF LEFT$(Y$,1) = "Y" THEN GOTO 20:PRINT
120 END
200 PRINT"LOWEST TERMS FRACTIONS"
210 PRINT"USE THIS PROGRAM TO HELP FIND LOWEST"
220 PRINT"TERMS FRACTIONS. BE SURE TO CONTINUE"
230 PRINT"DIVIDING UNTIL THE NUMERATOR AND"
240 PRINT"DENOMINATOR HAVE ONLY 1 AS A COMMON":PRINT "FACTOR."
250 RETURN
```

Medians

Mary Ann liked to read about baseball teams and players. She saw this list of National League baseball stadiums showing the seating capacities. She could search through the numbers and find the largest and smallest stadiums. To find the stadium with the median seating capacity required arranging the numbers in order and finding the middle number.

What is the median seating capacity for these baseball stadiums?

It is sometimes difficult to sort a long list of numbers and place them in order of size. The computer program below will sort the numbers and compute the median of the numbers quickly and accurately.

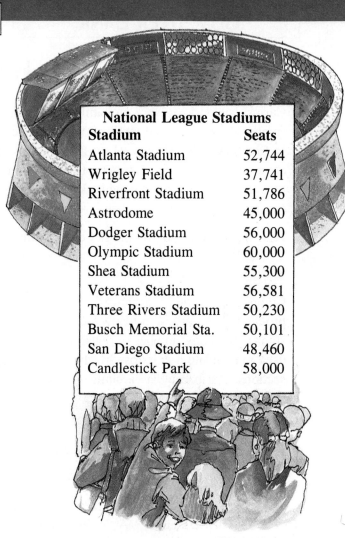

National League Stadiums	
Stadium	**Seats**
Atlanta Stadium	52,744
Wrigley Field	37,741
Riverfront Stadium	51,786
Astrodome	45,000
Dodger Stadium	56,000
Olympic Stadium	60,000
Shea Stadium	55,300
Veterans Stadium	56,581
Three Rivers Stadium	50,230
Busch Memorial Sta.	50,101
San Diego Stadium	48,460
Candlestick Park	58,000

```
10 PRINT:PRINT:PRINT"MEDIANS":PRINT"GIVE HOW MANY NUMBERS YOU WANT AND
   TYPE":PRINT"THEM IN ANY ORDER. THE COMPUTER WILL":PRINT"SORT THE
   NUMBERS AND GIVE THE MEDIAN."
20 PRINT:INPUT"HOW MANY NUMBERS DO YOU WANT?";N:DIM X(N)
30 PRINT"TYPE EACH NUMBER AND PRESS <RETURN>".
40 FOR I = 1 TO N:PRINT I;:INPUT X(I): NEXT I:PRINT
50 FOR I = 1 TO N − 1
60 FOR J = 1 TO N − 1
70 IF X(J) < = X(J + 1) THEN GOTO 90
80 T = X(J):X(J) = X(J + 1):X(J + 1) = T
90 NEXT J
100 NEXT I
110 PRINT"THE" N"NUMBERS IN ORDER ARE:"
120 FOR I = 1 TO N:PRINT I,:PRINT X(I): NEXT I
130 PRINT:IF INT (N/ 2) < > N/ 2 THEN PRINT"THE MEDIAN IS ";X(INT (N/ 2) + 1):
    GOTO 150
140 PRINT"THE MEDIAN IS "(X(N/2) + X((N/2) + 1))/2
150 END
```

Simulating a Probability Experiment

Carlos wanted to solve a probability problem with a
spinner divided into 10 sections of equal size. He wanted
to find how many times each of the numbers 1–10 would
come up in 100 spins. He did not have a spinner and
thought this experiment would take him a long time to
finish.

How many times do you predict each number will occur?

Computers can be programmed to simulate probability
problems. The program below can be used to simulate a
spinner with any number of equal sections. It can be
used to simulate a coin toss by choosing a spinner with 2
sections. It can simulate a number cube toss by choosing
a spinner with 6 sections. You can choose any number of
trials for the spinner.

```
10 PRINT"PROBABILITY SPINNER":PRINT"THIS IS AN EXPERIMENT IN
   PROBABILITY.":PRINT"CHOOSE A SPINNER WITH ANY NUMBER OF":PRINT
   "EQUAL PARTS. CHOOSE ANY NUMBER OF":PRINT"SPINS. THE COMPUTER
   WILL QUICKLY GIVE":PRINT"THE OUTCOME."
20 PRINT:INPUT"HOW MANY SECTIONS OF EQUAL SIZE?";X
30 DIM D(X)
40 FOR N = 1 TO X:D(N) = 0:NEXT N
50 INPUT"HOW MANY SPINS DO YOU WANT?";Y:PRINT
60 FOR I = 1 TO Y:R = INT (X*RND(1)) + 1
70 LET D(R) = D(R) + 1:NEXT I
80 PRINT"NUMBER","FREQUENCY"
90 FOR N = 1 TO X:PRINT N,D(N):NEXT N
100 PRINT:INPUT"DO YOU WANT TO TRY AGAIN?";Y$
110 IF LEFT$ (Y$,1) = "Y"THEN PRINT:GOTO 10
120 END
```

Prime Factorization

A large business was going to give a prize
to their millionth customer. Rita's number
was next in line. She said "I think 1,000,001
is a prime number so I should also get a
prize." Was Rita correct about 1,000,001
being a prime number?

It may be difficult to decide if a large number such as
1,000,001 is a prime number. The computer program
below will find the prime factors of any number that you
may choose. You can check 1,000,001 with the program.

```
10 GOSUB 200
20 INPUT"FIND PRIME FACTORS OF WHAT NUMBER?";X:X1 = X
30 PRINT:PRINT"DIVIDE "X" BY WHAT PRIME NUMBER?"
40 INPUT D:IF D = 1 THEN 160
50 IF D = 2 THEN 70
60 GOSUB 120
70 Q = X/D
80 IF Q < > INT (Q) THEN PRINT D"DOES NOT DIVIDE"X:GOTO 30
90 N = N + 1:F(N) = D
100 PRINT X"/"D" = "Q:IF Q = 1 THEN 170
110 X = Q:GOTO 30
120 FOR C = 2 TO D − 1
130 IF D/C = INT (D/C) THEN 160
140 NEXT C
150 RETURN
160 PRINT D"IS NOT A PRIME NUMBER.":GOTO 30
170 PRINT:PRINT"THE PRIME FACTORS OF "X1" ARE:":FOR J = 1 TO N − 1:PRINT
    F(J)",";:NEXT J:PRINT F(N): PRINT:INPUT"DO YOU WANT TO TRY AGAIN?";Y$
180 IF LEFT$ (Y$,1) = "Y" THEN PRINT:GOTO 10
190 END
200 PRINT:PRINT:PRINT"PRIME FACTORIZATION"
210 PRINT"USE THIS PROGRAM TO HELP FIND THE PRIME"
220 PRINT "FACTORS OF A NUMBER. USE THE RULES OF"
230 PRINT"DIVISIBILITY TO CHOOSE PRIME DIVISORS.":PRINT"GOOD FIRST
    CHOICES ARE 2 OR 3.":PRINT
240 RETURN
```

MORE PRACTICE BANK

Set A   For use after page 5.

Write the numbers in expanded form.

1. 748   **2.** 3,602   **3.** 4,500   **4.** 7,468

Give each number in standard form.

5. 8,000 + 500 + 30 + 8   **6.** 9,000 + 600 + 20 + 7

Set B   For use after page 7.

Write the numbers in standard form.

1. 3,000,000,000 + 800,000,000 + 40,000,000 + 6,000,000

2. six hundred forty-nine million, three hundred fifty-four thousand

Set C   For use after page 9.

Write >, <, or = for each ⫿⫿ .

1. 1,043 ⫿⫿ 1,403   **2.** 36,455 ⫿⫿ 36,455   **3.** 9,003 ⫿⫿ 8,973

Order from greatest to least.   Order from least to greatest.

4. 408,577; 488,700; 48,980   **5.** 98,501; 10,999; 103,275

Set D   For use after page 13.

Use compatible numbers to find each sum mentally.

1. 25 + 16 + 6   **2.** 40 + 58 + 80   **3.** 15 + 55 + 35

Break apart the numbers to find each product mentally.

4. 4×14 **5.** 3×19 **6.** 18×5 **7.** 64×6

Set E   For use after page 14.

Solve.

1. $21 \div (8 - 1)$ **2.** $5 + 15 \div 3$ **3.** $36 - 4 \times 8$ **4.** $6 \div 3 \times 2$

MORE PRACTICE BANK

Set A For use after page 17.

Estimate by rounding to the nearest thousand.

1. 1,050	**2.** 2,500	**3.** 1,329	**4.** 6,117	**5.** 7,277
+ 3,760	+ 1,431	+ 6,727	+ 5,089	+ 3,941

Estimate by rounding to the nearest dollar.

6. $1.48	**7.** $7.75	**8.** $3.80	**9.** $1.85	**10.** $4.27
+ 6.72	+ 3.25	+ 4.50	+ 9.17	+ 1.88

Set B For use after page 19.

Find the sums or differences.

1. 7,264	**2.** 18,426	**3.** 33,427	**4.** 7,563	**5.** 4,920
+ 1,966	+ 54,219	+ 18,916	− 2,088	− 1,377

Set C For use after page 33.

Write the decimal.

1. seven tenths   **2.** one and three tenths   **3.** twenty-one hundredths

Write the word name for each decimal.

4. 0.6   **5.** 3.7   **6.** 32.6   **7.** 40.16

Set D For use after page 35.

Write the decimal.

1. five hundred eighty-nine thousandths   **2.** two and five hundred six thousandths

Write a word name for each decimal.

3. 3.678   **4.** 0.525   **5.** 0.402   **6.** 8.005

Set A   For use after page 37.

Give the missing numbers.

1. 2 cm = ▓ m

2. 7,500 cm = ▓ m

3. 350 cm = ▓ m

4. 4,500 m = ▓ km

5. 4.3 km = ▓ m

6. 2,400 dm = ▓ m

Set B   For use after page 41.

Write the decimal.

1. seven and six hundred twenty-three hundred-thousandths

2. twenty-four and seven thousand sixty-two ten-thousandths

3. nine hundred seventy-five hundred-thousandths

4. eight hundred fifty-six thousandths

5. five and twenty-seven ten-thousandths

Set C   For use after page 43.

Write >, <, or = for each ▓

1. 0.44 ▓ 0.43   2. 3.98 ▓ 3.89   3. 1.99 ▓ 1.0   4. 7 ▓ 8.7   5. 1.6 ▓ 1.4999

Order from greatest to least.

6. 3.206; 3.026; 2.930; 1.500; 4.086   7. 0.677; 0.855; 0.760; 0.078; 0.541

Set D   For use after page 44.

Round to the nearest tenth.

1. 6.25   2. 0.19   3. 5.917   4. 0.08   5. 0.459

Set E   For use after page 49.

Estimate by rounding to the nearest whole number.

1. 20.35	2. 9.768	3. 16.3	4. 14.7	5. 17.89
+ 8.76	+ 6.547	− 8.9	− 6.8	− 9.42

Set A   For use after page 51.

Add or subtract.

1.	17.2	**2.**	42.1	**3.**	7.335	**4.**	1,546.12	**5.**	$798.05
	11.8		118.06		0.862		− 996.85		− 36.54
	+ 9.5		+ 1.97		9.577				
					+ 1.086				

Set B   For use after page 63.

Find the products.

1. 9 × 10   **2.** 300 × 4   **3.** 6 × 2,000   **4.** 7 × 100   **5.** 4,000 × 9

Use rounding and mental math to estimate each product.

6.	267	**7.**	195	**8.**	55	**9.**	366	**10.**	92
	× 3		× 4		× 54		× 42		× 45

Set C   For use after page 75.

Multiply.

1.	0.03	**2.**	0.004	**3.**	0.05	**4.**	15	**5.**	0.6
	× 0.2		× 8		× 0.6		× 0.003		× 0.02

Set D   For use after page 77.

Multiply.

1.	3.4	**2.**	0.005	**3.**	0.04	**4.**	1.5	**5.**	0.4
	× 0.6		× 6		× 0.03		× 0.6		× 0.04

Multiply.

6. 424 × 0.006   **7.** 0.67 × 10   **8.** 40 × 0.06   **9.** 0.009 × 8   **10.** 1.28 × 0.70

Set E   For use after page 81.

Find the standard form.

1. 3^5 **2.** 11^5 **3.** 23^2 **4.** 34^3 **5.** 5^4

MORE PRACTICE BANK

Set A   For use after page 83.

Write all the factors of each number. Then write *prime* or
composite for each.

1. 7   **2.** 36

3. 23   **4.** 87

Set B   For use after page 95.

Divide and check.

1. 630 ÷ 9   **2.** 450 ÷ 5   **3.** 360 ÷ 4   **4.** 540 ÷ 6

5. 1,200 ÷ 3   **6.** 2,400 ÷ 8   **7.** 4,200 ÷ 6   **8.** 3,000 ÷ 5

Set C   For use after page 97.

Estimate the quotients. Choose compatible numbers.

1. 4)172   **2.** 5)361   **3.** 7)222   **4.** 9)537   **5.** 8)423   **6.** 3)266

Set D   For use after page 99.

Divide and check.

1. 4)184   **2.** 7)457   **3.** 2)130   **4.** 3)232   **5.** 5)194

Set E   For use after page 103.

Find the averages to the nearest whole number.

1. 34, 22, 29   **2.** 17, 11, 25, 26   **3.** 43, 26, 25, 33

4. 48, 26, 15, 34, 60   **5.** 23, 19, 71, 22, 42

Set F   For use after page 107.

Find the quotients.

1. 75)11,400   **2.** 43)23,944   **3.** 67)385

4. 25)28,591   **5.** 52)18,627   **6.** 34)43,207

Set A   For use after page 108.

Estimate each quotient. Use rounding.

1. $41.98 \div 7.16$ **2.** $16.43 \div 3.98$ **3.** $19.997 \div 5.08$

4. $62.76 \div 6.84$ **5.** $48.11 \div 6.43$ **6.** $26.50 \div 2.84$

Set B   For use after page 113.

Divide.

1. $2\overline{)1.888}$ **2.** $5\overline{)15.6}$ **3.** $3\overline{)20.4}$ **4.** $4\overline{)217.2}$ **5.** $6\overline{)14.88}$

6. $7\overline{)9.59}$ **7.** $9\overline{)4.41}$ **8.** $2\overline{)17.04}$ **9.** $9\overline{)248.4}$ **10.** $4\overline{)6.92}$

Set C   For use after page 117.

Find the quotients. Round to the nearest tenth.

1. $3\overline{)14}$ **2.** $6\overline{)17}$ **3.** $17\overline{)6.35}$ **4.** $23\overline{)85}$

Round to the nearest hundredth or cent.

5. $7\overline{)36}$ **6.** $17\overline{)5}$ **7.** $5\overline{)\$2.17}$ **8.** $28\overline{)\$78.22}$

Set D   For use after page 121.

Divide. Round to the nearest hundredth when necessary.

1. $4.3\overline{)14.85}$ **2.** $0.5\overline{)28.06}$ **3.** $0.53\overline{)3.352}$

4. $3.4\overline{)108}$ **5.** $0.75\overline{)8}$ **6.** $0.64\overline{)5.893}$

Set E   For use after page 135.

1. What is the approximate range of numbers represented in this graph?

2. How many intervals are there?

3. What is the number of units in each interval?

4. Create a scale for the data in this graph if the scale is to omit the numbers less than 80.

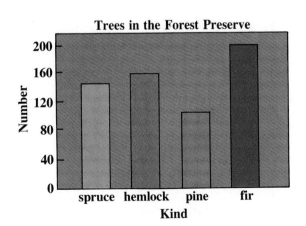

Trees in the Forest Preserve

MORE PRACTICE BANK

Set A   For use after page 137.

1. This table shows the number of sit-ups Anne did over five weeks. Use the data to make a line graph.

2. In which week did Anne improve the most over the week before?

Week Number	Number of Sit-ups
0	0
1	6
2	18
3	22
4	31
5	21

Set B   For use after page 139.

1. This table shows how Juan spent all of his after-school time on Tuesday. Use the data to make a circle graph.

2. Which activity did Juan spend the most time doing? Which activities did he spend about the same amount of time doing?

Activity	Time
Playing with dog	0.24
Reading	0.38
Listening to music	0.13
Playing kick-the-can	0.25

Set C   For use after page 147.

Find the mean, median and mode for the following sets of numbers.

1. 42, 54, 31, 33, 54   **2.** 23, 19, 14, 23   **3.** 25, 30, 29, 18, 22, 29

Set D   For use after page 163.

Give the next three equivalent fractions.

1. $\dfrac{3}{5}$ **2.** $\dfrac{1}{6}$ **3.** $\dfrac{2}{7}$ **4.** $\dfrac{1}{5}$

Give the missing numerator.

5. $\dfrac{1}{3} = \dfrac{}{18}$ **6.** $\dfrac{3}{8} = \dfrac{}{16}$ **7.** $\dfrac{1}{4} = \dfrac{}{20}$ **8.** $\dfrac{3}{5} = \dfrac{}{15}$

Set A   For use after page 165.

Give the greatest common factor.

1. 9, 18   **2.** 12, 21   **3.** 5, 30   **4.** 9, 16   **5.** 12, 18

6. 32, 36   **7.** 20, 30   **8.** 7, 21   **9.** 36, 48   **10.** 15, 27

Set B   For use after page 167.

Reduce to lowest terms.

1. $\dfrac{9}{12}$ **2.** $\dfrac{10}{12}$ **3.** $\dfrac{3}{24}$ **4.** $\dfrac{10}{15}$ **5.** $\dfrac{14}{21}$ **6.** $\dfrac{4}{16}$

Set C   For use after page 169.

Find the least common denominator of each pair of fractions.

1. $\dfrac{1}{6}, \dfrac{2}{3}$ **2.** $\dfrac{1}{4}, \dfrac{1}{12}$ **3.** $\dfrac{1}{10}, \dfrac{4}{15}$ **4.** $\dfrac{2}{3}, \dfrac{4}{8}$ **5.** $\dfrac{1}{3}, \dfrac{3}{5}$ **6.** $\dfrac{2}{3}, \dfrac{1}{4}$

Set D   For use after page 171.

Give the correct sign, $>$, $<$, or $=$ for each ⫿ .

1. $\dfrac{3}{9}$ ⫿ $\dfrac{3}{4}$ **2.** $\dfrac{3}{4}$ ⫿ $\dfrac{1}{16}$ **3.** $\dfrac{2}{6}$ ⫿ $\dfrac{3}{9}$ **4.** $\dfrac{2}{5}$ ⫿ $\dfrac{3}{4}$

Order from least to greatest.

5. $\dfrac{2}{3}, \dfrac{3}{4}, \dfrac{2}{5}$ **6.** $\dfrac{2}{5}, \dfrac{1}{3}, \dfrac{5}{9}$ **7.** $\dfrac{6}{7}, \dfrac{3}{5}, \dfrac{2}{3}$

Set E   For use after page 172.

Write as a whole or mixed number. Reduce to lowest terms.

1. $\dfrac{9}{4}$ **2.** $\dfrac{15}{2}$ **3.** $\dfrac{12}{10}$ **4.** $\dfrac{11}{4}$ **5.** $\dfrac{10}{3}$ **6.** $\dfrac{6}{2}$

Write each mixed number as an improper fraction.

7. $5\dfrac{1}{6}$ **8.** $1\dfrac{3}{10}$ **9.** $8\dfrac{3}{5}$ **10.** $9\dfrac{1}{3}$ **11.** $6\dfrac{2}{7}$ **12.** $3\dfrac{4}{9}$

MORE PRACTICE BANK

Set A For use after page 179.

Write these fractions as decimals.

1. $\frac{1}{2}$　　　　**2.** $\frac{1}{4}$　　　　**3.** $\frac{1}{5}$　　　　**4.** $\frac{1}{8}$　　　　**5.** $\frac{2}{5}$

6. $\frac{3}{5}$　　　　**7.** $\frac{4}{5}$　　　　**8.** $\frac{3}{8}$　　　　**9.** $\frac{5}{8}$　　　　**10.** $\frac{7}{8}$

Set B For use after page 191.

Find the sums and differences. Reduce answers to lowest terms.

1. $\begin{array}{r} 2\frac{1}{3} \\ + \ \frac{1}{3} \\ \hline \end{array}$　　**2.** $\begin{array}{r} 3\frac{2}{10} \\ + \ \frac{1}{10} \\ \hline \end{array}$　　**3.** $\begin{array}{r} \frac{2}{8} \\ + \ \frac{4}{8} \\ \hline \end{array}$　　**4.** $\begin{array}{r} \frac{1}{6} \\ + \ \frac{3}{6} \\ \hline \end{array}$

5. $\begin{array}{r} 4\frac{5}{12} \\ - \ 2\frac{1}{12} \\ \hline \end{array}$　　**6.** $\begin{array}{r} 6\frac{4}{5} \\ - \ 1\frac{2}{5} \\ \hline \end{array}$　　**7.** $\begin{array}{r} 1\frac{7}{8} \\ - \ \frac{3}{8} \\ \hline \end{array}$　　**8.** $\begin{array}{r} 2\frac{1}{6} \\ + \ 1\frac{5}{6} \\ \hline \end{array}$

Set C For use after page 195.

Estimate each sum and difference.

1. $1\frac{1}{4} + 2\frac{1}{5}$　　　　**2.** $6\frac{2}{5} + 4\frac{3}{10}$　　　　**3.** $10\frac{1}{2} + 1\frac{7}{8}$

4. $5\frac{2}{3} - 3\frac{1}{4}$　　　　**5.** $8\frac{1}{3} - 2\frac{1}{12}$

Set D For use after page 199.

Add or subtract.

1. $\begin{array}{r} \frac{1}{6} \\ + \ \frac{1}{3} \\ \hline \end{array}$　　**2.** $\begin{array}{r} \frac{3}{4} \\ + \ \frac{1}{2} \\ \hline \end{array}$　　**3.** $\begin{array}{r} \frac{1}{4} \\ + \ \frac{3}{8} \\ \hline \end{array}$　　**4.** $\begin{array}{r} \frac{7}{8} \\ - \ \frac{5}{6} \\ \hline \end{array}$　　**5.** $\begin{array}{r} \frac{7}{10} \\ - \ \frac{33}{100} \\ \hline \end{array}$

Set A   For use after page 203.

Add. Reduce to lowest terms.

1. $3\frac{1}{10}$
$+ 2\frac{3}{5}$

2. $8\frac{1}{6}$
$+ 2$

3. $21\frac{7}{10}$
$+ 19\frac{1}{5}$

4. $8\frac{3}{10}$
$+ 62\frac{1}{4}$

5. $20\frac{1}{6}$
$+ 40\frac{1}{4}$

Set B   For use after page 205.

Subtract. Reduce to lowest terms.

1. $35\frac{2}{3}$
$- 1\frac{1}{12}$

2. $37\frac{7}{10}$
$- 24\frac{1}{2}$

3. $26\frac{4}{5}$
$- 12\frac{1}{2}$

4. $20\frac{5}{8}$
$- 14\frac{3}{16}$

5. $67\frac{5}{8}$
$- 14\frac{1}{3}$

Set C   For use after page 207.

Find the sums and differences mentally.

1. $2\frac{3}{5} + \frac{1}{5} + 7\frac{2}{5}$

2. $6\frac{3}{4} + 6\frac{5}{8} + \frac{1}{8}$

3. $\frac{7}{12} + 2\frac{1}{6} + 5\frac{2}{3}$

4. $6 - 5\frac{5}{6}$

5. $15 - 4\frac{7}{10}$

6. $22 - 10\frac{5}{8}$

Set D   For use after page 219.

Use mental math to find each answer.

1. $\frac{2}{3}$ of 9

2. $\frac{3}{5}$ of 25

3. $\frac{1}{8}$ of 32

4. $\frac{3}{8}$ of 72

5. $\frac{5}{6}$ of 36

6. $\frac{3}{4}$ of 36

7. $\frac{1}{4}$ of 20

8. $\frac{1}{2}$ of 50

9. $\frac{3}{8}$ of 24

MORE PRACTICE BANK

Set A   For use after page 223.

Multiply. Write the product in lowest terms.

1. $\frac{2}{3} \times \frac{1}{4}$ **2.** $4 \times \frac{1}{2}$ **3.** $\frac{2}{5} \times \frac{5}{8}$ **4.** $\frac{2}{3} \times 6$

5. $\frac{3}{5} \times \frac{5}{3}$ **6.** $5 \times \frac{3}{10}$ **7.** $\frac{4}{7} \times \frac{7}{4}$ **8.** $\frac{5}{8} \times 24$

Set B   For use after page 226.

Estimate each product by rounding.

1. $19\frac{7}{8} \times 4\frac{5}{6}$ **2.** $8\frac{3}{4} \times 5\frac{1}{2}$ **3.** $7\frac{5}{8} \times 5\frac{5}{7}$

4. $31\frac{9}{12} \times 4\frac{3}{7}$ **5.** $1\frac{9}{10} \times 8\frac{1}{8}$ **6.** $16\frac{7}{9} \times 12\frac{6}{11}$

Set C   For use after page 229.

Multiply.

1. $1\frac{1}{2} \times 3\frac{1}{2}$ **2.** $2\frac{1}{3} \times 2\frac{1}{2}$ **3.** $\frac{2}{3} \times 1\frac{1}{4}$ **4.** $1\frac{1}{2} \times 3\frac{2}{3}$

5. $4 \times 1\frac{2}{5}$ **6.** $3\frac{1}{3} \times 1\frac{1}{5}$ **7.** $2\frac{2}{5} \times 1\frac{1}{9}$ **8.** $1\frac{2}{3} \times 3\frac{1}{5}$

Set D   For use after page 233.

Divide.

1. $\frac{1}{6} \div \frac{1}{8}$ **2.** $\frac{1}{2} \div \frac{2}{3}$ **3.** $\frac{3}{4} \div \frac{1}{3}$

4. $6 \div \frac{5}{8}$ **5.** $\frac{7}{10} \div 8$ **6.** $\frac{9}{10} \div \frac{2}{5}$

Set E   For use after page 235.

Divide.

1. $3\frac{3}{5} \div 2$ **2.** $5\frac{3}{4} \div 2\frac{2}{3}$ **3.** $4\frac{1}{2} \div 1\frac{1}{3}$

4. $8\frac{1}{2} \div 3\frac{1}{5}$ **5.** $\frac{1}{8} \div 3\frac{1}{6}$ **6.** $7\frac{1}{5} \div 1\frac{1}{5}$

Set A For use after page 249.

Give the number of faces, edges, and vertices

1.

Triangular prism
▦ faces
▦ vertices
▦ edges

2.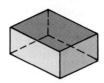

Rectangular prism
▦ faces
▦ vertices
▦ edges

3.

Hexagonal prism
▦ faces
▦ vertices
▦ edges

Set B For use after page 251.

Draw the following space figures. Give the number of faces, edges, and vertices.

1. triangular pyramid
▦ faces
▦ vertices
▦ edges

2. rectangular prism
▦ faces
▦ vertices
▦ edges

3. hexagonal pyramid
▦ faces
▦ vertices
▦ edges

Set C For use after page 253.

Draw the front, top, and side views of the following space figures.

1. triangular prism

2. cylinder

3. hexagonal prism

Set D For use after page 255.

Which plane figure is suggested by the objects given?

1. stop sign

2. box

3. tip of a nail

Set E For use after page 257.

Name these figures.

1. ─────────
─────────

2.

3.

MORE PRACTICE BANK

Set A For use after page 259.

First estimate the measure of each angle. Then measure to check
your estimate. Tell if the angle is right, acute, or obtuse.

1.

2.

3.

Set B For use after page 261.

Write *square, rectangle, parallelogram, rhombus,* or *trapezoid* to
describe each quadrilateral below.

1.

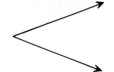

2.

3.

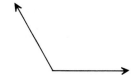

Set C For use after page 265.

Which figures are congruent? Trace a figure and turn it, flip it, or
slide it if necessary to see whether it matches another figure.

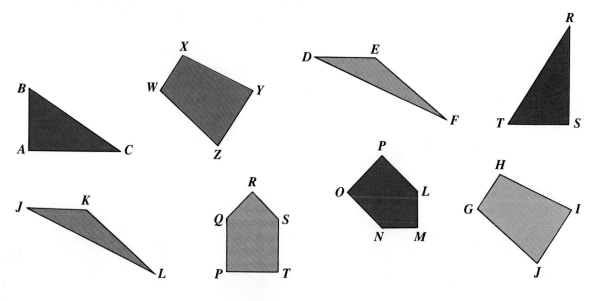

512

Set A   For use after page 267.

Are the figures similar? Write *yes* or *no*.

1.   2.    3.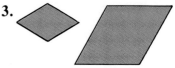

Set B   For use after page 269.

The figures formed by connecting these points are symmetric figures. Graph each figure and draw its line (or lines) of symmetry.

1. (1, 2), (3, 9), (5, 2), (1, 2)   **2.** (4, 8), (10, 8), (9, 4), (5, 4), (4, 8)

Set C   For use after page 281.

Use this favorite summer camp activity tally chart. Write each ratio using all three forms.

1. swimming to volleyball

2. crafts to fishing

3. fishing to crafts

4. hiking to total votes

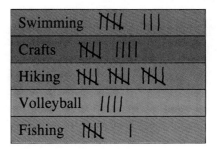

Swimming	ⅢⅡ			
Crafts	ⅢⅡ				
Hiking	ⅢⅡ ⅢⅡ ⅢⅡ
Volleyball					
Fishing	ⅢⅡ	

Set D   For use after page 283.

Copy and complete each ratio table.

1. 12 to 1

12	24	▒	▒	▒	▒
1	▒	▒	▒	▒	▒

2. 7 to 3

7	▒	▒	▒	35	42
3	▒	▒	▒	15	18

MORE PRACTICE BANK

Set A   For use after page 289.

Using a scale of 1 m : 1 cm, make a scale drawing of the
following.

1. the doorway to your classroom   **2.** your desk in math class

Set B   For use after page 295.

Write each ratio as a percent.

1. 32 : 100   **2.** $\frac{63}{100}$ **3.** 27 to 100   **4.** $\frac{98}{100}$ **5.** 56 out of 100

Write each percent as a ratio.

6. 31%   **7.** 17%   **8.** 48%   **9.** 67%   **10.** 94%

Write each percent as a fraction in lowest terms.

11. 75%   **12.** 20%   **13.** 45%   **14.** 24%   **15.** 60%

Set C   For use after page 297.

Replace the percent with a compatible percent and use mental
math to estimate the answer.

1. 26% of 24   **2.** 19% of 25   **3.** 48% of 82

4. 35% of 27   **5.** 52% of 98   **6.** 21% of 150

Set D   For use after page 299.

Write each decimal as a percent.

1. 0.15   **2.** 0.29   **3.** 0.75   **4.** 0.62   **5.** 0.20

Write each percent as a decimal and as a fraction in lowest terms.

6. 75%   **7.** 20%   **8.** 45%   **9.** 24%   **10.** 60%

Set A   For use after page 301.

Find the percent for each fraction.

1. $\frac{1}{2}$ 2. $\frac{3}{5}$ 3. $\frac{1}{4}$ 4. $\frac{9}{10}$ 5. $\frac{1}{20}$

6. $\frac{7}{10}$ 7. $\frac{36}{50}$ 8. $\frac{2}{5}$ 9. $\frac{9}{20}$ 10. $\frac{3}{50}$

Set B   For use after page 303.

Give these fractions as percents. Round to the nearest percent.

1. $\frac{5}{8}$ 2. $\frac{2}{3}$ 3. $\frac{5}{6}$ 4. $\frac{7}{16}$

Set C   For use after page 313.

Find the percent of each number.

1. 10% of 90   2. 50% of 60   3. 18% of 300   4. 25% of 84

5. 20% of 80   6. 75% of 200   7. 23% of 400   8. 5% of 90

Set D   For use after page 315.

Find the percent of each number mentally.

1. 10% of 60   2. 25% of 28   3. $33\frac{1}{3}$% of 300   4. $12\frac{1}{2}$% of 48

5. 75% of 24   6. 25% of 96   7. 10% of 850   8. 15% of 200

Set E   For use after page 317.

Use mental math to estimate the percent of the numbers.

1. 21% of 45   2. 24% of 44   3. 9% of 80

4. 53% of 124   5. 21% of 55   6. 32% of 150

Set A   For use after page 323.

Find the interest.

1. Borrow: $550
   Interest Rate: 11% per yr
   Time: 1 yr

2. Borrow: $275
   Interest Rate: 7% per yr
   Time: 1.5 yr

3. Borrow: $1,300
   Interest Rate: 17% per yr
   Time: 3.3 yr

Set B   For use after page 325.

Tell how much has been discounted from the original price.

1. $150 at 30% off

2. $32 at 10% off

3. $7.98 at $\frac{1}{4}$ discount

4. $16 at 15% discount

Set C   For use after page 337.

Give the opposite of each integer.

1. $^-18$ **2.** $^+75$ **3.** $^+327$ **4.** $^-1$ **5.** $^+92$ **6.** 0

Set D   For use after page 339.

Write > or < for each ▦ .

1. $^+12$ ▦ $^+2$ **2.** $^+18$ ▦ $^-12$ **3.** $^-17$ ▦ $^-16$ **4.** $^-6$ ▦ $^+1$

Order from greatest to least.

5. $^+12$, $^-2$, $^-7$, $^+6$, $^+8$

Order from least to greatest.

6. $^+22$, $^-16$, $^-7$, $^+18$, 0

Set E   For use after page 340.

Copy each column of equations. Follow the pattern from top to bottom to give each sum or difference.

1. 7 + 3
   7 + 2
   7 + 1
   7 + 0
   7 + $^-1$
   7 + $^-2$
   7 + $^-3$

2. 6 − 2
   6 − 1
   6 − 0
   6 − $^-1$
   6 − $^-2$
   6 − $^-3$
   6 − $^-4$

MORE PRACTICE BANK

Set A   For use after page 343.

Find the sums.

1. $^+16 + ^-4 = n$

2. $^-8 + ^+3 = n$

3. $^+12 + ^-6 = n$

4. $^-11 + ^+12 = n$

5. $^+20 + ^-13 = n$

6. $^-5 + ^-15 = n$

7. $^+4 + ^+3 = n$

8. $^-9 + ^-8 = n$

9. $^-6 + ^+3 = n$

Set B   For use after page 345.

Find the differences.

1. $^+5 - ^-8 = n$

2. $^-6 - ^+6 = n$

3. $^-8 - ^-10 = n$

4. $^+11 - ^-8 = n$

5. $^+2 - ^-6 = n$

6. $^-11 - ^-10 = n$

7. $^-9 - ^-8 = n$

8. $^+6 - ^+9 = n$

9. $^-7 - ^-7 = n$

Set C   For use after page 349.

Give the ordered pair for each point
on the graph.

1. A

2. B

3. C

4. D

5. E

6. F

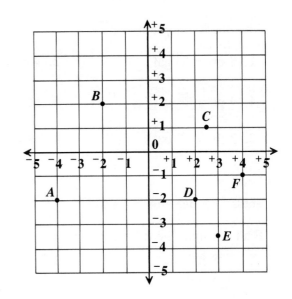

Set D   For use after page 361.

Give the number for each changed unit.

1. 6.3 m = ▐▐▐ dm

2. 86 dm = ▐▐▐ m

3. 4.63 m = ▐▐▐ dm

4. 693 cm = ▐▐▐ m

5. 347 mm = ▐▐▐ m

6. 6.336 m = ▐▐▐ mm

MORE PRACTICE BANK

Set A   For use after page 367.

Find the volume. Use the cubic centimeter (cm³).

1.

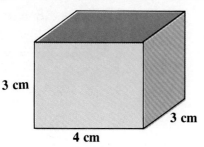

3 cm

3 cm

4 cm

2.

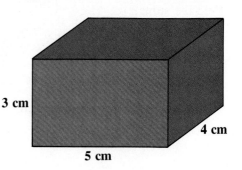

3 cm

4 cm

5 cm

3. 1,000 mL = ▨ L   **4.** 2,000 mL = ▨ L   **5.** 8,000 mL = ▨ L

Give each weight in grams.

6. 2 kg   **7.** 23 kg   **8.** 475 kg

Give each weight in kilograms.

9. 8 g   **10.** 67 g   **11.** 999 g

Set B   For use after page 375.

Give the missing numbers.

1. 8 qt = ▨ gal   **2.** 4 c = ▨ qt   **3.** $\frac{1}{2}$ qt = ▨ pt

4. 4 pt = ▨ qt   **5.** 16 c = ▨ gal   **6.** $\frac{1}{2}$ pt = ▨ c

7. 3 lb = ▨ oz   **8.** 48 oz = ▨ lb   **9.** 6,000 lb = ▨ T

Set C   For use after page 377.

Find the sum, the difference, or the product.

1. 8 ft 2 in.
   + 3 ft 6 in.

2. 3 ft 4 in.
   − 2 ft 8 in.

3. 6 ft 9 in.
   ×   3

4. 7 lb 3 oz
   ×   4

5.   6 oz
   ×   20

6. 2 lb 15 oz
   + 3 lb 9 oz

518

Set A   For use after page 391.

Find the area of each figure.

1.

3 in.

3 in.

2.

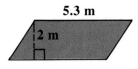

5.3 m

2 m

3.

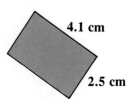

4.1 cm

2.5 cm

Set B   For use after page 393.

Find the area of each figure.

1.

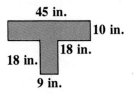

25 m

30 m

2.

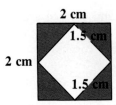

28 mm

33 mm

65 mm

Set C   For use after page 394.

Find the shaded area of each figure.

1.

45 in.

10 in.

18 in.

18 in.

9 in.

2.

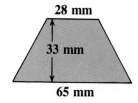

2 cm

1.5 cm

2 cm

1.5 cm

Set D   For use after page 397.

Estimate the area of each figure in square centimeters. Then calculate to check your estimate.

1.

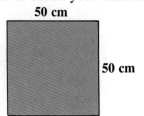

50 cm

50 cm

2.

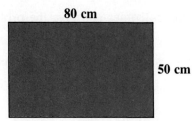

80 cm

50 cm

Set A For use after page 399.

Find the circumference. Use 3.14 for π.

1.

$d = 5$ in.

2.

$d = 12$ m

Set B For use after page 401.

Find the area of each circle. Use 3.14 for π. Round to the nearest hundredth when necessary.

1.

7 cm

2.

4.2 cm

Set C For use after page 403.

Find the volume and surface area of each box.

1.

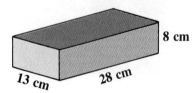

8 cm

13 cm   28 cm

2.

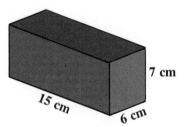

7 cm

15 cm   6 cm

Set D For use after page 419.

List all the outcomes and give the probability of each.

1. Spin a spinner.

2. Toss a cube with these faces.

3. Spin a spinner.

MORE PRACTICE BANK

Set A For use after page 425.

Find the expected value.

1. Trials: 200
Probability: $\frac{3}{5}$

2. Trials: 956
Probabilty: 0.25

3. Trials: 1,612
Probability: $\frac{1}{2}$

4. Trials: 25,000
Probability: 0.14

Set B For use after page 427.

Use these samples to predict.

1. Sample: 5 out of 50 are marked
Sack: 50 out of n are marked

2. Sample: 2 out of 60 are marked
Sack: 30 out of n are marked

3. Sample: 8 out of 320 are marked
Sack: 40 out of n are marked

4. Sample: 10 out of 40 are marked
Sack: 40 out of n are marked

Set C For use after page 441.

Solve. Use guess and check.

1. $a - 25 = 32$

2. $25 \times k = 125$

3. $m + 82 = 645$

4. $3 \times n = 96$

5. $r - 62 = 131$

6. $p - 8 = 112$

Set D For use after page 443.

Solve and check.

1. $d - 18.5 = 36.2$

2. $r + 3 = 259$

3. $67 + m = 385$

4. $b + \frac{3}{4} = \frac{7}{8}$

5. $a + 25 = 100$

6. $0.5 + n = 0.5$

7. $s - 17 = 28$

8. $9 - k = \frac{3}{8}$

Set E For use after page 449.

Solve and check.

1. $6y = 522$

2. $\frac{n}{4} = 18$

3. $r \div 3 = 99$

4. $4 \cdot x = 96$

5. $a \times 6 = 90$

6. $7b = 63$

7. $\frac{g}{25} = 4$

8. $h \div 24 = 1$

MORE PRACTICE BANK

Set A   For use after page 11.

Name the operation you need to use. Then solve.

1. Brenda planted 16 corn plants, 5 snap bean plants, 2 pepper plants, 2 tomato plants, and 3 cucumber plants. How many vegetables did Brenda plant?

2. Jason got 15 people to agree to each pay $1.50 a mile for every mile he rode in the bike-a-thon. He rode 12 miles. How much did Jason collect in the bike-a-thon?

Set B   For use after page 21.

Solve. Use the 6-point checklist.

1. At 7:00, 5 of Tina's friends came to her record party. At 8:00, 7 more friends arrived. How many people were at the party then?

2. Jeff had $14 to buy presents for 3 friends. He spent $5 for a record for 1 friend. How much money did he have left to buy presents for his other 2 friends?

Set C   For use after page 39.

Solve. Draw a picture if you need help.

1. Alton, Benton, Clinton, and Dunlap are towns on the same highway. Dunlap is between Alton and Clinton. Dunlap is 189 km from Alton. Clinton is between Dunlap and Benton. Clinton is 237 km from Benton. Alton and Benton are 671 km apart. How far apart are Dunlap and Clinton?

Set D   For use after page 47.

Solve.

1. In 1978, Richard J. DeBarnardis bicycled completely around the mainland United States! His trip took 180 days. How many weeks less than a year did his trip take, to the nearest whole number of weeks?

Set A   For use after page 53.

Tell which calculation method you choose. Then solve.

1. Boyd must put 10 cans on each section of a shelf. How many cans does he need for 35 sections?

Set B   For use after page 67.

Solve.

1. Les sold 3 fewer tickets to the school play than Nico. Together the boys sold 17 tickets. How many tickets to the play did each boy sell?

2. Marla told Sandy, "If you give me a nickel, each of us will have the same amount of money." Together they have 36¢. How much money did Marla have at the beginning?

Set C   For use after page 79.

Solve.

1. In 1939 Tommy Godwin set out to average 1,500 miles per week on a 1-year bicycle trip. However, he averaged 1,444 miles per week. If he had averaged 356 miles per week more he would have reached his goal. How far did Godwin travel?

2. The bicycle trip across the United States is about 3,000 miles. On the average, how many miles would you need to travel each day to complete a 2,660-mile trip in 4 weeks?

Set D   For use after page 105.

Solve. Copy and complete each table. Then give the answer.

1. Darrel needs 4 cups of pancake mix for every 3 cups of milk. How many cups of mix does he need for 15 cups of milk?

Cups of mix	4	8	▓	▓	▓
Cups of milk	3	6	9	12	15

2. Marsha can buy 2 theater tickets for $7. She needs 10 tickets. How much will they cost?

Tickets	▓	▓	▓	▓	▓
Cost	▓	▓	▓	▓	▓

Set A   For use after page 119.

Solve.

1. Armando paid $40 for a pair of roller skates and $35 for outdoor wheels. What was the cost if the tax was $4.50? What was the cost of these items, without tax?

2. The skating coach bought 24 knee pads and 30 elbow pads. How many pads did the coach buy? If each pad costs $6, how much did the coach pay before tax was added?

Set B   For use after page 123.

Solve. Use a calculator.

1. At Bill's Market, you can get 5 oranges for $1.95. At Maximart you can get 3 for $1.29. Are the oranges cheaper at Bill's or at Maximart?

2. You can get 3 cans of Bell's soup for $1.23 and 2 cans of Mom's Soup for $0.84. Which brand of soup costs less per can?

Set C   For use after page 143.

Solve.

1. There are 8 teams entered in the all-school tennis finals. If each team plays every other team, how many games must be played to find teams for the championship games?

2. The city tennis league has 5 Blue teams and 5 Red teams. Each Blue team plays each Red team twice. How many games are played?

Set D   For use after page 175.

Solve.

1. Jan works in a small sandwich shop. A customer can have rye bread or whole wheat bread and one kind of meat— chicken, beef, ham, or turkey. How many different kinds of one-meat sandwiches can be ordered?

2. In a certain part of a state only the letters J, K, L, M, and N, can be used to form a 2-letter beginning for a license plate. How many different 2-letter beginnings are possible?

Set A   For use after page 181.

Do not solve the problem. Decide if the answer given is reasonable. If it is not reasonable, explain why.

1. London has an average daily temperature of a high of 64°F and a low of 35°F. One Monday, the high temperature in London was 64°F. The next Monday, the high temperature was 48°F. What was the average temperature for the two Mondays?
   Answer: The average temperature for the two Mondays was 50°F.

Set B   For use after page 209.

Solve.

1. If Gary multiplies his dog's age by 5 and subtracts 37, he gets 28. How old is his dog?

2. Joyce bought some picture post cards for $0.29 and a ball-point pen that cost 3 times as much as the cards. She has $3.18 left. How much money did she have at the start?

Set C   For use after page 225.

Solve.

1. Each of 8 friends says "Hello" to everyone else at a party. How many hellos are spoken? (Note: When 2 friends meet, there are 2 hellos.)

2. It takes 1 block to make 1 step, 3 blocks to make 2 steps, 6 blocks to make 3 steps, and so on. How many steps can be made with 36 blocks?

Set D   For use after page 239.

Before solving the problem, write your estimate of the answer. Then solve the problem and decide if your answer is reasonable.

1. A local newspaper earned $4,867 for classfied advertisements, $25,543 for grocery store advertisements, and $58,425 for other advertising. How much more did the other advertising earn than classified and grocery combined?

Set A   For use after page 271.

Solve.

1. Mel and Dan each have two hobbies. Neither has the same
hobby as the other. The hobbies are drawing, collecting rocks,
taking photographs, and making model cars. Mel does not
collect rocks. Dan does not draw. The boy who draws does
not take photographs. Which hobbies does each boy have?

Set B   For use after page 287.

Solve.

1. A tree is 4.5 m tall and has a shadow
5.4 m long. How tall is a bush that has a
shadow 1.5 m long?

2. A truck 3.5 m tall has a shadow 4 m
long. How tall is a car that has a shadow
1.6 m long?

Set C   For use after page 327.

Find the total cost for each purchase.

1. Purchase: $7.50
Tax rate: $6\frac{1}{2}\%$

2. Purchase: $8.79
Tax rate: 5.5%

3. Purchase: $23.69
Tax rate: 6.3%

Set D   For use after page 350.

List at least 2 strategies that you think might help you solve each
problem. Then solve the problem.

1. There are 28 students in a class going on a field trip. If
4 students can ride in each car and 8 in each van, find the
least number of cars and vans needed so that every seat is
taken.

Set E   For use after page 365.

Should you estimate or measure precisely for each of the
following situations?

1. You are running a kilometer for
recreation. You are running a kilometer
in a timed contest.

2. You are purchasing an amount of roast
beef at the store. You are putting an
amount of roast beef in a sandwich.

MORE PRACTICE BANK

Set A   For use after page 379.

Solve.

1. At the football game, a team scored 44 points. They scored
   3 points for each field goal and 7 points for each touchdown
   and its successful conversion. How many of each did they
   make?

Set B   For use after page 389.

Solve.

1. A rectangular yard is 36.7 m long. The
   width is 12.9 m less than the length.
   How many meters of fence are needed to
   go around the yard?

2. The length of a rectangular playground
   is 26.5 m more than the width. The
   width is 137.8 m. What is the perimeter
   of the playground?

Set C   For use after page 429.

Solve.

1. It is 4,647 miles from Tokyo to Moscow. It is 5,871 miles
   from San Francisco to Moscow. Ms. Huffman flew from San
   Francisco to Tokyo with a stop in Moscow on the way. How
   many miles did she fly?

Set D   For use after page 447.

Read the following problem. Then follow the directions to solve
the problem.

Twenty-five 11-year-olds in the ski club want to go skiing this
weekend. There are a total of 123 11-year-olds in the ski club.
How many members do not want to go skiing this weekend?

1. Let c be the number of 11-year-olds who do not want to go
   skiing this weekend.
2. Write an expression involving c that shows the total number of
   11-year-old ski club members.

3. What is the total number of 11-year-old ski club members?

4. Write an equation for this situation.

5. Solve the problem.

TABLE OF MEASURES

Metric System	Customary System

Length

Metric System		Customary System	
1 centimeter (cm)	10 millimeters (mm)	1 foot (ft)	12 inches (in.)
1 decimeter (dm)	100 millimeters (mm) 10 centimeters (cm)	1 yard (yd)	36 inches (in.) 3 feet (ft)
1 meter (m)	1,000 millimeters (mm) 100 centimeters (cm) 10 decimeters (dm)	1 mile (m)	5,280 feet (ft) 1,760 yards (yd)
1 kilometer (km)	1,000 meters (m)		

Area

Metric System		Customary System	
1 square meter (m^2)	100 square decimeters (dm^2) 10,000 square centimeters (cm^2)	1 square foot (ft^2)	144 square inches $(in.^2)$

Volume

Metric System		Customary System	
1 cubic decimeter (dm^3)	1,000 cubic centimeters (cm^3) 1 liter (L)	1 cubic foot (ft^3)	1,728 cubic inches $(in.^3)$

Capacity

Metric System		Customary System	
1 teaspoon	5 milliliters (mL)	1 cup (c)	8 fluid ounces (fl oz)
1 tablespoon	12.5 milliliters (mL)	1 pint (pt)	16 fluid ounces (fl oz) 2 cups (c)
1 liter (L)	1,000 milliliters (mL) 1,000 cubic centimeters (cm^3) 1 cubic decimeter (dm^3) 4 metric cups	1 quart (qt)	32 fluid ounces (fl oz) 4 cups (c) 2 pints (pt)
		1 gallon (gal)	128 fluid ounces (fl oz) 16 cups (c) 8 pints (pt) 4 quarts (qt)

Mass / Weight

Mass		Weight	
1 gram (g)	1,000 milligrams (mg)	1 pound (lb)	16 ounces (oz)
1 kilogram (kg)	1,000 grams (g)		

Time

Metric System		Customary System	
1 minute (min)	60 seconds (s)		
1 hour (h)	60 minutes (min)	1 year (yr)	365 days 52 weeks 12 months
1 day (d)	24 hours (h)		
1 week (w)	7 days (d)	1 decade	10 years
1 month (mo)	about 4 weeks	1 century	100 years

GLOSSARY

a.m. A way to indicate time from 12:00 midnight to 12:00 noon.

absolute value The number of units from a point on the number line to the origin. The absolute value of a number is never negative. Absolute value is shown by vertical lines.
$$|^-3| = 3; \; |^+6| = 6; \; |0| = 0$$

acute angle An angle that has a measure less than 90°.

acute triangle A triangle in which each angle has a measure less than 90°.

addend One of the numbers to be added.

addition An operation that gives the total number when two or more numbers are put together.

algebra A branch of mathematics in which arithmetic relations are explored using letter symbols to represent numbers.

algebraic expression An expression (name for a number) that contains at least one variable.
Example: $n + 5$

and When the word *and* connects two statements, both statements must be true for the combined statement to be true.

angle Two rays from a single point. Types of angles include acute angles, obtuse angles, and right angles.

area The measure of a region, expressed in square units.

associative property When adding (or multiplying) three or more numbers, the grouping of the addends (or factors) can be changed and the sum (or product) is the same.
Examples: $2 + (8 + 6) = (2 + 8) + 6$
$3 \times (4 \times 2) = (3 \times 4) \times 2$

average The mean. See *mean*.

bar graph A diagram that uses vertical or horizontal bars to show information.

base A number that is used as a factor several times.
Example: $7 \times 7 \times 7 = 7^3$ ← exponent, base

base five A numeration system based on groupings of fives. Base five uses the digits 0, 1, 2, 3, and 4.

benchmark An object of known measure used to estimate the measure of another object.

bisector A ray from the vertex of an angle that cuts the angle into two angles of equal measure.

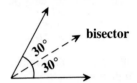

breaking apart Breaking a number into addends or factors in order to make mental calculations easy.
Example: $7\frac{5}{8} - 3\frac{2}{8} = 7 - 3$ plus $\frac{5}{8} - \frac{2}{8}$

calculator A device that performs arithmetic calculations.

capacity The volume of a space figure given in terms of liquid measurement.

center The point from which all points on a circle are equally distant.

chances The probability that a particular event will occur.

circle A plane figure in which all the points are the same distance from a point called the center.

circle graph A graph in the form of a circle that is divided into sections showing how the whole is broken into parts.

circumference The distance around a circle.

clustering Finding addends or factors that are nearly alike in order to make estimation easy.
Example: $28 + 31 + 29 + 32 \rightarrow 4 \times 30 = 120$

common factor A number that is a factor of two different numbers is a common factor of those two numbers.

common multiple A number that is a multiple of two different numbers is a common multiple of those two numbers.

529

GLOSSARY

commutative property When adding (or multiplying) two or more numbers, the order of the addends (or factors) can be changed and the sum (or product) is the same.

Examples: $4 + 5 = 5 + 4$
$2 \times 3 = 3 \times 2$

compass An instrument used to draw circles.

compatible numbers Pairs of numbers that "go together" so that computing with them mentally is easy.

Example: $2 + 8 + 4 = 10 + 4$

composite number A whole number greater than 1 that has more than two factors.

cone A space figure with one circular face and one vertex.

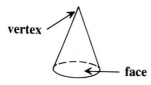

vertex   face

congruent figures Figures that have the same size and shape.

coordinates Number pair used in graphing.

cross products Products obtained by multiplying the numerator of one fraction by the denominator of a second fraction, and the denominator of the first fraction by the numerator of the second fraction. Cross products can be used to compare fractions and ratios or to solve proportions.

Examples: $\frac{2}{3} \times \frac{5}{8}$ $15 < 16$

cross section A view of a space figure obtained by "slicing" the space figure with a plane.

cube A space figure whose faces are all squares.

cubit A unit of length used by early civilizations, based on the length from a man's elbow to the tip of the middle finger.

customary units of measure See Table of Measures, page 528.

cylinder A space figure with two faces that are circles the same size.

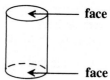

face

face

data Information

data bank An organized collection of information.

decimal Any base-ten numeral written using a decimal point.

3.2 ← decimal
↑
decimal point

degree A unit of angle measure.

degree Celsius (°C) A metric unit for measuring temperature.

degree Fahrenheit (°F) A customary unit for measuring temperature.

denominator The number below the line in a fraction. $\frac{3}{4}$ ← denominator

diagonal A segment, other than a side, connecting two vertices of a polygon.

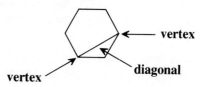

vertex

diagonal

vertex

diameter The distance across the interior of a circle through the center.

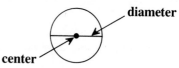

diameter

center

difference The number obtained by subtracting one number from another.

digits The symbols used to write numerals 0, 1, 2, 3, 4, 5, 6, 7, 8, and 9.

discount An amount of money subtracted from the regular price of an item when the item is on sale.

GLOSSARY

distributive property Multiplying a sum by a number is the same as multiplying each addend by the number and then adding the products.
Example: $3 \times (2 + 4) = 18$
$(3 \times 2) + (3 \times 4) = 18$

dividend A number to be divided.

division An operation that tells how many sets or how many in each set.

divisor The number by which a dividend is divided.

double bar graph A bar graph that uses pairs of bars to compare information.

edge One of the segments making up any of the faces of a space figure.

equality (equals, or =) A mathematical relation of being exactly the same.

equally likely outcomes Outcomes that have the same chance of occurring.

equal ratios Ratios that give the same comparison.
$\frac{9}{27}$ and $\frac{1}{3}$ are equal ratios.

equation A mathematical sentence that uses the equality sign (=) to say that two expressions stand for the same value.
Example: $9 + 2 = 11$

equilateral triangle A triangle with all 3 sides the same length and all angles the same measure.

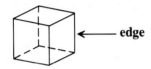

equivalent fractions Fractions that name the same amount. Their cross products are equal.
Example: $\frac{1}{2} = \frac{2}{4}$ $(1 \times 4) = (2 \times 2)$

estimate To find an answer that is close to the precise answer.

Euler's formula A formula about edges, faces, and vertices of polyhedrons: $E = F + V - 2$.

evaluate To find the number that an algebraic expression names.

even number A whole number that has 0, 2, 4, 6, or 8 in the ones place.

expanded form A way to write numbers that shows the place value of each digit.
Example: $9,000 + 300 + 20 + 5$

expected value The predicted outcome based on probability and a known number of trials.

experimental probability The number of times an event actually occurred divided by the number of trials.

exponent A number that tells how many times another number is to be used as a factor.
$5 \cdot 5 \cdot 5 = 5^3 \begin{matrix} \leftarrow \text{exponent} \\ \leftarrow \text{base} \end{matrix}$

face One of the plane figures (regions) making up a space figure.

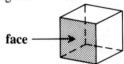

factors Numbers that are multiplied together to give a number called the product.
$6 \times 7 = 42$
$\uparrow \quad \uparrow$
factors

factor tree A diagram used to find the prime factors of a number.
Example:

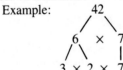

fair game A game in which each player has the same chance of winning.

flip To turn a figure to its reverse side. A flip and a slide results in a reflection image.

formula A general fact or rule expressed by symbols. For example, the area (A) of any parallelogram with base b and height h is given by the formula $A = bh$.

fraction A number that expresses parts of a region or a set.
Example: $\frac{3}{4}$

GLOSSARY

front-end digits The digits in the whole number part of a decimal, used to estimate sums and differences.

Example:
$$62.38$$
$$+\ 78.76$$
$$\overline{130}$$

graph A diagram that shows information in an organized way. Types of graphs include bar, circle, line, and pictographs.

graphing the point Marking a point for the coordinates on a grid.

greater than (>) The relationship of one number being larger than another number.
Example: 6 > 5, read "6 is greater than 5."

greatest common factor (GCF) The greatest number that is a factor of each of two numbers.

improper fraction A fraction in which the numerator is greater than or equal to the denominator.

inequality statement A mathematical statement that uses the symbol for "greater than" (>) or the symbol for "less than" (<) to say that two expressions do not stand for the same value.
Examples: 9>7   7<9

infinity Without end. The symbol for infinity is ∞.
Example: When it represents the fraction $\frac{1}{3}$, the decimal 0.33 repeats the same digit forever.

integers The whole numbers together with their negatives.
Examples: ... ⁺2, ⁺1, 0, ⁻1, ⁻2, ...

interest A fee paid for the use of money. The amount of interest depends on the amount of money loaned, the rate of interest, and the length of time before repayment.

intersect Lines that intersect are lines that meet each other.

interval The number of units between spaces on a graph's scale.

inverse operations Operations that "undo" each other. Subtracting 3 is the inverse of adding 3.

investigation An experiment or study done to find out information.

isosceles triangle A triangle with at least 2 sides the same length and at least 2 angles the same measure.

least common denominator (LCD) The least common multiple of two denominators.

least common multiple (LCM) The smallest nonzero number that is a multiple of each of two given numbers.

less than (<) The relationship of one number being smaller than another number.
Example: 5 < 6, read "5 is less than 6."

line A straight path that is endless in both directions.

line graph A diagram that uses a rising or falling line to show increases or decreases over a period of time.

line of symmetry A line on which a figure can be folded so that the two parts fit exactly.

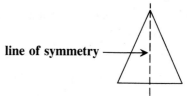

line of symmetry

line segment Part of a line that extends from one point to another point.

lowest terms A fraction is in lowest terms if the numerator and denominator have no common factor greater than 1.

mass The amount of matter that something contains.

mathematical probability The probability of a certain outcome if a very large number of trials were to be done.

mean The quotient obtained when the sum of two or more numbers is divided by the number of addends.

median The middle number of a set of numbers that are arranged in order. If there is no one middle number, the median is the average (mean) of the two middle numbers.

mental math Performing calculations in your mind, without using pencil and paper or a calculator.

metric system A system of measurement based on 10 like our place value system, making it easy to change from one unit to another.

metric units of measure See Table of Measures, page 528.

micron A length of 1 ten-thousandth centimeter (0.0001 cm).

mixed decimal A combination of a decimal and a fraction, such as $0.4\frac{1}{3}$.

mixed number A number that has a whole number part and a fraction part, such as $2\frac{3}{4}$.

mode In a list of data, the number or item that occurs most often. There may be more than one mode.

multiple A number that is the product of a given number and a whole number.

multiple choice A type of question that gives a person a choice of several answers.

multiplication An operation that combines two numbers, called factors, to give one number, called the product.

negative integer Any number in the set:
$^-1, ^-2, ^-3, \ldots$

number line A line that shows numbers in order.
Example:

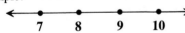

number properties Number properties include the Associative (Grouping) Property, the Commutative (Order) Property, the Distributive Property, the One Property of Multiplication, the Zero Property of Addition, and the Zero Property of Multiplication.

numeral A symbol for a number.

numerator The number above the line in a fraction.
$\frac{3}{4}$ ← numerator

numerical expression An expression (name for a number) that contains two or more numbers.
Example: $4 + 5$

obtuse angle An angle with a measure greater than 90° and less than 180°.

obtuse triangle A triangle with one angle measuring more than 90°.

odd number A whole number that has 1, 3, 5, 7, or 9 in the ones place.

one property In multiplication, when either factor is 1, the product is the other factor.

operation A mathematical procedure: addition, subtraction, multiplication, or division.

or When the word *or* connects two statements, the combined statement is always true unless both parts are false.

ordered pair Two numbers that are used to give the location of a point on a graph.

order of operations Rules about the order in which operations should be done:
Compute inside parentheses first.
Multiply and divide next, from left to right.
Add and subtract last, from left to right.

outcome A possible result in a probability experiment.

p.m. A way to indicate time from 12:00 noon to 12:00 midnight.

parallel lines Two lines that lie in the same plane and do not intersect.

parallelogram A quadrilateral with two pairs of parallel sides.

percent (%) Per 100; a way to compare a number with 100.

perimeter The distance around a figure.

period In large numbers, a group of three digits that is separated from other groups by commas.

533

perpendicular lines Two lines that intersect at right angles.

pi (π) The ratio of the circumference of a circle to its diameter. π is about $3\frac{1}{7}$ or 3.14.

pictograph A kind of graph that uses pictures or symbols to represent numbers.

place value The value given to the place a digit occupies in a number.

Example:

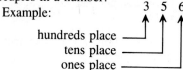

hundreds place
tens place
ones place

plane figure A figure that lies on a flat surface.
Examples:

square   triangle   circle

point A single, exact location, often represented by a dot.

polygon A closed figure formed by line segments.

polyhedron A space figure whose faces are polygons.

positive integer Any number in the set:
$^+1, ^+2, ^+3, \ldots$

prediction An educated guess about what will happen.

prime factorization Expressing a composite number as a product of prime factors.

prime number A number that has exactly 2 factors (the number itself and 1).

prism A space figure whose bases are congruent polygons in parallel planes and whose faces are parallelograms.

probability The ratio of the number of times a certain outcome can occur to the number of total possible outcomes. Probability can be mathematical (theoretical) or experimental.

product The result of the multiplication operation.

proportion A statement that two ratios are equal.
Example: $\frac{6}{9} = \frac{2}{3}$

protractor An instrument used for measuring angles.

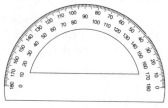

pyramid A space figure whose base is a polygon and whose faces are triangles with a common vertex.

quadrilateral A four-sided polygon.

questionnaire A list of written questions given to people in order to gather information about a topic.

quotient The number (other than the remainder) that is the result of the division operation.

radius A segment from the center of a circle to a point on the circle.

radius

range The difference between the highest and lowest numbers in a set of numbers.

rating response A type of question on a questionnaire that asks a person to answer on a scale, such as 1 to 5.

ratio A pair of numbers used in making certain comparisons. The ratio of 3 to 4 can be written 3 to 4, 3:4, or $\frac{3}{4}$.

ratio table A table that displays a set of equal ratios.

ray A part of a line, having only one end point.

reciprocal Two numbers whose product is 1.
Example: $\frac{5}{1}$ and $\frac{1}{5}$

rectangle A quadrilateral that has four right angles.

reflection image The new figure obtained by sliding and flipping a figure.

region A specific area.

regular polygon A polygon with all sides the same length and all angles the same measure.

GLOSSARY

remainder The number less than the divisor that remains after the division process is completed.

repeating decimal A decimal with digits which from some point on repeat periodically. 6.2835835... and 0.33333... are repeating decimals. They may also be written 6.2$\overline{835}$ and 0.$\overline{3}$ respectively.

rhombus A quadrilateral with all sides the same length. A rhombus is a parallelogram.

right angle An angle that has a measure of 90°.

right triangle A triangle that has one right angle.

rotation image The new figure obtained by sliding and turning a figure.

rounding Replacing specific numbers with numbers expressed in even units, such as tens, hundreds, or thousands.
  Example: 23 rounded to the nearest 10 is 20.

sale price A lowered price on an item, obtained by subtracting the discount from the regular price.

sales tax A percent of a purchase price to be paid to a government.

sample A small group of people or objects that is part of a much larger group. Information gathered from the sample is used to make predictions about the larger group.

scale Numbers along the side or bottom of a graph. Also, a ratio that shows the relationship between a scale drawing and the actual object or between distances on a map and actual distances.

scale drawing A drawing of an object made so that distances in the drawing are proportional to actual distances.

scalene triangle A triangle with no sides the same length and no angles the same measure.

scattergram A graph of a set of points representing two sets of data. By looking at how all the points are arranged, you can see if the two sets of data are related.

scientific notation A system of writing a number as the product of a power of 10 and a number between 1 and 10.
  Example: $2{,}300{,}000 = 2.3 \times 10^6$

segment Part of a line from one point to another.

sequence A set of numbers in a particular pattern or order.

set A group of items.

similar figures Two figures that have the same shape.

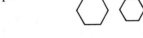

simulation A way of acting out or creating a situation like one in the real world to see what is likely to happen in the real world.

skew lines Lines that are not parallel and that do not intersect.

slide To obtain another figure by moving a figure without flipping or turning it. A slide results in a translation image.

solution To find the solution to an equation means to find a value for the variable that makes the left side of the equation stand for the same number as the right side.

space figure A figure that has volume.
  Examples:

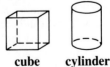

  cube   cylinder

sphere A space figure in which all the points are the same distance from a center point.

535

GLOSSARY

square A quadrilateral with four right angles and all sides the same length. A square is a rectangle.

standard form The form in which numbers are usually written.
Example: 794,502

subtraction An operation that tells the difference between two numbers, or how many are left when some are taken away.

sum The number obtained by adding numbers.

surface area The sum of the areas of all the faces of a space figure.

survey A method of obtaining information by collecting facts or opinions from a number of people.

symmetric figure A plane figure that can be folded in half so that the two halves match.

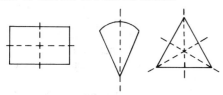

table A method of displaying information in rows and columns.

tally A mark used to keep track of items when counting. Tally marks are arranged in groups of five, with the fifth mark across the first four.
Example:

terminating decimal A decimal in which digits do not show a repeating pattern. A terminating decimal results when the division of the numerator of a fraction by the denominator leaves a zero remainder.

trading To make a group of ten from one of the next highest place value, or one from ten of the next lowest place value.
Examples: one hundred can be traded for ten tens; ten ones can be traded for one ten.

translation image The new figure obtained by sliding a figure without flipping or turning it.

trapezoid A quadrilateral with exactly one pair of parallel sides.

tree diagram A special kind of diagram that helps determine probability by showing the number of equally likely outcomes.

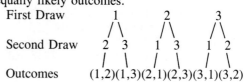

First Draw   1   2   3
Second Draw   2 3   1 3   1 2
Outcomes   (1,2)(1,3)(2,1)(2,3)(3,1)(3,2)

trial A test in a probability experiment.

triangle A polygon with three sides.

turn To obtain a new figure by rotating a figure into a different position. The result of a turn is a rotation image.

twin primes A pair of prime numbers that have a difference of 2.
Examples: 3 and 5   11 and 13

unit One of something. An amount or quality used as a standard of measurement. See Table of Measures, page 528.

unit fraction A fraction with a numerator of 1.
Examples: $\frac{1}{4}, \frac{1}{3}, \frac{1}{2}$

unit price The price for one unit (one ounce, one pound, etc.) of an item.

variable A letter, such as n or x, that stands for a number or for a range of numbers in an algebraic expression.

vertex (plural vertices) The point where the two rays of an angle meet. Also, the point where two sides of a polygon meet.

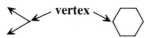

volume The number of cubic units of space that a space figure holds.

weight A measure of the force that gravity exerts on a body.

whole number Any number in the set 0, 1, 2, 3, . . .

zero property of addition The sum of a number and zero is that number.
Example: $21 + 0 = 21$

zero property of multiplication The product of a number and zero is zero.
Example: $94 \times 0 = 0$

ACKNOWLEDGMENTS

Illustration Acknowledgments

Dave Blanchette p. 8T, 18, 19M, 64, 65, 83, 112M, 190, 199, 208T, 212, 224, 242, 252M, 255T, 274B, 287R, 288, 292, 308, 315, 324, 325, 327, 330, 338, 339, 360, 362, 364, 367, 368, 376, 377, 379, 389, 393, 398, 399T, 401, 403T, 404B, 418, 442, 443, 447, 451, 456, 466, 489, 492, 497

Alex Bloch p. 68, 231, 238, 270B, 271, 340, 382, 384, 394, 414, 416, 420, 440, 441, 446, 448, 449, 450T

Bill Colrus p. 56, 88, 164T, 165, 239, 268, 326

Rick Cooley p. 467, 491, 495, 496

Don Dyen p. 128, 143, 202T/(Background), 202B, 203, 225, 344, 345, 346, 347, 400, 404T, 485, 488

Andrea J. Fong p. 478, 479, 481

Simon Galkin p. 184, 208B, 244, 274T, 306, 380, 381, 399B, 410, 419, 422, 423, 429, 432, 460, 462, 499

Betty Gee p. 468, 469, 470, 471, 472, 476, 477, 482, 483

Ignacio Gomez p. 14, 19T, 20, 22, 39, 43, 69, 76, 95, 102, 103, 122T, 136, 140, 151, 164B, 171, 193, 195, 200, 214, 222, 223, 226, 280M, 293, 365, 371T, 373, 465, 494

Celeste Henriquez p. 38, 46T, 52, 179, 191, 204, 205, 206, 218, 234, 284, 285, 300, 302, 303

Arlan Jewell p. 132, 142, 144T, 146, 150

Kay Life p. 36, 49, 80, 81, 82, 126, 154

Ruth Linstromberg p. 45, 110M, 111, 133, 141, 148, 152, 175, 259T, 280T, 281, 286, 287L, 297, 316, 317, 370

Jane McCreary p. 26, 192B, 323, 363, 372B

Deborah Morse p. 473

Michael O'Reilly p. 46M, 228, 314

Bill Ogden p. 8B, 9, 12, 13, 17, 28, 33, 51, 66, 70, 72, 77, 79, 94, 104T, 110B, 112T, 113, 116, 121, 160B, 161, 162, 168, 169, 192T, 196, 219, 220, 241, 354, 374, 375B, 408, 426, 427, 428T, 444, 450B, 454, 463, 464, 484, 487, 490, 493, 498

Frederick Porter p. 58, 90, 144B, 145, 160T, 198, 207, 209, 236, 237, 322, 378

Eileen Rosen p. 73, 235, 375M

Ed Sauk p. 75, 104B, 110T, 122B, 123, 172

Sally Schaedler p. 270T, 318, 371B, 403B

Dennis Schofield p. 134, 229, 336, 337, 372T, 405

Nancy Spier p. 475

Lazlo Vespremi p. 6, 16, 42, 48, 74

All other artwork by PC&F, Inc.

Photo Acknowledgments

Chapter 1: 4 Bill Gallery/Stock, Boston; 5 John G. Ross/Photo Researchers; 7 Brian Brake/Photo Researchers; 11 Lawrence Migdale/Stock, Boston; 13 Carol Palmer/Andrew Brilliant*; 23 The Granger Collection; 24–25 Carol Palmer/Andrew Brilliant*

Chapter 2: 34 John Walsh/Photo Researchers; 35 Arthur M. Siegelman; 40 Cary Wolinsky/Stock, Boston; 41 (pot): Jack Spratt/The Image Works; 41 (box): Charles George/H. Armstrong Roberts; 41B: Sam Sweezy/Stock, Boston; 44 NASA; 47 Peter Fronk/TSW-CLICK, Chicago; 53 Carol Palmer/Andrew Brilliant*; 54–55 Carol Palmer/Andrew Brilliant*

Chapter 3: 62 NASA; 63 Cosmos-Kubasik/Photo Researchers; 66 Animals Animals/Ray Richardson; 67 Animals Animals/C. Baldwin; 72 Carol Palmer/Andrew Brilliant*; 78T: Francois Gohier/Photo Researchers; 78B: (c) Kent Wood/Peter Arnold, Inc.; 79 NASA; 84 A. Geisser/H. Armstrong Roberts; 85 David Schaefer/The Picture Cube; 86–87 Carol Palmer/Andrew Brilliant*

Chapter 4: 96T: Don Eastman Photo/The Stock Solution; 96B: Bob Daemmrich; 97 Charles Gupton/Stock, Boston; 98 Jeffrey C. Marienthal/ASK Design; 99 E. Simonson/H. Armstrong Roberts; 100T: Fredrik D. Bodin/Stock, Boston; 100B: James P. Rowan/Tony Stone Worldwide; 101 Ken Cole/The Stock Solution; 106 Scott Ransom/Taurus Photos; 107 Francois Duhamel/Sygma; 108T: Bob Daemmrich/Stock, Boston; 108B: Mikki Ansin/The Picture Cube; 114T: Don and Pat Valenti/Taurus Photos; 114–115B: Carol Palmer/Andrew Brilliant*; 118T/B: (c) Jan L. Wassink/Pintler Photos; 119 COMSTOCK, Inc./Bruce Hands; 124–125 Carol Palmer/Andrew Brilliant*

Chapter 5: 148 Carol Palmer/Andrew Brilliant*; 152–153 Carol Palmer/Andrew Brilliant*

Chapter 6: 166T: (c) Ralph Wetmore/Photo Researchers; 166B: (c) Gregory K. Scott/Photo Researchers; 167 (c) Bob Daemmrich/The Image Works; 174T: (c) Joe Sohm/The Image Works; 174B: COMSTOCK, Inc./David Lokey; 175 Carol Palmer/Andrew Brilliant*; 180 Grant Heilman/Grant Heilman Photography, Inc.; 181 Carol Palmer/Andrew Brilliant*; 182–183 Carol Palmer/Andrew Brilliant*

Chapter 7: 196 Carol Palmer/Andrew Brilliant*; 210–211 Carol Palmer/Andrew Brilliant*

Chapter 8: 220 Carol Palmer/Andrew Brilliant*; 232T/B: Carol Palmer/Andrew Brilliant*; 236 Carol Palmer/Andrew Brilliant*; 240–241 Carol Palmer/Andrew Brilliant*

Chapter 9: 248 Lenore Weber/Taurus Photos; 250 (c) Kip Peticolas/Fundamental Photographs, New York; 252 (c) Manfred Kage/Peter Arnold, Inc.; 254 (c) Paul Silverman/Fundamental Photographs, New York; 266 Dr. David Schwimmer/Bruce Coleman, Inc.; 272 (apartment): (c) Steve Allen/Peter Arnold, Inc.; 273L: Jon Feingersh/Stock, Boston; 273R: Pam Hasegawa/Taurus Photos; 272–273 (composite): Carol Palmer/Andrew Brilliant*

Chapter 10: 282T: Don and Pat Valenti/Taurus Photos; 282B: Eric Neurath/Stock, Boston; 283 Milton Feinberg/Stock, Boston; 288 William Floyd Holdman/The Stock Solution; 290 (c) Tom Till/TSW-CLICK/Chicago Ltd.; 294 Carol Palmer/Andrew Brilliant*; 298 Donald Dietz/Stock, Boston; 299 Royce Bair/The Stock Solution; 303 Carol Palmer/Andrew Brilliant*; 304–305 Carol Palmer/Andrew Brilliant*

ACKNOWLEDGMENTS

Chapter 11: 312 (c) Mitchell Bleier/Peter Arnold, Inc.; 316 Dick Durrance/Woodfin Camp & Associates, Inc.; 321 L.L.T. Rhodes/ Taurus Photos; 328–329 Carol Palmer/Andrew Brilliant*; inset photo on pg. 329 by Gerald Gitlitz

Chapter 12: 340 Carol Palmer/Andrew Brilliant*; 349 (c) Wolfgang Kaehler; 350 Animals Animals/G.L. Cooyman; 351 (c) Wolfgang Kaehler; 352–353 Carol Palmer/Andrew Brilliant*; 356 Carol Palmer/ Andrew Brilliant*

Chapter 13: 380 Carol Palmer/Andrew Brilliant*

Chapter 14: 388 Photo Researchers; 389 Patrick Montagne/Photo Researchers; 406–407 Carol Palmer/Andrew Brilliant*

Chapter 15: 424 Barbara Alper/Stock, Boston; 425T: M. Murayama, Murayama Research Lab./BPS; 425B: Carol Palmer/Andrew Brilliant*; 430L: Animals Animals/C. Roessler; 430R: Animals Animals/W. Gregory Brown; 431L: Animals Animals/Zig Leszczynski; 431R: D.J. Wrobel, Monterey Bay Aquarium/BPS; 430–431 (composite): Carol Palmer/Andrew Brilliant*

Chapter 16: 438 Carol Palmer/Andrew Brilliant*; 439L/R Carol Palmer/Andrew Brilliant*; 452–453 Carol Palmer/Andrew Brilliant*

Chapter Opener and Data Bank: 2–3 Giraudon/Art Resource; 30–31 David Cannon (Allsport)/West Light; 60–61 NASA; 92–93 NASA; 130–131 Kevin Horan; 134–135 Culver Pictures; 158–159 R.F. Head/Earth Scenes; 188–189 Janice Sheldon*; 216–217 Ted Horowitz/The Stock Market; 278–279 Craig Aurness/West Light; 246–247 Barry L. Runk/Grant Heilman Photography; 310–311 Stephen Frisch*; 358–359 West Light; 386–387 Robert Harding Picture Library Ltd.; 412–413 (c) Lennart Nilsson from BEHOLD MAN/Little, Brown & Co.; 436–437 John G. Ross/Robert Harding Picture Library; 472 Eric Crichton/Bruce Coleman, Inc.; 477T E.R. Degginger/Earth Scenes; 477M Barry L. Runk/Grant Heilman Photography; 477B C.L. Heyer/Grant Heilman Photography; 478 Janice Sheldon*

*Photos provided expressly for the publisher.

Production/Art and Photo Direction by PC&F, Inc.

Special thanks to Ruggles Mine in Grafton, NH for use of their facilities for the photos on pages 452–453.